T0055469

Letters to his Parents

THEODOR W. ADORNO

Letters to his Parents 1939–1951

Edited by Christoph Gödde and Henri Lonitz
Translated by Wieland Hoban

polity

First published in German as *Theodor W. Adorno: Briefe an die Eltern 1939–1951* and copyright © Suhrkamp Verlag, Frankfurt am Main, 2003.

This English translation © Polity Press 2006

Polity Press
65 Bridge Street
Cambridge CB2 1UR, UK

Polity Press
350 Main Street
Malden, MA 02148, USA

ISBN-10: 0-7456-3542-3
ISBN-13: 978-07456-3542-3

A catalogue record for this book is available from the British Library.

Typeset in 10.5 on 12pt Sabon
by Servis Filmsetting Ltd, Manchester
Printed and bound in Malaysia by Alden Press, Malaysia

For further information on Polity, visit our website: www.polity.co.uk

Contents

Editors' Foreword   vi

Letters

    1939   1

    1940   33

    1941   67

    1942   78

    1943   122

    1944   164

    1945   210

    1946   242

    1947   273

    1948   312

    1949   347

    1950   379

    1951   383

Index   386

Editors' Foreword

When Adorno saw his parents again in June 1939 in Havana, they had only been in Cuba for a few weeks. Oscar and Maria Wiesengrund had managed to escape from Nazi Germany at the last minute. At the end of 1939 they moved first to Florida, then to New York, where they lived from August 1940 until the end of their lives. It is only with his move to California at the end of 1941 that Adorno's letters resume once more, coming almost consistently once every two weeks, reporting on work and living conditions as well as friends, acquaintances and the Hollywood stars of his time. One finds reports of his collaborations with Max Horkheimer, Thomas Mann and Hanns Eisler alongside accounts of parties, clowning around with Charlie Chaplin, and ill-fated love affairs. But the letters also show his constant longing for Europe: Adorno already began to think about his return as soon as the USA entered the war.

The *Letters to his Parents* – surely the most open and direct ones he ever wrote – not only afford the reader a glimpse of the experiences that gave rise to the famous *Minima Moralia*, but also show Adorno from a previously unknown, extremely personal side. They end with the first reports from the ravaged Frankfurt to his mother, who remained in New York – and from Amorbach, his childhood paradise.

The occasional harsh comments about the family of his uncle Louis – *the brood* – can be attributed to a strong spleen on Adorno's part, which was well known and indeed criticized in the Wiesengrund family, and which he only seems to have been able to control in the immediate presence of his relatives.

Unfortunately, of the equally numerous letters sent by his parents during their emigration in Cuba and America, only two from his father, from 1945 and 1946, were found among Adorno's belongings; of his mother's letters, those written from March 1948 onwards have survived. Excerpts from these have been cited where it assists the reader in understanding Adorno's letters.

The letters written by Theodor and Gretel Adorno are reproduced with diplomatic faithfulness; words written unclearly are marked with a question mark in square brackets. This also applies to any additions or alterations made by the editors.

The notes serve to explain events and names found in the letters. The editors have sought to supply information also about those friends and acquaintances, both from Frankfurt and then America, whose names never became well known. Unfortunately this was not always possible; in some cases the notes could not ultimately be as comprehensive as intended, or the editors were even forced to give up entirely.

The following collected editions are referred to in abbreviated form:

Theodor W. Adorno, *Gesammelte Schriften*, ed. Rolf Tiedemann in collaboration with Gretel Adorno, Susan Buck-Morss and Klaus Schultz, vols. 1–20 (Frankfurt am Main: Suhrkamp, 1970–86): GS [1–20].

Max Horkheimer, *Gesammelte Schriften*, ed. Alfred Schmidt and Gunzelin Schmid Noerr, vols. 1–19 (Frankfurt am Main: Fischer, 1988–96): Horkheimer, *Gesammelte Schriften* [1–19].

Max Horkheimer, *Gesammelte Schriften*, vol. 17: *Briefwechsel 1941–1948*, ed. Gunzelin Schmid Noerr (Frankfurt am Main: Fischer, 1995): Horkheimer, *Briefwechsel 1941–48*.

The editors would like to thank the following persons for assisting them in their research: Wolfram von Boxberg (Meckenheim), Volker Harms-Ziegler (Institut für Stadtgeschichte, Frankfurt am Main), Joachim Heimannsberg (Munich), Rüdiger Koschnitzki (Deutsches Filminstitut), Ingrid Kummels and Gundram Kunz (Amorbach), Fritz-Bernd Leopold (Deutsches Literaturarchiv, Marbach am Neckar), Michael Maaser (Universitätsarchiv der Johann Wolfgang Goethe-Universität, Frankfurt am Main), Susanne Neis (Stadtarchiv Neunkirchen), Frau Neugebauer (Amorbach), Reinhard Pabst (Bad Camberg), Elisabeth Reinhuber-Adorno (Oberursel), Klaus Rheinfurth (Institut für Stadtgeschichte, Frankfurt am Main), Manfred Schäfer (Amorbach), Joachim Seng (Hofmannsthal-Archiv, Freies Deutsches Hochstift, Frankfurt am Main) and Jochen Stollberg (Stadt- und Universitätsbibliothek, Frankfurt am Main).

Oscar and Maria Wiesengrund, *c.* 1939

Theodor W. Adorno, *c.* 1939

1939

12 May 1939

My dears:
 this is but a brief note to welcome you to the new world, where you are now no longer all too far away from us. Our anxiety will not cease until we know that you have arrived safely, and we are putting off everything else until the moment we receive your telegram. I only wish to add that it is my firm intention to visit you as soon as possible. I cannot name a date at present, as this depends not on my wishes, but partly on the radio project.[1] But I shall not wait a day longer than absolutely necessary.

We received your letter from Antwerp,[2] to our greatest joy, and are relieved to know that everything has gone smoothly so far. I hope with all my heart that you will now truly have a peaceful time, and that you will experience your emigration, now that it has become inevitable, somewhat in the manner of an extended Amorbach.

We will discuss the matter of how to get you over here as soon as I am with you.

Otherwise, I would only like to give you two pieces of advice today: 1.) do not eat any *uncooked* pork, as the risk of trichinosis is very high throughout America, 2.) take great care from the start to protect yourselves against the sun, which must be considerable now in Cuba, 3.) be very careful in your dealings with other emigrants. Frenkel's business partner[3] will soon be looking after you, and the brother of Frau Dr Herbert Graf[4] will also be turning up in Cuba soon; going on what his sister told me, he should be pleasant company. Furthermore, Carry Sinn[5] will recommend some American families, whom I would at least

1

prefer to someone like the Wendriners.[6] But I hope that the whole Cuban expedition will be no more than a brief transitional episode. I need hardly tell you how happy we shall both be when we know that you are nearby and have escaped the horror. Or rather: I hardly dare say so, out of superstition, until your telegram is brought here. Gretel and I are already envisioning how it will be when I tell you all the stories about the hippos, giraffes and hyenas that have meanwhile dissolved into a mirage in the American desert.

A Frankfurt acquaintance of ours by the name of Ganz,[7] who had to spend a few months in Cuba before his immigration here, told us a few things we would like to pass on to you, as they will perhaps be useful. I would particularly like to draw your attention to the possibility of Viennese food, as I do not know whether our tummies[8] are up to Cuban food. During the summer months, however, one can perhaps recommend *North American* food, which is relatively rich in vegetables.

Heartiest kisses from your now audibly whinnying horses
Hottilein and Rossilein[9]

Warmest regards to Julie.[10]

Hotel Abos Mundos (roof garden)
Obispro good, c. $ 60 per month, good food, but not cheap.
The addresses of the German guesthouses can be obtained from the Joint Relief Committee.
Restaurant Orbe Chinese, good, c. 35–40 cts.
Very much worth seeing: Tropical Garden
Nice: Playa (bus number 32).
Elegant restaurant, very good food: Petit Miami.
Nice: Veradero blue beach, c. 3½ hours by bus from Prado.
Non-German guesthouse in Havana: Paseo de Mart 104
Hotel Trocha, very good, pretty garden.

Original: typewritten letter signed by Theodor W. and Gretel Adorno.

1 The project, which concerned 'The Essential Value of Radio to All Types of Listeners' (mostly referred to as the Princeton Radio Research Project), was under the direction of Paul F. Lazarsfeld, who taught at Princeton, and was funded by the Rockefeller Foundation. In autumn 1937, Max Horkheimer had suggested Adorno as musical advisor, thus making it financially possible for Adorno to emigrate to the USA.

2 This letter, written during the forced exit from Germany, before boarding the ship bound for Cuba, has not survived; only three letters from Adorno's parents have been preserved from the period between 1939 and 1948. Maria Wiesengrund's letters to her son from March 1948 onwards have mostly survived.

2

3 It was impossible to gain further information about either Leo Frenkel, who seems to have lived in New York as an insurance salesman and was on friendly terms with Oscar Wiesengrund, or his business partner.

4 The brother-in-law of the Vienna-born director and music writer Herbert Graf (1903–73), who was head of the Städtische Oper in Frankfurt from 1929 to 1932 and worked as director at the Metropolitan Opera in New York from 1936 onwards, could not be traced.

5 Née Frenkel; her name is also spelt 'Carrie' elsewhere.

6 A married couple created by Kurt Tucholsky, who devoted a number of satirical tales to them in the 1920s.

7 Difficult to trace; possibly the actor and writer Rudolf Hermann Graf (1901–1965).

8 Translator's note: in English in the original (henceforth: EO).

9 The pet names of Theodor and Gretel Adorno. Translator's note: both names are generic (albeit doubly diminutive, and thus especially 'cutesy') names for horses, rather like 'Fido' or 'Rex' for dogs. They have therefore been left untranslated.

10 This is Julie Rautenberg (1882–1960), a senior employee of Oscar Wiesengrund and signing clerk of the wine shop 'Bernhard Wiesengrund', who emigrated with them. Julie Rautenberg was a relative of the Frenkels.

2   NEW YORK, 21.5.1939

New York, 21 May 1939. My dear, faithful Wondrous Hippo Cow,[1] here a few words of welcome – may you continue to live with the same contentment, the same security, and the same stubborn superiority as the hippo cow overleaf. I shall be visiting you in the first days of June; the precise date will depend on my work, I will inform you in good time, only tell me how I can best avoid delay in this quarantine, i.e. as a visitor with American first papers.[2] I am happy that everything has gone smoothly now. Meanwhile had great success at Columbia University.[3] Heartiest kisses – fond regards to you both Your old Archibald
Fond regards Giraffe Gazelle wearing negligee

Original: photo postcard: Rose the Hippopotamus, Central Park Zoo, N.Y.C.; stamp: NEW YORK, MAY 2, 1939 (see fig. 1). Manuscript.

1 Translator's note: the original pet name is *Wundernilstute*. It should be noted that, while in English the male and female hippopotamus are termed 'bull' and 'cow' respectively, they are referred to in German as *Hengst* and *Stute*, i.e. 'stallion' and 'mare'. In the light of the Adorno family's clear penchant for horses, this can be seen as connected to the various other horse-related pet names that appear in the correspondence.

2 This refers to the 'Declaration of Intention' to become a citizen of the United States of North America, i.e. the application for naturalization.

3 Adorno had given a lecture entitled 'Husserl and the Problem of Idealism' (see Theodor W. Adorno, *GS* 20.1, pp. 119–34).

3   NEW YORK, 11.6.1939

11 June 1939

My dear Wondrous Hippo Cow,
dear Willibald:
   a thousand thanks for the delightful red waistcoat, which fits me perfectly; Giraffe Gazelle is very happy with her new saddlecloth – dear Archibald rolled up here in good health and spirits, albeit a little tired at present. New York had just put on a gentle cooling shower to welcome him. – I am glad you are so well, and that you have some peace and are comfortable there. I would so love to get dear Marinumba a few light clothes here, but I need to have her measurements first. Perhaps it would even be possible to find out the exact American size (I am size 16, for example) in a shop there. I have not yet seen any wild silk here at all, people wear artificial silk (rayon) or cotton (even for evening dresses). What sort of colours were you thinking of: grey, blue and black with white?
   Do send us more news soon, with kisses from your
                              Gretel-horse

My dears, having arrived in good shape after a somewhat adventurous ride, I still see the terribly brave and yet terribly sad face of the Hippo Cow on the pier before me – and I felt no different, but was merely less heroic! And yet I am so happy about those 6 days. More soon, for today just fond and hearty greetings from your Archibald.

Original: handwritten letter.

4   NEW YORK, 8.7.1939

8 July 1939

My dears:
   we are anxious at not having had any reply to our lengthy letter of 21 June,[1] nor any confirmation that you received the book packets we sent you around the same time. We hope you are well, and that the

Cuban postal service has simply treated itself to a feast – although I can scarcely imagine that those robber-chieftains had much fun with Stifter's studies and Beethoven's sonatas, to say nothing of my own utterances.

There is an altogether inhuman heat here, and I do not know whether I should fear that it might be even hotter where you are, or console myself with the assumption that it cannot get any hotter. At any rate, we decided yesterday to go on holiday after all, to Bar Harbor once again at the end of the month, for 4 or 5 weeks. Max and Maidon[2] originally wanted to come too. But Dée's condition is such that Fritz was unable to decide on the westward journey she had so dearly wished for, and he will also go to Maine, which means that Max and Maidon cannot leave Fritz and Dée[3] and come with us. But we shall certainly meet. Lazarsfeld[4] proved most friendly and accommodating with regard to the holiday. We have been invited, either on the way there or the way back, to go to Maine to visit Professor Lynd,[5] the world-famous author of Middle Town, whom you have probably also heard of, on his property in New Hampshire. I have known him for a long time and am on good terms with him; he has meanwhile read a substantial amount of my work and is, as Lazarsfeld told me yesterday, most impressed by it. I tell you this not for the sake of prestige, as the worth of my efforts is not to be measured by the opinions of some celebrities, but only to show you that, for all the accusations of Jewish-Hegelian dialectics[6] directed at me, I am clearly coping well with Americans of even the most Aryan blood.

Aside from this, I am in such an exhausted and overworked state as I have perhaps never before experienced. The holidays are truly not a luxury. I cannot refrain from telling you in brief all the things I have done since my return from Cuba:

1) a 20-page essay[7] for the journal that brings my jazz theory up to date with the current American discourse, in the form of an examination of two newly published books.

2) a long, 40-page memorandum[8] for the radio project on pop songs and monopolistic propaganda with suggestions for research I have worked out, and which are now to be carried out – by Lazarsfeld's very pleasant wife, among others.

3) two further reviews[9] for the journal, among them one whose length is equivalent to around 8 columns in the FZ features section.

4) completely revised, i.e. rewrote, a long essay by Max[10] on the Jewish question together with him and Gretel. We spent the last week working literally day and night on this most interesting piece of work, at such a pace that Max broke down immediately after its conclusion and went to bed with a fever.

5) briefed all the employees for the radio project, who are now fully available for the music study,[11] about their new tasks.

6) carried out the 'drive'[12] for the research project on anti-Semitism[13] with Max.

If that's not American! I hope to send you some of my English output soon. I daresay you will understand that I am a little drowsy after all this. The peaceful calm of the noise of Havana lies behind me like a lost paradise.

On Wednesday evening we had an official institute do at our place, which went extremely well, with Rudi and Josie.[14] Yesterday evening we were invited to Max and Maidon's place together with the Frenkels, as well as Fritz and Dée, and it was very pleasant. Only I think that dear Leo was a little taken aback at the names we use for each other. For we have now adopted the names of Indian chiefs: Max is called 'Soft head', Gretel, in keeping with an older tradition: 'Three Lamb-vultures', and I am simply 'Big Ox'. As you see, I shall soon have lost my wits, and if I carry on like this I will surely soon be given the professorship in Oxford for which I was previously too highbrow.[15] Gsh.

Do write soon, and in particular also tell me – as is fitting in a letter to a dialectical materialist – whether you are really getting enough to eat from Miss Laidlaw,[16] which I doubt somewhat, as I ate like a pig for a few days after my return here, and whether you are coping with the climate.

Heartiest kisses from your old and somewhat America-weary child,[17] also from Mrs Hippo King Archibald, the dear Giraffe Gazelle with the little horns.

Your faithful Teddie.

Original: typewritten letter.

1 As the next letter reveals, it never reached Adorno's parents.

2 Max (1895–1973) and Maidon (1887–1969) Horkheimer.

3 Friedrich Pollock (1894–1970) and his first wife Andrée.

4 The Vienna-born sociologist Paul Felix Lazarsfeld (1901–1976) had gone to America in 1933, and decided to remain there in 1935. From 1937 to 1939 he was director of the Office of Radio Research, which was initially resident at Princeton and moved to Columbia University in New York in 1939. Adorno had been an employee of this research institution – also known as the Princeton Radio Research Project – since 1938. In 1936, Lazarsfeld had married his second wife, also born in Vienna, the social scientist Herta Herzog (1910–1999).

5 The sociologists Robert S. Lynd (1892–1970) and his wife Helen Merrell Lynd (1896–1982) had published the study *Middletown: A Study in Contemporary American Culture* in 1929, and in 1937 the follow-up *Middletown in Transition: A Study in Cultural Conflicts*. Robert S. Lynd taught at Columbia University in New York.

6

6 See also Horkheimer's essay 'Die Juden und Europa' [The Jews and Europe], which begins: 'The "Jewish-Hegelian jargon", which once began in London and made its way into the German Left, and which even then had to be translated into the full-bodied rhetoric of trade unionists, is now considered well and truly worn out' (Max Horkheimer, *Gesammelte Schriften* 4, p. 308).

7 Adorno's review of Wilder Hobson's *American Jazz Music* (New York, 1939) and Winthrop Sargeant's *Jazz, Hot & Hybrid* (New York, 1938) appeared only in 1941, in the ninth volume of the *Zeitschrift für Sozialforschung* (henceforth: *ZfS*); see GS 19, pp. 382–99.

8 There is a memorandum headed 'Plugging, Likes and Dislikes in the Field of Light Popular Music' among Adorno's belongings in the Theodor W. Adorno Archiv (Ts 51499–51537).

9 The three unpublished reviews, all from 1939, deal with the collective introduction to philosophy *Knowledge and Society* (New York, 1938), Maximilian Beck's *Psychologie. Wesen und Wirklichkeit der Seele* [Psychology: Essence and Reality of the Soul] (Leiden, 1939), and Richard Laurin Hawkins's *Positivism in the United States 1853–61* (Cambridge, MA, 1938) respectively. It is not clear which two are meant here. See GS 20.1, pp. 238–43.

10 See Max Horkheimer, 'Die Juden und Europa', in *ZfS* 8 (1939–40), pp. 115–36; now in Max Horkheimer, *Gesammelte Schriften* 4, pp. 308–31.

11 *music study*: EO.

12 *'drive'*: EO.

13 This was originally published in English in 1941, in vol. 4 of the *ZfS*, which at that time bore the name *Studies in Philosophy and Social Science*. For the German translation see Max Horkheimer, *Gesammelte Schriften* 4, pp. 373–418.

14 The violinist and leader of the Kolisch String Quartet, Rudolf Kolisch (1896–1978), who had been Adorno's friend since 1925, and his first wife, the pianist Josefa Rosanska (1904–1986).

15 *highbrow*: EO.

16 The landlady of the Havana guesthouse in which Oscar and Maria Wiesengrund resided, Miss Estella Laidlaw.

17 An allusion to Ferdinand Kürberger's novel *Der Amerikamüde* [The America-weary One], first published in 1855.

5   NEW YORK, 15.7.1939

15 July 1939

My dears:
a thousand thanks for your telegram, letter and card. The telegram came just as Gretel was copying my letter from the shorthand. To

answer the question from the card: the exact words of the Jack Smith[1] record should be: '*are you sorry*, really sorry?' I hope this is sufficient to win the bet.

As you did not receive my dramatic travel report: during the night of my crossing to Miami, my cabin neighbours sought to infiltrate my room through the connecting door, and even continued their attempts after I had begun to protest vigorously, until I finally called the night-steward to my aid. It is unclear whether they were simply drunk or entertained the vain hope of robbing me; to be truthful, however, I suspect the former. Then I almost missed my train, as the Americans kept me on board for hours: for they had lost my papers, and there-fore sent me to the back of the queue. It was only because I smelled a rat, and, generally hostile towards authority, did not 'comply' (as Annachen[2] would say), that I managed to catch my train after all. On the return journey I was freezing like a dog, especially while passing through Florida, as the train was so thoroughly air-conditioned that my tropical clothing offered entirely inadequate protection against Western civilization. My subsequent cold took me a fortnight to recover from.

You should never worry if our letters fail to arrive. If anything were the matter, we would wire you *immediately*; and, on the other hand, one should constantly expect surprises from the Cuban postal service.

And dear WK[3] should not be anxious about Regius[4] – he has now long been in safety.

It is now fairly certain that we shall go on holiday at the end of July, once again to the Hotel de Gregoire, Bar Harbor, Maine.

We had arranged with the Wondrous Hippo Cow to get her a few clothes here, and now she writes that she does not want any. But why not? What are her measurements?

We are now taking things at a much slower pace until the holidays – having a semi-holiday, so to speak – and I have already recovered somewhat; unfortunately, however, my poor Giraffe Gazelle has had another migraine.

Aside from these matters, I can think of nothing special to report: I shall send our dear Hippo Cow a few songs. It has cooled off slightly here, and it is very pleasant in our apartment. Fond regards to you both, and to Julie; we had Bea[5] over here a few days ago, together with the Pollocks and a big-shot Jew who is in charge of the Alaska project[6] (which, by the way, is very interesting and sensible).

Please give my best to Miss Laidlaw, and tell her, as the old Pachulke[7] joke goes: 'carry on like that, and you'll go far in life'.

Kisses from

your old child
Teddie.

The money will be wired to the old whore on Monday by Tratte: no simple matter.
Enclosed: 1 Archibald with trap wide open.

Original: typewritten letter with handwritten postscript.

1 The singer and film actor 'Whispering' Jack Smith, born in 1919 in Seattle.

2 A maidservant of the Wiesengrunds in Frankfurt.

3 Translator's note: This is the abbreviation for *Wildschweinkönig* (Wild Boar King), the pet name for Oscar Wiesengrund.

4 This refers to the collection of aphorisms entitled *Dämmerung. Notizen in Deutschland* [Twilight: Notes in Germany] published by Max Horkheimer in 1934 under the pseudonym Heinrich Regius.

5 Presumably the wife of the architect Ferdinand Kramer (see letter 13 and the corresponding note).

6 The name could not be ascertained; Alaska, together with the Virgin Islands, was one of the places vaguely mentioned as a new location for Jews forced to flee from Germany. The Roosevelt administration's intention was presumably to reduce the strain on the USA resulting from Jewish immigrants.

7 Pachulke (in Polish: *pacholek*) refers to a peasant, farm hand, or generally rough type. The figure Pachulke came from a Berlin joke.

6   NEW YORK, 25.7.1939
    429 WEST 117TH STREET
    NEW YORK, N.Y.

25 July 1939

My dears!
A thousand thanks for your letter. I am sending you these words today by air mail, so that you might still receive a line or two from New York, and above all to convey to WK the very heartiest of birthday greetings.[1] May the first in exile at once be the first in a long line of agreeable ones – on holiday, so to speak. And may you both continue to cope with fate as bravely, naturally and free of bitterness as you have until now. Beyond this, my hope for us all today is simply that we can soon see each other again, and in calmer circumstances than those days in June, as rewarding as they were.
   We have little to report. Work is progressing slowly – in recent weeks mainly the project once more, now that the long essay by Max

9

and various smaller matters have been completed. But I am still only working at half-speed, so to speak, and will interrupt my work completely and absolutely in August. Gretel has had a whole series of migraine attacks, I am afraid, with ever-increasing frequency; though she is feeling better today, a holiday is very much overdue, and for this reason I am dictating at the institute today. We are labouring under a truly infernal heat here, with 60 per cent air humidity – I swear, it is scarcely bearable. We are leaving on Sunday, and will spend the whole of August at the Hotel de Gregoire, Bar Harbor, Maine. It is quite possible that Max and Maidon will visit us there, and the Pollocks are also considering Maine, though in the case of Frau Pollock there are some doubts on account of the sea climate.

Regarding Alaska, my dear WK, you are as mistaken as all of us here were until recently. Alaska is an entire continent. The northern parts are arctic, while the climate in the southern and south-western regions – due to what is known as the Japan Current – is considerably milder than most of the American Midwest, or indeed Chicago. The temperature does not drop more than a few degrees below zero, and in the summer it is apparently as warm and agreeable as southern Norway, for example. If I am not much mistaken, Alaska – which is after all part of the USA, and economically still entirely untapped – genuinely looks to become the main refuge for exiled Jews. Our source on the matter,[2] incidentally, is a charming man who has proven especially friendly towards us, and is involved in the project together with Max Warburg (Anita's father).[3] Economically speaking, the aim of the project is to develop a lumber industry that would make American newspaper production largely independent of raw materials from Germany, Canada and Scandinavia. The whole of Alaska is inhabited by no more than 60,000 people – 30,000 of them white, the rest a mixture of Eskimos, Japanese, Chinese and negroes. The southern, fertile parts of Alaska are very easy to reach from Seattle. On the whole, the project seems to me incomparably more solid and healthy than the Guyana project, for example, to say nothing of Shanghai.[4] The things one hears about that are truly horrendous.

As far as Kreisler[5] is concerned, I agree entirely. He has long since gone to the dogs and lost all sense of good measure. This whole sort of music-making should be liquidated, and one often wonders whether the current German barbarism contributing to that liquidation is not perhaps involuntarily serving a most just purpose.

I was deeply touched by the correspondence between Hofmannsthal and George, which I shall review in detail for the journal.[6] In the next two weeks you will be receiving two manuscripts in English: Radio Voice,[7] the completed second part of my theoretical book about the radio project, and the extensive project of a scientific study of anti-Semitism; Max had the idea to begin with, and then the two of us wrote it together with Gretel and my old American secretary. I would ask that you return both manuscripts to me once you have read them: the anti-Semitism project should be treated absolutely confidentially – that means that no one other than you, my mother and Julie should under any circumstances lay eyes upon it. I am most eager to know what you both make of it. The matter of carrying out the anti-Semitism project, that is to say of carrying out the investigations planned for it, will preoccupy us in the next few months to the same extent as the practical basis of the study. We are absolutely convinced, however, that the only meaningful way to counteract the persecution of Jews is to get to the heart of the matter, rather than simply reeling off the customary phrases. Admittedly such attempts will not always meet with approval – least of all from those in whose interests it is being undertaken.

Please forgive the remarkable stupidity of this letter, but I am melting away in this heat, and am no more than a shadow, albeit a well-nourished one.

Heartiest kisses
from

your old
Teddie

P.S. Please convey my warmest greetings to Miss Laidlaw, and a particular expression of sympathy to the new cook. Does Ophelia still cry out 'aï', and can Julie still imitate her so wonderfully?

Original: typewritten letter with printed letterhead.

1 Oscar Wiesengrund's birthday was 30 July.

2 Unknown.

3 The Hamburg banker Max Warburg (1867–1946), who was chairman of the supervisory board of I.G. Farben for some time, had insisted until his emigration to the USA in 1938 that the German Jews should continue to defend their economic positions under the Nazi regime. From 1929 onwards he had supported Jewish aid organizations. No further information was found on his involvement in the Alaska plan. Anita Warburg (b. 1908) studied violin in Berlin after completing school in Salem, and later began to work as a sculptress. She moved to London in 1935, and worked in an aid organization for Jewish refugees. In 1940 she married the Swiss journalist Max Wolf; they both emigrated to the USA.

4 After the foundation in January 1939 of the Reichszentrale für jüdische Auswanderung [National Centre for Jewish Emigration], which Heydrich directed, the idea of creating Jewish settlements outside of Europe and Palestine

11

was popular for a while. Shanghai was an option because of its loose regulations on visas and passports. And Dutch Guyana had been recommended by the Dutch fascist Anton A. Mussert (1894–1946). 'Thus, for example, Mussert thought that the Jewish question should be resolved "properly", as "the Dutch despised vandalism and injustice". He developed a Guyana plan as an alternative to the Madagascar plan. Surinam, as well as British and French Guyana, would be handed over by their respective mother countries (the Netherlands, England and France) for the foundation of a national Jewish homeland. In this arrangement, England and France would not be allocated any other regions as compensation, as they still had enough other colonies left over' (Hans Jansen, *Der Madagaskar-Plan. Die beabsichtigte Deportation der Europäischen Juden nach Madagaskar* [Munich, 1997], p. 257).

5 The Vienna-born violinist Fritz Kreisler (1875–1962), who also composed and had received tuition from Anton Bruckner as a boy, was one of the most famous virtuosos of the first half of the twentieth century. Kreisler, who had lived in Berlin between 1925 and 1932, emigrated to France in 1933 and became a French citizen; in 1939 he left France for America.

6 The correspondence, published in Berlin in 1938, induced Adorno to write a substantial essay that first appeared in 1942, in the mimeographed volume *Walter Benjamin zum Gedächtnis* [In Memoriam Walter Benjamin], published by the Institute of Social Research; see GS 10.1, pp. 195–237.

7 A chapter of the unfinished book *Current of Music*, which is to appear in the series *Nachgelassene Schriften* [Posthumous Works].

7 BAR HARBOR, 1.8.1939

Bar Harbor, 1 August 1939.

My dears, after travelling and arriving well, being received as old friends, and settling in superbly, we are finding it more beautiful than ever here, and are recovering with all our energy, utterly abstaining from work. Today we spent the whole day outside – aside from a long siesta – and are both already looking quite different. The last two weeks in N.Y. were unbearably hot and exhausting, and we have truly earned our rest. Gretel is wearing the red waistcoat with great zeal. Fondest regards to you both and to Julie from the old child Teddie

There is an old lady here who has been coming to B.H. for the last 60 years.

Fond regards from your Gretel
it is much busier here than it was last year, maybe this indicates a boom.

Original: photo postcard: Hotel de Gregoire, Bar Harbor, Maine. 'ONLY HOTEL ON THE SHORE'; stamp: AUG 2, 1939. Manuscript.

Bar Harbor
7 August 1939.

My dears, we are *seriously* concerned at not having heard from you for so long once again, despite writing to you fervently. Is everything all right? Leo F. also wrote to you at my request. We are increasingly recovering – quite literally – spending the whole day outside, with at least 10 hours of sleep and good seafood.[1] Utter peace and quiet, and nothing, absolutely nothing new: that is the best news we have to report. Kisses from your old child Teddie

We have already had an adventure too: the tide came in more quickly than we expected, and we were beginning to become uneasy, but a friendly seaman saved us just in time for lunch.[2] Warmest regards Gretel

Original: picture postcard: Cliff at Great Head Bar Harbor, Me.; stamp: AUG 8, 1939. Manuscript.

1 seafood: EO ('sea food').

2 *lunch*: EO.

Bar Harbor, 14 August 1939.

My dears, a thousand thanks for your lengthy letter – we are happy that you are continuing to feel at ease, even in this heat, of which the temperatures here these last few days give us an idea. Regarding Busch-Serkin,[1] I am entirely in agreement with you, my enormous Marinumba. Nothing new here, absolutely nothing – nor any visitors yet, and our recovery is progressing well and steadily. The radio project will continue for the time being; its longer-term status will only be decided on in December. The day before yesterday we managed to drive a horse-cart ourselves for 2 hours, with a real live horse, albeit an old one. It is indescribably beautiful, peaceful and lonely here, and I am sure you would also like it. Hugs from Hippo King Archibald and his beloved Giraffe Gazelle with the little horns.

Original: picture postcard: Thunder Cave. Bar Harbor, Maine; stamp: AUG 15, 1939. Manuscript.

1 The Austrian-born pianist Rudolf Serkin (1903–91) had played with the violinist Adolf Busch (1891–1952) since his youth, until the Nazis forbade

him to perform with Serkin, a Jew. Busch subsequently left Germany for good. Busch and Serkin, who had married Busch's daughter in 1935, moved to the USA in 1939.

10   BAR HARBOR, 17.8.1939

Bar Harbor, 17 August 1939.

My dears, at the same time as WK's sweet card came, we also received the news that poor Dée Pollock had passed away; she suffered no pain. Do write him a few lines c/o International Institute of Social Research, 429 West 117th Street, New York City. Perhaps Max and Maidon will now come here after all. We made up for your tornado with a nocturnal storm between 10 and 5:30 – without interruption. But, although the infernal racket prevented us from sleeping, we are so refreshed that it made no difference to us. Hugs from Archibald and Giraffe Gazelle.

Original: picture postcard: Anemone Cave Bar Harbor, Maine; stamp: AUG 18, 1939. Manuscript.

11   BAR HARBOR, 23.8.1939

23 August 39

My dears, a thousand thanks for the letter: these are the oft-mentioned Porcupines, which really do look like their namesakes. – I am very curious as to whether Leo followed my advice in time – it would not be good any more *now*, of course. Frau Täubler[1] is nice enough, and a possible contact for you, but careful: a real gossip (friend of Lotte Lenja[2] and Pussy Heimann).[3] Telegram today: Max, Maidon and Fritz are coming here on Sunday. We should be back in N.Y. on the 4th. With the splendid weather and our complete idleness, we are continuing to enjoy an excellent recovery. Gretel wrote to Frau Seele immediately about Jenny.[4] Simply carry on as you have been doing, and you could get far in life. Fond regards, many kisses from your big ox. Archibald is looking well, and is making incredible progress at 66, which we play every evening, competition for your rummy. Fond regards, Giraffe Gazelle

Original: picture postcard: The Porcupine Islands, Bar Harbor, Maine; stamp: AUG 24, 1939. Manuscript.

1 Unknown.

2 The actress and singer Lotte Lenya (real name: Karoline Charlotte Blamauer; 1898–1981), who was originally from Vienna and lived and worked in Berlin

14

from 1921 onwards. Lenya, who had played the role of Pirate Jenny in *The Threepenny Opera* to great success in 1928, emigrated to the USA in 1933.

3 Referred to in later letters as 'Heymann'; unknown.

4 Jenny Leonore Wiesengrund (1874–1963), who lived in Hamburg with her husband Arnold Villinger; no Frau Seele is known. Translator's note: it is unclear whether 'die Seele' refers to a woman named Seele or rather simply 'the soul' (in its application to a person), as the word *Seele* (soul) is a female noun. As the former seems slightly more probable, however, all further references to 'die Seele' in the original text will henceforth be translated as 'Frau Seele'.

12   BAR HARBOR, 28.8.1939

28 August 39

My dears, I enclose a letter that Sadie wrote to Gretel, and from which you can recognize that our lovely brown-skinned lady is on a higher cultural level than all the German Annachens and their wider surroundings.

Max, Maidon and Fritz are here with two cars, and we drive around all day. Now we are showing them our island at the lowest tide. We are very glad to be able to follow the events in Europe[1] – which are enervating enough – here together, which I should add is no easy thing, as secluded as it is here. We still do *not* believe that there will be war, although the show is certainly costing enough this time. We had predicted Russia. We are determined to remain in America, even if war breaks out. Chamberlain – or J'aime Berlin, as the French say – was certainly in no hurry to go to war for us when Hitler threw us down the stairs. – I would advise WK both warmly and urgently to resist any fits of imperious emotion and remain calm in H. Do not guard German prisoners, but rather the Wondrous Hippo Cow, and water her with Cervera (?) tropical![2] We are well rested and will stay here 2 days longer, arriving in N.Y. on 6 Sept. Kisses from the horses the big ox

The dear horse barked in its sleep like a dog the other day. Kisses from your Gretel Horse

Fri. at 1:30 P.m.

My Dear Mrs. Adorno:–

Your letter and was very glad to hear from you and the Dr. So far my vacation has been 'Lousy'. I've had company every night up untill Wed. night. and now I am as tired as I can be.

I haven't been out of N.Y.C. other than the 13th I went on a boat ride up the river, but I do expect to rest up from now on and maybe go to Philadelphia for Labor day week end.

15

I hope you both are very much rested and are feeling very fine by now.

When I closed the Apt. I was very satisfied with the painters work only they were so dirty.

I shall go in Mon. and start to getting things in order for your return.

Sorry not to have written you before I have the receipts for the chowders but couldn't get one of Lobster Stew.

Hope you both continue to rest on.

My kindest regards to the Dr and Yourself.

I am as Ever.

Sadie

Original: handwritten letter on the same sheet as Sadie's letter. Translator's note: Sadie's letter written in English (with spelling and grammatical mistakes).

1 On 23 August, Hitler's Germany and the Soviet Union had signed a pact of mutual non-aggression, and in England the mobilization for war had begun with the conscription of reservists; the English–Polish pact of alliance was signed on 25 August.

2 Adorno unquestionably wrote 'cervera', but presumably meant *cerveza*, the Spanish word for beer.

13   NEW YORK, 8.9.1939

8 September 1939

My dears:

it seems that the great times[1] have begun once more. I still cannot really believe it, and would not be the least bit surprised if, after the conquest of Poland, Hitler were to appoint a new Polish government and form an alliance with it, Mussolini held a peace conference, and the Louischers[2] allied themselves with the Siegfrieds in the Maginot Line, with the pope swinging his gas-mask above it all as a censer. I know that this notion mocks all reason among all reasonable people, but hardly any more than this war itself, which ultimately nobody believes in, and which the newspapers and radios incessantly tell us is 'a reality', mocks true reason. We are now left with our theory as the disgraced Hebrews, but those Hebrews who turned out to be right, all the Walter Rosenthals[3] who view Hitler as a madman and hail the peace front against him as a blessing, are nonetheless wrong in a more profound sense. If it really is true, then the world spirit has had an occupational accident, and the world of appearances has gained

16

control over the intrinsic order – or rather disorder – of the present historical phase in a truly demonic fashion.

Nonetheless, it goes without saying that, for all our disillusionment at the saviours of democracy, who have now also been joined by the Polish pogrom instigators, destroying Hitler would spare the world the worst, leaving only the second-worst, and we hope with every bone in our bodies that he will be defeated. Why he began the war is beyond all rational explanation; after the pact with Russia, he could have had everything he wanted peacefully, and his victory is by no means out of the question, but still rather improbable – especially as America will be unable to keep out of it if it goes on for a long time, which one should absolutely reckon with. The Blitzkrieg method will not work in the West; England's resources are inexhaustible, and England and France should be able to force at least the right of passage from the Italians, assuming they do not break through the Siegfried Line[4] before then. You can see how this madness works; even partly reasonable persons such as myself are transformed by an irresistible force into alehouse politicians, simply because true thinking proves powerless in the face of the absurd senselessness of this war. One cannot imagine the suffering and horror it will cause.

Your situation, at any rate, has been transformed in the most peculiar fashion: you are now no longer the emigrants, but rather the most envied people among your whole circle in Germany. Even Annachen will have some thoughts drummed into her head, assuming she has not already died an Aryan death by then.

As I imagine that your thirst for news is as great as our own, and as I have no more faith in Cuban radio than I do in any other public institution there, I have compiled an exact list of all the American stations run by the two big broadcasting corporations that you can pick up with a decent radio in Cuba. NBC (National Broadcasting Company), whose trademark is the three consecutive notes of a second-inversion chord, is the largest, richest and most powerful of the companies, and has the quickest news service. CBS (Columbia Broadcasting System) is not quite as big, and perhaps a little bit slower sometimes, but younger and less bureaucratic, with better commentators (Kaltenborn).[5] But the most important thing for you will be to receive the United Press and Associated Press news, which are broadcast at regular times. They are normally broadcast by NBC, in connection with Esso petrol advertisements.

We returned one day earlier together with Max, Maidon and Fritz. We spent two whole days going on very pleasant drives, spending the night in Concord, New Hampshire. We are both fully rested, and Bar Harbor made an excellent impression on our visitors. The next few days I will be incredibly busy with the radio project, for which I have

17

to prepare an extensive report.[6] Aside from this, I have no news; but the present news is quite enough as it is.

I am very sorry about poor WK's illness; I assume that the cause was not poisoned *laurel*, but rather poisoned [*sic*] *ivy*, something that is very common here, and very unpleasant, but completely harmless – and which, incidentally, depends on a particular allergic disposition. Certain individuals, e.g. Ferdi Kramer,[7] are entirely immune to it. I wish you a swift recovery.

Write soon, and at length; our attitude that this war was primarily an act of revenge on your behalf would admittedly be unworthy of our theory, but after the failure of theory it can at least be excused as the most tangible idea. In any case, one cannot even seriously enjoy one's lust for revenge. One had hoped for this war a thousand times, but, now that it has become real, all that remains is naked horror: as if a terrible black funnel had opened, and is now sucking everything in. The fact that humanity has come far enough to wage such a war, but not far enough for such a war to be unnecessary, is cause for nothing short of absolute despair.

Heartiest kisses from

> your two horses
> Hottilein and Rossilein

PS. We would naturally like to know if Hermann Levi[8] and brother Samson[9] still managed to get out in time. Franz Adorno[10] and Franz Villinger[11] have been conscripted, and equally Bolly, Bummel and Rüsselacko[12] on the other side. A shame they cannot wage the war among themselves. Then England's victory would at least be guaranteed – assuming one put Bummel in the right mood at the right moment. Redvers[13] is in Massachusetts; he had invited us to come, but we could not delay our return any longer. I hope he cannot go back.

I will have your papers checked again; it is possible that *a great deal* can be earned if one reaches a *quick* decision. I shall wire you then, and ask that you wire back *immediately*. I am absolutely in favour of making the most of this opportunity, i.e. *selling out* at a certain point. The boom is so fantastic that it *cannot* last. One *must* not get out too late.

Original: typewritten letter with a partly handwritten postscript.

1 Allusion to Karl Kraus's essay 'In dieser großen Zeit' [In These Great Times], from the issue of *Die Fackel* published on 5 December 1914.

2 This name originates from that of Adorno's maternal uncle Louis Prosper Calvelli-Adorno (1866–1960), and at once refers to his uncle's entire family; Adorno's 'Louis complex', as his father once termed his stylized aversion, was

well known in the Wiesengrund family. Translator's note: *Louische* is a diminutive of 'Louis' in Frankfurt dialect.

3 A fictitious figure used as a parodistic projection by the members of the Institute of Social Research.

4 In the First World War, this was the defence system set up in February 1917, extending from Arras to La Fère (Aisne). In the Second World War, this name was also used for the West Wall, or the Siegfried line, a fortification that was the scene of important battles in 1944–5.

5 Hans von Kaltenborn (1878–1965) worked for CBS as a news commentator from 1928 onwards; his commentaries were not scripted.

6 'On a Social Critique of Radio Music'.

7 The Frankfurt architect Ferdinand Kramer (1898–1985), who worked with Ernst May, the town councillor and head of the planning department, designed, as director of the typography department, appropriate and reasonably priced interior furnishings, and later worked as a freelance architect; the Nazis banned him from his profession in 1937, and he emigrated to the USA in 1938 with his wife Beate. Kramer had close relations with the members of the institute. In 1952, Max Horkheimer made him director of the reconstruction of Frankfurt University; the university library in Frankfurt was also built according to his plans. In the USA, Kramer worked as an architect and industrial designer.

8 Connected to the Herzberger family by marriage.

9 Samson was the brother-in-law of Julie Rautenberg, whose will mentions two men by the names of Ernst and Ludwig Samson (probably father and son); it is unclear which of these is meant here.

10 Franz Calvelli-Adorno (1897–1984), who had studied law and was an excellent pianist and violinist, had lost his post as district court administrator in Frankfurt, which he had held since 1928, in 1933. He taught as a private music tutor in Dortmund in 1945, and played in the orchestra of the Jüdischer Kulturbund [Jewish Cultural Association] from 1934 to 1938. He was conscripted at the outbreak of war, and dismissed again in June 1940.

11 Franz Villinger (b. 1907) is the son of Jenny Villinger (1874–1963) and the doctor Arnold Villinger (1869–1962). The Villingers lived in Hamburg.

12 'Bummel' was the nickname of Adorno's English cousin Alexander Louis Wingfield (1908–69), and it may have been his brother Bernard Theodore Wingfield (1903–57) who was known as 'Bolly'. Rüsselacko was probably a further relative of Adorno – this time on his mother's side – namely Anton Calvelli-Adorno (1911–69), Louis Prosper Calvelli-Adorno's son from his second marriage, i.e. Franz Calvelli-Adorno's stepbrother. Anton Calvelli-Adorno served in the British Army.

13 Adorno had made the acquaintance of the economist Redvers Opie (1900–84) in Oxford.

13 September 1939

My dears:

a thousand thanks for your letters and good wishes,[1] and for the pictures. How charming of Estella to make those for us – please extend the warmest thanks to her from both of us. They are much better in the smaller format than they are enlarged, and we found the photograph by the car in particular delightful and lively.

We hope the Hippo Cow has meanwhile become a little calmer about the war. Even if one cannot expect the likes of ourselves to remain as cool as Daladier or Chamberlain, who still convey the impression that they are afraid of harming a hair on Herr Hitler's head. Things have become somewhat more serious these last few days, but there is a peculiar feeling to this whole war that one cannot quite shake off. It reminds one of those sorts of dreams[2] where the most terrible things occur, but without entirely becoming a reality. A dream in which the world is ending, for example, and one then strolls out of the cellar and onto the road.

I was most jealous to hear that the Hippo Cow is now thinking of Louis again. I had hoped that he would have sunk into oblivion once and for all after your emigration, to live on only in my songs; instead, I now see the shadow of his beard covering the Hippo Cow's letter. I am the only one you should be worrying about, and in my case there is no immediate reason.

We wrote to Melly[3] immediately from Bar Harbor about the 300 RM. However, I do not now under any circumstances wish to write to her about the division of the remaining sum. You probably do not know that Germany is now in a state of martial law, with every conceivable offence punishable by death, and I would find it irresponsible to put Melly at such risk. Foreign correspondence, let alone between Aryans and Jews, is probably suspect in itself, and if there is even talk of money, whatever camouflage we might use, the Gestapo will strike immediately. I have truly never been a scaremonger myself, but under no circumstances would I wish to bear the responsibility for endangering Melly's life on account of a few hundred Marks, and would urge you also to refrain from doing so. Gretel and Max are of the same opinion.

As far as the proletarianization hinted at by WK is concerned, the current state of the stock market certainly does not give cause for any immediate fears. I have not had anything sold yet, and will certainly wait for your general opinion on the matter before I undertake anything. Everything is pointing to a war boom par excellence.

20

I am working strenuously on that report for the Rockefeller Foundation with a new and quite intelligent assistant.[4] One of the other assistants seems, once again, to be a real mental case. We celebrated my birthday in utter peace and quiet, only Gretel, Max and I, and thought of you. Meanwhile Rudi has re-formed the quartet, and Khuner[5] is staying after all. I am dictating these lines in great haste between work. Write soon, and heartiest kisses

from the two horses
Hottilein and Rossilein

Original: typewritten letter.

1 On the occasion of Adorno's thirty-sixth birthday on 11 September.

2 See also the aphorism 'Eigentumsvorbehalt' [Reservation of Proprietary Rights] from *Minima Moralia*.

3 This is Amalia Karplus (1878–1956), née Jacak, from Neuheusel in Czechoslovakia, the second wife of Gretel Adorno's father, Albert Karplus (1863–1936).

4 George Simpson (1904–98), whose collaboration on the report 'On a Social Critique of Radio Music' Adorno explicitly mentions. This report was read to the members of the Princeton Radio Research Project on 26 October 1939.

5 The Moravian-born violinist Felix Khuner (1906–91) had been a member of the Kolisch Quartet since mid-1926. The other members of the re-formed Quartet were Jascha Vlissi and Stefan Auber.

15   NEW YORK, 1.10.1939

the most reverent congratulations[1] to the venerable mother MARI-NUMBA VON BAUCHSCHLEIFER[2] from her faithful children HIPPO KING ARCHIBALD and wife THE DEAR GIRAFFE GAZELLE WITH THE LITTLE HORNS known as GAZELLE-HORNLETS

Original: telegram.

1 On the occasion of Maria Wiesengrund's birthday, which Adorno customarily dated as 1 October, whereas the birth certificate records 30 September.

2 Translator's note: this means 'belly-dragger', a reference to the hippo-potamus.

14 October 1939

My dears:

a thousand thanks for your kind letters. It is a great pity that Estella is not coming here; we were already greatly looking forward to hearing at length from her about you. We hope she is not having any more troubles with her little arm.

We had had especially good intentions with the money, as we thought that Leo, who after all sends money to Julie, would transfer the amount to you in the most convenient fashion. You are doing me a monstrous injustice by assuming 'idleness' on my part. I would only ask the following of you: 1) tell me in which form you would most like to have the money (after my visit to Cuba I am very much against a money order) and 2) always inform me well enough in advance to rule out any possibility whatsoever of such an exceptionally regrettable delay.

Melly: we have also heard nothing from her since August. – Leo's last bank statement went out to you by recorded delivery. A document contained in the previous statement has meanwhile turned up. Incidentally, I agree with you that one should not sell anything at present, and I have informed Leo accordingly.

I daresay that after the preliminary vote there can no longer be any doubt about the lifting of the arms embargo. America almost certainly has much stronger ties to the Allies than you know over there. We avoid speaking German in public, and at the institute also on the telephone.

Various old friends have turned up: Redvers is business advisor for the English embassy in Washington, the only one. You can imagine what that means. I am glad he escaped the disaster. We spent a lovely day together. He told me, incidentally, that suitable positions had been found for all Oxford dons, so that hardly any of them had to go to the front, which is most reassuring. Then Paul and Gabi[1] came here on a visitor's visa. They left before the war broke out, and are now preparing for a longer stay here, though emigration is naturally unthinkable. We often see each other; they have been over here for lunch, and I took Gabi out one evening, as our old tradition has it – but to Harlem, to some of the darkest negro bars.

On 1 November I shall be speaking in front of a number of representatives of the Rockefeller Foundation about my music study in connection with the project, so keep your fingers crossed. You will receive a copy of the lecture[2] as soon as I have given it. I would, incidentally, be grateful if you could return Radio Voice once you have read it; I am short on copies. But you can keep the anti-Semitism project – which is now lying dormant – and my Columbia lecture, which you should have received by now.

I am in bed with flu and am dictating. I had a fairly high fever (39), but I am feeling much better now, though I still have a slight temperature – not a cold, but rather an infection. There was a veritably infernal heat here at the start of the week. I hear that the fairest months are now beginning where you are; but if they are similar to here, then it will not be a particularly enjoyable experience.

Write soon to your poor child.

We send you all fond, warm regards, and do be good and learn your Spanish: compared to such a language as the American, where it is possible to write in an obituary: 'he was a very swell guy', that Romance and Catholic language must already be like a promise of happiness.

Hugs and kisses from

Hottilein and Rossilein
Teddie

Original: typewritten letter.

1 Gabrielle Oppenheim-Errera, born in Brussels, and her husband Paul Oppenheim (1885–1977), who lived in Frankfurt until 1933. Paul Oppenheim had studied chemistry in Giessen, and had a leading position in the company N. M. Oppenheimer Nachfolger in Frankfurt from 1908 to 1926 before working for I. G. Farben. From 1927 onwards he was also an outside lecturer. The Oppenheims emigrated initially to Brussels in 1933 and then to the USA in 1939.

2 A copy of the typescript of this untitled lecture, which was largely identical to the essay 'On a Social Critique of Radio Music', however, has survived among Adorno's possessions; see Theodor W. Adorno Archiv, Ts 49667–49690.

17   NEW YORK, 17.10.1939

17 October, 1939

We just paid a visit to Mrs. Adorno[1] and we all send you her devotest regards. Love

Teddie

Gabrielle Oppenheim Errera
Gretel   Paul Oppenheim

Original: art picture postcard: Paola Adorno. By Anthony van Dyck (1599–1641). The Frick Collection, New York; stamp: OCT 17, 1939 (see fig. 2). Manuscript. Translator's note: the original is in English.

23

1 In her letter of 6 September 1948, Maria Wiesengrund writes that she had seen this painting in Genoa, in the Palazzo Adorno, and refers to the Genoese Adornos as the direct ancestors of her father.

18 NEW YORK, 6.12.1939

New York, 6 December 39

My faithful old Wondrous Hippo Cow, you are doing me a frightful injustice – you probably cannot imagine how busy I am with the radio project, and I am now recovering from a *very serious* bout of flu with a very high fever, which confined me to my bed for 10 days, all because I did not take the time to convalesce properly after the last one. I was out with Gabi for *one single* evening, and I should add that it was purely out of obligation. So do not be rough with your child, for he cannot bear it. The only way to make him write more – and I shall truly do my best to write more now – is to treat him well. Franchement: if I am silent, then it is almost always because I have been scared off by an unpleasant or unfriendly undertone. You understand me, and certainly know how to remedy the situation. For there is nothing I wish for more than to receive letters from you, and am happy to reply to them. But: when will you write me an *individual* letter? Is this whole business of writing family letters from everyone to everyone not inhuman, rendering any truly spontaneous utterance impossible? Far be it from me to reproach you, but I am at least not alone to blame for my silence.

I am happy at the prospect of your coming soon, and only hope that you will feel as well in the U.S.A. as in Cuba (I daresay one can *live* much more pleasantly over there, but it would be irresponsible to miss the chance of immigrating here). I shall write to WK at length about this. I am *against* California (too far away) and against N.Y., for I absolutely do not want to see you leading the emigrant life here. Best of all probably a little towards the south (*west* coast of Florida? Georgia?): pleasant climate, easy to reach from here, and cheap. But we shall discuss all this in detail.

I have an idea for dear WK that I would ask him to consider *very* seriously. He should write an English book about *wine*, about the knowledge and the treatment. Very quickly, for these reasons:
  (1) this culture is dying out: one should at least hand it down in such a way that it can be taken up again some day.
  (2) I am convinced that I could find a publisher for it here, precisely *because* nobody here knows anything about it. I would do everything in my power.

24

(3) WK would have an activity he enjoyed, one that is worthy of him and, in a sense, would be a review of his professional life.
(4) he could easily find some expert position afterwards.
Am I being practical?

Very sad that you and Julie had to part ways – the Frenkels found it inexplicable. Send her a thousand greetings from me, and let me know in good time when she is arriving, for I want to collect her at all costs.

And the time when we shall see each other again is approaching. Look after yourself over there in the fair coming months, together with our good old bad Tusker[1] and Julie, and

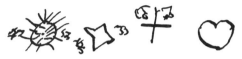

(Shakespeare)[2]
Your old child Teddie

Gretel is on a fattening diet and is not eating anything anymore. (overleaf)

PS for WK: regarding economic matters. The situation in Europe is *completely opaque*. Anything is possible: even the collapse of Hitlerism – and some things point precisely to that. I consider it extremely important to be thinking already now about what to do under such circumstances – it is possible that *everything* depends on acting quickly. Have you thought about that? Would *you* – or should *I* go then? Things should not escalate before the spring – I do not, in my heart of hearts, believe that the war will be long; the English tactics allow certain conclusions about Germany.

As far as German property is concerned, I would avoid worrying about that at present. Keep quiet, wait and see,[3] let sleeping dogs lie, then there is a chance of slipping through. I would not sign *anything* for *anyone*.

Love[4]
Teddie

Original: handwritten letter.

1 A further family name for Oscar Wiesengrund, the Wild Boar King.

2 Picture puzzle: Suggested solution: *A Midsummer Night's Dream, Measure for Measure, As You Like It.*

3 *wait and see*: EO.

4 *Love*: EO.

19 December 1939

My dears:
a thousand thanks for such kind and lengthy letters. I have mean-while recovered completely, but am fighting a constant risk of catch-ing cold, which is presumably mainly a result of the appalling weather conditions. But this is not the only reason that I can understand why it is difficult for you to bid farewell to Havana. If one did not have to be in the USA to earn a living, or whatever else, by being part of some company where the only honourable thing would be to have no part in it, then a southern, human, unhygienic, in a word: sympathetic city like Havana would be a thousand times more preferable. – We have discussed moving there on countless occasions, at least temporarily, and have often considered this together with Max. But I nonetheless consider it best for you to avoid further delaying your immigration; not simply because of the 2 x $500, but above all because one cannot know what the Cuban policy on foreigners will be like in the future, so one should not squander one's right to immigrate. I consider it an excellent plan to spend at least part of the year in Cuba after immi-grating here. But I would urgently advise you against Miami, one of the most ghastly places I have ever seen, a desert littered with house palm-trees and rip-off bars. The completely non-tourist west coast of Florida, on the other hand, according to everyone and especially Carrie Sinn, is genuinely beautiful and serene. I heard the same thing from Robert de Neufville,[1] who lived in Florida for years as a school-teacher; unfortunately I cannot reach him at the moment, as he is searching for employment with his little car somewhere in the west. (I fear he lost the job in Florida due to his unstable mental state, and is therefore having difficulty in finding a new one.) I would definitely get in touch with Carrie right away about Florida, and not spend more than 24 hours in Miami. You will see that I am right.
I consider it highly unlikely, by the way, that you will be deprived of your German citizenship; this only happens to political persons, and even then entirely by chance: e.g. Fritz and Leo L.,[2] but otherwise none of us yet.
As far as the crisis is concerned, we will send you à part Churchill's wonderful speech,[3] one has to read it in English, as it loses its flavor[4] in any German translation. The English lion seems to be stirring some-what – let us hope that it was not merely stretching about in its sleep. It was also not without satisfaction that we registered what was obvi-ously an utter failure on the part of Stalin's Red Army, although their opponent, the Finnish general Mannerheim,[5] is one of the most raging

pogrom heroes of all time (which is not in any of the papers), whom I actually wish a particularly sticky end. If Mr Stalin continues in this manner, then maybe there will even end up being something like a real socialist revolution in Russia. But the world has become so dialectical that one cannot even hope for that without reservation, for then Chamberlain and Hitler would reach an agreement in 24 hours. In short, it is a joy to be alive. The East, I might add, is not an acute problem, and Japan is in a similarly drained condition to Italy, with incredible inner conflicts to boot, and will not be capable of action for years.

As far as my literary wine idea is concerned, I do not consider this a crackpot idea.[6] I think you are really being too modest in this respect. I have practically unlimited faith in your technical competence, and as for the literary aspect, you still have me too, with my herd of secretaries and assistants. I share your belief that you would have chances as an adviser or in some similar position in the USA without any untoward optimism, and all the more for your not being dependent on acquiring such a position. It is purely a matter of getting started at the right level, i.e. at the top, through higher connections, and not as a 'job-seeker'. I am sure the Frenkels will gladly be of assistance, and I could think of a few other people besides. But precisely in this context it would be extremely advantageous to have some thoughts on paper. It is only since being here that I have discovered the magical powers of memoranda. New techniques and specialized economic competence are valued to an almost superstitious extent here, and I doubt that you would have many equal rivals in this field. The fact that there is no wine culture here has no great bearing on this: on the contrary, one would have to work towards exploring new sales possibilities through new methods (both in the actual production and in advertisements for 'wine appreciation'[7] – a slogan I invented myself, and which I hereby lay at your feet). The grander the better. This is the land of self-promotion – all you have to do is find an American radio station. I entirely agree with you, however, that you should by no means get anything started at your own expense. But the thought of your finding an appropriate activity without having to go to much effort is surely a tempting one. It need not, and should not, turn into work. Regarding the question of where you should go in the summer, we still have plenty of time to correspond on this. We intend to discuss this in depth with Julie in January – we are so looking forward to her coming here, as sad as we are that you are to lose her. It will certainly be a great relief to be closer together. I have my eye – for all sorts of reasons – on Virginia and North Carolina, where the climate is very consistent in summer and winter, and seems to resemble that of Germany.

27

How darling the Hippo Cow's letter was. It made me frightfully happy. The birthday photograph was a sweet gesture, but do not be angry with me if I say that one can see rather clearly that it was made by the premier photographer in Havana, one who could just as easily be the premier photographer in Miltenberg: I infinitely prefer the little amateur pictures, especially the one with the three of you standing by the car.

You too will only receive our Christmas parcel once you are in Florida, for the same reason. But we send you all our best wishes for Christmas and the New Year today: perhaps that fat, round Hippo Cow number 1940 will bring us all something good and pleasing at long last. For everything is so unclear that even something good is not beyond the realm of possibility.

We are living together happily and peacefully; the horse's treatment seems[8] to be working well. I have completed a long critical study[8] on the educational music programme hosted by Walter Damrosch[9] on NBC, in English, for the radio project; in it I combine my criticisms of this ghastly undertaking with positive suggestions showing how one could introduce children and laypersons to music. If I have a spare copy I shall send it to you; but it may still take a few weeks. At the moment I am working on a big German essay[10] for the journal that I had already sketched long ago, and which I now finally want to get done. On Saturday Max, Maidon and Fritz will be here for our Christmas dinner, and we will all drink your health. Our New Year's Eve party will be at the institute. Aside from this, we intend for the holidays to be as quiet and undisturbed as possible.

I expect you do not know that Alfons Herzberger's wife has a bastard child by Gottfried Salomon. We heard this story from Else;[11] but to tell you about that would itself require a long letter of its own, one whose contents you can imagine yourselves by now – it was all exactly the way you think, only even a little more so. Among other things, she would have liked to get some money out of us, but we pretended not to notice anything. She is consumed by envy, towards both you and us. I doubt she is at all well off financially any more, and my theory is that she is going to Argentina to order Grünebaum[12] into the creaking marital bed once and for all and, while exposing her mature charms to him, snatch away the remnants of his fortune.

Heartiest kisses from the two horses, whinnying a faithful WELCOME at you.

Hottilein and Rossilein

Original: typewritten letter.

1 Erich Sebastian Robert de Neufville (1907–1989), who was born in Frankfurt but showed a preference for the family residence in Kronberg im

Taunus, studied law in Marburg and subsequently worked for a law firm in Berlin. He fled to England soon after the Nazis' rise to power on account of his mother's Jewish descent, where he met Adorno again in Oxford. Both frequented the Oxford University Musical Club; Robert de Neufville, a lover of music, had taken violin lessons in his youth. After gaining his BA at Oxford University, he moved in 1936 to the USA, where two of his brothers and his sister were living. He became a teacher for foreign languages there at a boys' college. During the war he served as second lieutenant in the US Army and worked for military intelligence. He was awarded the Purple Heart, the American Campaign Medal and the French Croix de Guerre. His daughter Julie Logsdon de Neufville said of him: 'My father was a brilliant man who loved languages, music, literature, history, and mathematics.'

2 Leo Löwenthal (1900–1993), who was born in Frankfurt and was a friend of Adorno and Kracauer in his youth, gained his PhD in 1923 with a dissertation on Franz von Baader, and subsequently worked as a secondary school [Gymnasium] teacher before joining the Institute of Social Research in 1930. Löwenthal was chief editor of the *Journal for Social Research* from 1932 to 1940.

3 This presumably refers to the speech made in the House of Commons on 6 December 1939. It was published in the German edition of Churchill's speeches under the title 'Unsere Seewege' [Our Sea Routes].

4 *flavor*: EO (American spelling).

5 Carl Gustav Emil Freiherr von Mannerheim (1867–1951), who had ruthlessly crushed the Finnish socialist revolution with his 'white army' in early 1918, became a Finnish marshal in 1933. The Finnish–Soviet war in the winter of 1939–40, which began on 30 November with the invasion of the Red Army, occasioned great losses for Finland, which sided with the Germans after their attack on the Soviet Union. As president of Finland, Mannerheim was forced to sign a truce with the Soviet Union in 1944.

6 Translator's note: the original expression for 'crackpot idea' is *Schnapsidee* – i.e. the sort of idea one would have when intoxicated with spirits (*Schnaps* not being restricted to 'schnapps', but actually a more general term for spirits) – which is clearly intended as a pun in the context of wine.

7 *wine appreciation*: EO.

8 This is 'The NBC Music Appreciation Hour', which then became the essay 'Die gewürdigte Musik' [The Appreciated Music].

9 The conductor Walter Johannes Damrosch (1862–1950).

10 'George und Hofmannsthal. Zum Briefwechsel' [George and Hofmannsthal: On their Correspondence].

11 The siblings Else (1877–1962) and Alfons Herzberger (b. 1879), whose family – originally resident in Neunkirchen in the Saarland – were co-owners together with Gretel Adorno of a leather factory in Berlin. Alfons Herzberger, who had been married, until 1932, to a Jewish woman living in Paris, had

emigrated with his sister in 1935 to Paris, where the Frankfurt sociologist Gottfried Salomon-Delatour (1896–1964) was living as an emigrant. Else Herzberger, a long-standing friend of Agathe Calvelli-Adorno and Maria Wiesengrund, was portrayed by Adorno in the aphorism 'Heliotrope' from *Minima Moralia*.

12 Director Grünebaum (1874–?), known to the Wiesengrund family since their Frankfurt days, did not marry Else Herzberger, at least not before 1949.

20 NEW YORK, 29.12.1939

New York, 29 December 1939

My dears,

I have meanwhile gathered information for you, taking your place of residence into account – initially for the winter and the transitional period. Alex Böker,[1] who was an assistant professor in the South (Tennessee) for a long time, visited us in Boston (where he is now an instructor at Harvard) over Christmas, as did Robert de Neufville, who taught for years at a boarding school in Florida. They all agree with me in urging you to avoid Florida, a ghastly place that is nonetheless shamelessly expensive during the season (i.e. during the coming months). They say that the west coast, however, is quite beautiful, as well as peaceful and cheap. As Florida is a very narrow peninsula, the distance from the east coast – where Miami is located – to the west coast is insignificant. By far the most beautiful place is *Sarasota*, apparently, which can be reached comfortably by bus in a 5-hour ride from Miami; I would strongly advise you even to go there as soon as you get to Miami and have a look. There are guesthouses etc. there. Other locations on the west coast of Florida rated highly include Fort Myers (which is even closer to Miami) and St. Petersburg. For now I would choose among these places, with Sarasota as the favourite.

In North Carolina there is *Ashville*, a quiet place among woodlands that seems to offer ideal conditions. But I would avoid going there right now, during the winter, but rather later and for a longer time. – And Virginia has the advantage of a climate that is almost identical to that in Germany, and of being much closer to New York (6–8 hours by train). The well-situated places worth considering for you there are Lexington and Charlottesville.

A further possibility would be New Orleans, which is evidently a quite wonderful, French-influenced city with extremely pleasant living conditions. I myself find it very attractive, and you would probably be best off there, but the one disadvantage is the considerable distance from New York. – Finally, I have been recommended a number of small towns between Florida and New Orleans in the state of Mississippi (New Orleans is the capital of Louisiana, the old French colony that fell to the English in the 18th century). The recommended places in Mississippi are Biloxi, Pass Christian and Bay St. Louis (not to be confused with St. Louis, an enormous city that is much closer to Chicago and probably horrible). – These places are pretty much the cream of the crop I have gathered so far, and I would advise dear WK to go to an American travel agency and gain further information about all of them. You can naturally find out anything about the places in Florida in Miami, as you have to land there in any case.

Our Christmas was not quite as peaceful as we had hoped, for people were constantly paying us visits. But it was pleasant and restful nonetheless; meanwhile I had to finish something for the radio project[2] *par force*, and New Year's celebrations will take place collectively at the institute. Aside from this, we have absolutely nothing new to report; Gretel's therapy seems as if it might be successful, at least she has not had any more real migraines since, but she is still terribly thin despite eating well – presumably due to a hypofunction of the pituitary gland. And precisely this can be treated with radiotherapy and injections.

We hope you have had pleasant holidays. Think of us at New Year as we shall think of you. Perhaps things will be more peaceful at last. We were already greatly worried about our oh-so-delicate war, but it seems to have recovered somewhat, and Hitler will be brought down if the English are serious about it. That, however, is the question – whether they want to or not. But one thing suggests that they do, at least: the fact that they have no reason to fear this Russia, and therefore need not hold on to so costly a henchman as Germany, even if they would like to. Forgive the atrocious appearance of this letter – my typewriter was crazy[3] to start with – apparently out of revenge, as I write so rarely myself since having secretaries swarming about me. This letter, however, I am writing myself.

Your dear letter just came – I am so glad that you had a pretty, albeit half-wild Christmas. We have not converted to turkey – we had a good, proper goose! – Hope to see you soon.[4]

Heartiest kisses from the old child

Teddie

Many kisses, happy New Year

Your old Gretel Horse

Original: typewritten letter with handwritten conclusion.

1 Alexander Böker (1912–97), born in Heidelberg, studied jurisprudence, political science, philosophy and economics in Munich, Königsberg and

Berlin, and continued his studies at Oxford on a Rhodes scholarship. He lived in the USA from 1939 onwards, and gained a PhD at Harvard under the tutelage of Heinrich Brüning. Besides his position as an assistant, he also worked as a journalist. Because Böker refused to assume American citizenship and serve in the army, he was only allowed to return to Germany in 1948, and worked there as a diplomat from 1949 onwards.

2 See letter 19, note 8.

3 *crazy*: EO.

4 *Hope to see you soon*: EO.

1940

13 January 1940
New York City

My dears,
we were overjoyed to hear from Leo Frenkel, who called us last night, that you have landed – and immigrated! – successfully. We send you our warmest welcome to this land that may be ugly, and inhabited by drugstores, hot dogs and cars, but is at least safe to some extent at the moment! Two *Tazzelwürmer*[1] have dashed ahead of this welcome; we hope you received them!

We were greatly saddened to hear that Julie is having difficulties, but with the Frenkels' capital power it should be easy enough to deal with them, so we shall expect to see her over here very soon, and are greatly looking forward to it.

You will now be setting off on your explorations – we hope you will already find what you are looking for in Sarasota. Incidentally, I have been invited for next Wednesday evening by a Southerner[2] (from Georgia) from a 'posh' but impoverished family (one of my assistants from the project), who I am sure will advise me well, and who might even be able to name a *family* that would be prepared to accommodate you. For this would be best, especially if Julie is really to be with you no longer. The prices you were told are surely exaggerated; outside of Miami, Palm Beach and Daytona Beach, it should hardly be much more expensive than in H – Dixieland is too broke for that!

Your idea of spending part of your time in Cuba strikes me as a very good one – and also feasible. Everything will be different once

33

you have your American First papers. I shall seek out precise legal information.

As for myself, I have given birth to a substantial baby: I finished the big piece on George and Hofmannsthal yesterday. By the way, were George's parents in Bingen rich, or were they petty bourgeois and it was only the brother who made something of himself financially? It would be quite important for me to know. – The Hippo Cow poem[3] was tremendously fine; it was only my preoccupation with George that prevented me from paying tribute to its metric beauty immediately.

Gretel was *greatly* pleased by your invitation to come to the South; but we are both overwhelmed by work at the moment, especially as Max is once again not getting along with his new secretary!! But we do hope to see you soon – and we are all living in *one*, albeit large country. Heartiest kisses
from the child Teddie

Not a word from Else,[4] whereas Felix Weil[5] and his wife, who were on the same ship, wrote immediately!

Original: handwritten letter.

1 Translator's note: according to legend, there is an Alpine dragon known as the *Tazzelwurm*; it is unclear, however, exactly what could have been meant here.

2 *Southerner*: EO; presumably George Simpson.

3 This has not survived.

4 Else Herzberger.

5 The economist Felix Weil (1898–1975), a co-founder of the Institute of Social Research, and his second wife, Margot Weil.

22 NEW YORK, 27.1.1940

New York   27 January 1940

My dears, it worries me a little that I have not heard from you. I gather it is freezing cold down south – here, we hardly dare step outside the hut. Are you dressed warmly enough? All well here. The new big essay is completely finished and checked, and I greatly enjoyed working on it. The Wagner text[1] now published, I will send you the latest issue as soon as it arrives here. We met up twice with Albert Hahn,[2] very pleasant and interesting. Anita Lothar[3] apparently getting divorced; Pussy's husband[4] locked up. Do write soon and at length. A thousand kisses from the two horses Hottilein and Rossilein

Original: photo postcard: The American Museum of Natural History, New York, USA; 'BALUCITHERIUM. The largest known land mammal. This gigantic beast was really a huge, hornless rhinoceros which lived in the Oligocene Period in Central Mongolia. Its fossilized remains were found there and also in Baluchistan. Its total length from nose to tip of tail was 34 feet. Its height at shoulder was 17 feet 9 inches'; stamp: indecipherable. Manuscript.

1 Five chapters of Adorno's book *In Search of Wagner* were printed in the first 1939 issue of the *Zeitschrift für Sozialforschung* (pp. 1–48) under the title 'Fragmente über Wagner'.

2 Between 1919 and 1933, the banker and economist Albert Ludwig Hahn (1889–1968) was on the executive board of the Deutsche Effecten- und Wechsel-Bank AG vormals L. A. Hahn, founded in Frankfurt by his great-grandfather Löb Amschel Hahn (1796–1856). Besides his work in the management of the bank, he also held an honorary professorship at Frankfurt University from 1928 to 1933, teaching monetary and credit systems. In 1936 he emigrated first of all to Switzerland and then to the USA, where he taught at the New School for Economic Research in New York.

3 Anita Lothar, the daughter of Milton Seligmann, married Hans Lothar in 1931. She studied philosophy, sociology and psychology in Frankfurt between 1924 and 1931. Before 1933, she had agreed with Adorno to write a dissertation on the philosophical interpretation of texts by Robert Walser.

4 Unknown.

23   NEW YORK, 2.2.1940

New York, 2 February 1940

My dears – we are happily together, and your ears must be ringing as loudly as the Alpine Symphony. Julie came as a veritable Christmas angel – a thousand thanks, the shoes are magnificent, the touchingly knitted Hippo Cow jumper suits and fits the horse perfectly, and *we* shall confiscate the cigars ourselves in order to offer them to our guests of honour, which Maidon would do otherwise, as Max and Fritz do not smoke themselves. You spoil us more than we deserve. Thank God you got it right there! More soon! Heartiest kisses from your Junior Hippo Archibald.

My dears – It is charming here in the horses' nest & we have had a proper cuddle and feasted very well! The gifts went down very well
1000 greetings and kisses Yours Julie

We were very happy to hear from you at such length. The jumper fits like a glove and the shape is delightful. A thousand thanks always
Your old Gretel-horse

Original: handwritten letter with additional note by Julie Rautenberg.

24   NEW YORK, 7.2.1940

New York, 7 February 1940

My dears:
we were overjoyed to hear from Julie that you are put up well and are as content as one can expect when one moves from the lands of the noble savages to the ignoble lands of civilization – and what a civilization! We were somewhat nervous about receiving your first messages, firstly because of hideous Miami, and secondly because you are living with emigrant German country Jews. But as you are evidently far enough outside to avoid seeing much of Miami and its horrors, and the Levis are such Columbuses that there is little risk of having any contact with them, we have accustomed ourselves to the idea. Apropos of Columbus: the Spanish historian Madariaga has just brought out a book[1] which shows in detail that Columbus was a Jew. The book has caused a great sensation here, and one should mention it as often as possible in America for reasons of apologia.

Two things were particularly reassuring for us: firstly, that you are getting decent German food, for that of the splendid Emeranja Sevilla would not have been the right thing in the long run; and secondly, that you are living on the ground floor, so that the Hippo Cow can get out often enough. She should make good use of it – the cold spell is over, and the climatic conditions down there should be extremely pleasant during the next months. But the Hippo should *be extremely careful*, especially when going out alone. For America is not a land of walkers, but of drivers; on foot, one is hopelessly in the minority, and one has to look both ways at least *three times* whenever crossing the street. Furthermore, I would avoid leaving larger sums of money in the house at all costs; either give them to the Jewish women's committee or a bank to look after, for there was an article in the Times today stating that the safety standards in Miami are particularly unsatisfactory. Speaking of which, would you like us to save the New York Times for you and send it every week, as you used to do with the FZ, or are you reading it daily over there?

36

It was quite especially lovely and pleasant with Julie. We had invited her again for last night, but she was unable to come, and generally has more social engagements than we do. So she will be here next Tuesday evening. Hopefully the Frenkels will realize that it is not quite appropriate for Julie, who is not so young any more, and is accustomed to an 'executive function',[2] to be doing 'clerical work',[3] as Leo once suggested to me. Incidentally, when Julie saw how strenuously Gretel was working for me, she offered in a *truly charming* fashion to relieve her of some typing work; but we naturally declined. Many people could take an example from Julie's behaviour. Not least Else, whose latest atrocities will no doubt be recounted to me in the next few days, as Felix Weil returned from Argentina yesterday. (Else's address: Canning 2886, Buenos Aires.) The idea of coming to Florida over Easter is very tempting, but the pace of my current work makes any Easter holidays utterly impossible. – We could not even go to Hartfort Con.,[4] let alone the sunny south. The Hofmannsthal has been copied and corrected in full, and now I have to do the following:

1) prepare a lecture on Kierkegaard[5] to be read to the internal union of philosophy lecturers at Columbia.

2) sort out Max's new essay,[6] a critique of contemporary Marxism, with him and Gretel, which requires, as he himself says, 'rolling one's sleeves up'.

3) put together a large internal text[7] on the problem of prima philosophia, which will form the basis of the next piece Max and I write together.

4) write a large memorandum[8] for the Rockefeller Foundation.

Even with my working capability, which is not exactly modest, this is certainly plenty. Max's excellent long-standing secretary, Frau Bloch,[9] whom I believe WK also knew, has been in a lunatic asylum since the summer of last year. She was incidentally a classmate of the unfortunate Ilse Maier[10] and the daughter of the neurologist Mannheimer,[11] who – as far as I know – once milked Zilchen.[12]

We sent you some pralinés as the first part of your Christmas package; we hope you will enjoy them, and do not let that Jewish lot gobble them up – I already had to raise an eyebrow at the mention of the delightful children. So I was all the happier that WK is now citing several Louische statements.[13] If they are welcome, I can send you a whole list of statements by Louische about the war that I invented. (Though it takes strong nerves to bear them.)

Write soon and tell us at length about your current life and your plans. As far as the future goes, we are in very frequent contact with Julie.

Heartiest kisses from the two horses

Hottilein and Rossilein

If you do not mind, we shall send Oscar another two pairs of Teddie's pyjamas, the ones of which you so kindly gave us such a rich supply back then.

I had quite an incident today. I discovered that one of our assistants, Dr Maier, is guilty of blatant plagiarism – in his PhD thesis,[14] which is already in print, he copied out *pages' worth* of Cassirer, and concealed the theft in a stupidly cunning manner. When I confronted him with it – half an hour ago – he even became impertinent, so that I literally had to throw him out. Max says quite rightly: country Jews. There is no blessing in it. The whole thing came out because I wanted to help M by reviewing his book for the journal, and upon reading the passage in question, with my unfortunately still reliable memory, recalled reading exactly the same thing, except in German, in Cassirer. Forgive the atrocity story.[15]

On 22 February, from 1–2 p.m. on the New York City radio station, WNYC, frequency 810 kilocycl., there is a concert of modern German music that I organized at the station's invitation. Among other things, Rudi's new quartet (Schönberg) and Eduard[16] (Eisler sonata) will be playing. I will be speaking about the music.[17] You should be able to pick it up on a decent radio; it is a very decent station, and you should try to receive it beforehand. I will think of you with every word I say over the airwaves! Fond regards once more!

Original: typewritten letter with handwritten postscript.

1 The book *Christopher Columbus* by Salvador de Madariaga was published in 1939.

2 '*executive function*': EO.

3 '*clerical work*': EO.

4 This is what Adorno wrote; it remains unclear whether he really meant Hartford, Connecticut.

5 Adorno gave the lecture 'On Kierkegaard's Doctrine of Love', which was published in the third 1939–40 issue of the *Zeitschrift für Sozialforschung*, on 23 February 1940 in an English translation; for the German original, see *GS* 2, pp. 216–36.

6 Horkheimer's essay 'Autoritärer Staat' [Authoritarian State], published in 1942 in the mimeographed typescript book *Walter Benjamin zum Gedächtnis* [In Memoriam Walter Benjamin]; see Horkheimer, *Gesammelte Schriften 5*, pp. 293–319.

7 Seventeen pages of handwritten notes on a small pad have survived of this.

8 Difficult to ascertain; this was presumably a memorandum for the study on 'Likes and Dislikes' within the radio project.

9 No further information about Trude Bloch was available.

10 Nothing could be ascertained regarding Ilse Maier, whose name is sometimes spelled *Maier*, sometimes *Mayer*; she possibly belonged to the Mayer family, who were related to Oscar Wiesengrund.

11 Jakob Mannheimer (1870–?) had been a practising neurologist in Frankfurt since 1906.

12 Unknown.

13 A series of these have survived among Adorno's possessions under the title 'Lebensmülle' [Life's Waste Products], some of which possibly date back to his time in America.

14 Josef Maier (1911–?) emigrated to the USA in 1933; from 1935 to 1939 he was an assistant at the Institute of Social Research, where he last worked on the radio project. Maier later became editor of *Aufbau* and worked for government agencies. In 1957 he gained a professorship in Newark. His dissertation, which was published in 1939 by Columbia University Press, was entitled 'On Hegel's Critique of Kant'.

15 *atrocity story*: EO.

16 The pianist and composer Eduard Steuermann (1892–1964), who studied with Ferruccio Busoni and Arnold Schoenberg, and was among the most important performers of the Second Viennese School, was Adorno's piano teacher during the latter's time in Vienna in 1925. See also Adorno's obituary from 1964 entitled 'Nach Steuermann's Tod' [After Steuermann's Death] (*GS* 17, pp. 311–17).

17 For Adorno's concert introduction, see *GS* 18, pp. 576–80. Aside from the compositions by Schoenberg and Eisler mentioned, the programme also featured Alexander Zemlinsky's Maeterlinck songs, op. 13, and Ernst Křenek's song cycle *Durch die Nacht* [Through the Night].

25 NEW YORK, 12.2.1940

New York, 12 February 1940

My dears:
  a thousand thanks for your two letters of 9 February. Meanwhile you should also have received our Hippo Cow present, for which Gretel made a particular effort to find a cross-stitched pattern in true Hippo Cow style.
  Regarding your country Jews, I seem to have prophesied correctly in my last letter. You will recall from what I wrote what sort of experience I had with my one.

39

Regarding Julie, we will discuss the situation with her tomorrow evening. I hope it will not be as bad with the relatives as it may seem to her at first, after receiving such delicate treatment from the gentle yellow boars. The two Frenkels certainly do not suit the Gratianic ideal of Cortegiano, but at least they are no brutes; I consider George very good-natured, and Leo may be a little morose, but is a helpful sort. And I do not have the impression that they intend to keep Julie down; I think they rather want to keep her there without letting her do any work, and I would find it better for them to do this in a decent fashion than to burden Julie with some more menial work that she might only consider beneath her. We have both offered Julie our full assistance in advising her on all these matters, and it goes without saying that we will do all we can. There is no hope of finding a position for Julie in the real-estate management, as the team of employees for that has – largely on Max's and our initiative – been reduced as far as possible (Franz Neumann[1] is consequently no longer involved in managing the real estate), so that now, after getting rid of all those employees who acquired their jobs through internal connections, we can hardly introduce new ones ourselves. Please maintain absolute discretion regarding this, not least towards Julie. Aside from this, I would not wish her such work any more than that for the Frenkels, as Felix Weil has a great say in the real-estate matters, and with his manner that would only end in tears.

Now for the matter of Germany. I spoke about this with Julie, and I had certainly not asked her to write anything like that to you.* It is equally incorrect that I might consider letting *you* go back to Germany after a possible collapse of Hitler's regime while *I* remained here. In any case, there is every reason to suppose that this war, in the entirely new forms it has assumed, will take endlessly long and possibly outlast all of us. Nonetheless, as the question has now been brought up, I would like to clarify my own position in the matter. I am fully aware of what you went through in Germany, and had myself, incidentally, been thrown out of the university and robbed of any opportunity for work already 5 years beforehand. But I still believe that we should not take the attitude of the cigarette salesman who walks about saying: 'In my heart, I have given up on Germany'. Not because I have any illusions about Germany, but rather because I have none about the *world*. Fascism in Germany, which is inseparable from anti-Semitism, is no psychological anomaly of the German national character. It is a universal tendency and has an economic basis, which you in particular,

* [Marginal note:] I had the idea because Paul Oppenheim had given me some information from Warburg – *strictly* entre nous, one must *not* talk about it – that negotiations between the leading Jewish organizations and the Allied governments about compensation for German Jews in the case of an Allied victory have already progressed very far.

40

dear WK, recognized relatively early on, namely the dying out of the sphere of circulation, i.e. the increasing superfluity of trade in the widest sense, in the age of monopoly capitalism. The conditions for it – and I mean *all of them*, not only the economic but also the *mass psychological* ones – are at least as present here as in Germany, however, and the barbaric semi-civilization of this country will spawn forms no less terrible than those in Germany (we shall send you the novel 'It Can't Happen Here' by Sinclair Lewis,[2] which should be of interest to you; moreover, it is no coincidence that Jack London's Iron Heel,[3] with its prediction of fascism, was written in America). I consider the solution dreamt of by WK, namely that the Jews could still mingle with the others, out of the question. It is too late; the business has taken on the character of catastrophe. Essentially, I am convinced that one is hopelessly trapped, regardless of where one may be. And it was this conviction that was the root of my resistance against emigration – first my own, and then yours. If one is definitely going to be struck dead, I thought, then at least in the place where one belongs most, according to one's whole nature and the character of one's insights. The only chance to survive the horror, and by no means one that I rate highly, is for fascism to collapse in Germany before it breaks out here. Aside from the fact that I would prefer not to die amid fear and horror, and believe that it would also be a shame in objective terms if I did. But I consider it pure ideology to speak of the 'insignificance of individual fate'. These are the considerations that lead me to think of Germany, where the institute, after all, still has great interests. If, against all expectations, the war should turn out for the best, however, I do intend to go back and see what can be salvaged. Here I am also driven by a deeper motive, one that I can perhaps best illustrate for you with a dream, which I recently dreamt in exactly the same way as I am now writing: I had asked WK to arrange for my corpse to be transferred to Germany as soon as the Third Reich had fallen, for the reason that I did not under any circumstances want to experience the Day of Judgement in America. This mirrors my sentiments in a drastic form.

Forgive me for speaking so gravely of these matters. But they are so grave, and you ultimately know that as well as I do. You have sometimes – and the Hippo Cow has often – said to me that all your worries apply to me. I have never doubted it. But if this worry is real, then it will no longer be able to avoid looking in the face of the matters I have intimated to you. If I may speak entirely frankly – I sometimes have the feeling that in a corner of your soul, entirely unbeknown to you, there is some authority (my tigress[4] dated it back to 4000 years ago) that considers all the misfortune of our times a form of just punishment for beings such as myself, who fly so completely in the face of everything that can be expected of useful members of a society. I am not afraid of this 4000-year-old authority, because I know very well that there are others – stronger ones – within you. I think I am acting in accordance with those in speaking of these matters. I can see nothing damnable in attempting to salvage some of that independence for myself about which you have always said – rightfully – that it is the deciding precondition for any true productivity.

We have had nothing to report since the last letter. Today is a wonderful spring day here, so yours is presumably summery. Max is very enthusiastic about my new essay, which is very pleasing to me, as I worked at it incredibly intensively.

Heartiest kisses from

your old changeling
Teddie

Original: typewritten letter with a handwritten footnote.

1 Franz Neumann (1900–54) studied jurisprudence in Breslau, Leipzig and Frankfurt, where he met Horkheimer and Adorno in 1921; after his PhD he worked as an articled barrister in Frankfurt and as assistant to Hugo Sinzheimer, as well as lecturing at the Academy of Work. In 1933, Neumann was expatriated and went to London, where he studied with Harold Laski at the London School of Economics and Political Science and obtained a PhD in 1935. From 1936 to 1942 he worked at the Institute of Social Research in New York. After that he was research director at the Office of Strategic Services and the State Department in Washington. From 1947 to 1954, Neumann taught at Columbia University. See also 'Franz Neumann zum Gedächtnis' [In Memory of Franz Neumann], in GS 20.2, pp. 700–2.

2 This novel was first published in 1935.

3 *The Iron Heel* was published in 1907.

4 Adorno's pet name for his aunt Agathe Calvelli-Adorno (1868–1935).

26 NEW YORK, 20.2.1940

New York, 20.II.1940

My dears, a thousand thanks for your lengthy letters, which were a source of infinite joy to me. I am still under ridiculous pressure for another few days – so wrecked I cannot even sleep. So it will take until the start of next week before I write to you properly. So the concert is on Thursday, 1 p.m., on WNYC, wavelength 810 kilocycles. But you should try to turn it on 10 minutes earlier, as we may be starting sooner. Though I sadly doubt that you will be able to pick up that station, as the big networks are too strong. Perhaps one of the many radio tinkerers here can help you. – You will receive the ZfS within the next few days, containing not only my Wagner and Benjamin's Baudelaire[1] and a *splendid* discovery (Jochmann),[2] but also the essay by Max,[3] into which I also put a great deal of work. Max has now been naturalized, incidentally, which is perhaps not unimportant for you to know. A thousand kisses from the old child Teddie

Original: handwritten letter.

1 Benjamin's essay 'On Some Motifs in Baudelaire'; see Walter Benjamin, *Illuminations*, trans. Harry Zohn (New York: Schocken, 1969), pp. 155–200.
2 Benjamin had printed excerpts from Carl Gustav Jochmann's 'Die Rückschritte der Poesie' [The Regressions of Poetry], with an introduction of his own, in that issue of the journal.
3 'Die Juden und Europa'.

27 NEW YORK, 7.3.1940

New York, 7 March 1940

My dears,
all this in haste now, to tell you that the people at the New York City radio station I mentioned to you the other day have now placed me in charge of their music education programme,[1] without the slightest effort on my part. Half an hour completely at my disposal every Sunday afternoon, the best time of all, with an audience of literally hundreds of thousands of young people. There will not – initially at least – be any payment, but it constitutes such an enormous success in terms of prestige and publicity that Max, Fritz and ourselves have decided to do it nonetheless, and to invest some time in it. I have an almost unlimited archive of recordings to draw on for musical examples, as well as a staff of collaborating artists. One cannot yet imagine the consequences it might have.
    Rudi is going to Florida within the next few days, will play in Miami, will call on you immediately and you must go to hear him.
    As far as the money via Allmeier[2] is concerned, we did not see any trace of it – in fact in general, since no longer being in Oxford, I have not seen a penny apart from a small sum from Rothschild that is in your savings account here. Incidentally, Julie said that you had instructed the embassy official to send the money not to us (on account of our address frequently changing at that time), but rather to *Leo F.* I think it would be wise to look into the matter. For as long as the payments were being made to me, I was still receiving them – perhaps the money has simply

43

been buried amid the piles of various Frenkel accounts. I would correspond with Julie regarding the modus procedendi.

My radio hour will already be starting in April; we intend to prepare it sufficiently in 3 weeks to go 'on the air'[3] at the start of April.

Dear Wondrous Hippo Cow, you are not *née* von Bauchschleifer,[4] but *to this day* still Marinumba von Bauchschleifer (not Baroness, but rather 'Frau von Bauchschleifer'. Her maidservant, the tapir Sophie, always says 'jawohl Frau v. B'). For the hippopotami have a matriarchy, and hippos bear their *mother's* name. E.g. Marinumba is named after her mother, Archinumba von Bauchschleifer, while her father was the hippo king Mammut von Elephants; equally, Archibald is named Archibald von Bauchschleifer, whereas his father is called Willibald von Climber (being so good at climbing up riverbanks). Upon Archibald's birth, Marinumba exclaimed: Willibald von Climber, come here quickly, I think I have spawned a hippo king (she speaks Frankfurtish).[5]

On that note, heartiest kisses from Hippo King Archibald, known as Hippo Oaf.

A thousand thanks for your invitation, but I am afraid I cannot come to you at Easter, for what should otherwise become of poor Archibald, especially now that Sadie comes only 3 times a week on account of her heart troubles. And Archibald is under such strain that he cannot even think about going away. I hope you are still well over there. The very fondest regards from

Your Gretel-horse

Original: typewritten letter with handwritten postscript.

1 The project, for which Adorno's exposé has been preserved among his belongings (see Ts 50426–50446), subsequently fell through.

2 Unknown.

3 '*on the air*': EO.

4 See letter no. 15, note 2.

5 Translator's note: three words in the original 'exclamation' are in Frankfurt dialect.

28 NEW YORK, 24.3.1940

New York, 24 March 1940
(Easter Sunday)

My dears, do not be cross with me for writing so meagrely these days. But I have so much work that I literally do not know whether

44

I am coming or going – and today, on my first day off, I am fit for nothing but dozing. Some exceedingly strenuous work with Max on state capitalism (still related to his essay on the Jews); preparing the first 12 radio lectures,[1] which will be augmented by a further 2. Then a new study[2] for the radio project on light music, which has to be finished by the end of May – it really is a tad too much. Gazelle wrote concerning the plans for WK[3] – I only wish to say that we are *not* guided by *any other* concern than a solution that is in every sense satisfactory to *you both*. – I am very glad that you had a lovely time with Rudi. He too was very enthousiasmé, and found that you were both in the best of form. Tonight we are seeing him and Josie.

I have invented a new hippo cow, a friend from Marinumba's youth, Espérance de Walros, whom she has now found once more. They constantly speak to each other in French about the glorious days of the old hippo society. Heartiest kisses from loyal

Archibald

Original: handwritten letter.

1 The 'outlines' form part of the exposé, which bears the title 'Plan of a New Type of Music Appreciation Hour' (see letter no. 27).

2 It dealt with 'Likes and Dislikes' in light music.

3 Gretel Adorno's letter has not survived.

29   NEW YORK, 21.4.1940

21 April 1940

My dears:
    thank you for your dear long letter, which eased our minds greatly. Max's essay on state capitalism is meanwhile finished, Teddie's lecture[1] at Columbia on Simmel last Friday was a very great success, and the rough draft for the Likes and Dislikes study for the radio project is finished. All this at least offers a certain relief, but there is still enough to be getting on with for the next while. The radio lectures have not yet begun, but will probably start next Sunday (28.IV.). – We haven't heard anything from Melly; she only writes to an aunt of mine in Sweden occasionally, complaining of too little news from us.
    Lottchen will most likely get married at the end of May or sometime in June: Dr Egon Wissing,[2] an old acquaintance of us horses, and incidentally a cousin of Benjamin. He is an excellent radiologist and has a post at the Massachusetts Memorial Hospital in Boston.

45

We do not have any summer plans as yet; I daresay we shall have to remain in New York at least until the end of July. Incidentally, there have once more been very serious discussions about moving the institute to the West Coast, as the cost of living there is simply so much lower. But this is all still unclear and entirely undecided, and I therefore ask that you mention it to no one. Take care of yourselves, and enjoy the spring and the sun; it has been raining here for 3 days now, and we are cold. Hugs from

Your old Gretel horse

My dears, Mac Iver seminar a great success, finally had a rest, but terrible weeks still lie ahead of me – never before in my life have I had such a workload. But believe me that I think of you faithfully even if I do not get around to writing. I do *not* consider the powder plan practical (monopolized!!!), don't let yourself be rushed into anything; wine *much* better. A thousand kisses from Archibald Stumpfnase[3] v. Bauchschleifer

Original: handwritten letter.

1 Adorno gave a lecture at the sociological seminar on 19 April entitled 'On the Problem of Individual Causality in the Work of Simmel'.

2 Egon Wissing (1900–84) was a maternal cousin of Walter Benjamin. Wissing had studied medicine, and worked in the USA at the Massachusetts Memorial Hospital. His second wife was the dentist Liselotte Karplus (b. 1909).

3 Translator's note: the English equivalent would be 'Bluntnose'.

30 NEW YORK, 8.5.1940

8 May 1940

My dears:

I cannot tell you how much joy your last letter brought me. Today is the first day – including Sundays – that I have been able to catch my breath again to some degree, and at once I am hastening to write to you at somewhat greater length. Yesterday Max and I finished work, once and for all, on our second joint child, the essay on George and Hofmannsthal, and it is already going off to the typesetter today. The new issue[1] will consist of our collaborative efforts: the piece on state capitalism, the George essay and the English project on anti-Semitism that we wrote last year. It is our private issue, so to speak, and will be identified as such in an introductory note. Working on it was a wonderful experience, but together with everything else it made incredible demands on us, and now we all want to take a little breather.

Admittedly, this breather will be rather a modest one in my case. The educational lectures on the city radio station have still not started yet, as all manner of technical things still have to be sorted out, and this sort of work requires endless tests, meetings and toing and froing. But I am introducing a concert broadcast by the same station tonight, involving a conversation with Bela Bartok about his music.[2] (The Second Violin Sonata will subsequently be played by Rudi and Eduard.)* I prepared this conversation yesterday with Bartok. He is the most curious person one could ever imagine, a cross between a child and an old man, a quite extraordinary musician, but so naïve and obstinate that every word, even about his own music, has to be put in his mouth for him.

Then I am busy finishing the Like and Dislike study for the radio project, and I hope to finish that within the next 14 days. It is now a matter of distilling an essence of about 70 pages from a raw text of 250; but this, against my expectations, seems possible.

I am well amid all this work, but Gretel is unfortunately having more ups and downs; last week she had another migraine attack. It is hard to say whether the therapy was of any use. She has not become much fatter, but I would nonetheless say that her overall condition has improved somewhat.

I am particularly pleased that your new housemates have turned out to be such a good choice. The fact that you were living with German country Jews had been a thorn in my side from the outset. I simply wanted to avoid any hounding. But I am certain that you will be incomparably better off with the Americans, if they are at least somewhat cultivated people, than with that sort, who simply assume that a common fate gives them the right to be intrusive and impudent.

And now to the main point, namely the question of the future. It is still unclear whether we shall remain in New York. It is a very difficult decision. California or some other western state would be favourable especially for financial reasons (the institute and its entire organization could be made much cheaper there) as well as climatic ones. One reason to stay here would be my meanwhile highly extended relations with the radio, which still promise all sorts of chances that one should certainly pursue before opting for solitude. Then there is also the pure institute inbreeding that would ensue in the West, which does not strike me as especially healthy intellectually.

The question is how you should act upon all this. In my opinion, your life in the South is so much more pleasant and sensible than it would be here in New York, so I would most urgently advise against

---

* [Marginal note, presumably added after the concert:] quite excellent

breaking it off before the situation here has been resolved. I would think it much better for you to decide on paying us an extended visit in September/October, when it is truly beautiful here. All further decisions will depend on how things continue to develop. If we should move to the West, then we could perhaps find a place to live together there.

What WK wrote about your financial situation is very reassuring. I would incidentally like to be given some credit for the fact that Leo finally sent you a decent statement, as I had Julie see to it. I myself preferred not to, as Leo would no doubt have found this intrusive coming from a non-businessman like myself. The reassuring figures should above all ensure that you want for nothing. After all, Florida is a land of such plenty that one can surely live in paradise there. Incidentally, have you ever eaten alligator pears?[3] If not, you must buy some in the nearest fruit shop for a few cents. One takes out the stone, and fills the hole with a dressing of vinegar, oil, salt, pepper and possibly a little Worcester sauce. It is one of the most delicious things one can obtain in America. They grow on trees in Florida.

I often feel a veritable yearning for Havana, and the few days I spent there remain unforgettable. I can imagine how you must miss that humane Romance city between the drugstores and Brooklyn Jews. If I had my way, we would come to Havana for an entire winter sometime and work there.

As far as an assessment of the war is concerned, I completely share your pessimism. The ineptitude of the English – or shall we say their secret sympathy for the barbarians – surpasses even my rather bold expectations. Though I do not believe in the likelihood of their extermination, but rather a sort of new Munich, where the English can then finally continue to bumble about under the Nazi yoke they have craved all along. To say nothing of the international consequences. But it is clear that, in a world where all that counts is diligence, the Germans not only have every chance but also all sympathies. One has to admit that they are truly so far superior to the decaying liberalism that their victory, for all its horror, does have certain progressive aspects. Evidently the world has to go through this hell completely and utterly first before it finds the chance to come to its senses.

The bravery of the Wondrous Hippo Cow Marinumba is a joy to me. As far as Toscanini is concerned, I agree with her that his performances of Romance music, especially Debussy and Ravel, are the best he has to offer. Everything else, admittedly, is ghastly. Next Friday we are expecting a visit from Klemperer, who has survived a terrible operation (brain tumour). – The opera by Weill that Marinumba asked about is called Mahagonny. Weill is here, but is avoiding me fearfully, as he has now completely devoted himself to writing pop

48

songs, towards which he was always strongly inclined. – Incidentally, Lotte's husband, Egon Wissing, was first married to Gertrud Feiß,[4] whom Herman Levi knew well, and whom I saw as a young girl at his place on various occasions. Wissing, a cousin of Walter Benjamin, is a quite excellent doctor, the only German to be made a member of the Board of Radiology. He was the first to recognize Dée Pollock's illness, and if the others had listened to him they might have been able to save her. You will no doubt soon make his acquaintance. (The wedding is on 30 May; we plan to go there, as do Max and Maidon. Lotte's address: Dr K. 400 Marlboro Street, Boston Mass. I am sure Lotte would be very pleased about the tin opener, she has a sense for gadgets in any case, but if you can't get one over there, buy her something else, perhaps a pretty tablecloth with napkins that can easily be washed and sent. After all, she can still use everything like that, as she is starting completely from scratch, and has nothing except for the few bits of furniture from us and some clothes and things she took along from E. That Gretel!).

I have not seen Julie at all these last few weeks, as we have had to work with Max almost every evening. But she is coming to lunch Saturday week, together with Max and Maidon, whose acquaintance she would like to make. I can very well understand that the two Frenkels – who would incidentally make an excellent circus act – are getting on her nerves, along with the mechanization of American business. Nonetheless, one should encourage her, for the Frenkels may be philistines, but not brutes. Precisely the fact that Julie is not herself mechanized, but rather shows spontaneity, should give her a head start on the psychologically crippled Americans with their pathological employee mentality.

Maidon gave me a quite wonderful hippo. It is so big that I can gather my previous ones around it in such a way that it looks like an ancient hippo cow suckling her young. On this note, heartiest kisses from

Your old child
Teddie

Original: typewritten letter.

1 This could not be published because of the German invasion of France, as the publisher (Felix Alcan in Paris) who produced the journal in German and the printing company (Presses Universitaires de France) had already been unable to edit and print the manuscripts they had for the third 1939 issue and the first 1940 issue under the conditions of the occupation.

2 A two-and-a-half-page transcript of this conversation, which dealt with the compositions played (five of the Hungarian Folk Songs and the Second Violin Sonata), has been preserved among Adorno's belongings.

3 'Alligator Pears (the fruit of *Persea gratissima*) is a curious corruption. The aboriginal Carib word for the tree is "aouacate", which the Spanish discoverers pronounced "avocado", and English sailors called "alligator", as the nearest approach which occurred to them' (E. Cobham Brewer, *Dictionary of Phrase and Fable*, 1898).

4 Gertrud (Gert) Feiß, a friend of Erika and Klaus Mann from their youth, had died in Paris in 1933.

31   NEW YORK, 20.5.1940

20 May 1940

My dears:
I cannot tell you how much I enjoyed your lengthy letters. They are a true ray of hope in these immeasurably horrific times, and I am not exaggerating when I say that the present time is worse for me than everything previous, except for the pogroms in 1938. I consider the war lost through the indescribable irresponsibility, incompetence and pettiness of the Allies – just as in Hebbel's 'Haideknabe',[1] even the most dreadful fear fantasies are still surpassed by reality. I am now unable to regain my balance even to a moderate degree, which has never happened to me before, am barely sleeping at all, and stare as if paralysed into the black abyss sucking everything into its eddies and destroying it. I am quite certain that the madness of fascism, once it has taken hold of the earth, will act in such opposition to the incredibly progressive elements also present in fascism that it cannot last forever, and that humanity will ultimately come to its senses. But I believe neither that we will have the chance to see that, nor that much will be salvaged of those things on which all possibility of a meaningful existence for us once depended. I do not like to use such grand words, but what is going on here is not simply a world war any more, but rather the collapse of that form of culture which has lived in the world since the Migration Age. And as I am fated to be a seismograph, and in a certain sense think more with my nerve-ends than with my calculatory faculty, I am at present completely disoriented by the shock, and wait for the hippo beast in me to gain the upper hand and give me some peace again.
I am glad that you are in such pleasant surroundings, and do not have to go through this horror amid the horror of the city. Before we see each other again in September, so many things will have been decided that we will somehow be able to adjust ourselves psychologically, even if it be at the level of deepest despair.
Your concern for the issue of our journal is touching, but unfounded, I fear; for it is unlikely that the journal will come out in

50

Paris once the Germans have marched in, and a great deal of water will flow down the Hudson yet before we have it printed anywhere else. Furthermore, the worries are also unfounded for the reason that the double issue coming after the next will not contain any long essay of ours. We simply wish to lay out, at least in one issue, our own position as unflinchingly and purely as possible. And, in addition, we unfortunately cannot expect much from the other members of the institute, Jews and Christians alike. Our goy Wittfogel[2] is writing the dreariest stuff about China, of which we have published too much already, and Pollock is not getting around to writing anything. You can believe me that Max and I do not do all the work ourselves for fun, but simply because, for a number of reasons, there is really hardly any spontaneity coming from the others. Except for Benjamin, but he is currently in the most terrible danger. He has long been locked up again, incidentally, like all other emigrants in France.[3] The emigrants seem to be the only Germans the French attack.

On the matter of anti-Semitism, I am unfortunately coming around to your view more and more. But I would be incredibly interested to become acquainted with your notes on our project, as there is a certain chance that the research tasks sketched there might be carried out. Please send them!

After a lot of toing and froing, we have not yet begun the regular educational broadcasts on WNYC after all, nor will I begin them before the autumn, as it would be too inconvenient in the next months. But I am giving regular introductory lectures for the modern concerts broadcast on that station, the next two of which are on 28 May and 11 June.[4] The Bartok interview turned out quite well, except that the available time was too short, and that Bartok is so incapable of any theoretical utterance that no great words of wisdom were spoken. Incidentally, Bartok has inexplicably returned to Europe.

Gretel has been feeling quite well these last few weeks, thank God, and I do not know how I could survive these times without her. (Giraffe sends a thousand thanks for the kind invitation, and she would love to come to you, but she does not under any circumstances wish to leave her Archibald alone, for then she could barely relax for one minute. She is essentially in perfect health, these crises are probably inevitable with her somewhat delicate constitution, but she will always pull herself up again soon enough.) We both consider it unwise to consult any other doctor than Egon; Liefmann[5] puts on a wise face, but almost certainly knows less than E.

I envy you the proximity of wild nature, and can very well imagine how one might draw strength from it in a quite literal sense. I myself feel more in need of nature than ever before. We spent two hours with Eduard Steuermann yesterday on a walk along the Hudson. One can walk down directly from our house and then properly along the bank, almost as if it were the Main, all the way up to 125th St.

The decision regarding the location of the institute has still not been made yet; we shall let you know immediately. This decision is in no way dependent on Felix Weil, and will ultimately be made by Max.

You are quite right: Gertrud Feis was the adoptive daughter. She died in emigration seven years ago.

We had Julie over here on Saturday together with Max, entertained them with a bottle of Deidesheimer, and it was very pleasant.

I am especially glad that the atmosphere with your landlords is so carefree and agreeable. One of the few things that one really can learn from the Americans, after all, is a certain independence from the security ideal.

I do not find the letter from Else[6] enigmatic so much as fairly stupid, but I shall write to her nonetheless. I must have told you that Felix Weil claimed she had attempted sexual assault upon him in Rio de Janeiro. He said that he escaped the attack by taking flight.

The Hippo Cow asked after Klemperer:[7] his visit was a rather sad one. The brain operation was successful, but at what expense! One half of his face is paralysed, his sight is very poor, his hearing too, he is unsteady on his feet, and seems much diminished mentally. Around 11 he suddenly crumpled together, and I had to escort him down to his car. He has now gone to California. Many people think he will recover once more; I cannot judge that myself, but I have the feeling that he is surrounded by a herd of people still seeking, be it directly or indirectly, to profit from him in the belief that they will not be able to do so for much longer.

The performance by the Kolisch Quartet must have been from a record, as Rudi is still here and the others already went to California weeks ago. But perhaps the announcement was wrong, or the Mighty Sow mistook *Coolidge* Quartet[8] for *Kolisch* Quartet. That would also explain the bad performance. Rudi does not release bad recordings. The Bartok performance was excellent. Bartok's English is less perfect, but he refuses to speak even one word of German.

We are already looking forward to September.

Heartiest kisses from

Your old Hippo King and his dear Giraffe Gazelle

Archibald

Original: typewritten letter.

1 Friedrich Hebbel's poem, written in 1844, was set by Robert Schumann. See also the aphorism of the same name in *Minima Moralia*.

2 Karl August Wittfogel (1896–1988), who worked at the institute from 1925 to 1940, published his work *Wirtschaft und Gesellschaft Chinas* [Chinese Economy and Society] in 1931 in the institute's own series of writings.

3 Benjamin, who was interned after the outbreak of war, was able to remain in Paris without further incarceration in May 1940 and to reach Lourdes in June.

4 The German manuscript of the introduction to the concert on 28 May, featuring Anton Webern's op. 12 songs and Alban Berg's Four Clarinet Pieces, op. 5, has been preserved among Adorno's belongings; for the introduction to the concert on 11 June, with Berg's Piano Sonata, songs by Gustav Mahler and two movements from the Sonata for Oboe and Piano by Stefan Wolpe, see *GS* 18, pp. 581–3.

5 The Frankfurt doctor Emil Liefmann (1878–1955) was still able to emigrate to the USA with his wife as late as 1938; he lived in New York and later treated Adorno's parents.

6 Not preserved.

7 Otto Klemperer (1885–1973) did very little conducting between 1939 and 1947 on account of his illness.

8 The Coolidge Quartet resided in the Chamber Music Hall of the Library of Congress, which had been funded by Elizabeth Sprague Coolidge (1864–1953); it existed, with various changes of personnel, from 1936 to 1943.

32 NEW YORK, 28.5.1940

28 May 1940

My dears:
    a thousand thanks for your letters, which truly fortified me. I do not intend to issue any prophecies of doom about the situation[1] today, only to say that the hole has not yet been plugged. If Weygand[2] were really such a marvel, then in my layman's opinion something should already have happened – at this rate of operation, the Germans must already have so many reinforcements around the Channel that the fate of the Northern Army is sealed, especially now that the Belgians have surrendered. It remains to be seen what happens next, but judging by what we have witnessed so far, only the very worst can be expected.
    I am keeping my head above water by working desperately, and will conclude my long like and dislike study with Simpson next weekend.[3] I worked on it all Friday, Saturday and Sunday, and the necessity of dealing exclusively with pedantic questions of formulation in a foreign language helped me, as I would hardly have been capable of truly productive thought. A further consolation, aside from your truly heroic

53

bearing and the horse, which guards me like a trusty hippo sentry, is Max, who will stand by us through thick and thin, and entertains the hope that one will perhaps find some hiding-place after all to survive the end of the world – for that is what it is, I have no illusions. To survive not purely to cling to life at all costs, although that is an interest too, but in order at least to secure some of our insights, which might in future times prove not entirely worthless for humanity. Our own lives are unlikely to last that long – in fact I imagine them as a permanent flight from danger.

Tonight I shall speak on the radio for the third time, introducing songs by Webern and the clarinet pieces by Berg. Tomorrow we will go to Boston for the wedding, and return on Friday.

Should the war drag on, against expectations, I daresay America's intervention will be inevitable. There is a veritable psychosis about foreigners here even now; in the street, and especially in the subway, we only speak English. I would recommend that you do the same. If I really were the brute that I am, then the letter about the saintly Elisabeth[4] would have made me very happy, and I am sorry indeed that I cannot send it to my tigress in heaven as a piece of evidence. But as it is, I find it very sad. The woman is surely, at least in her conscious layers, what one generally calls a sensible and decent person, and there is no reason to distrust her claims. (The fact that things probably look bleak with Frau G., and that she has that whole pragmatic resentment towards dreaming, as I experienced with Else, is another matter.) But if one accepts her account, then it indeed seems to suggest that something is amiss with poor Elisabeth. And I am thinking not of the symptoms of puberty, but rather something far more serious – a psychosis. (Nascent schizophrenia.) A whole series of traits point to this, such as the simultaneity of intellectual talent and childishness, the tendency towards a lack of bodily cleanliness, but above all the obvious lack of contact with her environment. I could be mistaken, of course. If it were only a neurosis, then it would be something that we have also observed in other emigrant children of exactly the same age, e.g. those of Leo Löwenthal and Marcuse. Evidently the shock of emigration under the present conditions and with inadequate parents is such that these already empty, atomized human beings are completely destroyed by it. The indifference of Elisabeth could perhaps be a symptom of this, i.e. a sort of protective measure against the excess of shock that this life would otherwise mean, even before it has shown its true face in aeroplane attacks with howling sirens.

It is good that you are among young and carefree people. – At 10 in the evening we listen to Raymond Graham Swing WOR (710) from commentators.[5] I would not worry about financial matters; even in the case of a great depression, I am convinced that a war boom cannot be put off for any longer than three years, and until then you can still live comfortably without having to sell a single security paper. (We even still have over $4,700 lying here for you.)

Write soon and at length – perhaps the old Hippo Sow's indestructible optimism will do the trick once again. I pray to the great Hippo Sow. We are heartily grateful for every letter from you.

Kisses
from your two old children
Hottilein and Rossilein

Original: typewritten letter.

1 In order to separate the French and the British troops, the Germans had invaded the Netherlands, Belgium and Luxembourg on 10 May, thus advancing to northern France while bypassing the Maginot Line. The Netherlands capitulated on 10 May, Belgium on 28 May.

2 The French general Maxime Weygand (1867–1965), who had been chief of staff for General Foch from 1914 to 1920 and ruled Morocco from 1931 to 1935, had been made commander-in-chief of all French troops in May 1940.

3 *weekend*: EO.

4 Nothing could be ascertained regarding these persons and the context.

5 *commentators*: EO.

33   BOSTON, 28.5.1940

28 May 1940

My dears, waiting in the hall to be collected for the wedding[1] – the horse is still packing – I send you these words as a sign of my most heartfelt love. Embraces and kisses from your child
Teddie
Your old Giraffe

Original: picture postcard: Old State House, Boston; stamp: Boston, Mass., MAY 30, 1940. Manuscript.

On the dating: according to the previous letter, the Adornos travelled to Boston only on the 29th.

1 Egon Wissing married Liselotte Karplus.

11 June 1940

My dears:
a thousand thanks for your birthday letters, which were a source of much joy to us. The birthday celebrations[1] were as fine as they could possibly have been in these dreadful times. Max treated us to lunch in a very nice restaurant, that same 'Caviar' to which he had previously taken WK. Then we drove home, Max, Horse and I, and drank a bottle from our well-guarded supply by ourselves, and finally Horse and I went to the cinema, for the first time in almost a year, to see a very pretty film, Brother Orchid,[2] with Robinson. Robinson is probably the best gangster comedian – and not only comedian – they have here. He plays the boss of a racket[3] who falls into the hands of an enemy racket, almost dies, escapes to a monastery and becomes a monk, and ends up saving the monastery's material existence by annihilating the enemy gang. The whole thing has a little touch of the joke that the whole monastery is murmuring, artificial and very harmless, but in fact overwhelmingly comical! Thus we managed to get through the day as well as can be hoped.

I need hardly say anything about the situation. France is definitely lost, and it seems extremely questionable to me whether England will somehow manage to set up a second line of defence[4] after the French and the Germans have bled each other to death. I consider it entirely out of the question that America will start an active military intervention within as short a time as would be necessary, and by the time they are armed and ready Hitler will presumably have pocketed the rest of Europe. We are trying at least to keep a cool head and not be dumbed down by horror. But this horror has meanwhile taken on such proportions that even that is no easy matter, and one falls into a sort of frozen state, like the bird staring at the snake. As for how you are feeling, I can sense that most clearly from the fact that the Hippo Cow is starting to refer to astrology.

Otherwise, we have nothing new to report. The next larger piece of work for me to tackle will now be the Beethoven[5] after all.

The Herzbergers have probably been ruined by the events, as St. Quentin and Amiens were at the centre of the fighting in Flanders.

Write soon and forgive this particularly stupid letter
from your semi-daft, but faithful and old child
Archibald

A thousand thanks for your kind letters, it is truly touching that our good Hippo Sow remembered. If I might make a wish, then I would love some coloured napkins, either monochrome or with a woven pattern. Without the tablecloth, just the napkins, as I almost always use coloured ones – the white ones get washed so badly over here.

Hugs from your Gretel-horse

Original: typewritten letter.

1 Gretel Adorno's birthday on 10 June.

2 In this film, made by Lloyd Bacon and Byron Haskin in 1940, Edward G. Robinson (1893–1973), whose breakthrough had come in 1930 with the film *Little Caesar*, played alongside Ann Sothern, Humphrey Bogart, Ralph Bellamy and Donald Crisp.

3 *racket*: EO.

4 *second line of defence*: EO.

5 For the notes to this book planned by Adorno, see Adorno, *Beethoven: The Philosophy of Music*, trans. Edmund Jephcott (Cambridge: Polity, 1998).

35 NEW YORK, 16.6.1940

16 June 1940

My dears:
today, in place of a letter, my Kierkegaard lecture, which is to appear in the next issue of the journal. Perhaps the essay will speak to you – it is, incidentally, not a duplication of any ideas from my book,[1] but rather entirely new, and in fact treats a material that does not even come up in the book. Aside from that we have no news, and we are making every effort not to be entirely engulfed by sorrow, yet without letting ourselves become dulled in the process. Combining these two is no easy matter.

Heartiest kisses
from your old child
Archibald

Fond regards from your dear Giraffe Gazelle with the little horns, little gazelle horns, little horns, little horns.

Original: typewritten letter with additional handwritten note by Gretel Adorno.

1 'On Kierkegaard's Doctrine of Love'; the book is Adorno's post-doctoral dissertation [*Habilitationsschrift*] *Kierkegaard. Konstruktion des Ästhetischen*, which had been published in early 1933 (see Adorno,

57

Kierkegaard: Construction of the Aesthetic, trans. Robert Hullot-Kentor [Cambridge, MA: MIT Press, 1993]).

36 NEW YORK, 30.6.1940

30 June 1940

My dears:
we made use of the few quiet days between the French catastrophe and the attack on England[1] to gather our strength and our wits a little, without succumbing to any illusions about what is to come. I lack the necessary insight to assess the military chances of an invasion of England. Going on the course of events so far, I assume that, if the Germans attempt the invasion, they will also succeed. Not that I doubt the determination and ability of the current English government;[2] but it is all too late, and I think that material superiority is more significant today than even the greatest determination. In addition, an appeasement[3] government is becoming apparent, with the Duke of Windsor[4] and my favourite, Chamberlain. The fact that I have essentially always viewed England in this way is a very poor consolation. In my opinion, the true reason for the débâcle is that the so-called democracies essentially thirst for fascism, and have virtually invoked the disaster themselves. I found a hundred examples of this in England, and those are actually what make me so suspicious of all things English.

As far as America is concerned, we think that the chances have improved a little through Willkie's nomination.[5] While Vandenberg[6] or Taft[7] would no doubt have proved all too amenable to some sort of fascist efforts along the lines of Lindbergh[8] or Coughlin,[9] Willkie is the most democratic, anti-fascist and pro-Allies of all the Republican candidates. One can assume, admittedly, that America will be forced to adopt significant elements of fascism – such as the replacement of unemployment benefit with some open or concealed form of labour service for the arms industry – but Willkie at least offers the best guarantee that the next four years will be free of all terror and racial persecution, and what will happen after four years really cannot be predicted. At any rate, I should think that there will be a certain breathing space. If fascism truly does succeed on the largest scale, it is still not out of the question that some territorial solution for the Jewish question will be found after all. – I do not share the hopes held by many regarding the supposedly anti-German policies of Russia. The Russian industry is probably already 'organized' by the Germans to such a degree that the Russians no longer have any liberty of action anyway, even if they wanted to. I do not even think they want it, but rather that they are themselves ¾ fascist.

58

So much for public matters. As for private ones, our holiday plans are still undecided. It is rather uncertain whether we shall go to Maine – it is rather expensive. We are now seriously considering spending our holidays with you in Miami. It is still not certain, for if the institute were really to move west in the autumn, we would presumably remain here for the summer. But it would be lovely if we could come – possibly in time to celebrate WK's 70th birthday together with you. In any case, we would be grateful if you could look around for possible accommodation (2 rooms with bathroom) and board (definitely breakfast, perhaps half-board) and inform us of the price. We would like to know if you would be able to find someone who would drive us around in the car a little for some money and kind words, and if you could advise us regarding clothing (elegance? Will we need warm clothes? How are the nights?).

We send you our warmest congratulations on your wedding anniversary, and enclose a few little snap shots[10] of Lotte's wedding as a little token.

The Hippo Cow must now brace herself for the most dreadful Louische stories. I look forward to atrocity reports about sweet little Elisabeth. The Times reported today that English bombers blew up the paint factory in Höchst, and that the flames were visible 50 miles away.

Heartiest kisses

from your old Hippo Oaf
Archibald
and your dear Giraffe Gazelle with the little horns

Original: typewritten letter with additional handwritten note by Gretel Adorno.

1 On 22 June, France had been forced to sign a cease-fire agreement with Germany after German troops had taken over the entire northern and western coasts of France, as well as Paris. The preparations for the German landing in England – Hitler had fixed the date of the invasion for 16 July – including a bombardment of London and Coventry, failed on account of the British air defence.

2 Winston Churchill had succeeded Neville Chamberlain as prime minister on 10 May, forming a grand coalition with the Labour Party and the Liberals. From that point, Churchill had sought to persuade the USA to join the war.

3 *appeasement*: EO.

4 This was the title of King Edward VIII (1894–1972), who was forced to abdicate following his enthronement in 1936 because his intended marriage to the divorced American W. W. Simpson was not approved by parliament or the Church.

5 On 26 June in Pittsburgh, Wendell Willkie (1892–1944) had been elected presidential candidate for the Republican Party.

6 Until the Japanese attack on Pearl Harbor, Senator Arthur Vandenberg (1884–1951) was one of the 'Isolationists'.

7 Senator Robert Alphonso Taft (1889–1953).

8 Charles Lindbergh (1902–1974) was an exponent of Isolationism.

9 Father Charles Edward Coughlin (1891–1979) – the 'Radio Priest' – was initially a follower, then an embittered opponent, of Roosevelt; in November 1936 he referred to National Socialism as 'a necessary defence mechanism against Communism' and supported the Nazi theory that Jewish bankers were behind the Russian Revolution. In his study 'The Psychological Technique of Martin Luther Thomas' Radio Addresses' (see *GS* 9.1, pp. 7–141), Adorno refers to Coughlin several times.

10 *snap shots*: EO.

37 NEW YORK, 8.7.1940

8 July 1940

My dears,
    I am afraid we must disappoint you. We cannot come to Miami, and cannot take any holidays at all at present. Reason: Max is going on an 'exploratory tour' of the West soon. He has asked me to carry out some extraordinarily important and urgent work at the institute[1] in the next eight weeks, and its possible consequences for the future are so great that I would not have been able to justify withdrawing from it. As we would hardly have had a quiet minute anyway until England's fate has been decided, and would simply have been glued to the radio for the whole time, we are in fact not so very disappointed. All the more so because, if all goes well, we shall be able to make up for missing that break in the winter, and you can surely imagine that we will not be travelling to icy regions. You really need not feel sorry for us on account of our decision, as we can reach the Hudson directly from our apartment, and will be outside for at least 1½ hours every day. (We have been keeping this up the whole time.)
    As far as the apartment[2] is concerned, incidentally, we will be staying in it. It has been decided that we will remain in New York for at least a further year, which is very pleasing to us, as resettling would be quite a business under the present circumstances. And the tradition-forming aspect of having an apartment one has grown into, and in which one truly feels at home, is of particular importance. Naturally, as WK correctly observed, all these questions are connected to financial

60

matters, as the institute has suffered considerable losses. But you need not worry on account of that. We will admittedly be earning a little less in the next year than we have previously, but still enough to avoid any genuine deprivation. Otherwise we would not have kept the apartment. Your offer to make a donation for our holidays is *touching* and truly moved us both. Accept our heartiest thanks. Fortunately, however, we will not have to take you up on your offer.

A few words regarding WK's linguistic suggestions for the Kierkegaard. *Deciding* is an error, and should read *decisive*; *sublates* is the customary term in English translations of Hegel for 'aufheben' in the Hegelian dual sense; *reification* is the translation of 'Verdinglichung', one can also say thingification, but I do not wish to use this semi-Latinate, semi-English brute of a word; Chthonian = chthonisch, 'earthy' in the demonic sense; hypostatize is the technical term in philosophy for 'hypostasieren', equally often used in English, i.e. illegitimately passing off a merely derived principle as an original one to base something on. You see, most of the words you incriminate belong to the specialized philosophical vocabulary. Incidentally, one can also use *content(s)* in the singular.*

Your somewhat restrained account of the joys of the Floridian summer makes us worry a little as to whether you truly feel comfortable there. Please do write a word or two about that. Heartiest kisses from

Your old Hippo King
Archibald and his
dear Giraffe
Gazelle

Original: typewritten letter with a handwritten greeting from Gretel Adorno.

1 Adorno's version of the 'Anti-Semitism Project' (see letter no. 4, note 13) has been preserved as a typescript among his belongings. See Theodor W. Adorno Archiv, Ts 52540–52598.

2 On Morningside Drive.

23 July 1940

My dears,

a thousand thanks for your most concerned and charming letters. Yes, it is unbearably hot here, and it is no pleasure to be in New York.

---

* [Marginal note in Oscar Wiesengrund's hand:] *n e i n!*

But, as we told Max we would stay, we cannot simply up and run. Though I should point out that it was a matter of agreement, not obligation. You have much too official and earnest a notion of the whole thing. If we were to bring Max a certificate, he would be amazed beyond measure at such a procedure, and rightly so. Our relationships with both Max and Fritz are so thoroughly non-official on all sides that we would only be making fools of ourselves. All the more so for having already arranged with Max that, if it becomes too hot here, we can get away for a few weeks after all. This brings me to my real point, namely: it would be impossible for us to leave *before* 15 August (and in the past we normally never left before the 1st). But if we were to leave in mid-August, then we would miss you when you pass through here on 23 August, and that is precisely what we hoped to avoid. In addition, it is possible that we may return here only a few days later than you intended to be here (assuming that, under these circumstances, you do not decide to stay on in the Adirondacks a few days longer than Julie after all). But nonetheless, if you are in agreement, we are now fairly intent on going to Bar Harbor for at least 2–3 weeks, and would therefore ask you to let us know. As far as financial assistance is concerned, it is touching that you are once again offering to provide some. But at present we are really not in need of it, even for funding our holidays. If we should at some point find ourselves in a situation where such a necessity arises, the horses will not hesitate to stretch out their long necks trustingly to you. You really need not worry at all about us. – I think you would only have to see fat Archibald to drive all fears of imminent starvation out of your minds for good.

The two letters enclosed were addressed to us, which is why we opened them. Why does little Elisabeth not train as a whore? I am sure that with the 2.5 million Tommies she would have excellent chances at her tender age, and perhaps then she would at least bring joy to a few people for *once* in her life. But I am probably overestimating her – no doubt she is surly and arrogant as well as everything else, and clings tightly to her maidenhead, as my dear tiger used to say.

Aside from the main tasks at the institute, I am also taking on increasing responsibility in other work – correspondences with foundations,[1] emigrant negotiations with the various committees[2] etc. I am spending a great deal of my time attempting to get severely endangered emigrants out of France. Benjamin is relatively safe in Lourdes; we are undertaking every conceivable effort to bring him here, and have made him a permanent member[3] of the institute. (It might perhaps interest WK to know that Erich Fromm[4] is no longer a member of the institute, on account of grave scientific differences, first between him and myself, then also between him and Max, which made any further collaboration impossible. He is earning a great deal of money as a psychoanalyst.) Friedel K.[5] also escaped from Paris – I managed to scrounge together $250 in one day to get him out of France, although we cannot take him on at the institute under any circumstances. We do not know what has become of Alfons and the other Herzbergers; nor have we heard anything from Hermann Grab[6] or Fred Goldbeck.[*7]

We had a very cosy evening outside at Fritz's place on Saturday; it was so hot yesterday that we literally barely moved, but simply lounged about in the lightest of clothes on the couch and the bed. If your weather is at all similar, it cannot be very enjoyable – in Cuba, the dryness of the heat made it incomparably more pleasant. We have been invited to Julie's for next Sunday evening – she is going to chase away her relatives especially for this purpose.

The next 2 weeks should be of decisive importance for the war. In my particularly inconsequential opinion, England probably *could* stand up to a German attack, unless the disintegration and the capitalists' yearning for fascism are already so far advanced – as in France – as to paralyse all resistance, despite Churchill and the evident will of the English masses, so that after a few successful German attacks (for example massive air-raids) they will come out with their hands up. Going on my knowledge of England, however, this danger is very great. Should things turn out differently, I would say that England has a good chance of making it through the winter; and anyhow, I doubt that the Germans would attempt the invasion if there were genuine resistance, in which case they would probably pounce on Spain and Portugal first. (Path of least resistance.) Naturally, one cannot rule out the possibility of a true military defeat of the English and the success of the invasion. But here my analysis approaches what we all know: if the cock crows on the dung-heap, then the weather will change or stay as it is.[8] Only I fear that, at present, no one in the whole world knows what is what anymore.

Heartiest kisses from your faithful
Hippo King
Archibald
and his thin Giraffe Gazelle

We are frightfully looking forward to seeing you!
Now *all* emigrants in England have been incarcerated, including Sohn-Rethel,[9] Donald v. Hirsch[10] etc.

Original: typewritten letter with handwritten postscript.

1 *foundations*: EO.

2 *committees*: EO.

* [handwritten addition:] What about Hermann Levi? I heard that the German emigrants in Brussels were in a bad state as they fled.

3 *permanent member*: EO.

4 The separation from the Frankfurt-born Erich Fromm (1900–80) had already taken place in the transition from 1939 to 1940.

5 Siegfried Kracauer (1889–1966) and Elisabeth Kracauer only reached New York on 25 April 1941.

6 The Prague-born musician and writer Hermann Grab (1903–49), who studied philosophy and music, gained a PhD in law, and then gave concerts and wrote, had travelled to Paris for a concert and subsequently remained in France. By the end of June 1940 he had already reached Lisbon. In December of the same year Grab arrived in New York, where he worked as a piano teacher and as director of the 'Music House', which he had founded. Adorno, who wrote an obituary for his friend, had known Grab since 1925.

7 The Dutch-born Fred (Frederik) Goldbeck (1902–81), who had gone to school in Frankfurt and, like Adorno, studied composition with Bernhard Sekles, had lived mostly in Paris since 1925, working there as a music writer and teacher of conducting. He was married to the pianist Yvonne Lefébure (1898–1986).

8 Translator's note: this German saying, which seems to have no direct equivalent in English, essentially means 'Do not trust proverbs or hearsay', the 'cock' being one who makes proclamations about the state of the world, which remains totally indifferent to his words.

9 Alfred Sohn-Rethel (1899–1990), who initially emigrated to Switzerland in February 1936, then moved to Paris and ultimately went to England, was interned on the Isle of Man from 30 June 1940 until the end of January 1941.

10 The diplomat Donald von Hirsch (1901–?) had gone to England in 1938 after years of emigration in Italy and Switzerland. Von Hirsch, who was director of the German Cultural Institute in London from 1956 to 1970, had married Katharina Bachert – who had previously been the wife of Felix Weil – in 1930.

39 NEW YORK, 28.7.1940

28 July 1940

My dear faithful old WK,

accept our heartiest and warmest congratulations on the occasion of your birthday. The seventieth is a solemn date – but if anything gives particular cause for joy on your seventieth, it is the fact that one is not aware of this solemnity for even a moment. It may sound like a cliché, but I genuinely think that no one ignorant of your age would take you for 70. And this is not only a fine thing for the present, in which you are able to live with such elasticity and naturalness under conditions that you were not brought up to live in, and that do not stem from the true intention of your existence, but have rather struck you with barbaric fortuity as something completely alien and external. And there is indeed cause to hope that you will, despite your 70 years, still remain young long enough to witness the traces of something better which, despite all the terror of the last months in particular, none of us have been able to stop hoping for.

We had so looked forward to celebrating your 70th together with you, just the four of us in Miami. This too came to nothing – the staggeringly great events are casting their shadows upon the most intimate plans in our lives. But at least here, the famous silver lining is visible. For the Wondrous Hippo Cow's 75th birthday is on 1 October, and we shall celebrate the two occasions together in our cave, in the most peaceful and pleasant manner possible. As you had requested, we have not sent you any present now, but will look for something proper with you once you are here. (Even chocolates would only arrive melted now)

I said that, with you, one hardly notices the solemnity of the occasion, and the current situation makes me particularly loath to emphasize this solemnity. But ultimately I am not feeling quite so unsolemn that I could abstain from thanking you, simply and with few words, but with all my heart: for everything. I know too how much in life you have forgone for my sake in all sorts of areas, from lacking, in me, one who could continue your work, to the restrictions you have both taken upon yourselves for the sake of my independence. And I simply wish to assure you with the greatest conceivable emphasis that my sentiment has not been affected in any way by the change of circumstances. I think I can presume to differ at least in one respect from the bourgeois: in the fact that I lack any kind of faith in success, and that for me it has never – in any respect – been an indicator of what is good or right. I learned this early on from the tigress. If you have not succeeded, then this only holds something more touching and human for me. For, deep in my soul, I have the suspicion that all things decent and good that one can find at all in the world as it is can only really prove themselves by *not* succeeding. You understand me. – And now: celebrate your birthday as merrily as you can. Perhaps the Wondrous Hippo Cow will be right after all, with her gift of prophecy gained from the source of the Nile,[1] and we shall still see a change.

Yesterday was the hottest day here in 60 years, almost 100 degrees,[2] and 10 degrees warmer than in Miami. But we got through it well. Mr Berlin[3] is here from Oxford on the way to a diplomatic mission in Moscow, which one can reach from England only via South Africa–Constantinople or America–Japan–Vladivostok. He travelled to Canada on an English ship without convoy that was attacked twice by German submarines that missed on both occasions, however. They

saw the torpedoes explode in the water. The joys of travel. But it is amazing what good spirits Berlin is in, and if what he says regarding England is true, which I have no reason to doubt, then they are truly determined to fight it through[4] over there.
Heartiest kisses and sniffs from
Your two Rozinantes
Hottilein and Rossilein

Original: typewritten letter.

1 Translator's note: it should be borne in mind that the German word for hippopotamus, *Nilpferd*, literally means 'Nile horse'.

2 Measured in Fahrenheit; equivalent to 37.78°C.

3 The philosopher Isaiah Berlin (1909–97), who had fled with his family before the Bolsheviks from Riga to England in 1919, had studied and taught at Oxford. Berlin spent the war as a diplomat in Washington and – briefly – in Moscow.

4 *to fight it through*: EO.

40   BAR HARBOR, 21.8.1940

Bar Harbor, 21 August 1940

My dears, this card is simply to welcome you – in our stead – to N.Y., and to wish you a wonderful time.[1] We had a pleasant trip, arrived here with glorious weather, have been recognized and greeted by all the natives, and have plunged headlong into full relaxation – and both already look different at our first lunch. Julie will report to you at length. A bientôt – fond regards from the two horses
Archibald and Giraffe Gazelle

Original: photo postcard: Hotel de Gregoire, Bar Harbor, Maine. 'Only Hotel on the Shore'; stamp: Aug. 21, 1940. Manuscript.

1 *a wonderful time*: EO.

Rose the Hippopotamus, Central Park Zoo, New York; postcard sent
21 May 1936

Paola Adorno. By Anthony van Dyck (1599–1641). The Frick Collection,
New York; postcard sent 17 October 1939

Handwritten letter on the back of the title page of *The Happy Hippopotamus* by Anne Heyneman and Hugh Kappel; 28 February 1944

Card with giraffe image; 23 December 1945

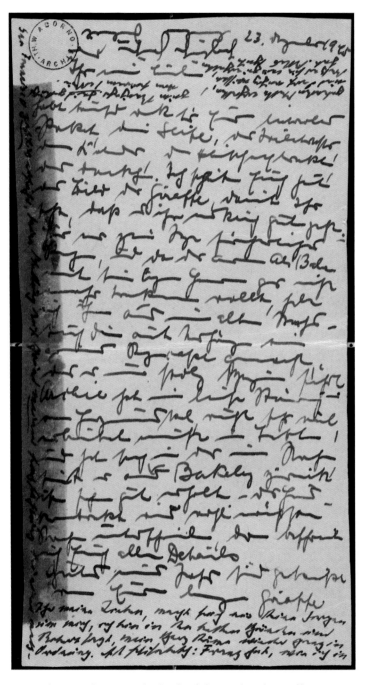

Handwritten letter on the back of the card with giraffe image;
23 December 1945

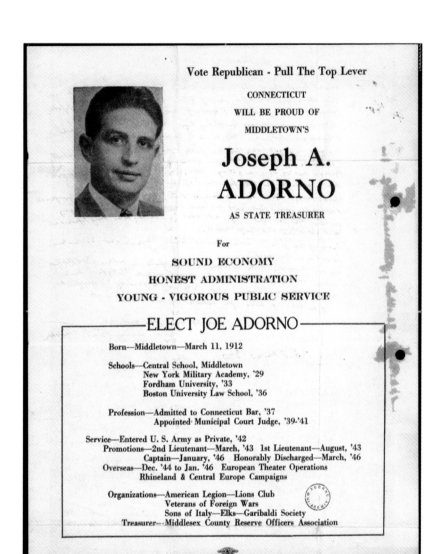

Vote Republican - Pull The Top Lever

CONNECTICUT
WILL BE PROUD OF
MIDDLETOWN'S

Joseph A. ADORNO

AS STATE TREASURER

For

SOUND ECONOMY
HONEST ADMINISTRATION
YOUNG - VIGOROUS PUBLIC SERVICE

ELECT JOE ADORNO

Born—Middletown—March 11, 1912

Schools—Central School, Middletown
New York Military Academy, '29
Fordham University, '33
Boston University Law School, '36

Profession—Admitted to Connecticut Bar, '37
Appointed Municipal Court Judge, '39-'41

Service—Entered U. S. Army as Private, '42
Promotions—2nd Lieutenant—March, '43 1st Lieutenant—August, '43
Captain—January, '46 Honorably Discharged—March, '46
Overseas—Dec. '44 to Jan. '46 European Theater Operations
Rhineland & Central Europe Campaigns

Organizations—American Legion—Lions Club
Veterans of Foreign Wars
Sons of Italy—Elks—Garibaldi Society
Treasurer—Middlesex County Reserve Officers Association

Joseph A. Adorno's election publicity; 28 October 1946

Handwritten letter on the back of Joseph A. Adorno's election publicity; 28 October 1946

Historic old Piper Opera House, built during the 1880s, Virginia City,
Nevada; postcard sent 17 September 1947

1941

Bar Harbor (Maine)
Hotel de Gregoire
July 28, 1941

My dear W.K.,
   happy birthday! Many happy returns! May all your wishes be fulfilled, Hitler crashed! good health for you (and fewer commentators!!!) and that sort of quiet life which, according to Espérance de
Walros, is the most important thing for a hippopotamus! We shall continue celebrating your birthday in N.Y.; we start doing it here tonight.
All my love to you and Lady Bauchschleifer! I hope you will enjoy
your vacation[1] as much as we do. Yours ever
                                            Archie

I hope Sir Willibald and Lady Bauchschleifer will do me the favor to
have lunch with me in September.
Good luck   yours ever
                                 Giraffe Gazelle

A very happy birthday and many returns yours   Lotte.

Best wishes to you and – cheerio. Is it possible to improve Old
Mr. Boston's Apricot Brandy? best yours Egon

Original: postcard; stamp: Bar Harbor, JUL 29, 1941. Manuscript with additional notes by Gretel Adorno and Lotte and Egon Wissing. Translator's note:
all written in English.

67

1 Oscar and Maria Wiesengrund spent their holidays in Swiftwater, Pennsylvania.

42 WEST LOS ANGELES, 19.11.1941

West Los Angeles (Cal.)
19.XI.1941

My dears, after a very smooth and pleasant trip[1] – we even slept – arrived well, collected by Max and Maidon early in the morning, welcomed charmingly, accommodated superbly in the 'motel' in which they lived for a long time – Max had already bought us a car, and Gretel drove us back home from Max's house, Max leading the way in his car. In the afternoon they took us on a big driving tour along the coast. Landscape of incomparable beauty, reminiscent of the French Riviera – we are happy and hope you will come soon.
    Hugs from your child Teddie
    Greetings and kisses Gi

Original: photo postcard: Brentshire Motel, 5 minutes to the beach. Located on the famous Wilshire Boulevard, most popular direct route from U.S. 101. Alternate at Santa Monica to Hollywood and downtown Los Angeles. 22 single and large party units, some with completely equipped kitchens with Frigidaire. Radios in all units. Closed, locked garages. No stamp. Manuscript.

1 Since August 1940, Oscar and Maria Wiesengrund had lived on West End Avenue in New York. The Adornos followed Max and Maidon Horkheimer to Los Angeles after the institute's activity had been restricted, and Horkheimer once again followed the principle of the subsidiary office.

43 LOS ANGELES, 23.11.1941

23 November 1941

My dears, a thousand thanks for the letter and in all haste the news that we have found a delightful little house with Max and Maidon, *fantastic* location, which, following a unanimous decision, we have now *rented*. We are moving there – already *before* our things get there – on 1 December. New address: 316 So. Kenter Avenue, Brentwood Heights, Los Angeles Cal. I am sure you will be here soon.
    With heartiest kisses from your child Teddie
We are two cheerful horses, and whinny loudly in your direction.

Original: photo postcard: Brentshire Motel; no stamp. Manuscript with additional note by Gretel Adorno.

44 LOS ANGELES, 30.11.1941

429 WEST 117TH STREET
NEW YORK, N.Y.

30 November 1941.
316 So. Kenter Ave,
Brentwood Heights,
Los Angeles, Calif.

My dears,
let us now attempt to tell you of the things we have experienced during these last twelve days. We departed on schedule, arrived in Cleveland without incident in the evening, spent a particularly good and pleasant night in a delightful establishment, Hotel Cleveland, directly by the train station, and travelled on to Chicago the following day. The ride through Indiana is pretty, and shortly before Chicago one passes a small subsidiary works belonging to United Steel, which seemed to me about ten times as big as Leuna, and which was in a state of full activity on Sunday, which did not a little to improve our humour. In Chicago we were met by Gräfenberg,[1] who showed us the city, which, despite some splendid streets by Lake Michigan, made a rather ghastly impression on us. Then, in his particularly attractive one-room apartment, Gräfenberg served us a supper he had been so cordial as to prepare himself, and then around 9 p.m. he took us to the 'Challenger', the train with the sleeping-car that brought us here. It is not luxurious, no Pullman train, but it is certainly practically comfortable and pleasant, so that we slept – I well, Gretel bearably – for three nights in real beds. Only the food is rather pitiful, but we were able to gain relief through the stock of gifts we had with us. On Monday we drove through Nebraska – very monotonous, nothing but cornfields. (Who eats all that corn?) We travelled through the Rockies in the state of Wyoming on Monday night, and did not see a thing or even notice the difference in altitude. Tuesday through snowy Utah with the big salt lake. The landscape seems strange, with those mountains that suddenly shoot up out of the plain like pyramids, and increasingly disappear as one approaches Nevada. Early on Wednesday morning we then reached the South with palms and orange groves, the latter admittedly all in the possession of Mr Sunkist.[2] Max and Maidon were awaiting us at the barrier; they had had to get up at 6 to do so. The journey from Los Angeles station to our motel (a group of cabins for automobile drivers, each consisting of two very nicely furnished rooms and a bathroom, kitchen and

69

garage) takes a good hour by car. Los Angeles is 30 miles or more from the sea, while the places around where we are now living still extend past Hollywood – so Santa Monica, Brentwood Heights, Pacific Palisades – in hollows that approach the sea and line the coast itself. The beauty of the region is so incomparable that even such a hard-boiled European as myself can only surrender to it. The proportion of mountains to sea initially reminds one strongly of the French Riviera, for example San Remo or Mentone, except that it is not so divided and 'privé', but rather much more long-lined and open. The shape of the mountains themselves, however, is more reminiscent of Tuscany. The view from our new house makes one think of Fiesole, even if there is of course no green dome to marvel at. But best of all are the incredibly intense, in no way reproducible colours; a drive along the ocean around sunset is one of the most extraordinary impressions that my – by no means highly responsive – eyes have ever had. All the red, blue and violet activity found there would appear laughable on any illustration, but it is overwhelming if one sees the real thing. As well as this, the more southern style of architecture, a certain reduction of advertising and one or two other factors combine to form something that is almost like a cultural landscape: one actually has the feeling that this part of the world is inhabited by humanoid beings, not only by gasoline stations and hot dogs. The entire wider vicinity here is somewhere between city and country (so more like Oberrad). The houses, all bungalows and never offensive to look at, are spaced far apart, the roads are paths, and only those great longitudinal veins known here as boulevards resemble what one is generally used to in America. One can take walks anywhere, only the distances are so great that it would be impossible for us without a car (Max, for example, who lives in our neighbourhood, so to speak, still lives 10 minutes' drive away from our house, and 15 minutes from the motel). But despite the problem of distances – the only serious one in the organization of external life – I would like to express my conviction – even so early on, and as a greenhorn – that you will find it ideally beautiful here.* Everything takes on a lightness that one could never dream of in New York, let alone the New York winter.

Max had already got us a car – an older one, very sensibly, so that we need not worry about every scratch until Gretel is truly experienced as a driver. In other respects, too, the Horkheimers have been looking after us in the most delightful and comradely fashion. Max does everything he can to make our life here as pleasant and smooth as possible, so that our work plans – for we hope to write our longer things together in the next years – have the best possible con-

* [Marginal note:] much more beautiful than Florida, and even than Cuba!!

ditions, assuming we do not fritter away all our earthly goods. We searched vigorously for a place with Max; he also had buying a house in mind, and had already found something very pretty, though just a touch too small, but after the most careful consultation we decided against it. The house we have rented is one half of a semi-detached house, two-storey. It belongs to an exceptionally pleasant and serious working woman who inhabits the other half – which is completely separate from ours, however – with her niece, and assists us in every respect in the most cordial fashion. On the ground floor we have our double garage (Mrs Colburn has a double garage for herself). On the upper ground floor a very large, bright living room, a small dining room, a kitchen with side rooms. Everything furnished in the most modern and practical fashion, and with genuinely useful gadgets[3] that WK will be enthusiastic about (the house is only about 2 years old). On the first floor: Gretel's bedroom, my bedroom, my study (wood) and the bathroom with shower.[4] Small garden; the water and the gardener are paid for by the landlady.[5] We have signed a contract for two years with the option[6] of leaving after one year if we are transferred somewhere else. As our contract begins on 1 December and we do not intend to pay double, we are already moving in tomorrow. The landlady will lend us the most necessary things. But naturally we have a great interest in getting our things over here as quickly as possible. Naturally, Max is here all the time. Aside from that, we are fortunately seeing rather few people for the meantime; the motel room without a telephone was a true relief. We were very diligent, finished the greatly expanded English version of the Veblen[7] with our American assistant,[8] and also the rough English translation of the first part of the music study.[9] Now we shall translate Max's new essay on the dialectic of reason[10] together with him. Then we shall be finished with our backlog and can begin the new things, which are no longer to take the form of essays. As soon as we have installed ourselves to some degree, we shall search with the utmost energy for a place for you, and inform you *as quickly as possible*. Max, and incidentally Fritz too, also consider it by far the most sensible thing for you to come here.

We were *so* very happy to read your kind and heroic letter. I did not tell you just *how* difficult it became for us to leave – you noticed it, and I did not wish to make our hearts heavier still. But: you must come here as quickly as possible. If you divide up the journey as we did, it is not so gruelling; it is as soothing and peaceful here as it could be anywhere in this world; the climate is *ideal* for you; we would be near, and in our garden there is a eucalyptus tree, like in Corsica. Heartiest kisses from your old child

Teddie

71

The journey is probably less exhausting by train than by car. But perhaps there is a different route to the Union Pacific, one on which you can see more. Our price was $75.86 with the sleeping-car. My driving gets better every day, and I am very careful, so you need not worry. Fond regards ever your old Gretel.

Original: typewritten letter with printed letterhead and handwritten post-script, as well as additional note by Gretel Adorno.

1 The gynaecologist Ernst Gräfenberg (1881–1958), who invented the contraceptive coil. Gräfenberg had managed to escape from Germany with the help of Adorno and Horkheimer as late as 1938.

2 This had been the registered trademark of united citrus fruit producers since 1908; there was no 'Mr Sunkist'.

3 *gadgets*: EO.

4 *shower*: EO.

5 *landlady*: EO.

6 *option*: EO.

7 See Adorno, 'Veblen's Attack on Culture: Remarks Occasioned by the Theory of the Leisure Class', *Studies in Philosophy and Social Science* 9 (1941), pp. 389–413 (no. 3). For the German version, see GS 10.1, pp. 72–96.

8 Unknown.

9 This is the section on Schoenberg in the *Philosophy of Modern Music*.

10 See Max Horkheimer, 'Vernunft und Selbsterhaltung', *Gesammelte Schriften* 5, pp. 320–50. The English version – 'The End of Reason' – appeared in the same issue of the journal as Adorno's 'Veblen'.

45   LOS ANGELES, 10.12.1941

Los Angeles, Brentwood H.
Dec. 10, 1941

My dear ones,
this is just to tell you that our furniture and everything has arrived yesterday in very good shape. Very few things broken: two jazz records, a record of Rudi, one glass, one coffee pot – some bruises on the furniture, that's about all. Gretel works like a commuter and we all feel it will be very lovely. I spent part of the time with Max, part with Norah Andreae who rang us up, as charming, amiable and

intelligent as ever. Her husband, (Hermann's colleague)[1] incidentally, has lost his position but is over there. She is with her parents. Here everything is quiet – this is country-side, above all. We are impatient to have you here. The wine has arrived without any loss! Let us have the first bottle soon!
All my love
and kisses

yours ever
Archibald
Max has been appointed air raid warden!

Love yours ever

Giraffe Gazelle

Original: handwritten letter with additional note by Gretel Adorno. Translator's note: written in English.

1 Norah Andreae (1888–1949). Her husband, from the Andreae family of Frankfurt, could not be identified.

46   LOS ANGELES, C. MID-DECEMBER 1941
     FRAGMENT

got on splendidly with Schönberg. She too is much nicer than she used to be. It would be superb if this relationship were to remain untroubled. Otherwise, we are still living a very reclusive life. We may be meeting Soma Morgenstern[1] tomorrow, who arrived here at more or less the same time as we did. The work with Max will also be starting from next week.

Regarding Christmas, we have absolutely no idea what to send you. The nearest bookshops are in downtown Los Angeles, where we never go, and you can get the California fruits just as well in New York. Please let us know what you need. We will be glad if we are all set up here by the 24th – officially, we have cancelled Christmas.

A thousand kisses fondest regards
Your Giraffe Gazelle

A great deal of work (aside from the big translation, the Veblen finished, and all sorts of things with Max). But I am in excellent shape, except for overeating on dates, my favourite fruit of those that grow here . . . On Sunday, Gretel and I went for a wonderful drive along the sea, very far – about as far as Amorbach from Frankfurt. How we are already looking forward to showing you all this! We had a sweet,

73

albeit somewhat embarrassed letter from Else; she acts – without reason – as if she has been offended (and is now reconciled). She and the difficult one[2] have made up again, and he is paying, thank God! (according to weight?)

I have only one wish: that world history, whose victims we have been for long enough now, will not delay your moving here. I daresay the Allmeier business[3] will hardly be feasible anymore, and I would *not* wait in N.Y. on her account.

Heartiest kisses
from the big fat
Hippo King
Archibald

Original: handwritten letter from Gretel and Theodor W. Adorno. The front page numbered 'IV' seems to belong to the letter which Gretel Adorno goes on to mention, and whose three preceding pages were evidently lost.

1 The writer Soma Morgenstern (1890–1976) had fled from Austria to Paris in 1938. After being interned several times after the outbreak of war, he was finally able to escape to the USA via several intermediate stops in 1941, and lived mostly in New York.

2 This presumably refers to Herr Grünebaum.

3 Unknown.

47 LOS ANGELES, 21.12.1941

21 Dec. 1941

My dears:

Let us send you our very best, fondest Christmas wishes. We shall have a very quiet time at home and think of you a great deal. Do not worry about us – we are well, as you will soon be able to see for yourselves. (I forgot to tell you in my last letter that the electric current here is the same as in New York, and our appliances are working; it was only in the old house in 113th St that it did not work). Today I would like to describe to you what our apartment looks like now that it is finished: the bottom floor is really a large flat area on top of the garage: one immediately enters the living room with a large window to the west, 2 to the north, the door to the dining room and stairs to the east. The pieces of Biedermeier furniture stand next to the fireplace (which we do not use, however), facing the entrance, the grand piano is in the diagonal corner that slopes into

74

the room, 2 comfortable armchairs against the south wall and in the middle the chest of drawers from Teddie's room with the gramophone on the magnificent Hippo Cow blanket. Dining room: in the middle the table and chairs in 2 corners your record cabinet and against the south wall the cupboard from my room that I used for the good crockery, which now contains sheet music. 1st floor: Teddie's bedroom: bed, bookshelf, 2 farmhouse chairs, bedside table, the little chest of drawers from my room with a Hippo Cow blanket, the little stool we were given; Teddie's study: bookshelf, manuscript (flour) box with the red and green Hippo Cow blanket, fireside armchair. Table, chair, fur blanket as a rug, my room: couch, typewriter desk, small table, mirror, salon door [?], leather cushion. Perhaps I can still hunt down a few rocking chairs or other armchairs in a used furniture shop for upstairs. We are still missing curtains, and the books, sheet music, records, manuscripts etc. still have to be ordered, but for the moment everything has been stored. Very hearty hugs and kisses from your faithful

Giraffe Gazelle (Gi)

please turn over, now it is Archibald's turn:

My dears, so now we are settled once again, and I think I can say much more pleasantly than in New York, in a spacious but not excessively large house that is also easy to manage; neither petty bourgeois nor ostentatious, wonderfully situated – ideal for us! If only you could see it *soon*. The view from my study over a southern property and the view of the mountains from the balcony are already worth the trip in themselves. To see something like the Bay District here when living in Europe would require a whole holiday and cost considerable effort. Considering that you are not tied to any one place, it would be absurd not to come soon. The Allmeier business is all over anyway. We have not found anything for you yet, but that would not take more than a few weeks, and I would already begin *energetically* with your arrangements for the trip etc. now (is permission from Washington necessary?). I completely forgot to write to you how much we laughed about your report on the rencontre with the old Gs.[1] It is in fact much funnier than you realize. Not only is it completely uncertain where Leo[2] will stay – the old man's question about his work must have been very embarrassing for Herman,[3] and it was not out of secrecy that he refrained from answering it . . .

Please dear WK do tell me at length, *openly* and critically, about your impression of the Columbia lectures.[4] – Fritz is coming here for 2 weeks on Thursday; Marcuse still in New York.

We are with you with all our thoughts and love. We must spend next Christmas together again. May the new year finally bring us closer to happiness – the course taken by the old one at least gives some hope.

Stay healthy and be glad that you are here – over in Europe, things are getting horrible *everywhere*.
Heartiest kisses
from your increasingly old child
Teddie

[Postscript by Gretel Adorno on the first page:]
The Horkheimers were very keen on WK's apricot brandy, and ask if you could perhaps send them and a few of their acquaintances 6 bottles altogether, but please not as a gift, only for an appropriate sum. (Giraffe Gazelle would advise you strongly to do so, if it is not too much work.)

Original: handwritten letter from Gretel and Theodor W. Adorno.

1 Unknown.

2 Leo Frenkel?

3 Frenkel?

4 Between 7 November and 19 December 1941, five members of the Institute of Social Research had given lectures on 'National Socialism': Herbert Marcuse spoke on 'State and Individual under National Socialism', A. R. L. Gurland on 'Private Property under National Socialism', Franz Neumann on 'The New Rulers in Germany', Otto Kirchheimer on 'Law and Justice under National Socialism', and Frederick Pollock's lecture was entitled 'Is National Socialism a New Social and Economic System?'.

Dec 25, 1941

My dear(s):
You cannot imagine how great our surprise was when your parcel arrived, a thousand thanks. We appreciate it very much. Yesterday night we spent with Mamuth's,[1] quiet and nice. Today it is raining but not too cold. Archie feels very happy and enjoys the work with Max tremendously.
Happy, happy new Year
Yours ever
Giraffe Gazelle

Kindest regards to Julie

Thousand thanks – you could not possibly [have] made me happier than by the liquor and the Nile filly's books. We spend the holidays very quietly, working with Max.
   All my love and kisses, the old hippopotamus king,
   Archie
Come very soon! Let the new year be a happy one.

Original: handwritten letter from Gretel Adorno with additional note by Adorno. Translator's note: written in English.

1 This refers to the Horkheimers.

1942

8 January 1942

My dear Wondrous Hippo Cow,
last week Salka[1] invited us over twice – once for tea, then an informal dinner, and the following evening together with Brecht.[2] Salka Viertel, as you know, is the sister of Eduard Steuermann, and has a very high position here in the film industry, scriptwriter for Garbo at MGM, very famous and influential, and a sort of business centre for the Hollywood intellectuals. She received us in the most charming and friendly manner. But that is not why I am telling you about it: we met Eduard's 74-year-old mother[3] there. It turned out that she knows you not only from the stage, as we thought, but also rather well personally. She related that she used to meet you every Sunday in Vienna, at the house of a lady by the name of Laura Briggs (?).[4] Her own maiden name was Amster; she told me simply to write 'the red-haired girl', then you would know who was meant. Incidentally, she also knew Rottenberg[5] well. She had an exact recollection of your singing,[6] and praised your high F; she had wanted to become a singer herself. She did not remember Agathe and your mother.[7] She is a quite delightful old lady, a veritable Espérance, with a truly exemplary bearing and energy, a true lady, even though she spent most of her life in Russian Poland as the wife of the mayor of Sambor. In this war, she first went through the German occupation, then the Russian, and journeyed here all by herself via Moscow, where she experienced the heaviest air raids, then through Siberia, Vladivostok and Seattle, and is a fantastic storyteller. She is frightfully happy that she will soon see you again, and sends her warmest greetings. She not only speaks five languages – in

78

addition to French and German also Russian, Polish and Ukrainian – but is now also learning English in the most systematic and eager fashion, though she does complain about the discrepancy between orthography and pronunciation.

We have little to report, except that it is wonderful here, we are very happy in our little house, and work a great deal with Max. Fritz, who is going back at the end of the week, will tell you everything. The only matter troubling us is that of your accommodation. As we have not been able to find out anything through personal connections, we have advertised in the Santa Monica paper. Gretel will take a look at the rooms and report back to you. Price *c.* $90 per month, so roughly the same as in New York. The difficulties here have become even greater through the defense work,[8] and in addition the enormous distances. Hotel rooms have become absurdly expensive through the accursed film industry. We need not tell you how happy we shall be to have you here (WK's reference to a 'bothersome object' can only have been made in a mild fit of unreason), but we do not want to rush you into something where you end up feeling uncomfortable. Despite all its climatic and scenic merits, living on the West Coast would involve a certain sacrifice of comfort and mobility compared to your lodgings in New York. The fact that you would have far fewer people here should also be considered. (Aside from Max, we only really see Schönberg and Salka now and again, but with our workload we do not mind that at all.) Nothing would make us happier than for you to come, but we do not want you to accuse us of chasing you out of your cosy hippo mud into an eternal spring that you perhaps do not like all that much. The Robinsonesque, colonialist quality of the whole existence here (the entire Bay District is no more than 10 years old) makes demands of one's improvisatory ability and independence that at your age, despite WK's energy, should not be taken entirely lightly. At any rate, do not make any final decisions until we have found something decent, and do write to us at length how you feel about the whole complex. But to make sure that dear WK is not struck with a further fit of unreason, let me say with the greatest emphasis that our only thought in all this is *your well-being*, and that we would rather have you here today than tomorrow.

I do not wish to end this letter without having it put on record that, since America's entry into the war and the Russian resistance, I am now convinced that Hitler will suffer an ignominious defeat. There will still be terrible setbacks, not only in the Pacific, but probably also in Russia and the Middle East, but the technical superiority of the democracies will ultimately prevail: for quantity really does turn into quality. In addition, Hitler not only has to keep up with America and an England that has remained almost unscathed for the last ¾ of a year, but he has also forfeited his advantage once and for all through the losses in Russia, regardless of how the Russian campaign progresses. As strongly as I believe that it will still take a long time, and that there will be much suffering yet for us all, I am nonetheless convinced that the whole thing will end with Hitler's downfall. As much as I also initially agree with WK in his assessment of the total historical perspective, the matter of Hitler is first of all a matter of life and death. Whatever might come later will be affected by the fact that Hitler did not succeed, as much as it may also be affected by the respects in which he *did* succeed.

I read WK's account of the lectures with gusto. Our Baldchen is running well; now he has to last for a long time and is looking forward to sauntering along the Pacific Ocean with you.

Heartiest kisses

from your two horses
Archibald and Giraffe Gazelle

Original: typewritten letter.

1 The actress Salomea Steuermann (1889–1978), who was married to Berthold Viertel (1885–1953), had gone to America with her three sons in 1928, and worked for the film industry there. She lived in Santa Monica.

2 Bertolt Brecht had reached California via Vladivostok in July 1941, and settled in Santa Monica.

3 Augusta Steuermann (1868–1953) had aspired to a career as an opera singer herself: '[. . .] as a young girl, my mother had prepared herself for this career for a while. Her clear, beautiful soprano voice and her great musical talent – she was also a very good pianist – justified this ambition. She would have been an ideal Else, Sieglinde or Senta. Her reddish-blonde hair, blue eyes and rosy complexion would have fooled the best experts in racial matters: this Nordic beauty came from a rich Russian-Jewish family' (Salka Viertel, *Das unbelehrbare Herz* [The Incorrigible Heart]. *Ein Leben in der Welt des Theaters, der Literatur und des Films* [Hamburg: Rowohlt, 1979], p. 13).

4 Unknown.

5 The composer and conductor Ludwig Rottenberg (1864–1932), born in Czernowitz, worked at the Frankfurt Opera from 1893 to 1926.

6 Adorno's mother was employed by the Vienna Opera from August 1885 until May 1886. In that season she sang the parts of Urban the Page in Giacomo Meyerbeer's *The Huguenots*, Angélique in *The King Said So* by Léo Delibes, and the wood-bird in Wagner's *Siegfried*. (Letter from Minna von Altha to Adorno of 5.12.1962)

7 Elisabeth Calvelli-Adorno, née Henning.

8 *defense work*: EO.

12 Jan 1942

Dear Maria, dear Oscar,
we received quite a number of responses to our advertisement, but of these there is only 1 woman worth serious consideration, a former teacher with a 16-year-old daughter. You could have a room with board there for $80 per month, or two (which I would advise) for $100 per month. There is another woman who plans to turn her house into a guesthouse, and demands $100 for one room, and another one whom I can only call at the weekend,[1] and who demands $24 per week for one room. As the new schoolterm[2] begins here on 1 Feb., Mrs Willes would like to be informed soon (the teacher) she might otherwise go to live with her other married daughter. Teddie has not seen the apartment yet, as I would first of all like to know what you think. I am sad that I have nothing better to report.
  Fond regards ever
                              Your Giraffe Gazelle

On Saturday evening we had dinner at the Dieterles,[3] where Max Reinhardt[4] was Gretel's dinner partner. Yesterday we were invited to lunch by Norah Andreae, who clings to us in the extreme, and who appeared here today for lunch. There goes our lovely solitude.
  Fond regards – Giraffe went to look at countless things! I hope you do find the right one in the end. Hearty kisses from your child
                              Teddie

Original: handwritten letter from Gretel Adorno with additional note by Adorno.

1 *weekend*: EO.

2 *schoolterm*: EO.

3 The director William (Wilhelm) Dieterle (1893–1972) and his wife Charlotte had moved to Hollywood in 1930, and Dieterle worked there first at the Warner studios, then for RKO. In 1940 his film *Dr Ehrlich's Magic Bullet* was shown in the cinema. Dieterle returned to Germany in 1955.

4 The Austrian director Max Reinhardt (1893–1943), who had emigrated to the USA in 1938 and lived in New York.

22 January 1942

My dears,

today I wish above all to tell of our further apartment-hunting. The one landlady about whom we had written to you slipped through our fingers before we received your response; she did not want to wait any longer, and besides that also the usual claptrap about preferring tenants who are away at work all day. This is all connected to the aviation industry; if, as our local paper writes, the aviation industry is genuinely being moved inland, completely away from the coast, then the situation could change for the better very soon. On Sunday we had a look at the only other place worth serious consideration. It is a house located in a very pretty street, all green and palms, barely three minutes' walk to the sea via the truly magnificent Ocean Avenue, where there are also many benches where you can sit down and take in the most splendid view during your walks. It is only a little further, 10 minutes' walk at the most, to the next shopping centre, down town[1] Santa Monica, and to the drug store.[2] So the conditions would be very pleasant. Price for full board (3 meals a day) for you both together, $90 per month. The lady who owns the house is a teacher, and promises excellent food. The downside: she has no car, and one is really a bit trapped here without a car, not least because we are mostly tied up during the day, and driving in the evening is no delight here on account of the complete absence of street-lamps. The room is much smaller than the one you have now, and much less well furnished, in my opinion somewhat oppressive, but perhaps you would feel differently about it. But above all: despite her obliging manner and a certain courtesy, the landlady[3] somehow makes a desolate, haggard impression. As you will be incomparably more isolated here, without Julie, than in New York, this should be considered. Among the fellow occupants is also the landlady's very old mother, whom you naturally may or may not find agreeable. In a word, it is genuinely quite difficult for us to decide, and the responsibility is greater than I can bear. Nothing is more hateful to me than the thought of chasing you over here, simply so that you can be near me, and placing you in an atmosphere that, compared to your current one, would impose sacrifices, loneliness and discomfort upon you. On the other hand, as well as being close to us, you would also have the exceedingly pleasant climate – one should particularly note that here, and even more as close to the sea as you would be living, it is on average about 20 degrees F cooler than in Hollywood, so that one would really not have to worry about the heat, while the winter is mild, often autumnally gentle; and we have

82

still not seen much of the famous rains (which supposedly keep one inside the house for three weeks).

Gretel's suggestion was that you might come here in February and stay until September or October. There would thus be no real travel expenses, as you would save the cost of the summer stay – it is real paysage here. My only reservation is that once you have taken the journey here, which is after all a very long one, and are with us, you may decide not to return to your stable if you find it somewhat bearable here, whereas it is precisely my wish to spare you anything somewhat bearable and see to it that you live as comfortably as possible. I know only too well how dear WK in particular tends to accept circumstances once they are given, and can already hear him clearly saying: 'I mog nit mehr weg',[4] even if in secret (and naturally, out of Corsican and Jewish pride, without telling us) you were desperately unhappy. In addition, with the greater distances, it would not be as easy for Gretel to slip out to you often as it was in West End Avenue, as she is rather tied up not only with our work together, but also with the house. I have tried to present the situation to you as well as I possibly can, but genuinely want you to make the final decision yourselves, and in consultation with Julie. I would only ask you to inform us of this decision as soon as you can, as the new sissy already seems to fear that her stable might remain uninhabited, and has a certain tendency to be pressing (I have already told her that a move would be out of the question before February on account of the legal difficulties). Let me say it again: we are happy for every day sooner that you come, but unhappy for every sacrifice thus forced on you. There are further imponderable matters, such as the feeling I have been observing quietly in myself, which will probably be stronger for you, that, after taking root – however weakly – in the rocks of Manhattan, yet another move makes the emigration situation all the clearer. On the other hand, it goes without saying that it would be wonderful to show you the new house and our well-behaved Baldchen in action.

We are working incredibly profusely and intensively. As well as the daily work with Max, I have written all my contributions to the Dictionary of the Arts[5] – in German first, admittedly, in the hope that the Runes[6] Organization will somehow relieve me of the burden of translating them. (This work is unrelated to the translation of Philosophie der neuen Musik already completed in December.) As there happened to be a total of 19 articles, we gave the collected German text (the size of a long essay) put together for domestic use the name '19-teat pig', and it is under this name that this latest work, if at all, should go down in intellectual history.

A few days ago I went with Max to my first film shoot, by Dieterle (synchronizing of images and music) in the RKO studios, very interesting. Otherwise, the only people we see quite a lot of are the Brechts, with whom we get on particularly well.

You need not worry at all about the dangers here. We have not had any alarms since the first days after the Japanese attack.[7] Los Angeles is much further away from the Japanese bases than New York is from the German ones – this, incidentally, would also be a reason for you to move. Naturally, it is always possible that they will make a nuisance[8] attack from an aircraft carrier,[9] but that is just one of those risks one has to take into account, and we have not worried about that for even a second. Ceterum censeo . . .

I am terribly sorry to hear about the death of Wohlauer.[10] I have a profound feeling of gratitude towards him: he treated me with gentleness, care and understanding in a matter that was not only painful but also very delicate psychologically, and if I think of the two big shots in Frankfurt, then I know what that means. Please send me his wife's address. I would like to add a further request. Wohlauer had told me upon my last visit in September that he would give me the name and address of a very diligent, likewise German specialist colleague of his in Los Angeles that I had asked for. Could you find out this name and address for me? I would also be pleased if I could somehow get hold of the record that Wohlauer kept about me and my constantly – albeit less strongly – recurring problem. That would be quite important for me, e.g. in the case of a military examination; I do not even know the English name for the condition. It would truly be a great favour to me if dear WK could take care of this matter.

As I have translated one of my longer past essays[11] for Virgil Thomson,[12] and a larger study of mine[13] has just been published, together with two that were carried out under my direction,[14] in the volume Radio Research 1941, and Thomson is likely to refer to these, I would be pleased if you could follow his Sunday column.

We do not have all our sheet music in the china cupboard, but rather one part of it in the chest of drawers from the tigress, and one part in a built-in bookshelf in the living room. I have had a second large bookshelf in natural finish installed in my study, and the room has turned out particularly nicely, just as the rest of the house is now completely set up. Giraffe even arranged the books and sheet music in the most touching fashion.

Look after yourselves, and keep up your patience and hope. You and we at least want to live to see how the change in the world becomes palpable, and now and again I am already sticking my head in the air to have a sniff.

Heartiest kisses

from your old

Teddie and Giraffe Gretel

84

I found the chemistry book among our books; it is a little more up to date than the Hoffmann, and you will no doubt soon become accustomed to the layout. It is possible that CN as a carbon bond is already classed under organic chemistry. The halogens are the salts of fluorine, chlorine, bromine and iodine. What is it that particularly interests you here – the reaction to iron?

Please do not do anything about the apricot brandy yet, I am still waiting to hear from Maidon. She then wants to have Fritz Pollock send you a cheque, and is now thinking of only three or four bottles. She would like to avoid the transport – do you think you could perhaps bring them, but really only if it causes no inconvenience, or can Fritz Pollock not bring them here in June?

I, Frau Hippo King Archibald, would be extraordinarily grateful for a new batch of the excellent laxative brand WK. A thousand thanks in advance, how much do I owe you?

Original: typewritten letter.

1 *down town*: EO.

2 *drug store*: EO.

3 *landlady*: EO.

4 Translator's note: This is either Bavarian or Austrian dialect (despite the fact that Oscar Wiesengrund came from Frankfurt) for 'I don't want to leave any more'. In High German it would be 'Ich mag nicht mehr weg'.

5 See *GS* 18, pp. 57–87. The project fell through, and only the article 'Jazz' was printed in English in the dictionary.

6 The philosopher and writer Dagobert David Runes (1902–82), who also owned the publishing house that planned to print the dictionary.

7 On 7 December 1941, Japanese carrier-based aircraft had attacked Pearl Harbor, the main base of the American Pacific fleet.

8 *nuisance*: EO.

9 *aircraft carrier*: EO.

10 Eric J. Wohlauer had died at the end of 1941; the obituary notice appeared on 12 December in *Aufbau*.

11 Unknown.

12 The composer Virgil Thomson (1896–1989), who studied with Nadia Boulanger in Paris, where he met Jean Cocteau, Erik Satie and Igor Stravinsky, composed two operas in collaboration with Gertrude Stein: *Four Saints in Three Acts* and *The Mother of Us All*. His music reviews appeared in the New York *Herald Tribune*. Thomson's review of the book referred to in the following note appeared in the Sunday edition of the New York *Herald Tribune* of 8 February 1942.

13 See Adorno, 'The Radio Symphony: An Experiment in Theory', in *Radio Research 1941*, ed. Paul F. Lazarsfeld and Frank N. Stanton, New York, 1941, pp. 110–39. Adorno's essay 'Über die musikalische Verwendung des Radios' [On the Musical Use of the Radio] from *Der getreue Korrepetitor* [The Faithful Repetiteur] (see *GS* 15, pp. 369–401) originated from this study.

14 See Duncan MacDougald, Jr., 'The Popular Music Industry', in *Radio Research 1941*, pp. 65–109, and Edward A. Suchman, 'Invitation to Music: A Study of the Creation of New Music Listeners by the Radio', ibid., pp. 140–88.

52 LOS ANGELES, 12.2.1942

12 February 1942

My dears,

a thousand thanks for kindly sending the Thomson article, and for your kind letters. You made me infinitely happy. The Thomson article is really extremely pleasant, and I accordingly sent Thomson a telegram of thanks.

So far we have not been especially affected by the restrictions (touch wood), aside from the one that has applied for months, namely being unable to travel. But naturally it is possible that the regulations will be slackened – there is a big press campaign going on, though it is admittedly not appreciated by the authorities. This will, incidentally, depend in part on the progress of the war. We registered immediately, and were treated in the most pleasant manner. We already have our passports. There is no animosity whatsoever among the populace.

We cannot undertake anything until central special measures for refugees[1] have been implemented. I can assure you that we tried it right away. We regard the development with a certain fatalism, but would naturally be glad if we could stay in our charming little house. It is simply indescribably beautiful here – the way one always imagines the Riviera, and the way it never actually is.

A few days ago, Max and I completed our first genuine joint text,[2] and are both very happy with it.

Old Frau Steuermann said that you had made a particularly great impression on her as Lucia;[3] did you sing that part in Vienna? But she speaks of you with such certainty that I can hardly imagine any misunderstanding.

Please do not scold me in letters.

If we are not chased away and sentiments become calmer once more, we hope with all our heart that you will come here soon.

Heartiest kisses

from your two horses
Archibald and Giraffe Gazelle

86

Original: typewritten letter.

1 *refugees*: EO.

2 The essay 'Vernunft und Selbsterhaltung' [Reason and Survival], published under Horkheimer's name, appeared in German in 1942 in *Walter Benjamin zum Gedächtnis*, and in the English translation in the last issue of the journal; see Horkheimer, *Gesammelte Schriften 5*, pp. 320–50.

3 The eponymous heroine of the opera *Lucia di Lammermoor* by Gaetano Donizetti.

53   LOS ANGELES, 26.3.1942

26 March 1942

My dears,
my main reason for not writing to you for so long was that I had not written to you for so long. The guilty conscience turns into a block, and in the general state of depression affecting me, in addition to the extreme effort I have had to expend, I simply did not have the energy to deal with this block. A further factor is my instinct to hide in the bushes until I can keep my chin up again. I urgently ask that you take this in exactly the way I have described, not as a sign of any lack of love, which God knows it is not, and forgive me.

The reason for the depression, aside from the general situation, is the completely uncertain state of affairs here. Officially, we are classed among those who are to be evacuated. On the other hand, there has been much talk of reclassification, but I am rather sceptical. At any rate, the situation is such that one really does not know what to do. To leave here sooner than absolutely necessary would be impractical, nay impossible; on the other hand, being ultimately chased away is a highly unpleasant prospect (we are reckoning with this around May). Then there are also the special terms already in force. From tomorrow onwards, we have to be home no later than 8 each evening, and are not allowed to go more than 5 miles away from the house, which, with the truly monstrous distances here, amounts to being completely locked up. We can no longer go to Hollywood, only just to Beverly Hills, and our wonderful drives, our only source of relaxation, are now a thing of the past. It is particularly inexplicable that these regulations should be most strict against emigrants – the most reliable enemies of Hitler in the whole of America – and the Japanese. We do not have the 'out with us' mentality,[1] no more here than anywhere else.

The whole thing is all the more grotesque because I have been spending all of these last weeks working like mad for a government agency in Washington, the last few days even at night; I sent out a long report[2] yesterday. It goes without saying that the institute cannot evade the defense[3] commitments, which are of course purely volunteer work. As Max is lying in bed with influenza, I, the 'enemy alien', had to direct all the work assigned to the Los Angeles branch. Gretel helped me truly fantastically with this.

In addition to all this, I donated a pint[4] of my oh-so-precious Corsican-Jewish blood 2 weeks ago. One hardly notices anything during the process, and all those involved – doctors, nurses and fellow donors – have a humanity and friendliness that would be completely unimaginable in a European office. In fact one generally encounters a truly democratic spirit of helpfulness and co-operation here in the emergency[5] that was a great surprise to me, and which truly has something to do with fundamental democracy. In this context I would like to mention that even the special measures as such do not at all have the character of harassment, that all individuals involved have the best intentions, and that the unpleasant aspects merely stem from the ponderousness of the whole monstrous machinery, which is only gradually starting to work properly.

If you were here, incidentally, you would not be affected by the regulations (old people over 70). But you should only consider moving once our own position has been clarified in a positive fashion.

If you want to be kind to us, then write to us more in these weeks of uncertainty, even if we are occasionally naughty and do not answer. We are both in good health, aside from the fact that Gretel had a heavy migraine attack, but fortunately she made a speedy recovery.

This afternoon we plan to go on our last longer drive. Next week we shall have Easter holidays.

Heartiest kisses

from your two old Rozinantes
Teddie and Gretel

Original: typewritten letter.

1 Victor Klemperer relates: 'Do you still remember the first scenes in 1933? When the Nazis held the great demonstration against the Jews? "One-way street to Jerusalem!" and "The white stag chases away the Jews", and whatever was on the rest of those banners and posters? There was also a Jew marching in the procession, carrying a sign on a long pole, and the sign read: "Out with us!" ' (Victor Klemperer, *'LTI' die unbewältigte Sprache. Aus dem Notizbuch eines Philologen* ['LTI' The Unsurmounted Language: From the Notebook of a Philologist] [Munich: dtv, 1969], pp. 205f.).

2 'Private Morale in Germany' was a report written by Adorno together with Herbert Marcuse; it was sent to the Office of the Co-ordinator of Information.

88

3 *defense*: EO.

4 *pint*: EO.

5 *emergency*: EO.

L.A. Easter Saturday, 4.IV.1942

My dears, a thousand thanks for your kind words. Today, as a little Easter greeting, a few photos of the 1939 summer holidays with Max, Maidon and Fritz in Bar Harbor. We are resting – *completely* – for a week, which is clearly having a positive effect on us and on my worn-out nerves.

Max had to go to San Francisco to see Lix.[1] Maidon over for lunch today, at hers on Monday. Leo did not come to stay with us for a week as planned, but spent the whole time at Max's house; it would have been too impractical otherwise. He will report to you, though I think he will only be back in a week. I think you will like Norah, who is *touchingly* kind to us in every respect, a great deal. In her absence, her very old parents[2] (father *84*) constantly ask how we are! She is at loggerheads with Albert Hahn, incidentally, and her husband is living with Husch,[3] so be careful!

If only we could show you our wonderful laurel-like tree in the garden, which is overflowing with blood-red blossoms. It is generally incomparably beautiful here at the moment, even within the five-mile zone.

We are glad that you are well, and will do our best to follow suit.

Kisses from your old Hippo King Archibald

and your Giraffe Gazelle

Original: handwritten letter.

1 This is Felix Weil.

2 Norah Andreae's father was Ludwig Arnold Hahn (1858–1946), the grandson of Löb Amschel Hahn (1796–1856) and the uncle of Albert Ludwig Hahn; her mother was Anna Gertrude Hahn (née Wertheimer, 1869–1952).

3 Elisabeth von Gans, née Keller (1879–1964). In her obituary for the *Frankfurter Allgemeine Zeitung*, Anna Schmidt writes: 'She was the child of a famous gardener from Darmstadt, and seems to have gone with him at a very young age to the Riviera, where she stayed for good and learned many languages. As a married woman she commanded a large household, and many scholars, poets and musicians worked there and found peace or help. She herself had a fine literary talent, for those of us who are older still see her

in our mind's eye, explaining Marcel Proust's secrets to us at a time when few others were in a position to do so. She did this while sitting before a small audience in a delightful grey fur coat, like a flower.'

11 April 1942

My dears,
this just to tell you that we are well, and are doing our best to keep our chins up, even though the state of the world is more horrible than it has ever been since June 1940.

Please give many thanks to Julie from us for her kind letters and the newspaper cutting from the Times.[1] Here too there are many rumours about efforts in Washington; keep your fingers crossed for us.

As long as Max was away, we took a holiday and relaxed, and I used the opportunity to complete a new song cycle.[2] Though it is not really new; one part of the songs dates far back, but I have now added a few more and revised the older ones. All six are short, and in a certain absurd sense quite pithy. They are entitled 'Bagatellen für Singstimme und Klavier'.

Max returned yesterday, accompanied by Felix Weil and his newest lady (not to be confused with the previous one, no. 3, whom I had introduced to WK in the institute, and from whom Lix has meanwhile separated). Lix and his Helen[3] were at our place yesterday, and he will call you. I think he would be very happy if you were to invite him to tea together with his Donna. You can talk to him just as well about politics as about all manner of gadgets[4] and contraptions. Such an invitation would surely not be an unwise move.

My draft number[5] is quite high, approximately in the ninth tenth of those to be called up.

I received my health insurance card from Dr Wohlauer.

I would like to thank you once again for the new schnapps.

Look after yourselves and think of us. Kisses
from your two horses
Archibald and Giraffe Gazelle

Tomorrow the old Hahns, Norah Andreae's parents, are to come to tea. The old man 84 years old, the mother 10 years younger, and has baked us an apple strudel that she intends to bring us. Quite amazing for the wife of the senior manager of the investment bank.

Original: typewritten letter with handwritten postscript.

1 Unknown.

2 Adorno's *Klage. Sechs Gedichte von Georg Trakl für Singstimme und Klavier*, op. 5; see Adorno, *Kompositionen*, ed. Heinz-Klaus Metzger and Rainer Riehn, vol. 1: *Lieder für Singstimme und Klavier*, Munich, 1980, pp. 48–65.

3 Helen Knoppnig became Felix Weil's fourth wife. The third wife was Lucille, née Jakobowitz.

4 *gadgets*: EO.

5 The number for possible conscription.

19 April 1942

My dears,
    I do not know how I can begin to thank you for the early birthday present, my dear new red waistcoat. It is much finer still than the old one, with such splendid buttons, and fits like a glove. Archibald is also very proud of the old Wondrous Hippo Cow Marinumba for managing such a thing. We have gradually become accustomed to the 5 miles, and now truly go to bed with the chickens. But then we are also often woken up early in the morning by a rooster. If we do not write more often, that is largely a result of our idyllic rural life: nothing happens, we do not get out, hardly see any people. It is more important how many new rose-buds there are, that there is a wonderful, big brown dog living diagonally opposite us, that due to the cool weather Baldchen Plymouth (our little car) once again refused to start, that the cat caught a gopher (a sort of prairie rat) and dragged it onto the balcony. Poor daft village children that we are, we are naturally ashamed of all our follies before our cosmopolitan parents. The hippos also have new inventions to report now and again, for example: Pamela von Winterschlaf,[1] the giraffe language Giraffe with the originary word Gi., the two black hearse horses Yorrick and Humbert. Regarding New York, all we know is that Rye Lake has been sold (no swindle this time). Did Beate and Ferdi[2] visit you again? They are naturally still very cross with us for not writing. Is Julie all right again? Because of my still ongoing insurance matter I have not heard from the Frenkels for a long time.
    Could you give me the recipe for Teddie's beloved butter soup?
    Dear Hippo Sow, a thousand thanks for all the effort and love that you have knitted into the waistcoat. I wear it with pride and cherish it highly. Teddie and Max are both working very happily on the schema for the big new study. Hugs and kisses from your Giraffe Gazelle with the little horns.

(please turn over,
you will find Archibald there)

91

My dears, we are well, we are keeping our horses' heads up, we are not *at all* afraid of planes (I find being treated as an enemy alien[3] *much* worse!) – and Max and I are well into the schemata for our book[4] (definitely: *not* about the Jews!). It will be very fine if we are allowed to stay, and as far as the war is concerned, I *do* actually think that Hitler will be beaten! If only we might live to witness it!

We also heard part of Mahler VIII, the end, roughly from 'es ist gelungen' onwards, but after all these years I was so moved by the music that I did not even get around to judging the performance, which I might add did not seem bad to me.

Your waistcoat, my Hippo Cow, has also proved a source of *great* joy to me. What a sweet and good person you are, and how grateful I must be to have you. Perhaps you will come here after all.

As far as people go (aside from Max), almost only Brecht. Do not miss having a *good* look at the New Yorker; it is very much worth the effort and a few laughs.

WK, please have Leo[5] give you Neumann's book[6] (to keep); you can say that Max and I asked for it. You will find it interesting. The journal is in print and should come out soon.

Heartiest kisses

from your old Archibald

Original: handwritten letter from Gretel and Theodor W. Adorno.

1 Translator's note: this fictitious surname means 'hibernation'.

2 Beate (née Feith) and Ferdinand Kramer.

3 *enemy alien*: EO.

4 I.e. for the *Dialectic of Enlightenment*. One three-page and one thirteen-page manuscript have survived in the Max-Horkheimer-Archiv (XI 7a.1 and 2).

5 Leo Löwenthal.

6 See Franz Neumann, *Behemoth: The Structure and Practice of National Socialism*, New York, 1942.

57   *LOS ANGELES, 24.4.1942*

24 April 1942

My dears,

a thousand thanks for your dear letter of the 20th. We have very little to report; Max and I are engrossed in drawing up the schemata for our new study. Besides this, he has also learned to ride a bicycle, so that he can still come to us when we can no longer drive. His car now stands in our garage all day, next to ours.

The razorblade sharpener (Twinplex $1.95) has so far proved an excellent acquisition. I shaved myself today with the very same blade for the 15th time. My only fear is that the sharpener itself will be worn down, but that leads to Kafkaesque problems which ultimately terminate in the metaphysical one that one actually dies as a result of living, namely through the wear to which the organism is subjected by the process of life.

I will send the Hippo Cow the new songs as soon as I have had them copied. The government agency in Washington received my big report[1] (which is in fact a 50-page brochure) 'enthusiastically'.[2]

Hanns Eisler[3] is here, and will have lunch with us on Sunday. The Dieterles will be coming on Monday – he is very big here now at MGM.

It is so incomparably beautiful here at the moment that I am sorry for every day that we are unable to show it to you.

The trash one has to listen to on the radio is a result of the monopoly structure partly of the radio, and partly of what are known as 'name bands'.[4] Such an incredible amount of money has been put into advertising the latter that these ads have to be presented constantly – partly to exploit them, and partly to keep their names on everyone's lips, like those of Ford or Chevrolet. Benny Goodman,[5] incidentally, began as one of the most talented swing musicians (an excellent clarinettist) and did a number of things with his chamber ensemble that were really very pretty, but was completely ruined by all the plugging[6] at CBS. (Avis au lecteur: the word 'plugging' is not in the dictionary, but most certainly in my study on popular music.) When they announce the 'most popular tunes',[7] this refers to a snake that bites its own tail: for these are the most popular tunes solely because they are propagated as such, and naturally because the public has long since lost all say in the matter.

I would be very curious to know what you do with liqueurs. Incidentally, Fritz had told me that he wanted to talk to you about the monetary evaluation of the liqueurs. Did he do so? Do remind him some time soon, as he was very enthusiastic about the schnapps. Gretel also thinks that your Stimula[8] would have good chances here, as the tea supply has been almost entirely cut off. Gretel would dearly like to sample the Stimula sometime.

As far as the war is concerned, I have – for some rationally inexplicable reason – been much more optimistic for a number of weeks now. Here, the planes hardly ever stop roaring over our heads.

Kisses

from your old child
Teddie

Both Norah Andreae and Leo[9] wrote enthusiastically about you. Lix must have called you the moment he got to New York, so to speak, which very much contradicts WK's theory. Underneath all his brashness, he is in fact a very loyal and devoted person.

The Hippo Cow should be interested to know that Max and I found out about a Visigoth king by the name of *Wamba*[10] who lived in Spain during the seventh century AD. No joke.

Have we introduced you to the Hippo Cow Mimosa von Borstentier[11] yet?

Hugs from the long-legged, tassel-tailed, colourfully spotted, cone-horned

Giraffe Gazelle

Original: typewritten letter.

1 *report*: EO.

2 *'enthusiastically'*: EO.

3 Adorno had first met Hanns Eisler (1898–1962) in Vienna as early as 1925. Hanns Eisler had emigrated to the USA in 1938 with his second wife, Lou Eisler (1906–1998).

4 *name bands*: EO.

5 As well as jazz, Benjamin David Goodman (1909–1988), who rose to fame in the 1940s, played the clarinet concertos dedicated to him by Aaron Copland, Paul Hindemith and Darius Milhaud. In 1940, Béla Bartók composed *Contrasts* for him. Later in his career, Goodman also made a recording of Mozart's Clarinet Concerto.

6 *plugging*: EO.

7 *most popular tunes*: EO.

8 Unknown.

9 On 17 April, Leo Löwenthal had written: 'I visited your parents. They are delightful people. My modest advice to you is to write to them regularly and *more cheerful*' [EO].

10 He reigned from 672 AD until his death in 680.

11 Translator's note: this is another word for 'pig' or 'swine', and literally means 'bristle-animal'.

58   LOS ANGELES, 2.5.1942

2 May 1942

My dears,

a thousand thanks for your letter. Yes, we have settled down somewhat again, even though the world is so full of Fenris wolves that one

94

does not know by which of them one will be devoured, but our work – in a very emphatic sense – keeps us going, through the hope of at least uttering that which one supposes one should live for.

Our work revolves, in the widest sense, around the question of 'enlightenment', in that both positive and negative analyses of the guise taken on by enlightenment in modern philosophical thought are to help us to develop in the conceptual medium the insights we presume to have gained regarding the present state of the world and the possibility of a way out. The first main section, which we are beginning to draft now, relates to the philosophical concept of enlightenment and its connection to myth and rule. But please do not speak to anyone of these matters, i.e. our choice of theme, as no one at the institute in New York knows about it for certain, and there would only be petty rivalry otherwise.

Our evening with the Dieterles yesterday was a very pleasant one.

My report for Washington related to the matter of 'private morale in Germany'. As this description left me as clueless as you probably are now, and I did not even have time to ask any questions, I simply decided to base the whole thing around the question of what powers keep the German masses on their feet despite all the suffering that is forced on them; and evidently that was exactly what had been desired. As the available material is very sparse (the American books on the internal German situation – I read almost all of them – all refer to information already manipulated by the Nazis, and the 'inside Germany'[1] reports are rhapsodic and of questionable value), I relied instead on what I myself had observed in Germany up to 1937, and essentially provided a theoretical representation that I believe does more justice to reality than the sort of documentary reports which cannot get enough of going on about the Nazis' encouragement of extramarital intercourse and the like. My basic argument was that, through a form of organized competitive mechanism, through their scrabbling for privileges and advantages, through affiliation with the Nazi system, and conversely also through the fear of not belonging to it, and finally through a more or less vague hope for a change in their fate in the case of successful expansion, people in Germany go along with the official line, while it is certainly not a case of 'being convinced' in the sense of believing in the ideology, but rather a complete absence of such things as conviction, unambiguity or unity of personality, behaviour and thought in the present Germany. Contrary to the misconception that the Germans are 'drunk' on Nazism, I presented the system and its followers as an eminently sober, practical and in truth extremely disillusioned business. I might add that the apparently irrational aspect of Nazism is in fact the unarticulated, but quite precise awareness of the outdated nature of certain existential conditions, or, to be more precise, of the contradiction between Germany's industrial productivity and the current living conditions. What is disastrous is simply the fact that the awareness of this contradiction then manifests itself in categories of rule and oppression.

If I am writing you such a theoretical letter today, then this – leaving aside my desire to tell you a little more concretely about my work – is the fault of our externally completely uneventful life, which provides me with nothing whatsoever to report. – I am already so looking forward to the execution of the fine butter soup recipe. I am still as unsuited to being an emigrant as anyone. Look after yourselves and do not give up hope.

Heartiest kisses

from your two horses
Archibald and Giraffe Gazelle

P.S. Salka Viertel, Eduard Steuermann's sister, is going to New York on Tuesday, and we shall ask her to call you (we are having lunch at her place tomorrow). It would be a fine thing if she could visit you for tea, she is very amusing (and one of the pillars of our social life here – at MGM, scriptwriter for Garbo. Perhaps you could invite her together with Eduard. You must naturally not mention Gottfried Reinhardt!!).[2] You can then also clarify the question of your acquaintance with Eduard's mother!

Original: typewritten letter with partly handwritten postscript.

1 *inside Germany*: EO.

2 The actor and director Gottfried Reinhardt (1911–1994), the son of Max Reinhardt, who worked in Hollywood and was Salka Viertel's partner.

59   LOS ANGELES, 15.5.1942

Los Angeles
May 15, 1942

My dear ones, we did not write for some days because Gretel is ill. She had an unusually heavy attack of migraena and failed to recover, so we asked the doctor who found an irritation of the gall bladder. He thinks that the gall may be responsible for all her migraena troubles. He is a quiet, experienced man and his treatment appears to be very sound, for to-day she is *much* better, no fever, no pains, only still very weak. But she will doubtless be alright after a couple of days, so do not worry.

Very many thanks for your letter. Yes, the Report was directly requested. The issue of the Studies will be out during the next days and so will our mimeographed issue in memoriam Benjamin. You will get both. – I heard a miserable performance of Mahler's IX. Symphony and the Song of the Earth over the air, recorded by Walter.[1] Otherwise I feel o.k. Max and I work with great pleasure and intensity.

All my love! Yours ever Teddie

Gretel gives you her love

Original: handwritten letter. Translator's note: written in English.

1 The conductor Bruno Walter (1876–1962) had left Austria in 1938, going first to France before emigrating to the USA in 1939.

60 LOS ANGELES, 5.6.1942

5 June 1942.

My dears,

a thousand thanks for your letter of the 29th.

First of all regarding the question of the holidays: persistent rumours were going around here that the curfew[1] was almost certainly to be lifted on 3 June. This did not happen, however, and nothing further was heard about the matter. It is still unclear whether we can stay or not. The evacuation regulation that applies to us has not been revoked, but no further measures have yet been taken, although the evacuation of the Japanese from Zone 1, to which we are also assigned, has been completed. As far as the curfew is concerned, it seems that it is being enforced more strictly now; e.g. the other night Brecht received a visit from the FBI at ½ past 9 to see if they were at home; and the same thing with the Reichenbachs.[2] On the other hand, it seems that Max's old secretary (Mendelssohn),[3] who has been in the country for barely three years, is being granted a permit to move here. The logical conclusion from this would be that at least no evacuation is planned, but evidently there is such an absence of any clear policy that even such conclusions cannot be drawn with any confidence.

It is naturally possible that the situation could change for the worse or for the better from one day to the next. If the latter were to be the case, then we would of course gladly give you the green light[4] to come here as quickly as possible. On the other hand, however, I would not like to be responsible for your sitting around in rather uncertain expectation in New York, which is probably unbearably hot now, and spoiling your holidays. A further problem here is the threat of petrol rationing, which, with the incredible distances and the lack of any decent means of transport (except car), can lead to complete isolation. Under these circumstances, I do not think that I can reasonably expect you to wait any longer for a change in the situation here. Should it change, however, I would telegraph you immediately, and perhaps we could still find a way after all.

Giraffe is feeling relatively well. She no longer has a fever, looks quite healthy and is also suffering from less of a headache. The doctor is a sensible man, more of the GP type, no specialist in quirky complaints, and the measures he took strike me as very sensible.

The psychoanalyst Mannheimer[5] is, as far as I know, the same one who milked Zilchen in former times. He is incidentally also the father of our excellent former secretary Trude Bloch, who has now been mentally ill for some years.

It is touching that you are looking after old Löwenthal, and Leo also wrote enthusiastically about that, as too about the lovely flowers you sent Golde. I daresay the old man is not much fun, for he gripes about everything and is full of bitterness, and his wife[6] is quite simply a monster.

Did you receive the Benjamin memorial issue and the Studies?[7] Max and I have given instructions several times for both of these to be sent. If you do not have them, you can simply ask Leo to give them to you. Please let me know if you are given the correct 'big' version of the Benjamin issue, which is over 160 pages long. Incidentally, the essay 'Vernunft und Selbsterhaltung' is identical to the English one entitled The End of Reason. What counts for us is the German version, so you do not need to read the English one.

I recall that, while we were still in Germany, you gave me a few details about the conflict that was going on at the time regarding the Leipzig Mendelssohn monument[8] and the mayor of Leipzig. Do you still remember when that was, and could you reconstruct the story from memory? I would be most grateful: a musicology professor here at the university asked me if I could find out anything about the matter.

And another request: when Ilse Maier sought us out half-mad in New York, she snatched away a red notebook containing a series of aphorisms entitled: Handbook for Emigrants, but above all also a series of notes on the myth of Oedipus following on from a piece by Cocteau. Ilse promised to return the book immediately, but disappeared with it. Now I urgently need the Oedipus notes for the joint work with Max, but I do not even have Ilse's address so as to admonish her. Would you be so kind as to play the part of Wuwatz![9]

And finally yet another request. Felix Greissle,[10] Schönberg's son-in-law, borrowed one of my Mahler scores for a common acquaintance over a year ago. Despite all admonitions from myself and others, I have not yet managed to recover it, even though Greissle now has this score. Could you perhaps call him: Academy 4–3152, 1 West 100 Str. and if necessary go there and take it from him by brute force. He lives right by Central Park, very near you. Greissle is not a bad or unfriendly person, just sloppy.

As far as the war is concerned, I am genuinely beginning gradually to gain somewhat more hope. You can imagine what fantasies I had following the bombardment of Cologne and Essen.[11] I am sniffing about intensely with regard to changes in the wind and silver linings.

The work with Max is now moving along nicely. Fritz will arrive here tomorrow, and Felix Weil soon after that.

Did you hear anything from Else and Grünebaum?

Heartiest kisses

From your old child Teddie
and Giraffe Gazelle Gretel

Please let us know as soon as possible what WK would like for his birthday, and what our good Hippo Sow would like in order to join him in his celebrations.

Give Julie many fond regards and wish her a good recovery from us. As far as we know, Buky[12] is one of the best radiologists in New York, E. also knows him. Have you seen E. again and spoken to him about the treatment?

In the 'Nation' of 30 May, p. 638, there is a furious attack on me[13] by someone I have never heard of.

Original: typewritten letter with a handwritten closing paragraph.

1 *curfew*: EO.

2 The philosopher Hans Reichenbach (1891–1953) had emigrated to Turkey in 1933, then to the USA in 1939; he taught at the University of California in Los Angeles until his death.

3 Margot von Mendelssohn.

4 *green light*: EO.

5 See letter no. 24, note 11.

6 Leo Löwenthal's father Victor Löwenthal (1864–1942), himself a medic, died the following month. The mother's name was Rosie Löwenthal (née Bing, 1878–1970).

7 *Studies*: EO.

8 In November 1936, the monument in front of the Neues Gewandhaus had been knocked down by the Nazis. The mayor of Leipzig, Carl Friedrich Goerdeler (1884–1945), subsequently resigned and became an open opponent of the regime; Goerdeler was executed as a member of the German resistance on 2 February 1945 in Plötzensee.

9 Translator's note: in the play *Eine Kartoffelkomödie* [A Potato Comedy] by Heinrich Hoffmann (1809–84), author of the famous book of cautionary children's tales *Der Struwwelpeter*, the figure named Wuwatz the Sixtieth is the authoritarian and irascible Emperor of China.

10 Felix Greissle (1894–1982) had gone to Arnold Schoenberg for private tuition in 1920, and married his daughter in 1921. He worked on and off as secretary of the Verein für musikalische Privataufführungen [Society for Private Musical Performances] in Vienna, and produced arrangements for smaller ensembles as well as piano reductions. Greissle emigrated to the USA in 1938; he worked in New York as reader for the music publisher G. Schirmer, and taught composition and music theory at Columbia University.

11 The first genuine mass bombardment by the Royal Air Force took place at the end of May 1942.

12 Unknown.

13 It was penned by B. H. Haggin.

61 LOS ANGELES, 15.6.1942

L.A. 15 June 1942   Isn't the card pretty?

My dears, our lengthy letters must have crossed. Today I shall merely say that we are well, that we celebrated Giraffe's birthday in the most lovely fashion with Max, Maidon, Fritz and Norah Andreae, are working a great deal, and otherwise see only Schönberg, Brecht and Eisler. Leo wrote an enthusiastic letter[1] saying how touchingly our good WK had taken care of old Löwenthal, whose death we learned of today. I too would like to thank you once more, my dear WK. Otherwise, nothing has changed here yet. Might you not perhaps be given a permit[2] to come here on account of your *age*? It would at least be worth the effort to find out. Heartiest kisses from your old Hippo King Archibald
A thousand thanks for your kind wishes Yours Gi

Original: photo postcard: Entrance to Hollywood Bowl, Hollywood, Calif.; stamp: JUNE 16, 1942. Manuscript.

1 On 12 June, Löwenthal wrote [in English]: 'I am enthusiastic about your father. During the present serious sickness of my father of which I am afraid it will be his last, he really behaves like an angel and everything he does and says is the expression of the highest intellectual and moral culture. I shall never forget it.'

2 *permit*: EO.

2 July 1942

My dears,
    on Saturday I donated my blood (1 pint) for the second time; it all went very well again, and I am now fully myself again. What is particularly noticeable on such occasions is the remarkable friendliness and humanity one is treated with, and which is pleasantly different not only from offices, but also from all clinic-related places in Europe, where people are constantly viewed as objects of administration.
    As far as the alien[1] situation is concerned, there has been no significant change, though it does seem fairly certain now that there will not be any evacuation. The other evening we were checked in a friendly manner by an official, to see if we were at home like good law-abiding citizens, but even this was carried out in the most friendly manner. Otherwise, we have very little to report. We now see a few more people than previously, as both Pollock and Steuermann have set up their summer residences here.
    As a novelty we have established a little seminar,[2] whose participants (aside from the four institute members) are Brecht, Eisler, Steuermann, Prof. Reichenbach, Günther Stern,[3] Ludwig Marcuse[4] and Ralph Nürnberg.[5] Our work is progressing well, and we are also working on a new memorandum[6] for Washington, which in turn is confidential.
    I have also written two new pop song analyses[7] for the Lazarsfeld Office in which I tried out some new methods, e.g. showing the technical factors that make imitations inferior to models, and whether there can be criteria at all for good and bad pop songs. So you see: we are kept busy,[8] but are quite rested thanks to the curfew, as we consistently go to bed between 9 and 10.
    The weather is rather foggy and humid here, as it has been these last few weeks. I hear in New York it is quite unbearable now. I hope you will soon come away from there to your mountains.
    I am naturally very eager to know what WK thinks of my texts. I find his actions in the cases of the Mahler score and Ilse Mayer veritably

101

heroic, and thank him most heartily. Tonight I dreamed of the Hippo Cow: I had called upon her with the words 'Mumma, Mumma', and she was moved to tears, which made me incredibly proud and happy. So: Mumma, Mumma. Heartiest kisses

from your old child
Teddie
and Giraffe Gazelle

Original: typewritten letter.

1 *alien*: EO.

2 The seminars, held between mid-July and late August and which bore the collective title 'Die Theorie der Bedürfnisse' [The Theory of Needs], were documented by Gretel Adorno and Friedrich Pollock; see Horkheimer, *Gesammelte Schriften* 12, pp. 559–87. The institute members who took part in the discussions were Adorno, Horkheimer, Herbert Marcuse and Friedrich Pollock. It was in connection with this seminar that Adorno wrote his 'Thesen über Bedürfnisse' [Theses on Needs] (see *GS* 8, pp. 392–6).

3 Günther Stern (1902–92), who went under the name of Günther Anders following his emigration, had studied with Husserl and Heidegger in Freiburg; he had fled to Paris in 1933 and then moved to the USA in 1936.

4 The writer and critic Ludwig Marcuse (1894–1971), who studied philosophy and literature in Berlin and Freiburg and gained his PhD under the tutelage of Ernst Troeltsch, had fled to France in 1933 and emigrated to the USA in 1939. Marcuse had been granted a scholarship by the institute.

5 The publicist Ralph M. Nunberg (real name: Rolf Nürnberg; 1903–49) had emigrated to the USA in 1936.

6 Presumably the 'Memorandum on the Elimination of German Chauvinism', completed by Adorno in collaboration with Herbert Marcuse in August 1942.

7 The analyses of 'The Bells of San Raquel' and 'Two in Love' form part of *Current of Music*.

8 *we are kept busy*: EO.

63   LOS ANGELES, 9.7.1942

9 July 1942

My dears,
a thousand thanks for your kind letter. I think I can be forgiven for emitting loud bestial roars upon reading your report about Lore

Fürth.[1] I said it all along. If one were to invite e.g. Erna Löwenthal,[2] Lore Fürth and Bea all at once, it would be enough to fill an entire school for backward children.

I am very glad that you are going on holiday; it must be pretty ghastly in New York at the moment, and the situation here is still the same, despite all sorts of promises.

Otherwise, we have absolutely nothing new to report. We are working with Max in the afternoons, and rest a little in the mornings. Because of the imminent rationing of clothes, we went to a shopping mall today and bought all sorts of things, including a blue Californian monkey waistcoat for Archie and three sports shirts, lucus a non lucendo.

Please be so kind and send me the Mahler score before you depart – I am crying out for it as a stag cries out for water.

We had the first truly hot days here, but in the evening things cool off very pleasantly – to such a degree that one can really catch a chill if one is out on the balcony. Furthermore, the heat is completely free of that famous humidity,[3] and in absolute terms probably not as great as in Cuba.

I wish I could show you the colours; the hills often seem completely violet and, at the same time, as if they were glazed with gold dust. One cannot describe it, and if one were to paint it, it would be the most ghastly kitsch; but in its real state it is simply very beautiful.

So recover well, have a good rest, forget about the world and the rightly named[4] General Auchinleck.[5]

Kisses from your child and the dear Giraffe Gazelle

Archibald, Hippo King, m.p.[6]

Original: typewritten letter.

1 An acquaintance of the Wiesengrunds from Frankfurt.

2 Leo Löwenthal's mother.

3 *humidity*: EO.

4 Translator's note: the German slang phrase *Du kannst mich mal am/im Arsch lecken* means 'You can kiss my arse'.

5 The British general Claude Auchinleck (1884–1981) had been sent by Churchill to the Middle East, where he was defeated by the German troops under Rommel in July 1942; he was replaced on 8 August.

6 Translator's note: this is (most probably) the abbreviation for *manu propria*, meaning 'written by his own hand'.

Tel.: Arizona 9-5473

16 July 1942

My dears,
a thousand thanks for your kind words, the Mahler score, the Low
caricatures[1] (both little volumes, I think I never thanked you for the
first) and especially for the fine liqueur, with which we shall drink to
your health. Hopefully the great hippo transport came off well, and it
is as pleasant there as it was last year.

Virgil Thomson sent me an exceedingly cordial letter, advising me
urgently not to take any action against Haggin. He said the matter was
simply good publicity, and if he wants to continue it, then H. will have
to expand on my ideas and develop arguments, which would only be
in our interests. As the worldly-wise Lazarsfeld, who as editor has to
bear the real responsibility for the book, said exactly the same thing,
I did not take any steps.

Our life continues unchanged. We are outside a good deal, and you
can rest assured that we are keeping our reproduction in mind. It is
very difficult to take a genuine holiday, as we cannot leave here
without permission from the FBI, and to be granted this permission
one requires a medical certificate. But it is so beautiful here that we do
not even miss that. Our garden shed has been expanded, and I have
been sleeping with the window open for some time now, and in the
morning I am woken by the effusive choir of birds that does not keep
to seasons any more than humans do, and e.g. now, while the birds in
Europe have already fallen silent, they sing their little hearts out.
Yesterday we spent the whole day outside with Eduard, and tomorrow morning we shall be going to the beach[2] with him. Our little
house is currently under siege from decorators, the kitchen is being
painted tomorrow, and at the same time our Betty is getting married
and going away for a few days, so we have arranged to eat out as often
as possible.

Felix Weil and his new wife are here now, living a few houses away
from us, and is being extremely friendly and trusting. E.g. he has
offered to do some shopping for Gretel too when he drives to town
etc. I only say this because I genuinely believe that WK has got him
entirely wrong. He is a good-natured person in need of a great deal of
personal warmth – essentially a big child, in spite of his beard. On
Tuesday we entertained them here, tomorrow we are at their place.

We shall be sending a parcel in the next few days – you can have
three guesses what it is.

Gretel, to whom I am dictating, has just said that I wrote about the birds exactly the way a Louische would; it is best if I come out with it myself, so that the Hippo Cow does not point it out right away and remind us of all those shrieking nightingales at the graveyard that Agathe once flung in Louis's face.

As far as the war is concerned, I would like to quote that Viennese head waiter[3] who said: there's only one thing for it: be a philosopher and don't think. And this applies equally to correspondence on the subject.

I am already looking forward to WK's comments on our youngest children. Have a lovely, peaceful time and get plenty of relaxation. Heartiest kisses

from your two old horses
Archibald and Giraffe Gazelle

Original: typewritten letter.

1 The New Zealand-born British cartoonist Sir David Alexander Low (1891–1963); in 1941 he published the volumes *Low's War Cartoons, Low on the War* and *The World at War*.

2 *beach*: EO.

3 Source unknown.

65   LOS ANGELES, 27.7.1942

Hogs Reach
22-Year Peak

27 July 1942

My dear WK,
this is to send you the heartiest congratulations on your birthday, the 72nd, which figure I swear before God and all men that no one would assume if they saw how alertly you hop about, and if one considers that you are agile enough even to endure the old Löwenthals, which would be beyond many younger people, myself included. At the moment the world is looking ghastly enough once again, and there is no telling how long this business will last and how it will turn out, but I stand by my opinion that in a technical war it is the side with the highest technical productivity that will win, and that, if nothing else, we will at least experience the joy of witnessing the end of Hitlerism. I would augment this wish with two others, namely that we should be together at that moment, and that you and our good

105

Hippo Cow continue to hibernate through this great ice age as well as you have managed so far. Hopefully our little present reached you in time.

Otherwise, we have absolutely nothing new to report. We have had a long, thoroughly peaceful weekend,[1] and Max and I now have to interrupt our big study a little in order to finish the new report I have planned for Washington, which the government agency in question is very keen on. On the side I have starting dictating something[2] to Gretel that has been preoccupying me for some time, and which I would like to wrap up as quickly as possible.

Make sure you read the book by Carl Dreyer,[3] 'The coming show-down', which in my opinion contains the most interesting facts about the present situation.

Continue to relax, and hold onto what Brecht, in a beautiful poem,[4] calls the refugee's occupation: hope.

Heartiest kisses
> from your old children
> Archibald and Giraffe Gazelle
> with the little horns and horn-covers

Original: typewritten letter.

1 *weekend*: EO.

2 This is 'Das Schema der Massenkultur'; see *GS* 3, pp. 299–335.

3 It had been published in Boston in 1942.

4 This presumably refers to Brecht's poem 'Hollywood': 'Jeden Morgen, mein Brot zu verdienen / Gehe ich auf den Markt, wo Lügen gekauft werden. / Hoffnungsvoll / Reihe ich mich ein zwischen die Verkäufer.' [Each morning I earn my daily bread / By going to the market where lies are bought. / Full of hope / I take my place among the sellers.]

66   LOS ANGELES, 23.8.1942

23 August 1942

My dears,

this is simply to let you know that we are well and that our life is taking its customarily quiet course. It seems – touch wood[1] – that we will *not* be evacuated, and that only certain people will be removed from here on account of procedures particular to each case. This once more lends a more positive complexion to the prospect of your coming here, which makes us very happy.

Imagine who was here the other day: Anna Loeb[2] and her niece, the wife of the actor Zilzer,[3] née Lotte Mosbacher;[4] it was truly a great pleasure for us. The old woman is not only charming and sophisticated, but at 78 also has a quite amazing mental agility and freshness, and the young woman is pretty, friendly and pleasant – a complete contrast to the rest of the young generation of Katzensteins. Old Rosa Cahn[5] (80 years old) lives here, very close to us; we stopped by there briefly yesterday.*

Aside from that, all we have to report is that an American singer[6] turned up here to sing my songs, she has a fine voice, and also learned something, but unfortunately looks like a widowed dwarf bulldog. Apropos of bulldogs, there is an animal of this breed from the neighbourhood, severely damaged through a car accident, that is a regular guest of ours, i.e. it eats its fill and rewards our modest hospitality through a most charming nature – one of the most pleasant dogs I have ever known, clever, worldly-wise, a true hobbling sage. It brings us much joy, and we incidentally also have good neighbourly relations with its owners (a professorial couple from UCLA).

We hope you have had a relaxing time. Gretel goes swimming almost every day, and it is doing her the world of good. She is tanned and looks well, you would be very pleased. I have meanwhile written about half of the rough draft for the piece on mass culture, though the real work will start only when I make the final text out of it; for the time being it is still over rough and smooth.

Heartiest kisses

from your old child
Archibald and Giraffe Gazelle

Original: typewritten letter.

1 *touch wood*: EO.

2 Unknown.

3 Wolfgang Zilzer (1901–91), who also used the pseudonym Paul Andor.

4 Lotte Andor-Palfi (1904–91), previously married to Victor Palfi, had last played in *Casablanca*.

5 An acquaintance of the Wiesengrunds from Frankfurt.

6 Unknown.

* [Marginal note:] the rest of the family, Grete Loeb etc., ghastly.

1 Sept 1942

My dears:
welcome back to New York. It has been cool here too for the last few days, so much so that I cannot swim at the moment. But I have been assured that September is the hottest month. Did you have a good rest? Was it still nice without the car?

Today I can finally send you a little picture of our little house, taken from the front. We live in the left half, so you can see the garage, the large living-room window and upstairs my room with balcony – Max will be going to New York tonight, and will naturally call you. You can probably reach him best at Morningside Drive 90, Tel: Monument 2-2845. He will be here again at the start of October. He has a little lunch novelty for you with him, we hope you like it. – Yesterday the Eislers moved into their little house quite near us; I rather like them, and they are staying here for another six months, as he still has some film music to write. Lix and wife will also be back in New York in mid-September, and Pollock a little later. Many eye-witnesses who can confirm to you that we are well.

The very fondest regards from your old Giraffe Gazelle
with the little horns

My dears – happily at home![1] Congratulations! Hopefully you are well recovered! We are very well, except that the weather is like Amorbach in October, so Giraffe has had to interrupt her daily swimming routine, which had done her such good. I have almost finished the rough draft of 'Massenkultur', and at the same time come up with a national-economic (!!) theory[2] in order to bring Marx's doctrine of impoverishment up to date.[3] Otherwise nothing new, we work mostly in the garden, go to bed with the chickens and meet with a small and, as Else would say, 'select' circle of people, aside from the institute Eduard, Eisler, Schönberg, Brecht, Norah Andreae, that's about all.[4] – Pray that the Russians can stand firm, then everything could still turn out well, so to speak. Heartiest kisses from your unshapely child Archibald, Hippo King.

Original: handwritten letter from Gretel and Theodor W. Adorno.

1 *happily at home*: EO.

2 This refers to 'Reflexionen zur Klassentheorie' [Reflections upon the Theory of Class]; see GS 8, pp. 373–91.

3 *up to date*: EO.

4 *that's about all*: EO.

429 WEST 117TH STREET
NEW YORK, N.Y.

9 Sept 1942

My dears:
  a thousand thanks for your kind letters. We are both seriously concerned about WK. I know too little about medicine to infer anything about the nature of the illness from the symptoms, but enough about psychology to know that our good WK (with the magical intention of the spell) is expecting the worst, and so I hope that they are genuinely no more than nerve-pains, which can be very unpleasant, after all, and not muscular atrophy. But I would advise you urgently to consult Egon in the matter, whom I trust more with my little finger than that pompous old fool Liefmann. Do write him a line or two; he comes to New York often enough. But make sure you really do it.
  We shall celebrate my birthday peacefully, with Maidon, Fritz and Norah Andreae here. As far as the allegedly very spoilt husband is concerned, incidentally, he takes great pleasure in eating two plates of butter soup according to the Hippo Cow's recipe for his entire supper, and it is utterly ridiculous to think that he should not be equally satisfied with something similar at your place, especially as he normally eats at the drugstore on the corner of 118th St in the New York rush.
  Lix has left, will be in New York on Saturday, and, if I know him, he will call you within the first half-hour. He is extremely eager to be invited round by you and to introduce his new wife, whom he married here. Aside from that, he also has a burning interest in WK's liqueurs, and would be most flattered to have a technically versed conversation about them. You would truly be doing me a great favour by inviting him to tea and treating him in a friendly manner. For all his childishness, he is a true friend.
  We have a few things for sweet little Elisabethchen and also for Ludwigelchen,[1] whom you were no doubt right to term mentally deficient (that passage was the high spot[2] of your letter): I am even prepared to sacrifice my suit known as 'The Truffle' upon the altar of the Louische religion. We shall give the whole bundle for Britain[3] to Fritz, who is leaving on the 18th. You should also write to Lotte and Egon about clothes, I am sure they will also have something.
  I have now completed the rough draft for my long text 'Das Schema der Massenkultur', the longest I have written since the Wagner. While Gretel is writing it out so that we can then produce the final version, I am writing a series of theses on the theory of class, and also undertaking certain historical studies in connection with these.

I would be interested to know if my contribution for *Aufbau* ('Träume in Amerika')[4] has appeared yet, or only been announced. If I were you, incidentally, I would overcome your entirely understandable aversion against the paper in this case, as this contribution is an extremely personal matter that should directly concern you too. You should also read Max's essay 'Betrachtung zum curfew',[5] which was in the West Coast issue. – Just one question: could WK's pains not be related to some over-exertion through walks, and ultimately with his heart? My layman's instinct tells me that such things, even if they seem to appear quite separately, suggest a common source. The possibility of rheumatic pains should also not be entirely dismissed. Have you tried a heat pad, or is that too painful?

It has been consistently rather cool here, and unfortunately Gretel can only go swimming occasionally.

We meanwhile have the new aliens regulations, which state quite clearly that there is *not* to be any evacuation. This should also be of no little significance for your decisions, especially as the current curfew regulations do not apply to you on account of your age. Taking into account the dangers of aerial warfare, I think it is safer here than in New York.

Heartiest kisses

from your two children
Archibald and Giraffe Gazelle

On the blue ribbon, the distance between the knots shows the diameter of the round table in the living room.

A kiss with my little horns

your old Gi

Original: typewritten letter with printed letterhead and handwritten postscript by Gretel Adorno.

1 Ludwig Calvelli-Adorno, born in 1927 as the son of Franz Calvelli-Adorno and Helene Calvelli-Adorno (née Mommsen, 1895–1988).

2 *high spot*: EO.

3 *for Britain*: EO.

4 Three dreams appeared under the title 'Träume in Amerika, Drei Protokolle' on 2 October 1942 in the New York issue of *Aufbau*; see GS 20.2, pp. 573–5.

5 See Horkheimer, *Gesammelte Schriften* 4, pp. 351–3.

27 Sept 1942

My dear old faithful Wondrous Hippo Cow,
Whenever I have congratulated you on past birthdays, though I saw you before me as a mature Hippo, one demanding not only love but also respect, I never actually thought of you as old. But now you are turning seventy-seven, three years short of eighty, and the number alone has such a commanding aura that I have no choice but to bestow the title of *Old Hippo Lady* upon you. May you be as happy as possible in your new dignity, gain ever more age, wisdom and shape, until your belly leaves an even deeper trail, and, as you rest upon the stone tower of your courageous and steadfast life, remain well disposed towards your child, who may be less courageous and less steadfast, but in other respects is perhaps not entirely unworthy of you. The year that lies before you will most probably be a decisive one for all our existences, and I hope that you get through it well, just as I hope that it will finally bring better fortune for us all. I am stretching out my head into the air and sniffing, and as I at least inherited a portion of your sanguinism, it seems to me that the world no longer looks so desperate. The baffling inability of the Germans to exploit their immeasurable advantages (it was much the same with Hannibal) should gradually become so palpable that the Allies' greater resources start to count, and the ghastly tide will turn. As I think that the Germans' victories were due less to their own strength than to the weaknesses of the others, they could certainly be deprived of their sting, and there are signs to suggest that the Germans are really not quite what they are cracked up to be. This all still sounds rather frivolous, but I cannot abandon my conviction, which has persisted for the last three years, that this war will be won by the greater capital power, which naturally cannot be expressed in terms of financial capital.
On Saturday I donated my blood for the third time, and once again I had no complaints whatsoever. Upon examining my blood, they found it better than the first time, so the whole procedure even seems to be healthy to boot. As a thirdtimer[1] I had to enter my name in a silver book, and received a little silver button. Perhaps it not only helps others, but also myself. In the afternoon, Norah and her ancient father,[2] the very pretty violinist Minghetti[3] and her husband, who plays much better, came to us, and we had a lovely time playing Bach and Beethoven, and did so quite well, I think; so you can see how little the blood business affected me. Yesterday at the Marcuses[4] with the Eislers, tonight Salka and old Frau Steuermann will be at our place – we can really have as much Hollywood as we want, but are rationing it carefully, for the people are much more boring than the work. We also

had Lotte Mosbacher here alone the other day, incidentally, but she appealed to us much less than when she came with the charming Anna Loeb. She is that type of pretty, icy blonde Jewess whose Aryan appearance and the resulting exchange value for followers of the black faith give rise to a pretension that has no other justification.

We are very glad that you had a nice afternoon with Max, and hope that you will see him again. We would have loved to have rehearsed the warthog's song with him, so that he could then have sung it to you with all its finesse, but it was already too late, so Gretel (not I) sang it to him as a greeting to you. She can even bring off the wail on 'froh' [joyful] authentically.

I think you should not call Felix Weil straight off, but rather wait until he makes a move.

The socks the Hippo Cow had admired are mostly Giraffe's, being the ones she bought for England but which I never allowed her to wear. The suit certainly is the Truffle; I should know what my Truffle is like. But: it is from New York. It served me well, and I found it very difficult to part with it.

Just think: Mé Salomon and Arthur Weinberg[5] have supposedly been deported to Poland; old Herr Salomon evidently died beforehand.[6] Thinking of these things makes one even more grateful for the way our fate has turned out than one already is.

We are glad with all our heart that our good WK is feeling better now, just carry on like that . . . Be particularly careful now, at the time of the unbearably abrupt change of weather in New York. Look after yourselves, enjoy your celebrations and think of your children, who sniff at you faithfully.

Kisses to you, my Old Hippo Lady, from your
now also aged child
                                    Teddie

The dear Giraffe Gazelle with the little horns folds her front hooves together to perform an extremely beautiful and reverent curtsey for the dear Wondrous Hippo Cow. And then she tries out the new horn-kiss for the first time   Gi

to
MARINUMBA
the
seventy-seven-year-old
Wondrous Ancient Hippo Cow
with
a thousand wishes
for
health happiness all the best

                    from her
              loving admiring faithful
                     child

                                          Archibald
                                          Hippo King
Many kisses   m.p.
your daughter-in-law
the dear Giraffe
Gazelle with the
little horns

Original: typewritten letter with additional handwritten note by Gretel
Adorno and a handwritten supplement.

1 *thirdtimer*: EO.

2 Ludwig Arnold Hahn.

3 Lisa Minghetti, who was born in Vienna in 1912 and died in California in
1961, studied in Vienna and Berlin, where she was taught by Carl Flesch. She
performed in Austria, Germany and England.

4 Ludwig Marcuse and his wife.

5 Arthur von Weinberg (1860–1943), a nephew of the paint wholesaler
Leopold Cassella, had been a partner in and managing director of the Cassella
works, together with his brother Carl von Weinberg, since 1892. Arthur von
Weinberg had been on the administrative board of I.G. Farben A.G. since
1926, but had been forced to leave in 1935 due to the Aryanization campaign;
in 1938 he gave up all his remaining duties and voluntary work, was forced
to sell his entire property to the City of Frankfurt, and moved to live with his
daughter, Countess Marie von Spreti, in Bavaria. He was arrested and
deported to Theresienstadt in 1942 and died there the following year after an
operation, before his planned release, which former colleagues had persuaded
Himmler to grant, could take place.

6 Mé Salomon was the wife of Bernhard Salomon (1855–1942), whose
daughter Margot had been a friend of Adorno in his youth (see also letter no.
171, note 4).

70   LOS ANGELES, 13.10.1942

    429 WEST 117TH STREET
    NEW YORK, N.Y.

                                        13 October 1942

My dears,
    we greatly enjoyed your merry letters and Max's report on you,
'Max brings good news'. I completed my plans exactly on time, and

                            113

Max and I were able to continue exactly where we left off six weeks ago.

How nice that 'Dreams in America' came out exactly in time for the Hippo Cow's birthday. I should point out that it is no literary piece of work, but rather a series of genuine, literal and entirely faithful dream reports written immediately after awakening. I have a substantial collection of such reports.[1]

We have little enough to tell; our life is continuing its peaceful course, except that our last maid ran off for good, not because of any conflicts, but simply because she can earn more in the defense boom.[2] The staff problem here has become insoluble, but Giraffe's powers of organization, together with her diligent hands and my meaningful watching, will soon master the situation. Aside from that, I have consumed my first lobster[3] from the calm ocean in your honour, while Gretel, who was in the middle of a migraine attack, was sadly unable to keep up.

Heartiest kisses from the two animals

Archibald, Hippo King
Giraffe Gazelle w/H.

Original: typewritten letter with printed letterhead.

1 Adorno was intending to publish them as a book. Translator's note: see Adorno, *Traumprotokolle* (Frankfurt am Main: Suhrkamp, 2005).

2 *defense boom*: EO.

3 *lobster*: EO.

30 October 1942

My dears:

thank you kindly for your lines. We were particularly happy to see that you are in good spirits and sniffing about in the air, as we are also doing. Here, after last week brought the hottest days of the whole year, we have had the first properly rainy day, which, as a contrast to the ever-blue sky, seemed like a very homely little ray of sunlight to me. Meanwhile, the unwavering sunshine has broken out once again.

There is little to report; we are continuing work on our sacred text, and are also involved in a fair number of research projects besides that. I am playing a little more music now: with Eisler, whom I see relatively often, and also with the excellent violinist Maskoff[1] (the husband of Minghetti, that violinist who was so beautiful ten years

114

ago), with whom I shall regularly play chamber music, and with whom I have studied the Debussy sonata. The night before last, old Frau Steuermann, who has just turned 75, was here with one of Viertel's nieces,[2] who is in turn distantly related to Gretel. After I had played the old woman all sorts of pieces, it turned out that she likes to play piano four hands, and we sat down together and executed the Pastoral Symphony. Frau Steuermann in fact played amazingly well. I thought to myself: how lovely it would be if I had been able to play instead with the Hippo Cow herself. Incidentally, I have rarely met anyone as well suited to you and to Agathe in every respect, even in her style of verbal expression, as Frau Steuermann.

Tonight a few people are coming here: the Eislers, Horenstein,[3] probably Soma Morgenstern and his friend Lester,[4] also the writer Gina Kaus and her husband.[5] The increase in social activity is a result of the impending petrol rationing, which we are all awaiting with bated breath. Together with the curfew, which has been lifted for the Italians but not for us, the distances and transport conditions mean that the rationing would result in a barely imaginable isolation.

To give you just a little idea: to reach central Los Angeles from here, it takes between 50 minutes and an hour of good driving, roughly twice as long as from Frankfurt to Cronberg.

What the Hippo Cow wrote about the various conductors matches my own judgement to the letter. Stiedry,[6] incidentally, who was the best musician of the whole bunch, lost his position at the New Friends, and is now living in New York with severe heart trouble and in deepest poverty. Mr Szell[7] drove him out with his machinations. Ilse Mayer gave us a prompt and very pleasant reply, yet cannot recall the book in question. I can even believe it – she was in a state of acute mental disturbance at the time, and I consider amnesiac lapses highly probable. But my Oedipus notes are lost.

According to the last letter we received from Fritz, there has been great progress in Washington, and I think that, after the lesson of the Solomon Islands,[8] the time of blunders[9] has been brought to an end.

Heartiest kisses

from your two horses
Archibald and Giraffe Gazelle

Original: typewritten letter.

1 Anton Maaskoff was born in New York in 1893, and studied there and in Manchester; he performed in Europe, South America and Africa.

2 This refers to Susi Bruckner-Karplus, born in 1918, the daughter of Viertel's older sister Helene, who was married to the opera tenor Wilhelm Bruckner-Karplus.

3 The conductor Jascha Horenstein (1898–1973) had conducted the Düsseldorf performance of Berg's *Wozzeck*. He was dismissed as musical director of the Düsseldorf Opera as a result of the Nazis' efforts, and subsequently conducted in Australia, New Zealand and Scandinavia. In 1938 he worked in Palestine. Horenstein had arrived in the USA in 1940.

4 From the autumn of 1941 until the spring of 1943, Morgenstern lived with Conrad Henry Lester (b. 1907), a specialist in German literature who had emigrated from Austria to the USA in 1938.

5 The writer Gina Kaus (real name: Regina Wiener; 1894–1985) had emigrated to Switzerland in 1938 and then to France; in November 1939 she went to America with her sons and the lawyer Eduard Frischauer, also born in Vienna, whom she married in California, and was successful as a scriptwriter in Hollywood.

6 The Austrian-born conductor Fritz Stiedry (1883–1968) had been principal conductor of the Städtische Oper in Berlin from 1928 to 1933. Stiedry had lived in America since 1938. In 1941 he worked at the New Opera Company in New York.

7 The conductor and pianist George Szell (1897–1970).

8 These islands in the western Pacific were occupied by the Japanese during that year, then retaken by the American forces in August.

9 *blunders*: EO.

1 December 1942

My dear Wondrous Hippo Cow,
I am not exaggerating when I say that no present I have ever received from you, in fact no present I have ever received from anyone, has made me as happy as the blanket. If, as the psychoanalysts say, time is love, then the amount of love that lies within the time invested to fashion this is truly unimaginable, and the fact that you did this now, as an aged Wondrous Hippo Cow, during the time of our spatial separation, makes it even more touching than it would have been at any earlier point. But the result of the endless work is truly worth it – a genuine work of art, admired by all who see it. It arrived on Saturday morning, and in the evening the Horkheimers and the Eislers were here and marvelled at it – Maidon immediately said that one could see from it how much you must love me. I send you a thousand heartiest thanks for it, and we shall faithfully honour this blanket as long as we live, as one only did with things in those times that are now forever past, when possessions were still handed down from one generation

116

to the next. You are the dearest, best and most active hippo ever to drag its belly.

As Max and I both felt a little tired and worn-out, we took a week off, and also used it to make the most of our cars one last time, as the petrol rationing is beginning here too today, and marks the start of meagre times for Baldchen. We recovered well during that week, and tomorrow we will resume our work with renewed energy. I slept a great deal, sometimes spending entire days in bed.

Aside from this we have nothing to report, except that Giraffe Gazelle had a migraine attack yesterday, but recovered once more thanks to my exceedingly selfless, considerate and concerned care (for I slept off her migraine). But there was something: through a very peculiar chain of events, I met a former lady friend[1] from Berlin again, and she was here last night.

As far as the war is concerned, I think it would be best to hold one's tongue and cross one's fingers out of superstition. But you can tell my opinion from the fact that I consider that necessary.

Heartiest kisses from
your old child
Teddie

My dearest Hippo Cow, you truly deserve your name 'Wondrous Hippo Cow', for with the blanket you have achieved more than a miracle. I find it magnificent and immeasurably beautiful, and am very proud and happy to have it. I yearn very much to see you, and would be glad if a trip here could be arranged for this summer, though the petrol rationing makes conditions here more difficult still. The calendar too is most splendid, and has become a dear and familiar object on Archie's desk. I shall still write to Julie. A thousand kisses from your old Gretel.

Original: typewritten letter with additional handwritten note by Gretel Adorno.

1 Renée Nell, with whom Adorno had once had an ill-fated love affair.

73   LOS ANGELES, 21.12.1942

   429 WEST 117TH STREET
   NEW YORK

21 December 1942

My dears,
   there was an enormous blaze at Los Angeles station a week ago that probably claimed incredible numbers of Christmas packages, and we

spent a few days worrying about what had become of the delicious fluid you had intended for us. But then, after we had already given up hope, the gigantic crate arrived – how much love went merely into the packaging, to say nothing of its contents – in good shape, and we were all the more glad for it. Accept our heartiest thanks. Last night we sampled the crème de cacao and found it quite excellent, worthy of the greatest tradition. Its consumption takes place in silence.

We wish you a happy Christmas with all our hearts.

We spent Christmas Eve as an afternoon at the Horkheimers, as we had to be home by curfew that evening. Fritz arrived today, and we interrupted our regular work a little to relax somewhat, having just managed – after repeated attempts – to get through a particularly difficult part of our book,[1] which cost us the greatest effort and patience.

We have meanwhile received a highly official letter of thanks from Washington for the studies I had suggested and subsequently carried out with Marcuse concerning the problem of German chauvinism,[2] a sign that I was tactically on the right track[3] with my idea, and it may prove of some significance for the future. Our Marcuse has meanwhile acquired a rather decent post in Washington,[4] which is quite pleasant for everyone involved (he has long been an American). We shall also be seeing to our naturalization business soon, admittedly in the knowledge that there is very little hope of achieving it during the war. Come February, we will have been here for five years.

I am exceedingly curious to see how the year 1943, which I consider the decisive one, will turn out. I assume you know that those over 38 will not be conscripted.

Norah Andreae's attempt to bring over her children, who are living on the hopelessly deserted negro island of Antigua, was unsuccessful, even though she went to Washington especially to arrange it. Now she is in New York, and I have advised her to consult with WK, who will perhaps know how to find a way, and has the necessary connections to get Anina and her husband to Cuba. (The husband is Herr von Marx, whose mother[5] – if I am not mistaken in my recollection – is a friend from the Wondrous Hippo Cow's youth, unless it was actually the grandmother; it is all just as muddled as our hippo legends.) This will seem a little strange to you, as the family has the intact assets of Hahn and Marx, but they evidently suffer from a strange inability (namely stupidity and miserliness Gi!). Norah told us the other day that during one of the heaviest aerial attacks on London, an acquaintance with whom she was sharing a cellar or God knows what told her – in their final hour, so to speak – that she had known May Weinberg[6] as a young girl in Frankfurt, while she was still called Miss Forbes and worked for the Oppenheimers[7] as a governess. She was most amazed to hear that I already knew the entire story, but please do not mention it to her.

We have had no reply to our letter or telegram from Paul and Gaby, and I am extremely worried about Gabi, for whom such a blow[8] was probably too much.

After making an inquiry, I had received a letter from Hilde Frenkel (Flesch),[9] saying that both she and Gabi had not heard a word from Carl[10] in a very long time. I am now trying to re-establish contact with him; I would be deeply affected if something had happened to him, and I think I can safely say that there are few people to whom I owe such gratitude – in vital layers of my personality – as I do to him, and yet I have no way of helping him, as he is not qualified for serious scientific work.

I do not know the lady whose card you sent, and I have never heard the name; it must be some sort of mix-up with Louis.

The Bloch affair[11] is an embarrassment for him, not for me, and has also been registered as such by the few people who have followed it; I should add that, when Max and I printed the article in response to a desperate letter from Bloch, we were already expecting to make an enemy of him by doing so. I am old enough for experience to have taught me that nothing damages a person's loyalty more than the help one grants them. If there are exceptions, as in Benjamin's case, then one can only be grateful for them.

Is your heating still working properly?

It is so warm here that today we went for a walk without an overcoat, and in my case even without a waistcoat (our walking attempts are progressing).

So, once again, we wish you an enjoyable Christmas. Have some decent fodder, think of us as we do of you, and cling to the idea of a limit to the disaster.

Heartiest kisses from

your two horse-children
Archibald and Giraffe

We have something pleasing to report: Hanns Eisler, with whom I am on very good terms (and Gretel with his *very* charming wife), and who, as you probably know, is director of the Rockefeller Film Music Project, and now has to write a book[12] about it, has asked me to write it together with him. The official confirmation from the publisher (Oxford University Press) came yesterday, stating that we both have the status of authors and will split the royalties 50:50. As I had made preparations long in advance, I will be able to manage it comfortably in my spare time. I think it will be a very substantial external success. Eisler is being *extremely* loyal. Fond regards once again!

Original: typewritten letter with printed letterhead and handwritten postscript.

1 Presumably the first excursus of the *Dialectic of Enlightenment*, dealing with 'Odysseus or Myth and Enlightenment'.

2 See letter no. 62, note 6.

3 *right track*: EO.

4 Herbert Marcuse had initially entered the Office of War Information (OWI), and soon afterwards switched to the political department of the Office of Strategic Services (OSS); both offices were subordinate to the American secret service in Washington, DC.

5 Nothing further is known about Norah Andreae's daughter Anina; her husband was the banker W. Ernst von Marx (1902–?), born in Bad Homburg vor der Höhe, who had been vice-president of the supervisory board of the International Germanic Trust Company, of New York and Berlin, and had also acted as a representative of the bank Blair & Co. in New York. Nothing is known about his mother.

6 Ethel Mary (May) von Weinberg (1866–1937, or, according to a different source: 1935), née Forbes, daughter of a royal British colonel, was the wife of Carl von Weinberg (1861–1943), who, following his forced exit from the administrative board of I. G. Farben A.G. in 1938, sold his entire property to the City of Frankfurt and fled to his sister, Countess Maria Paolozzi di Calboli; Carl von Weinberg died in Rome.

7 Presumably the family of Sir Charles Oppenheimer (1836–1900), who had established himself as a businessman in England and returned to Frankfurt in 1875; he had been made a British honorary consul in 1880. The Oppenheimer family – Frau Oppenheimer, née Berta Goldbach (1847–1919), and her seven children, among them the painter Sir Francis Oppenheimer, who was made British Consul General in 1900 – lived in a palatial house near the opera house.

8 It could not be ascertained what fate befell the Oppenheimers.

9 Unknown. She probably came from the family who owned the Frankfurter Farb- und Gerbstoffwerke Carl Flesch [Carl Flesch, Frankfurt Paint Factory and Tannery].

10 Carl Dreyfuss (1898–1969), who had worked at the Flesch factory following his university studies, had done occasional work for the Institute of Social Research before 1933. In that year he published a study entitled *Beruf und Ideologie des Angestellten* [Profession and Ideology of the White-Collar Worker], in which he was able to draw on his experience as a leading industrial manager. Using the pseudonym Ludwig Carls, he worked in Berlin as a dramatic adviser to the Berlin film industry at least until 1935 (aside from a stay in Stockholm in 1933). Dreyfuss, who later spelled his name Dreyfus, emigrated to England in 1937, then in 1938 – with the financial assistance of Paul Oppenheim – to Argentina, where he lived in Buenos Aires until 1962. Following his arrival there, he appears to have earned a living through a company he managed that distributed magazines in cinemas. Dreyfuss returned to Germany around the start of 1963, and lived in Munich until his death.

11 In a private letter to Adorno from 18 September 1942 (see Ernst Bloch, *Briefe*, ed. Karola Bloch [Frankfurt am Main: Suhrkamp, 1985]), Bloch had written – in the hope of receiving financial aid from the institute – that he had lost his employment as a dishwasher, and was now packing parcels. Adorno took this literally, and published an appeal for funds in *Aufbau* entitled 'Für Ernst Bloch' (see *GS* 20.1, pp. 190–3) that caused Bloch to protest publicly.

12 See Adorno and Hanns Eisler, *Composing for the Films* (London: Athlone Press, 1994).

1943

74   LOS ANGELES, *c*.1.1.1943

A Happy New Year

May your New Year
be rich in opportunity,
Blest by fortune,
Cheered by friendship
And crowned
with health
and happiness!

My dears,
thank you for your lovely long letter. So, at the start of the new year, we are sending you a cheque for $10 for your brood, a good boy Archie. What did Santa Claus bring our good Oscar for Christmas – the precision scales or the cards? We were given a number of nice things privately, from the horse a cocktail table that we had urgently needed since moving into our house, and a very pretty green speckled bowl from Maidon that looks quite splendid upon the Hippo Cow blanket; in fact, it was bought especially for that purpose.

We were sent rather a nice blue/red horse from Boston, and from one of our friends here we received a sweet little glass giraffe. But it was the government[1] that really topped it all: for Christmas they lifted the curfew, and for New Year[2] they gave us a B card for petrol, which grants us twice the previous ration, and thus a degree of mobility once again. On New Year's Eve we had a large party, *c*.18 people, there was coming and going, and we are still a little tired but very happy.

We hope you too have started the new year well. The very fondest regards
ever your old Gretel

My dears, *such* a shame that you were not here on Christmas Eve, for it was quite splendid, and I played a great deal of chamber music with the excellent violinist Maaskoff and his wife (Lisa Minghetti). Gretel's arrangement was a succès fou – well, Fritz will tell you about that. The last guests left at half past four.

Through the lifting of all regulations here and the double petrol ration, the matter of your holidays here is now looking much finer and better, which certainly makes us happy!

Happy New Year, and:
> Tout le vent qui gonfle la voile
> Soit de désirs obéis!

That is by Mallarmé,[3] whom Giraffe is currently using to wind me up quite frightfully!

Heartiest kisses
wishes sniffs patters

from your child
the unshapely hippo
Piggybald.

Original: handwritten letter on a printed New Year's card.

1 *government*: EO.

2 *New Year*: EO.

3 The lines cited are taken from a quatrain entered by Mallarmé in the album of an unidentified lady named Helga: 'Tout le vent qui gonfle la voile/Sera de désirs obéis/Et que se lève votre étoile/Au phare de chaque pays.' It is unclear whether there was a printed version whose second line begins with 'Soit', or whether Adorno, who was presumably citing the lines in allusion to his unattainable mistress, was simply mistaken.

75   LOS ANGELES, 10.2.1943

10 February 1943

My dear Wondrous Hippo Cow,
your letter made me very sad and I have now become very little in my feeling of guilt and creep around you sniffing in the hope of being granted a sniff from your indescribably large nostrils once again. All I can do is to appeal to your inexhaustible supply of motherliness and

beg you to forgive my silence. Though I do think that you should know me well enough to realize that, whenever I fall so silent, it is not out of egotism, coldness, busyness or the like. Though I cannot give you any concrete information about what was happening to me during the last two months, you must believe me that I was in a state that made any human utterance on my part (except for the extremely demanding and serious work) practically impossible – only a few days ago I told Giraffe that I felt as if picking up the telephone receiver would be as strenuous for me as it was for Atlas to bear the weight of the world. I do not think I am opening my hippo mouth too wide in claiming that these months, since the end of November, have been a time of the most difficult inner crisis for me; a crisis affecting only myself and my most intimate emotional regions, and unrelated to external matters. Often I literally did not know how I would survive this experience, and if Gretel and Max had not stood by me with indescribable love and truly undeserved understanding, I really do not know how things would have continued; but I think that I can now consider myself to be gradually recovering, even though the trauma still extends to the innermost layers of my soul. I was so proud not to show any of this, and it was only the true gravity of the accusation I sensed in your letter – and also indirectly in what our good WK wrote – that have forced me at least to tell you this much: I beg you earnestly not to ask or insist; perhaps, when you are here, I will tell you something about the admittedly extremely strange events, which, I am almost inclined to say, have stirred up the entire burden of the past once more and somehow merged with it. All I ask you to believe is that this is truly not some story that has been thought out after the event, and that, if anything, it sooner falls short of the truth than inflates it. If not, you would be doing me the most bitter injustice. But you should not worry about me at all, for I am a resilient hippo: first comes the thick skin, then the layer of fat which enables it to float in the water, then the enormous mass of flesh, and only then the substance. And, apart from everything else, my work – and the conditions under which I am able to carry it out – is not only a great joy to me, but also, I am firmly convinced, such a serious objective duty that nothing private could get me down. My only misfortune is that I would probably not have those qualities which perhaps make my work something special if they were not coupled with a boundless capacity for suffering, for abandonment of self-control, for losing myself. As I am compelled to think and react with every part of myself, and above all with the most subtle sensory responses, it is not inconceivable that these reactions should assume an intensity that can be reconciled neither with what common sense tells us a philosopher should be nor even with the famed sense of proportions[1] expected in anglophone countries. You

124

should by no means imagine that I was merely unhappy during these months, on the contrary: in accordance with my manic-depressive nature, there were also times when it was exactly the opposite, but I was simply not able to live in the normal fashion. To avoid any mis-understandings on your part, I will say this much: it was an erotic matter concerning my person, but the relationship between Gretel and myself is such that it can even withstand such shocks – to say nothing of the fact that, on the surface, practically nothing happened, and that the scene of this novel is essentially my own mind, though this did not make things any easier for Giraffe, but only harder.

Norah immediately greeted me with a kiss from the Wondrous Hippo Cow, and we were frightfully happy to receive the truly delightful menu and the account of the invitation. It made me so vain and proud of my two cultivated, restrained and composed parents – I am sure you would never act as your child does, but you must simply take him as he is, and he does, after all, do his best to lay the finest eggs he can. The first long section of the joint book with Max, which is in fact supposed to repre-sent our entire philosophy, the one about myth and enlightenment, is finished, as well as a further section – conceived by Max and subse-quently formulated together word for word – on Kant, Sade and Nietzsche; and also a correspondingly extensive sketch of mine regard-ing a historico-philosophical interpretation of Homer, which we shall be ploughing through together, as well as the mass culture draft com-pleted last autumn. I think I can say – with the corroboration of my two wardens (Mammoth and Giraffe) – that I have not gone daft quite yet (Gi!). At the moment I have to do some more work for Washington.[2]

Last night we had a large gathering here, the biggest so far, to honour the actor Granach,[3] who read excerpts from his extraordinarily signi-ficant autobiographical novel, which one could probably best compare to a modern Pojatz.[4] There were 27 of us, including Max and Maidon, Norah, Berthold Viertel, old Frau Steuermann, Gina Kaus, the Maaskoffs, and Lou Eisler. The reading was particularly fine and suc-cessful, and I kept thinking of our tigress, who would have enjoyed it greatly; and everything went very smoothly indeed, even though Giraffe had arranged and organized everything by herself. Lou Eisler, with whom Gretel is on quite good terms, still remained here for half the night, whereas Hanns was unable to come on account of a bout of flu.[5]

I do not have much else to report. No, I do: Felix Weil's second wife, Motte, died of laryngeal cancer, and Lotte Gumperz,[6] whom the Hippo Cow knew in Frankfurt as Lotte Schneider, the red-haired wife of the cellist Mischa Schneider,[7] is also dead; Gumperz[8] was a colleague of mine at the institute, and we were on good terms with both of them for a while until he fell out with the institute. While Motte Weil was on her death-bed, we even considered sending our good WK a cable telling him to come to Colorado Springs to see her, for she had been deserted by everyone; he is the only one whom we would have trusted to handle the situation, but then we decided not to burden him with that journey, which would have been extremely strenuous under the present conditions. In the end it was Motte's sister who went.

Forgive me for writing so much and so little about myself, both of which are unlike me, but I am sure that you will understand me this once, and you seriously do not need to worry about me at all. Heartiest kisses from your old child

Teddie

Original: typewritten letter.

1 *sense of proportions*: EO.

2 Unknown.

3 Alexander Granach (1890–1945) had studied in Berlin in 1909 with Reinhardt, to whom his first teacher Emil Milan had recommended him, and entered the film business in 1920. After stays in Warsaw and Kiev, Granach emigrated to the USA, where he first lived in New York, then moved to Hollywood. Regarding the autobiographical novel *Da geht ein Mensch* [There Goes a Human], published in Stockholm in 1945 [and in English by Doubleday, Doran & Co. the same year as *There Goes an Actor*], Berthold Viertel (1885–1953) wrote, presumably quite shortly after the reading: 'No one would have thought that Granach would ever write. And now he has written a book, this unique, rich and beautiful book. He dared to do it; he was able to do it. He immigrated to literature, into the poetic realm. This took place in Hollywood, when the imposition of the 'curfew' forced him to spend one evening after another at home; when he, with his gipsylike, loose lifestyle, had unwanted leisure time forced upon him. [. . .] Granach sat down and wrote his book. Whoever reads it will learn, with great emotion, what kind of reaction it is: a reaction to the Hitler era and to all the inhumanity resulting from it' (Berthold Viertel, 'Alexander Granachs Autobiographie. Einführung eines ungedruckten Buches' [Introduction to an Unpublished Book], in *Die Überwindung des Übermenschen. Exilschriften* [Overcoming the Superman: Writings From Exile], vol. 1, ed. Konstantin Kaiser and Peter Roessler in collaboration with Siglinde Bolbecher, Vienna, 1989, pp. 163–7; for the passage cited here see p. 164).

4 Translator's note: this presumably refers to the novel *Der Pojaz* (published in 1905) by Karl Emil Franzos (1848–1904), also known for editing the works of Georg Büchner. The name of this tragicomic novel's eponymous hero, a figure in a Jewish ghetto, is the Yiddish word for 'jester' (derived from 'Bajazzo').

5 *flu*: EO.

6 Unknown.

7 Unknown.

8 The American-born economist Julian Gumperz (1898–1972) had worked together with Pollock at the Institute of Social Research since 1927.

19 February 1943

My dears,
I cannot tell you how happy your letters made me, and how grateful I am to you for them. I do not think anyone could have reacted with more tenderness or a greater measure of understanding than you did, and I found it especially comforting that you avoided any words of 'encouragement'. Attendons patiemment la réorganisation des tramways.[1]
Today I donated blood for the fourth time and, although I felt like Tristan at the end of Act III this time, it once again went just as smoothly, rationally and well, as one tends to say, as the other times. After lunch I lay down and slept, and just now Giraffe fed me with oranges. They said that all the blood would be restored within three days.
I had a lengthy letter from Rudi,[2] whose professional problems seem to have found a satisfactory solution. Hermann[3] had already told me that he had got married before I heard about it from Norah. We had once seen the girl in New York and urgently advised him not to marry her, simply because she is so grey, bland and sober – a true piano teacher – that one really cannot imagine her in a marriage. But perhaps he is right; at any rate, he will be spared any dangerous adventures. Aside from that, he was so closely connected to her through their music school – the basis of his professional existence – that we already realized in New York that he could hardly turn back.
We hope very strongly that your plan to spend the holidays here will be carried out. There is time yet to talk about how and when to do it. We did, incidentally, have a few days of the most splendid midsummer weather here. That is all we have to report.
Heartiest kisses, my dears,
from your old, evidently very old
Archibald, Hippo King, m.p.
and his dear Giraffe Gazelle with the ridiculous little horns
Gi

Original: typewritten letter.

1 A remark made by Max Horkheimer.

2 No letters written by Rudolf Kolisch during this time have been preserved among Adorno's belongings.

3 Hermann Grab and the Ghent-born Blanche Smullyan had married in September 1942.

8 March 1943

My dears,

a thousand thanks for your terribly kind letter, and especially for the convalescent's book[1] with the giraffe and hippo. I cannot tell you how happy you made us both with it. It now stands on the mantelpiece[2] next to a golden giraffe, a present from Max. You cannot imagine how perfectly the idea of a convalescent hit the mark, or rather: it proves what an extraordinary instinct – oh, how tremendous – you have for the situation. And the 'patient' is now gradually recovering, albeit with occasional relapses at poor Giraffe's expense.

The most important external event I have to report is that the anti-Semitism project[3] has now been financed by a grant[4] from the American Jewish Committee, initially on a modest scale. We are taking care of the psychological part here. I consider the matter especially urgent at the moment, and we intend to do everything in our power to make something decent of it, and to contribute to a serious counteraction, not just idle talk. Yet at the same time we are trying to continue doing our own things.

Last night we went to a very nice house warming party[5] at the Eislers with a great number of people, some of whom were genuinely stimulating and interesting, and there was even a somewhat unified and serious theoretical discussion, which is really very rare at parties. On Friday we will be at a gathering at Gina Kaus's place. If we wanted to join in, we could float with the Hollywood current and have a different celebrity every evening; but as our work is very serious and strenuous we do not have the nerves for it, and keep out of things to a considerable extent, which, however – such is the world – only serves to increase our value as an object of invitation.

We see Norah quite often. The business with her children has still not worked out. Though the children must, admittedly, be quite remarkable idiots. I agree all too heartily with WK in his assessment of both Mr Gould[6] and Jules Lehmann.[7] Lehmann, whom we know through Elisabeth Beit,[8] is a pompous, self-important ox, Gould is probably even worse, and the worst thing about the whole business is that one cannot even advise Norah to break it all off, which would probably be the most sensible option, as Gould probably does not have the power to be of genuine help, but has at least enough to cause trouble out of malice (even the most pathetic people always have sufficient power for that). Otherwise we have little to report. I am currently concluding some of the most difficult sections of my historico-philosophical excursus on Homer, a supplement to our main text, and have been reading various anthropological and ethnological material, with the reward that a 'theoretical' thinker always has when devouring in true hippo fashion something that is as neutral as possible, and has not already been pre-digested by clever Jews. In addition, my work with Eisler has progressed rather nicely this last week. This project would in fact be going superbly if both he and I had as much time as it requires. But as it is, we have to squeeze it into our hours of leisure.

Heartiest kisses

from your two old horses
Archibald and Giraffe Gazelle

Do you ever listen to the Saturday broadcasts from the Met? I heard a bit of *Die Valküre* – wonderful – and Aida, *ghastly*, but it is worth while.[9] It is broadcast by NBC, for you probably around 2 p.m.

Original: typewritten letter with handwritten postscript.

1 Not preserved.

2 *mantelpiece*: EO.

3 Since 1939, the Institute of Social Research and its employees had undertaken efforts to gain funding for a study on anti-Semitism. Numerous sketches, memoranda and notes were produced towards it. It was only in April 1943 that they found a sponsor for such a research project, namely the American Jewish Committee. The main work in that year was on the 'agitator studies', which Adorno and Leo Löwenthal wrote together. In spring 1944, following the expiry of the funding arrangement with the AJC, the Jewish Labor Committee took over the financing, and the Californian arm of the institute worked on the *Labor Study*, which was completed but never published. Only in 1945 did work begin on the renowned *Studies in Prejudice*, which were published in 1949. One part of these studies was the no less renowned work *The Authoritarian Personality*, in whose production Adorno played a substantial part, while Horkheimer, as research director of the AJC, was in charge of the entire project. It was produced in collaboration with the Public Opinion Study Group in Berkeley.

4 *grant*: EO.

5 *house warming party*: EO.

6 Unknown.

7 Uncertain; possibly the Frankfurt-born jurist Julius Lehmann (1884–1951), who emigrated to Switzerland in 1933, then to the USA in 1941.

8 Possibly a member of the Frankfurt family Beit von Speyer.

9 *worth while*: EO.

Brentwood, 29 March 1943

My dears,
the news that the enormous and warm Hippo Cow heart did not offer its honourable owner quite the service it owes her made me more than a little uneasy – I was on the point of packing my things and going to her. But I absolutely cannot leave here on account of the anti-Semitism project, which involves not only the actual scientific work, but in addition all sorts of contacts, above all to find helpers who can take care of the technical matters. For I am simply no longer an independent person, but a member of an organization – but aside from this it would also be inconceivable to leave Max on his own, especially in this phase, for we both hardly know if we are coming or going, as, at the same time, we also have our big theoretical works, which we do not expect to complete, of course (this is out of the question for lack of time alone), but at least to bring to a provisional close and mimeograph. So I must stay here and see if I can find an opportunity in the foreseeable future to go to New York. Unless you do decide to come here after all, which would make me happier than I can tell you – but can Marinumba take the considerable strain of such a long journey upon herself, with the additional discomforts of war? Please write to us at length, and also tell us roughly when you intend to come, *if* you intend to come. And also whether WK's heart is functioning normally and was only polished up as a matter of form, or whether it was once again expressive of his justified dissatisfaction with the state of the world.

I assess said state as follows: defeat of Germany, with the danger that Hitler's system and all it implies survives on the other side. And it could still take a long time, as no possible blunder is being left out, and it is a laborious process for the material superiority of the Allies to overcome the organizational and military experience of the Germans. We are now also feeling the effects of the war more strongly due to the scarcity of food, above all of meat, though that does not matter to us in the slightest; I think I can say that we are really very independent of such things. We spent weeks living mostly off what

130

our sausage-Jewess brought us, without any adverse psychological effects.

I probably wrote to you that my historico-philosophical study on the Odyssey is essentially finished – I read countless works of classical philology for it, and even brushed up on my Greek. – Tonight at Max's place with a few bigwigs, including Thomas Mann and his dear lady wife.

It is four months ago today that my horror novel – half Balzac, half monologue intérieur – began. I have not seen my Baudelairean mistress and Manon Lescaut, or whatever one might wish to call her, since mid-January; we are cross, as the children in Frankfurt would say. And yet I go on living, albeit with a very small capacity for self-denial (the Homer study is a critique of self-denial). The anti-Semitism project is a true blessing. Incidentally, I agree entirely with WK that abolishing the racial distinction would be the only right thing to do, and God knows our study espouses no less. But: the *others* do not want to. And at a time when millions of Jews are being murdered, it would not be so appropriate to reproach those people for isolating themselves. The problem lies with the Christians. I hope with all my heart that we really can do something – however modest – to help.

I send the Hippo Sow my heartiest wishes for a good and thorough recovery – I simply trust in her imperturbable nature, and expect to see her in good health and spirits once more – and the sublime beast should jolly well abide by that.

Heartiest kisses from your old Hippo King
Archibald Stumpfnase Kant von Bauchschleifer

Gretel is at the market[1] hunting for meat.

Original: typewritten letter.

1 *market*: EO.

79 LOS ANGELES, 15.4.1943

Happy Easter

Some of the cards were
kinda big.
And some were kinda small,
But then it's not the size
of cards
That matters, after all –

The thing that really matters
Is the wishes that
they bring –
And this one hopes you'll
always have
The best of everything!

15 April 1943

My dears,

despite the cold weather I met the Easter Rabbit yesterday and placed an order for you; I hope he is reliable and will deliver it on time. I had a terrible attack of lumbago, could hardly move, but now I am better, though greatly ashamed at these signs of ageing – or perhaps it is only the much-loved Californian climate which actually makes me rather suspicious. As always, there is no lack of work, and the maid business gets harder by the week, it is a matter of chance whether she or any other will turn up or not. It often happens that Teddie does not like the food I have got together quite as much as he used to, but he still eats up like a good hippo, and I do what I can. How is your health? What did Liefmann say? I would so love to see you, 1½ years is long enough for a separation – how on earth can one overcome those 3000 miles? If there is no other way, Teddie will have to come to you and I shall meanwhile look after our little house. The hippo cub urgently needs a good sniffing from the old Hippo Cow and the Boar. I hope you have the finest of weather at Easter, with the very fondest regards from

your old Gretel

My dears, today in all haste just this greeting and the hope that we might see each other again soon either here or over there (better here, for it is so much more beautiful here!)! Hopefully your two hearts are beating Andante Moderato, à la Haydn (but without the drum roll!), so that you can come after all! I am totally Jewified i.e. have nothing but anti-Semitism on my mind. It is hard to find anything new because Jews are so clever – 'Jews know everything'! Yesterday I hired an (Aryan) assistant,[1] I hope it will work out. Otherwise, I am feeling *much* better. I am reconciled with Madame, and the business has lost its sting. So you can rest assured on that count. I would not be telling you if it were not *truly* the case. Heartiest kisses from your child, who truly is what she only pretends to be: born again. Your old Archibald

Original: handwritten letter on a printed Easter card.

1 This is presumably the psychologist R. Nevitt Sanford (1909–95), who later taught at Berkeley; he was not Adorno's assistant, but in fact co-director (with him) of the Berkeley Opinion Study, which conducted the studies for *The Authoritarian Personality*.

80 LOS ANGELES, 29.4.1943

Thursday

My dear Wonder-Nile-Stute, this is just to tell you how happy I am that you feel better. I was worried more than I could tell you – You are the best and only Marinumba on earth. I hope you will soon recover completely. And I hope to see you in the none too distant future. I do everything I can in order to achieve this. Take all my love! Yours ever

Teddie

1000 kisses best and quickest recovery love yours
Giraffe

Original: photo postcard: Joshua tree silhouetted against a California sunset. Against the glowing desert sunset, the grotesque Joshua tree spreads its shaggy branches. Many desert birds nest in these spiny trees and Indians use the small roots for basket weaving; stamp: APR 30, 1943. Manuscript. Translator's note: written in English.
On the dating: 29 April 1943 was the Thursday before the date of the postal stamp.

81 LOS ANGELES, 14.5.1943

429 WEST 117TH STREET
NEW YORK, N.Y.

316 So. Kenter Ave.
Brentwood Heights,
West Los Angeles
14 May 1943.

My dear faithful old Wondrous Hippo Cow,
I waited with my letter until I was able to give you definite information. Today I can: I shall, in all probability (i.e. when I receive the travel permit etc.), come in July, stay for about 2 weeks, and go with you to the Poconos or wherever, if that is all right with you. I shall either pass through N.Y. very cursorily or not at all; and be entirely

independent of the project and do nothing, only be there for you. Giraffe will not be coming, unfortunately, for financial reasons, as the house etc. has to continue here. But we both have the feeling that the Wondrous Hippo Cow will be happy to have her Hippo King to herself this once. All this, of course, is subject to one condition: that your doctor does not advise you to go to the West on account of the Hippo Cow's heart, as the climate there is supposed to be especially good for high blood pressure. In that case I would naturally not wish to foil your plan with my own, and would be happy to show you the little house and the truly indescribable beauty of southern California.

I cannot tell you how happy I am that our plans to see each other again are now being realized.

Regarding WK's question about my military status:[1] I have not heard any more since being written 4h, but my work is so deeply connected to the war effort[2] and the institute so lacking in employees that Max and I do not think I shall have to pick oranges, not that that would be the worst thing in the world.

As far as the war – in the specifically military sense – is concerned, there seems now to be ample justification for my optimism, which is based on the basic thought that an industrialized war will be decided by the total industrial capacity, and that the Germans have lost their initial head start – rather like a medium-sized industrialist who introduces a revolutionary invention but is ultimately overtaken by the larger firm, which is able to produce the invention on a larger scale. In terms of the political prognosis, both Max and I have exactly the same view as WK. All the more so in the light of my current work[3] on anti-Semitic propaganda.

Yesterday we had a successful party with the Eislers, Helli Brecht and son[4] (B.B. is still in New York), Maidon (Max has gone to San Francisco for a few days for the project, to rummage around in the big libraries), the Viertels with old Frau Steuermann, two Americans, Ludwig Marcuse and wife, Lotte Mosbacher and husband. Everything fitted together well and went nicely, and I think you would have enjoyed yourselves too.

You will probably be called upon – either alone or with Egon and Lotte – by my friend and student Irina Coryan,[5] alias Ira Morgenroth, a pleasant and pretty woman whom I would ask you to receive cordially (as you do not have a piano, you will be spared her unpleasant side, namely her piano playing*). She is *not*, I should add, the Baudelairean mistress, but rather her closest friend, followed the whole affair and acted exceedingly loyally and fairly, for which I am

---

* [Marginal note in Adorno's hand:] do not mention this, as she knows that I consider her untalented and is particularly sensitive.

grateful. It goes without saying that you should not mention that. The Baudelairean mistress, incidentally, from whom I am now wholly emancipated, is called Renée Nell; Ira lived with her. The two women put on a big party for us on the occasion of Ira's farewell.

I am happy that the Hippo Cow is back in good shape again – she must make the most of the fine weather, get plenty of fresh air, and take a sit by the Hudson – and a deep, conscious breath. It was boundlessly reassuring to hold her handwriting in my hands again.

Do you know that Anna Löb is coming here again? Astonishing. Eduard Steuermann will also be coming here at the end of June – in case you do decide to travel after all.

So, God willing, à bientôt!

Heartiest kisses from your old but once more very cheerful, albeit incorrigibly romantic child

Teddie

Fritz asked after the Hippo Cow with great concern. He is ridiculously overtaxed, and mostly in Washington, in a quite responsible position.[6]

A thousand kisses Giraffe. I am so glad that Archie can soon tell you all our new animal stories and sing you the songs. Have you both fully recovered? Many regards also to Julie.

Original: typewritten letter with additional handwritten note by Gretel Adorno.

1 *military status*: EO.

2 *war effort*: EO.

3 'The Psychological Technique of Martin Luther Thomas' Radio Addresses'; see GS 9.1, pp. 7–141.

4 The actress Helene Weigel (1900–1971) had been married to Brecht since 1929; her son Stefan was born in 1924.

5 Unknown.

6 On the invitation of Eleanor Roosevelt, Pollock took part in discussions dealing with aspects of the rebuilding of Europe after the war.

82   LOS ANGELES, 31.5.1943

31 May 1943

My dears,

a thousand thanks for your lengthy letter; we were already slightly concerned at your long silence. Today I must disappoint you a little, for I would like – if it is not all too inconvenient and you do not have very serious arguments against it – to come not at the start of July, but rather at the start of August. For Fritz will only arrive here around the end of July. Max is therefore taking his holiday in August, and it would cause a sensitive disturbance in our work if we lost two months. In addition, we are in the middle of something very promising[1] in our project at the moment, and I could go with much greater peace of mind if I had brought the current study to some sort of conclusion. I should add that it was not Max who had the idea of changing our plans, but rather I myself. But I feel quite sure that it would be better like this. It would be nicest if you could make the necessary arrangements for us to meet in the Poconos at the start of August; but I would also come to New York, although I can hardly imagine that you will be in New York when it is so hot.

A thousand thanks for inviting me there – I accept the invitation on the condition that you can genuinely arrange it without any inconvenience. But I would ask, for very good reasons, that you tell no one, especially Fritz, that I will be visiting you there (though Fritz has been very friendly regarding the trip).

Please let me know exactly[2] what you will do to get the travel permit from the FBI, as I also have to apply for that. Possibly a certificate from Liefmann would speed things up, though it would probably be more practical to wait another few weeks before having it written, so that no one says that the Wondrous Hippo Cow's illness will already have passed by August.

I am happy that you are both back in shape, and hope that the May by the Hudson, which is one of New York's most pleasing institutions, will soon restore the Sea Sow to the shape[3] of blessed Marinumba. We have little to tell. Leo has arrived, quite pleasant and truly effusive in his gratitude to WK, who evidently proved a true blessing during old Löwenthal's illness (the wife is a scourge of God). My work on the anti-Semitism project is *exceptionally* interesting, and I think one could in fact do some good through it in a crisis – more on that when we speak.

Something curious: Norah has made me an executor of her will, together with her daughter and Paul Oppenheim, an honour that I could never have predicted. She has attached herself to us incredibly. I probably wrote to you already that the Gould–Jules Lehmann business has meanwhile been exposed; it happened exactly as we had predicted. But now she finally has a Mexican visa for her children, and if they are not total half-wits (which they are, however) they should be on the way to Mexico by now. On Friday evening at Max's a big official party for our head Jew, who will incidentally be working with me on a big study.[4]

Heartiest kisses from your old Hipposchleifer
Archibald m.p.

136

Are you already acquainted with the horn-shark or the giraffe-fish? From a distance, its skin is reminiscent of a giraffe's coat, and it has two peculiar horn-like continuations on its head. It grows to a length of 12 to 15 feet. Kiss from your

Giraffe

Original: typewritten letter.

1 Unknown.

2 Oscar Wiesengrund noted at the foot of the letter:

'Suggestion for Teddie's trip:
leave Los Angeles: 31 July
in N.Y.   3 August
spend the night in our room (if spending the night is opportune) which we will keep. –
leave Hoboken – N.Y. 3 or 4 August
in Swiftwater   3 or 4 ″
travel permit: we will give him precise information in good time c. 2 weeks before the trip: *no sooner*'

3 *shape*: EO.

4 Both unknown.

New postal address: Los Angeles 24
316 So. Kenter Ave. (*without* Brentwood)
10 June 1943

My dears,

I am making use of a free minute to tell you about one of the most peculiar people – were it not for Walter Benjamin, I would say *the* most peculiar – we have ever encountered in our lives. It is the film actress Luli Deste,[1] whose real name is Countess Goerz, née Baroness Bodenhausen. In the last 4 weeks we have both developed an exceedingly intense friendship with her, as intense as I would not have thought it still possible, old silly that I am, to have with any 'new' person.

We met her – and this already sounds like a joke – at the 'reconciliation party' that Renée put on for us. She seems to have invited Luli and ourselves to impress each of us with her refined acquaintances. It all started at the party, when a ghastly film guy and an equally ghastly psychoanalyst (the confidant of Dr Rosane, ça suffit,

137

a certain Dr Meyer, whom Renée seems to be living off now, incidentally) got into a fake[2]-scientific conversation while Luli and I were talking, until she asked me to go into a different room with her and Gretel in order to be undisturbed, which we did (I can scarcely describe the anger of my former grande passion). Luli is our age, just a year younger than myself, but quite simply the most beautiful, noble and enchanting being that I have encountered in my entire life. Imagine roughly the Lenore Zickel[3] type, only much smaller, very delicate and with an indescribable charm and magic that only grows through the fact that her beauty is just on the point of fading (she has a grown-up son). She comes from not only an exceedingly affluent family (her father was president of the Krupp works) but also an equally cultivated one: that same father had very intimate relations with Hofmannsthal, Borchardt and Rudolf Alexander Schröder. I was able to check all this in Hofmannsthal's correspondence, where she is also mentioned as a child. Yet equally delightful, astute, open and modest in a deeper sense, for all her mondanité, and of such aristocratic bravery as I have never encountered in anyone save the Hippo Cow. This being, which today still looks like a dream of a girl (I had made her up during the worst time, under the name of Schnurz Hellingrath, long before I knew her, and now both I and she herself use that name for her, but that is another story), and of a beauty whose radiance is matched only by Marlene Dietrich – I kid you not – became an actress at a young age (the material circumstances at home must have changed), was offered very big film contracts owing to her beauty, first in London and then here, and was subsequently left high and dry on account of her evident lack of acting ability (which she herself admits with the absolute openness of everything she tells us about her whole difficult life), had no contract for 4 years, bought a ranch, went bankrupt, and now lives in the deepest poverty with the most indescribable poise in – Annachen would say: a garden shed, the tiny wooden back-house of a little worker's house at the start of Hollywood, whose every corner she has furnished with the greatest imaginable culture. So she lives there with two dogs, a tiny little Afghan and a magnificent black one, hardly has anything to eat, only the finest dresses, all of which she showed us one evening while the mice quite literally ran over the trains. She is so unreal and fairy-like that each morning one fears she may have dissolved into thin air during the night. And bursting with talent, also as a writer; she has written poems that contain, alongside teenie verse, the most ingenious lines, and a children's fairytale novel, which Gretel is currently working through with her. Otherwise: desperate search for a new engagement, as well as dealings with the most abhorrent film guys, heroically withstanding an existence that even she herself essentially

138

finds incomprehensible. On Sunday, for Gretel's proper birthday party, we had her here officially for the first time with 'celebrities', including the Dieterles; on Friday we shall introduce her to the Brechts – may God grant that something comes of it for her: she arouses such hatred, simply because she is different, truly different to everything under the sun here, just like our theoretical writings. We spend as much time with her as possible – she has become incredibly attached to us, simply because we are the only ones who do not want either to get something out of her or to harm her, because she really is like something I might have thought up. I know you would react just as effusively as we have. Of course, there are enough dark spots in her life that I do not even wish to explore, but her nature is such that one automatically forgives everything that could be held against her, and is simply grateful that she exists. I have not, incidentally, observed the slightest reaction on her part that would alter the image of one who, even in the utmost degradation, has not been degraded one iota. And after all, Giraffe and Archibald are very hard-boiled animals that do not become enthusiastic easily or without scepticism.

We celebrated Gretel's birthday most enjoyably with just Max, Gretel and myself, and a bottle of the finest WK-Forster, and Max read us a wonderful prose piece by Victor Hugo. Last night we also went to see Luli, because she was down,[4] and sat with the princess, her dogs and mice and spoke of the horrors of the world, which none of us have understood for a long time, and in which we all intend to stick together. Incidentally, Luli is a cousin of Count Beroldingen,[5] whom I used to meet every Friday over Husch's[6] lentil soup . . .

Main event otherwise: our adoptive dog Torro, who had been a great source of joy to us for the last 1½ years, was hit by a car (he always limped as a result of an earlier car injury) and died of internal bleeding; Gretel still brought him to hospital. We miss his begging and barking and his Socratic dog's head more than I can express. Being thus damaged had turned him from an animal into an individual. We were so proud of how we had fed him back into shape and how shiny his fur was. Now we are saving the little bones and bowls for the countess's dogs to feast on – such is life.

I am happy to accept dear WK's itinerary on the whole, and am looking forward terribly to seeing you – we still have to correspond regarding the details. How long will you still be in N.Y.? – A few sweet sad lines from Gabi. Otherwise much with Norah, who is being especially pleasant and friendly. I think I wrote that she has made me (not A.H.)[7] an executor of her will, together with her daughter and Paul Oppenheim – you should naturally keep that to yourselves.

As I am also partaking of the wonderful Hippo Cow blanket and the meat-extract, allow me also to send you the heartiest thanks for those.

Kisses and sniffs from your faithful and now fully restored child

Teddie

On the property opposite here, which is magnificent, children are playing about with two unsaddled horses – an image of the most peaceful Wild West.

Original: typewritten letter with handwritten postscript.

1 According to information written on the back of photographs of her taken by A. L. Schafer, who was director of still photography at Paramount (he worked for Columbia Studios before 1942), Luli Deste was born in Vienna, was a dancer and singer, and brought three Afghan hounds with her to America from Europe. In 1937 she played alongside Edward G. Robinson in *Thunder in the City*, in 1938 in *She Married an Artist*, and in 1940 in *South of Karanga* and *Flash Gordon Conquers the Universe*. Luli Deste was the pseudonym of Julie von Bodenhausen, the daughter of Eberhard von Bodenhausen – director of the Krupp works from 1907 to 1910, then on the supervisory board and in 1918 chairman of the supervisory board – who was born in 1902 and married a certain Count Schlitz, known as Goertz; she died in 1952.

2 *fake*: EO.

3 The wife of Reinhold Zickel (1885–1953), Adorno's German teacher; see *GS* 20.2, pp. 756–67.

4 *down*: EO.

5 After the founding of Frankfurt airport, Count Egon von Beroldingen (1885–1933) was its director, and from 1926 to 1928 he was president of the football club Eintracht Frankfurt.

6 See letter no. 54, note 3.

7 Alfons Herzberger?

84 LOS ANGELES, 7.7.1943

429 WEST 117TH STREET   Los Angeles, 7 July 1943.
NEW YORK, N.Y.

My dears, this is just to tell you – amid a mad rush of work – that, aside from being very tired, we are all well. If everything goes smoothly, I shall be going to San Francisco with Gretel on *1 August* to spend 3 quiet, undisturbed days, and on the 4th will travel on to N.Y. and to you, where I shall stay – without doing any work whatsoever – until the end of the month. Perhaps a few days of N.Y. after that, but I have to be back at the start of September. We have completed our first long report ad Antis.

On Saturday we had our first hearing,[1] with Max and Mrs Colburn (our landlady) as witnesses; it all went very well, but it could still take a year until the naturalization is final. One consolation: emigrants *are* now being naturalized.

In the evening there was a massive gathering at the Dieterles, with lots of big shots[2] and the Russian film about Stalingrad.[3] On Sunday we were at the Zilzers (Lotte Mosbacher) with a small but especially pleasant group of people. Next Sunday a big party at our place in honour of Davidson Taylor,[4] the chief programme director at CBS.

Next week Max is going 'away' for 10 days, i.e. to a suburb, so that they can have a little rest.

As well as everything else, Luli has constant (justified) nervous breakdowns, and Gretel has to comfort her.

We are extending the contract on our house for another 2 years – hopefully you will be able to see it soon after all.

Forgive my stupidity – I hope soon to become more intelligent again once I am at your place.

Fond regards, also to Julie
kisses from your old child
Teddie

The business with the statement of assets is known here too. Fritz will register the German institute's assets (buildings and giant library). Everything that belongs to Gretel is under Melly's name.

Fond regards, I am waving with my little horns
Your old Giraffe Gazelle

Original: handwritten letter with printed letterhead.

1 *first hearing*: EO.

2 *big shots*: EO.

3 The documentary film *Stalingrad*, directed by Leonid Varlamov, had been shown in the USA with the title *The City That Stopped Hitler: Heroic Stalingrad* and an American commentary.

4 Davidson Taylor (1907–79) later became director of the Arts Center Program at Columbia University.

please turn over

July 12, 1943
6600 Luzon Ave. N.W.
Washington 12, D.C.

YOUR MAJESTY ARCHIBALD KING AND EMPEROR
YOUR MAJESTRICE ARCHIBALD QUEEN AND EMPRESS

Greetings in humble humility. May the sun be lucid to you And the moon soft on your imperial hearts.

No sooner had I received your letter than I proceeded to fulfil your wish and desire. I am enclosing the two sheets with my insignificant signature affixed, and I sincerely hope that you two will have joined the great community of the citizens of this great country before the leaves of autumn fall. Amphibious operations of a peculiar complexity will be set in motion to expedite the process.

As a matter of fact, I really enjoy the thought of seeing you here East in the near future. There are many things that must be talked over. Since I am cut off from all activity which calls for my brain (if any), I have to be contented with learning what I can learn about the so-called world in which we so-called live. Since this world is most certainly bound to deteriorate at an ever accelerated pace, we should get together and talk it into order.

I am glad to hear that you are able to get some theoretical satisfaction out of the anti-Semitism project sotto voce and volta face. I keep track of the New York output, and I must say that it is much better than I expected. I am anxious to see your contribution: it is promised to me for this week.

On one point you are wrong: the supply of pretty girls here at least equals that of Los Angeles, and I don't make use of it anyway.

If you want anything more in your naturalization matter, please let me know.

Best regards, and alles gute
Yours
H. M.

Los Angeles, 16 July 1943

My dears,
so everything is fine and dandy now, if you will pardon the expression. This morning, on the basis of the Liefmann statement and

a statement from Max, we were granted the travel permit for San Francisco, New York and the Poconos without any problems. The tickets have also been reserved, and we hope to have them by Monday. The plan is: on the morning of 1 August we go to San Francisco, where I have to see a professor for the project. On 5 August Giraffe is going back while I go on to New York, where I should be arriving on the morning of the 9th. I shall then strive to go directly to you in the Poconos on the same day, and would ask that you give me the most precise directions. I shall cable you about when to pick me up as soon as I reach the station in New York; it would be difficult to arrange now, as the trains are sometimes severely delayed on account of the war. In fact the entire trip is complicated, and hunting down the tickets was a full time job[1] in itself. I am very happy that we managed to sort it out.

I am writing to you on the reverse of a letter sent by Herbert Marcuse from Washington, which he sent with his additional statement for the naturalization procedure. The letter is so delightful that we wanted you to laugh with us.

Otherwise we have little to report, a great deal of work, especially on the Jewish project. On Monday Max, who is terribly overworked, is taking a week's holiday, but shall still see each other a few days before he leaves. Leo, who had mumps for almost 4 weeks and was under quarantine, is still here – and particularly agreeable, as it happens.

On Sunday we will be visited by Virgil Thomson, who had us over for tea a few days ago; he is taking his holidays in Los Angeles. Besides him, and a very important film producer he is bringing along, the Palffys[2] will also be coming – he is the former husband of Lotte Mosbacher (through whom we know him), and she is an enchantingly beautiful Dutch-Javanese half-breed. And naturally Luli, whose move to New York is impending, though I cannot advise her all too seriously against it under the circumstances, even though we will miss her terribly. Well, I daresay you will encounter Her Grace somewhere or other. I am already eager to know what the Hippo Cow will think of that natural spectacle (my word, what a pair). – On Tuesday the Dieterles had us over for dinner together with Davidson Taylor, and Dieterle announced himself for one evening next week as a grass widower; the poor little horses are in such great demand, among people who earn as much in a week as we do in a year, which is all but inexplicable to me and an utterly excessive burden on my poor half-dead Giraffe. None of us have had maidservants for a long time now, not even Max, after we had got by for some time in combination with the Brechts, the Eislers and the Kortners. Now we are trying to get a permanent one together with the Horkheimers (she would live there upstairs), but without much of a chance. Gretel is quite touching, and continues with our real concerns despite the immense work in this actually not-so-little house and the herds of guests.

But I will soon be able to tell you about everything face to face, and at length. I am overjoyed that my visit is taking place in a friendlier aspect of the world.

Heartiest kisses from your soon-to-be-snorting-along child, Hippo King

Archibald

Original: typewritten letter on the back of a letter [in English] by Herbert Marcuse.

1 *full time job*: EO.

2 Nothing is known about the second wife of the former theatre director Victor Palfi.

86 LOS ANGELES, 26.7.1943

Los Angeles, 26 July 1943

My dear WK,

this is just to wish you the very best with all my heart on your birthday, the seventy-third – who would believe that you are already 73! If I am not entirely mistaken, it will be the most joyful birthday in a long, long time – the famous silver lining is gradually taking quite clear shape, and it is glorious that Mussolini, the first one to try out fascism, is now also the first to be dispatched.[1] Even if the thugs have rigged the whole business with the clever intention of neutralizing Italy *without the Allies occupying it* (and God forbid that the reaction here is already so strong that people let themselves in for it), the fact that they had to resort to such a bold manoeuvre would prove what a desperate situation they are in. And more probably they simply toppled him in the old Roman way once he turned out to be unsuccessful. So, Cheerio![2] – Max, who still called us late last night from his holiday spot, and who is normally consistently pessimistic about the war, was now also prepared to concede my theory for the first time.

The last few days have still been terribly busy; I shall be glad to leave on Sunday. We were Thomas Mann's guests on Tuesday, unfortunately with music, otherwise very nice; Dieterle had announced himself for Thursday, and we served him the Brechts, a few of the Viertels (with Eduard) and Luli; on Saturday we were at Leo's place

144

in Hollywood, today at the Eislers with a herd, on Thursday at Leon Lewis'[3] . . . I am feverishly dictating my big study; we had to hire an additional secretary here for a few days, and I am awaiting her at the moment. In addition, I still have to conclude the studies of our assistant, who is going to the O.S.S. (Donnovan)[4] in Washington on the 1st. As you can see, there is plenty to do. Max is returning on Wednesday.

We heard the news of the invasion of Sicily[5] just as we were drinking a bottle of WK wine (the first in months) with Luli. Yesterday afternoon, Sunday, we slept peacefully once Frau Eisler had told us on the phone about Musso's deposition.

As I shall be arriving in N.Y. around 9 in the morning, I hope very much that I can still reach you on the same day. I am looking forward to it quite terribly – and to the peace!

Enjoy the festivities, both of you
with heartiest kisses
from your approaching
child
Teddie

My dear WK,

the very fondest birthday greetings, and at least another 30 years. Sadly, I cannot get hold of any nice pyjamas here in California, the shopkeepers think I am as barmy as if I were asking for the moon. Forgive the coldly objective cheque and please let Julie buy them for you in New York. It is quite ghastly that we will not see each other, at least you will have Archie for a while.

Heartiest kisses from your
Giraffe Gazelle

Original: handwritten letter.

1 Mussolini was given a vote of no confidence by the fascist parliament on 25 July; King Victor Emmanuel III subsequently decreed his dismissal and arrest. Mussolini was freed again by German paratroopers on 12 September.

2 *Cheerio*: EO.

3 A New York lawyer.

4 William Donovan (1883–1959) had been director of the Office of Strategic Services since its founding in 1942.

5 American and British troops had landed in Sicily on 10 July without meeting any substantial resistance.

Tuesday
San Francisco

My beloved ones, we are both very happy here, and the huge hippopotamus is on the march!!! A bientôt
Yours ever Teddie

We spent a very nice afternoon and evening with Milton,[1] Mietze[2] and
Walter Herbert.[3] Anita[4] is unfortunately away with the children. Love.
Yours ever your daughter in law[5] Giraffe.

Original: photo postcard: Hotel Mark Hopkins, Nob Hill, San Francisco. The
Top of the Mark is located high in the sky on the topmost floor of Hotel Mark
Hopkins. The luxury and glamour of this unique room and the breathtaking
panorama from its windows combine to make it America's most spectacular
cocktail lounge. D. Smith, Gen'l Manager; stamp: AUG 4, 1943. Manuscript.
Translator's note: written in English.

1 The jurist Milton Seligmann (1866–1948) was the son of Hermann
(Henry) Seligmann, who had founded the Frankfurt bank Seligmann &
Stettheimer with his brother and his brother-in-law in 1867. Milton
Seligmann, who was a member of the supervisory board of I.G.
Farbenindustrie, had good connections to the USA through his ancestors and
relatives, who had gone to America in the nineteenth century. (Jens Ulrich
Heine, *Verstand & Schicksal. Die Männer der I.G. Farbenindustrie A.G.
[1925–45] in 161 Kurzbiographien* [Reason & Fate: The Men of I.G.
Farbenindustrie A.G. (1925–45) in 161 Short Biographies] [Weinheim, New
York, Basel and Cambridge, 1990], p. 274.)

2 Pet name for Milton Seligmann's wife, Marie Bernhardine, née Gans
(b. 1867). Her father was the co-owner of Cassella, Adolf (according to a different source: Fritz) Gans (ibid.).

3 Walter Herbert Seligmann (1893–1985), who was born and grew up in
Frankfurt, and took private tuition in counterpoint and musical form with
Schoenberg from 1919 to 1922, conducted the first performance of
Adorno's Six Short Orchestral Pieces (16 February 1929 in Berlin), which
were dedicated to him. Herbert was married to Rudolf Kolisch's sister
Maria.

4 Anita Lothar-Seligmann.

5 This could not be deciphered with certainty due to smudged ink.

New York, Saturday
28 August 1943

My dear good huge animals, this is just to send you my love, to tell you how happy I was with you and how sad I am without you, to thank you for everything and to let you know that I am o.k. A Maelstrom of people: Institute, Rudi, de Neufville, Krac,[1] Martha Everett,[2] Lazarsfeld and God knows who else. Julie very kind and charming, had breakfast with her to-day. Appartment agreeable; I behave like a good Roy. The fort-night with you did lots of good to me. I hope you will enjoy the rest of the vacation and come back in high spirit. Monday lunch with D. Taylor. – Ali Baba[3] behaves well and sends you his kindest regards. It is nice to be in N.Y. again, I have a load of Heimatsgefühle, notwithstanding the beauty of the West coast.

Take good care of yourself.
All kisses from the old big hippopotamus king
Archibald Stumpfnase Kant von Bauchschleifer.

Original: handwritten letter. Translator's note: written in English.

1 Siegfried Kracauer.

2 Unknown.

3 Luli Deste's Afghan hound, which was in Los Angeles with Gretel Adorno at the time, however. Adorno had probably received a letter from his wife in which she mentioned the dog.

89   LOS ANGELES, 6.9.1943

6 Sept. 1943

My dears,
    we found your house key in Teddie's wallet, and are returning it to you immediately by registered mail, with many thanks. Archie arrived here in good shape with a 2-hour delay, and by today had already recovered entirely from the strain of the journey; the last remnants of his cold should most likely also be gone soon. As Pollock stayed here a few days longer, Teddie still met him after all, but we also have a week of after-holidays, so to speak, which is especially nice after being separated for so long. Today we immediately took a long walk with

Ali Baba, which Teddie found exceedingly enjoyable. With all this 'news', I have still not thanked you for the delightful little blanket. It is so sweet of Marinumba always to think of me and give me such lovely gifts. What have I done to deserve this? A thousand thanks my dear good animal. Hugs and kisses from your old
                              Giraffe Gazelle

My dears, the return journey went absolutely smoothly and according to plan. In Michigan I met E[1] and Lotte; E with a heavy cold, while my own – perhaps an allergy after all – broke out immediately amid the greenery, and accompanied me quite heavily all the way here (much better now). The day with the two very nice, in the evening to Chicago. Next morning met Luli punctually at the train, she was incredibly happy and cried like a child. She looked bad and stressed. In the 3 hours I had with her discussed her affairs, in which I had assisted as far as possible. Very sad farewell. Afternoon and evening with Miss Reinheimer,[2] whom we shall probably employ. Return journey very interesting with a labour leader of the CIO[3] and a cowboy who reads Schopenhauer (!) and Nietzsche, 2¼ hours delay, collected by Giraffe, who looks excellent and truly well recovered. In the car Ali Baba, with whom things are going well. In the evening then Max and Maidon. Yesterday peace and air. In the evening at a meeting[4] with Jewish bigwigs.

Dear WK, you must report the lost possessions as precisely and *comprehensively* as possible. There is no doubt that very *serious* efforts are being made for a full restitution for Jews over there. List Hippo Cow accounts as *yours*, WK (joint property). I seriously consider this *extremely* important and *know* that the entire complex is already being widely supported.

It was so enjoyable to stay with you – another thousand thanks for that. I hope you have meanwhile recovered *from* me as well as I did *with* you.

I urgently hope that we shall see each other again soon. Everything can happen much more quickly than it seems at present. That is also Max's opinion. At any rate, everything is looking much brighter.

Take good care of yourselves, and may the good but obstinate daughter of the giant Archinumba (– a wonderful, truly good-hearted woman) follow her seasoned warden and not get up to any mischief, which also goes for him. So that you are in good shape next time.

Heartiest kisses from your old,
                      reluctantly world-travelling child
                      Teddie

Original: handwritten letter.

1 Egon Wissing.

2 Jane Constance Reinheimer worked as an assistant on the anti-Semitism project in 1943 and 1944; she was still studying sociology in Chicago at the time.

3 Committee for Industrial Organization, an American trade union, founded in 1935, that also accepted coloured people and untrained workers.

4 *meeting*: EO.

Los Angeles, 26 September 1943

My dear faithful best old Wondrous Hippo Cow Marinumba,
     when I congratulated you on your birthday one year ago, I wrote that I believed our fate would have been decided by the time of your next – the present – one. Now it looks as if I was not promising too much. I think that, in military terms, Germany's fate is sealed – even now, before the power of the Allies has reached its pinnacle, and one must almost hope that it does not happen too quickly: that there is not a political collapse which would spare the Germans an open military defeat instead of making them feel themselves what they have done, to prevent them from hatching any new mischief and infecting the world, which is so open to infection . . . But in any case, I would not even give them another year, and thus solemnly wish for you and for all of us that we might witness the fall of Hitler and the revenge[1] within the next 12 months. For I have nothing against revenge as such, even if I do not wish to be its executor – I object only to its rationalization as justice and law. So: may the little Horst Günthers revel in their own blood, and the Inges be handed over to the Polish brothels, with extra vouchers for Jews. And may they return to us, as to the others, what they have stolen: for there is about as much similarity between organized theft by the oppressors and socialism as there is between heaven and hell. And may you live in good health, wisdom and mobility, to experience all that with full consciousness, and to feel your homeland given back to you at least morally, even if the practical side might take a while yet, despite the fall of the racket.[2] And may the wave of victory lead your Hippo King – who in absolute terms is perhaps heavy, but relative to events still rather light – and his wife, the dear Giraffe Gazelle with the ridiculous little horns, to undertake an extensive visit to New York that is not filled with conferences, if the journey here is still too strenuous for you (this will be one of the first things to change once the war is over). You see, Marinumba my animal, daughter of the wonderful Archinumba and friend of Espérance de Walros, I have a great

149

deal to wish you this time, but the extent of what happened, after all, justifies such energetic wishes. And we shall view your next birthday in 1944 as the springboard for your 80th. Enjoy your celebrations and think of us, as we too thought quite especially of you on my 40th with a bottle of Forster (this time only Max and Maidon were there). I am heartily looking forward to the apricot, but WK should not for God's sake rush or put himself out, especially as I am abstaining from alcohol for a few weeks, as in the Poconos, which is doing me a lot of good. I hope the giant mother-animal received her little present.

Otherwise, my health has not been so good – hence my infrequent letters. The mysterious cold, probably allergic = hay fever after all, which was gone entirely in New York, took strong hold of me in Michigan and then in Chicago, and tormented me to such a degree, especially on the journey here, that I arrived in a quite pitiful condition. Then the cold shifted to the head, with the most incredible headaches and a quite unnatural drowsiness, until I went to the doctor – something I decide upon most reluctantly – who diagnosed neuralgia, so not the frontal sinuses. With the aid of 3 Vitamin B1 injections, which my body received especially well, then vitamin tablets, Empyrine and heat pads, we managed – as they say here – to 'fix' me again, so that I am now quite fit again and working all day with Max (on the side I am completing an analysis of the fascist agitator Thomas, i.e. correcting it and making some additions). My work with Max is proceeding especially well.

Otherwise there is little to tell – we have been seeing as few people as possible due to my health, albeit still too many. We were invited to a premiere at Warner[3] as prominent refugees,[4] without knowing why, along with Max, Thomas Mann, the Brechts and very few others, and the day before yesterday we visited the old Hahns and Norah, who sends you many fond regards. Rather sad letters from Luli, consisting mostly of curses upon the world, which in essence are perfectly justi-fied, but in her case sometimes directed at the wrong people, like the good Otto de Neufville.[5] From this distance it is very difficult to help her; I would have to 'coach' her, and that is a lifelong job for which I lack the time. She seems to have struck up quite a friendship in N.Y. with Martha Lehner and her husband, to whom I had recommended her. Ali Baba is a source of endless joy to us. He is the most beautiful and noble dog I have ever seen – so devoid of greed that almost all the people I know would do well to take him as an example, and com-pletely innocent with us. The leopard-hunter most likes drinking milk. On the other hand, he passionately loves driving in the car; as soon as he hears it he comes along and pounces in with a single jump. You really cannot imagine his exotic elegance. Most of the time he looks like Marquis Posa, sometimes like Pierrot lunaire, sometimes like an African sorcerer and sometimes like a great cocotte. Wherever we take him there is sensation – from enthusiastic people who want to stroke him (which he tolerates with complete indifference) to children who – quite unjustly – run away, or youths who taunt him for his peculiarity, to which he no more reacts than we do. Anna Loeb, incidentally, whom I found particularly appealing once again, also saw him. That morning, at the beach, Ali and I encountered an Afghan *bitch* – the two magical animals were quite entranced by one another for some minutes. – Zilzer, incidentally, Lotte Mosbacher's husband, is currently playing Goebbels in a film about Goebbels,[6] and in another one our friend Granach is playing Streicher and Kortner is playing Gregor Strasser – so we know the whole gang in their mirror-images.

Aschaffenburg, respect: tomorrow we are invited – by ourselves – to dinner at the house of Thomas Mann.[7] He read my 'Philosophie der neuen Musik', and was so impressed that he wants to discuss it in detail with me and read me parts of his new novel, about a musician (the protagonist is somehow based on Schönberg), on which he would like to know my opinion. Well, perhaps he will become Reichspräsident . . . He is very pleasant, friendly and cultivated, in any case, even if he is no longer at the height of his intellectual powers, and we enjoy his company.

But now I have filled your poor heads with enough of my words, and can already see our good WK complaining about the lack of paragraphs, although he can see from this letter that few paragraphs do not necessarily go hand in hand with theoretical difficulty. But I will gladly promise you to divide the next letter (not my texts . . .) into more paragraphs. Enjoy yourselves and think of me with love, even if I do not know what oil-heating is (if only there were enough oil in the winter . . .)

Heartiest kisses to both of you from your now also
forty-year-old, old child

Teddie

The key is for the institute – please give it to Leo when you have the opportunity, when he drops in, and forgive the muddle. It was well meant.

Should I send Lina[8] some of my texts in English?

Original: typewritten letter with handwritten postscript.

1 In an aphorism from *Minima Moralia* dated autumn 1944, Adorno writes: 'I have only two possible answers to the question of what to do with Germany after its defeat. One would be: I do not under any circumstances wish to be an executioner, or to supply legal justification for executioners. The other would be: I do not wish to prevent anyone – least of all by means of the law – from taking revenge for what happened. That is a thoroughly unsatisfactory and contradictory answer, and one that defies both generalization and actual practice. But perhaps the error already lies in the question, not only in my answer.'

151

2 *racket*: EO.

3 Further details unknown.

4 *refugees*: EO.

5 Hermann Otto de Neufville (1897–1979), a brother of Robert (see letter no. 19, note 1).

6 John Farrow's *The Hitler Gang* of 1944, which retraced the histories of the highest-ranking Nazis.

7 On 27 September, Thomas Mann noted in his diary: 'In Adorno's text./– He came to dinner with his wife./At the table discussed details of the philosophy of music./Afterwards reading of the chapter of lectures./Intimacy with music confirmed with praise./Objections to details, some of which can easily be taken into account, others hardly at all. On the whole served to reassure me. Appointment for Friday' (Thomas Mann, *Tagebücher 1940–43*, ed. Peter de Mendelssohn [Frankfurt am Main, 1982], p. 631).

8 Presumably the doctor Lina Wingfield (1899–1968), Adorno's English cousin; see Evelyn Wilcock, 'Adorno's Uncle: Dr Bernard Wingfield and the English Exile of Theodor W. Adorno 1934–8', *German Life and Letters* 49 (3 July 1996), pp. 324–38, here p. 327.

91   LOS ANGELES, AFTER 5.10.1943

Schwäbische Eisenbahn.[1]

Auf de schwäbische Eisenbahne
Gibt's gar viele Stazione:
Stuggert, Ulm ond Biberach,
Meklabeura, Durlesbach.

Auf de schwäbische Eisenbahne
Gibt's auch viele Restauratione,
Wo mer essa ond trinka ka,
Alles was der Maga ma.

Auf de schwäbische Eisenbahne
Dürfe Küh ond Öchsle fahre,
Büble, Mädle Weib ond Ma,
Ond der wos verzahle ka.

Auf de schwäbische Eisenbahne
Derf nit mit, was hot en Fahne
Sonst könnt man im Wage gerbe
Ond das Wägele verderbe.

Auf de schwäbische Eisenbahne
Wollt amol a Bäuerle fahre,
Geht an d' Kaß ond lupft de Hut:
'A Billetle! Sind so gut!'

Einen Bock hat er gekauft,
Ond damit er net verlauft:
Bindet ihn der gute Ma,
Hinten an de Wage na!

Böckle tu no wacker springe,
Z' fresse wird i dir scho bringe,
Also schwätzt der gute Ma,
Ond zündet sich sei Pfeifle an.

Als des Zügle wieder staut
's Bäuerle nach sein Böckle schaut.
Findet er bloß Kopf und Seil,
Hinte an dem Wageteil!

Do packt de Baure a arger Zora,
Er nimmt de Geisbock an de Hora,
Schmeißt en was er schmeiße ka,
Dem Schaffner an de Ohre na!

Des ist des Liedle von dem Baure,
Der sein Gaisbock hat verlaure:
Gaisbock ond sein traurigs End.
Himmel Stuegert Sapperment!

So jetzt wer des Liedle gsonge,
Hots Euch recht en d' Ohre klonge,
Stoßet mit de Gläser an,
Uffs Wohl der schwäbische Einsenbahn!

My dears,

Max found this in the 'Californian Staatszeitung', and we are sending you a transcription, as you were always looking for it. Everything o.k. here. More soon!

Kisses from Archibald and Gazelle

Walter Herbert and Anita Lothar were here. We had a look at his Rose Masque (the English west coast[2] version of Die Fledermaus), the musical performance was, with provincial mise en scène, carried out with infinite care, very pretty, with a delightful Adele and an excellent Ostrofsky. Marinumba would have enjoyed it.

Our dinner for the Thomas Manns was a great success. Resulted in the letter enclosed.[3] Please return it when you get the chance.

Fond regards

ever

your Giraffe

Original: handwritten letter – alternately by Adorno and Gretel Adorno – on the typescript of 'Schwäbische Eisenbahn'.

On the dating: the 'dinner for the Thomas Manns' had taken place on 4 October, and Mann's letter dates from 5 October.

1 Translator's note: this traditional song ('Swabian Railway') in Swabian dialect has been left untranslated in order to avoid contriving any far-fetched dialectal equivalents. A brief summary: after some verses praising the railway and its culinary resources, the song tells the story of a farmer who boards the train with a newly bought goat and ties it to the back of the carriage in order not to lose it. After smoking a pipe, the farmer goes to see to the goat, but finds only the rope and its head left, presumably as a result of the goat's hazardous position. In a fit of rage, he goes to the conductor and throws the goat's remnants in his face. The song concludes with a toast to the Swabian railway.

2 *west coast*: EO.

3 Thomas Mann's first letter to Adorno, see Theodor W. Adorno and Thomas Mann, *Correspondence 1943–55*, ed. Christoph Gödde and Thomas Sprecher, trans. Nicholas Walker (Cambridge: Polity, 2006), p. 9.

92 LOS ANGELES, 20.10.1943

20 October 1943

My dears,
a thousand thanks for your kind letter of the 16th with the lines by Thomas Mann. Kretzschmar, whom you had asked me about, is neither a reader nor a publisher nor any sort of real person, but rather a figure from Thomas Mann's new novel, about a musician, from which he has read me a good deal and for which I am acting as a manner of musical advisor (he rewrote an entire section after a discussion with me,[1] but that is strictly confidential, do not even tell dear Julie, as I absolutely want to avoid any of the Jewry getting wind of it somehow).

I find it moving that you are investing such effort in the statement of assets, and hope that something comes of it for you and for us – though the stately figures give cause for hope, even when considerably reduced. As both Milton Seligmann and old Hahn are doing exactly the same, and with the greatest vigour, and the latter at least has had a sort of sixth sense for money his whole life, it is surely no Don Quixotery to pursue the matter. I consider it very important to make several copies of the detailed list, and perhaps also have these certified by a public notary.[2] For the copy one hands in most likely ends up in a file,[3] where it can easily get lost. We have insisted that Fritz should do the same. Make sure you do not put yourself out with

154

the completion of the Ration Book,[4] and generally be careful under the present weather conditions. I would advise you to chew Aspergum, a chewing gum impregnated with Aspirin, which is very good for infections and even acute colds. I certainly found it very helpful.

Our work is proceeding at a good pace. We went to Laguna Beach the other day in connection with the Jew project, an indescribably beautiful southern lakeside spot in the middle between San Diego and here. And we are generally keeping up good connections with our Jewish bigwigs. I received Julie's sweet letter without any problems, and Giraffe also got the crocheting thread. I have not heard from Virgil Thomson yet,[5] but Berlin was here; he is now at the English embassy in Washington, and we spent a very pleasant evening with him. He was in England recently, and said that everything, especially in Oxford, was unchanged. I would be very grateful for the article 'Silence of the Sea'[6] – it has been a long time since I had a copy of Life. I expect you already know that the Musicological Society has made me a member – they approached me, not vice versa.

Otherwise we have little to report, I am in full health again and feeling so well that I intend to donate some more blood.

Heartiest kisses

from your old Hippo King
Archibald, m.p. and
his royal consort
Giraffe Gazelle

Original: typewritten letter.

1 Thomas Mann revised Kretzschmar's lecture on Beethoven's final Piano Sonata, op. 111, in the eighth chapter of *Doktor Faustus*, between 5 and 8 October.

2 *public notary*: EO.

3 *file*: EO.

4 *Ration Book*: EO.

5 No correspondence with Virgil Thomson from that time has been preserved among Adorno's belongings.

6 In the issue of *Life* from 11 October (pp. 102–14), there was an article about the novel *Le Silence de la Mer*, published secretly in occupied France in 1942. The author Vercors – the pseudonym of Jean Bruller (1902–1991) – was co-founder of 'Les Éditions de Minuit'. An American translation was published in 1944.

11 November 1943

My dears,
a thousand thanks for your letter. We would have answered immediately, but there was such a frightful amount of work to do – this is
literally our first free minute.

The story about Hermann Grab[1] is indescribably funny, and
vaguely reminiscent of Jewish jokes of the type 'für mein Gesund ist
mir nix zu teuer'.[2] I thoroughly despise that way of establishing personal connections[3] as soon as one 'needs' them for something, and not
for the people themselves, and I find it difficult to reconcile such
impropriety with Hermann's usual fine behaviour. Unless there are
scores of barbaric merchants hiding behind a thin layer of refinement.
The only thing which excuses him is a truly neurotic fear of not coping
with life, which can lead him to behave in the most unworthy and tact-
less fashion as soon as he glimpses a chance of improving his lot,
which is not even an especially hard one. Incidentally, I had introduced
him to Julie in a manner that did not leave room for any doubt either
about the nature of the relationship or about Julie's 'social status'.[4] She
will no doubt confirm this to you.

Aside from my work with Max, which is very intensive and proceeding well, I am also taking care of my part of the anti-Semitism
project, the analysis of speeches by Martin Luther Thomas,[5] which
spans about 150 pages of type. There is very little in it about anti-
Semitism in the more specific sense; I have rather shown, as systematically as possible, all the typical tricks and twists of fascist propaganda
and assigned keywords to them, so that they can easily be identified
and dispatched whenever they occur in propaganda speeches. I hope it
is genuinely a contribution, however small, to the fight against this evil,
which even a victorious end to the war will naturally not eliminate.

The war itself truly seems to be going better than ever, and I would
not be surprised if Germany fell soon, even if I do not consider it a certainty. But, at any rate, the only ones who could really profit from
drawing out the war are those at the upper end of the Nazi hierarchy,
and despite the terror they are able to unleash I can hardly imagine
them continuing for long, with all the country's real interests – the
population's yearning for peace and the fear of the ruling cliques –
against them. The situation is not dissimilar to the Robespierre dictatorship of 1794, which also had the power to behead anyone but
practically collapsed overnight, as its only foundation was an isolated
power separated from any social basis. Politically speaking, things
should also be looking up now after Moscow.[6]

As for our private life, there is little or nothing to report. It is a shame that the Hippo Cow will not even have the chance to hear our violinist friend Maaskoff, who would enthusiasmize her. We played the Grieg sonata together on Saturday – he was so outstanding that sometimes I merely punctuated on the piano, so that I could listen to him better. Kreisler could not have done it any better. Otherwise, we are seeing very few people except a few Jewish bigwigs, who correspond roughly to what one in Germany so charmingly used to term 'business friends'.

Sometimes we go to the cinema as research for the big project with Max.[7] On Sunday we saw Sweet Rosie O'Gradie.[8] You should go to see this completely harmless and meaningless but very sweet film sometime, especially because of the quite enchanting colours. (It is incredible what advances there have been in Technicolor technology and how much can be done with it.) The main role was played by the very pretty Betty Grable.

Ali Baba is a source of endless joy to us. He is the sweetest, prettiest, most benevolent and noble animal I have ever seen, a true sheep in wolf's clothing, and we spoil him to the best of our abilities, while members of our neighbourhood have also been paying tribute with worthy offerings of pigs' and sheep's bones. He has grown much fatter, one cannot feel his ribs anymore, and his fur is shiny. He feels absolutely at home, and is quite attached to us (Gretel's association: he is an attaché, after all). As far as that is possible with his weak and ephemeral sentiments: he often runs towards us, full of joy, to leap up at one of us, but then he forgets his intention around halfway from fatigue, and lies down with a noble gesture. We have not noticed any of his martial traits; even when he is stepped on, which happens all too easily in darkened rooms on account of his blackness, he grunts a little and leaves it at that. There is only one thing that rouses his temperament: if a car drives past with a dog sitting in it (he himself is a passionate driver). Then he runs after the car, and with his greyhound qualities he can catch even the fastest car with ease. Within three seconds he is already so far off that one can no longer see him, and only his martial barking is to be heard. Then he comes trotting back awkwardly like a bear, with a look of complete innocence on his face.

We have not heard from Luli in some time; she is evidently angry with me because I replied appeasingly to a letter in which she had poured scorn upon the harmless Otto de Neufville. Aside from financial problems, she does not seem to be badly off.

Give Julie our very warm regards and heartiest kisses to you
from your two old horses
Archibald and Giraffe Gazelle

157

Today we received your letter with the announcement of the parcel. We are both eagerly awaiting it already, and send you a thousand thanks for all the love and effort you have packed into it. We too will send off our Christmas things earlier this year: the book by Huxley – from 1928[9] – is an outstanding extrapolation of the conditions in America, and is sure to be very enjoyable for Oscar. But perhaps the Hippo Cow can read it too, or else Oscar will have to tell her all about it. The sweets will probably come directly from New York again. A little something for Julie. I wonder whether Oscar will approve of my new punch–? or is it rather a cocktail recipe: tea, orange and lemon juice, sugar, ice, rum, and apricot brandy. It really tastes very good, and enjoyed great popularity. We shall enclose a cheque for the brood. Goodnight ever your old Giraffe Gazelle

I am concerned about our good WK's eyes – and glad with all my heart that the result of the examination was a reassuring one. 'Keep up the good work' etc.

We still have no photo of Ali – heard nothing from Thomson; I will write to him in the next few days.

Musicology [Eng.] = Musikwissenschaft [Ger.]. Very boring (Peter Epstein's[10] field . . .).

Fond regards! T

Original: typewritten letter with handwritten postscript by Adorno.

1 Unknown.

2 Translator's note: this colloquial remark translates as 'when it comes to my health, no price is too high'.

3 See the aphorism 'Fish in Water' from *Minima Moralia*: '. . .' Adorno, *Minima Moralia: Reflections from Damaged Life*, trans. E. F. N. Jephcott (London: Verso, 1974), p. 23.

4 *'social status'*: EO.

5 The radio preacher Martin Luther Thomas was the founder of the West Coast fascist group 'Christian American Crusade'.

6 On 19 October, the foreign secretaries of the Soviet Union, the USA and the United Kingdom had met in Moscow and passed a resolution both for the prosecution of the Nazi regime through an international court of law and the cession of German territory.

7 Adorno and Horkheimer were evidently working at the time on the part of the *Dialectic of Enlightenment* entitled 'Culture Industry: Enlightenment as Mass Deception'.

8 The director of the film *Sweet Rosie O'Gradie*, which starred Betty Grable (1916–73), was Irving Cummings.

9 Aldous Huxley's novel *Point Counter Point*, published in 1928, does not fit the characterization here. The reference is most likely to *Brave New World*, first published in 1932.

158

10 Peter Epstein (1901–32), the younger son of Adorno's aunt Alice Epstein (née Wiesengrund; 1873–1935) and the mathematician Paul Epstein (1871–1939), who had taught in Strasbourg before the First World War, had taught in Breslau.

94 LOS ANGELES, 16.11.1943

429 WEST 117TH STREET
NEW YORK, N.Y.   Los Angeles, 16 November 1943.

My dears,
the birthday present arrived properly, well and unscathed – a thousand thanks. The packaging alone was such wondrous work and made with such care that it was almost blasphemous to take apart the huge box and all its contents, but in the end we did it after all. And everything in it was most welcome. The dressing-gown is so magnificent that I will not be using it for some time – I still have a very decent brown/coloured one. We will also be storing the liqueur for the time being. We used the meat-extract immediately, however, to make bouillon with egg precisely according to the Hippo Cow recipe, and it truly tasted superb. It helped us to devour the leftovers of a turkey,[1] which had already lasted more than a week, without ennui. May God reward you!
Otherwise no news from us, a *great deal* of work. Tomorrow Norah is coming to lunch with Mietze, who is staying with the old Hahns for a week. We were there on Sunday. – Fräulein v. Mendelssohn will no doubt have passed on our greetings to you. We have still not heard from Leo Frenkel.
Take good care of yourselves, do not forget us and write soon. We are well – cheerful and lively.
Heartiest kisses
from your old Hippo King
Archibald and his
Giraffe Gazelle

Original: typewritten letter with printed letterhead.

1 *turkey*: EO.

95 LOS ANGELES, 1.12.1943

Los Angeles, 1 December 1943

My dears, a thousand thanks for your telegram and letter. We were naturally extremely concerned about the problem with our good WK's nose. Even though I know nothing about medicine and abstain from any

159

amateurish dabbling in matters of health, I am not too stupid to be thoroughly suspicious of things that appear so suddenly and violently. It would be very kind if WK could inform us about the nature of the attack – and also about what it could have been, but ultimately was not. At any rate, we are very glad that it passed so quickly, and hope with all our hearts that it will not return, and that there is nothing more to it. We for our part have also had some health worries, like Frau Herlé and Frau Föh.[1] About 2 weeks ago poor Giraffe had a sudden attack of what we assumed to be lumbago, with the most incredible pains at the base of the spine and then in the whole leg down to the toes. After applying heat proved useless and the pains grew ever stronger, we had an x-ray carried out and diagnosed. The result: mechanical changes in the spine, making a vertebra press against the sciatic nerve and cause symptoms of sciatica. We feared an operation would be necessary. According to the report by the first orthopaedist, Dr Wilson, it seems we can get around that, but Gretel has to *stay* lying down for 4 weeks with weights attached to her so that the spine can be straightened out again, and then wear a corset for a while. The business is *harmless*, as all doctors say, with no mortal danger or other serious consequences, but extremely painful and unpleasant, and requires thorough treatment. It is still unclear whether she can be treated here at home or will have to go to hospital. We are rather sad and dejected, as you will understand, but we simply have to grit our teeth and get through it.

Otherwise nothing – under the present conditions, we were naturally doubly pleased about the naturalization. The last hearing[2] was a mere formality. There were roughly 800 people being sworn in together, the judge gave an exceedingly friendly and humane speech – the individual case had been decided long beforehand. I think the naturalization will be of some importance for our German claims – it remains to be considered what steps we should take. Incidentally, I do not believe – unlike many others (including Max, who has changed his view) that Germany's defeat is directly imminent. The ruling class has become too involved with Hitler to get out of it so easily. It will still cost a great deal of blood, probably also a German civil war. I have no doubts about the outcome, although the Russians seem to have taken on too much and Italy is strangely static.

A nice letter from Luli today, after quite a long silence – I would not want to change places with her. – Receive Frau Mendelssohn kindly, for she makes a great effort and is a faithful soul, despite her prickly old-maidishness. She is copying out my Thomas study at the moment, which is to be handed over to the committee on 8 December – a manuscript of 170 typed pages.

Heartiest kisses from your old child
Teddie

Leo Frenkel called and announced himself, but sadly did not turn up. Naturally I had invited him immediately. With the naturalization, our name change has been legalized.

Please do not fret on my account – it is a nuisance, but despite the pains it is perhaps actually less abhorrent than a proper migraine attack. Enjoy the Christmas sweets

ever your old Giraffe

Original: typewritten letter with handwritten postscripts by Theodor and Gretel Adorno.

1 Unknown.

2 *hearing*: EO.

96 LOS ANGELES, 20.12.1943

Los Angeles, 20 December 1943

My dears,

a thousand thanks for your so kind and concerned letters. The thought mentioned by WK in his first letter: namely whether Gretel's illness is really connected to a mechanical change in the spine, or rather to her overall constitution, and especially her thinness, had occurred independently to all of us, Gretel, Max and myself, and we have therefore decided not to put her through the painful, laborious, uncertain and not entirely harmless clinical orthopaedic treatment at present. We were supported in this decision by Egon, to whom we had sent the x-rays, and who had the most serious doubts about the diagnosis. Almost all people experience slight changes to the spine, and the causal connection between this change and Gretel's leg pains (supposedly due to the vertebral pressure on the sciatic nerve) is so indirect that it does not seem at all convincing to us. So Max went to a GP, an American named Alter – an experienced man of the Liefmann type, who may still not conform to the ideal of the European GP, but at least inspires confidence and does not belong to one of those rackets that are only after specialized exploitation (suffice it to say that the orthopaedist had insisted that Gretel have a *tooth* with an atrophied nerve – as a possible cause of the illness – pulled, and not by our own dentist, but rather one specifically chosen by the orthopaedist, which she then did. But if, in the orthopaedist's opinion, a tooth is responsible – why should it then be the spine? . . .). He* now also thinks that the business is related to

* [Marginal note in Adorno's hand:] Dr Alter

161

Gretel's constitution, the composition of her blood and her thinness, and is therefore treating her with injections. She is there for the second time now. Naturally it is too early to tell how successful the course is proving, but Gretel's overall condition has been decidedly better during the last week than during the previous one, part of which can certainly be attributed to psychological reasons. We now also have a maid here sometimes to do the necessary work, a pleasant Mexican girl whom we have had before and are sharing with the Kortners, who, like everyone else, have been extremely kind and helpful (Frau Brecht offered to cook for Gretel, Maidon and Norah bring food etc., so you need not worry). Gretel is in good spirits, and is also working together with me – she takes down my dictation in shorthand and then dictates it back for me to type, which still saves time. Naturally it is very tedious for her to have to lie down so much, but she crawls around a little at mealtimes, which the doctors have allowed. Once she even drove to the doctor herself, 3/4 of an hour from here. But we normally avoid that. We are learning bridge and play every Saturday evening with the Horkheimers, often till late at night, and are greatly enjoying it – though it is extraordinarily difficult to play truly well, a science of its own, as highly rationalized as modern chess.

It was terribly sweet of you to welcome the Mendel maiden, whom, to read between the lines, you do not find particularly likeable, which I can entirely understand. But for all her cyclist's qualities (I expect she flattered you blatantly, with occasional signs of awkwardness –), her reliability and tirelessness are merits that one learns to appreciate through working with other secretaries. She will also have one or two things to tell you about the general living conditions here, especially our own, that might interest you, and which I would not know so much about. Essentially she is a poor creature from a good family whom life has treated badly.

I would be happy to send you the Thomas if it genuinely interests you (which is by no means necessarily the case: it is, I hope, a successful study, but one that is essentially technical and which was conducted for external reasons, so that I was unable to burden it with any of my own ideas), but at present I do not have any available copies either here or in New York. When I find a spare one, and if you would like it, avec plaisir. I hope it will be of some help in the struggle against fascism. I consider the danger here very serious – much more serious than the sheep would dream of.

A lovely picture of Luli for Christmas and a very happy letter. Ali Baba has the patience of an angel, which, with his long black coat, he has all too frequent occasion to prove now during the almost unbearable rainy season. Whenever he comes home wet he whimpers like a child until one dries him off, and is in bliss once this has happened.

We are already trembling with fear to think that we shall have to return him one day.

Have an enjoyable Christmas – we will spend Christmas Eve up at the Horkheimers, where Giraffe can lie down. The year to come will now truly be the decisive one for us. – Incidentally: my *official* name is now simply Theodore Adorno, no W. (sadly) and also without the Ludwig . . .

Heartiest kisses – at Christmas I think of you with particular yearning, and of home –

Your old child
Teddie

Results of medical examination[1] (blood): *uric acid too high* (otherwise causes gout as sediment in limbs)

CO_2 *containing power bordering alkalosis* (presumably means too alkaline, not acidic enough)

Thinness causes ptosis of the organs, especially the right kidney, which probably also presses against the sciatic nerve.

Treatment: *Sodium Salycilele* (which I have been taking anyway for the last 5 weeks)

Diet: no citrus fruits, no proteins (beef, pork) and chicken or lamb chops

no raw fruit or vegetables

no sugar

Injections: *tissue extract combined with supra veneral cortex* (which I do not understand, will probably have to get E to explain it to me)

A girdle a sort of little corset with an extra cushion for the kidney.

Have a very nice Christmas Eve, we will think of you very much

ever your old Giraffe

Original: typewritten letter with handwritten postscript by Gretel Adorno.

1 Translator's note: as the following report frequently switches between English and German, it has been considered most practical to italicize those parts originally written in English.

1944

Los Angeles, 17 January 1944

My dears,

do not worry, and above all: do not be too cross if our messages are a little more sporadic than they should be (though I should add that the long pause was not our fault, the post simply lost our letter). It is simply a result of that exceedingly unfortunate coincidence of Gretel's illness and a particularly great amount of work. Regarding Gretel, she had a rather unpleasant week. For she had a tooth pulled that had been troubling her for a long time (and which possibly has something to do with the sciatic business), and her general condition was so poor that the wound would not heal and she had to endure the most unbearable pains, which gave her a migraine attack on top of everything else. But now it is over, and not only is the tooth better, but also – and I am very happy that I can tell you this – the leg. The pains have gradually slid down from the back of the spine through the entire leg all the way to the foot, and we are hoping that they will soon disappear to the tips of the toes. She has now also regained a sensation of warmth in the lower leg, which had long seemed dead, and the pains are generally becoming noticeably less. It may also be connected to the weather (a particularly hot day yesterday, which she made the most of on the balcony). It could still take a while, but I think the worst is behind us. Naturally she is still quite handicapped, and crawls, but drives around nonetheless. Our Mexican girl is sick again . . .

We have very little else to report, terrible amounts of work on the project and also on our own things. As it happens, there is very little mention of Jews as such in the Thomas study; it is an analysis of fascist propaganda psychology as a whole, where anti-Semitism is one motif among many others, and one that can itself only be understood in the overall context. I think WK has very much got the wrong idea about the whole study, or is rather so negatively inclined towards it that he has no idea at all. But I certainly do not intend to force it upon him.

We have been seeing relatively few people, as we cannot invite anyone here and Gretel only goes out in the most urgent cases, and to people where she can lie down. One such exception was an invitation (only ourselves and the Horkheimers) from Thomas Mann,[1] who read us long excerpts from his novel. It should interest you, but must remain confidential *at all costs*, that he not only made use of a whole series of explanations I gave him, but also cited entire passages – literally or almost literally – from an essay about Beethoven's last works[2] that I published 10 years ago. He showed me his gratitude, which God knows would not have been necessary, in an exceedingly gracious manner: in the respective chapter, where he describes certain explanations I gave him (he also portrayed me a little in the way I play and explain at the same time), he weaves in the name Wiesengrund in an extremely artful fashion on three occasions – a rather nice compensation for the loss of that decent Jewish name through the bone-headed pedantry of the authorities, which I was unable to prevent once they had got it into their heads (I always had an aversion to the name change, as you know, but it is practical – the naturalization document at least makes explicit reference to the old name). Incidentally, Thomas Mann studies every text I give him to the letter, and also takes down excerpts from most of them, for which I give him much credit (he is your age, almost 70). So evidently it is not *only* a misfortune that I did not become Franz Villinger[3] . . . However, I do not wish to nag, but rather to tell you frankly that I am a little sad at your indifference towards my work, when persons who are relatively remote from me, even those who, like Thomas Mann, are known for being particularly 'frosty', sometimes appear to have a greater sense for what is specific about me than you, the closest. Though on the other hand, I can also understand that your weary old heads want to have some peace, especially after what you have been through. Even the simplest things in life are just so damned dialectical.

The new year has started fairly well for us – may it be a friendly one for you and finally show you the prospect of an end to the present horror (– one hardly dares hope for any more). I consider it a possibility that anti-Hitler groups have already been organized in Germany and are prepared to do away with the Nazis as soon as the Allies set foot on the continent. I rather doubt that Hitler will hold out for another year – as does Max, in fact, despite his general pessimism. It can still take a while with Japan – they know they will be exterminated if they lose, and will fight with the courage of desperation.

On Thursday I will be speaking to a group of Jewish workers about our project[4] for the first time, with discussion. It will be an interesting experience.

Write soon and accept these kisses from your incorrigibly intellectual, malicious, and yet good-natured child

Teddie

Endless fun with Ali Baba. I take him for a half-hour walk every day, and in the evening, when I put him to bed with 4 dog biscuits, I sing him the lullaby by Brahms (both verses), as well as a few songs made up for him. It hardly bears thinking about what people I have promised to feed to him if he should return there. Sadly, he does not appreciate it, but is otherwise the sweetest, most beautiful and most distinguished animal one could ever imagine.

He is not malicious at all, but rather a true dear

Fond regards ever your old Giraffe

Original: typewritten letter with additional handwritten note by Gretel Adorno.

1 On 5 January; see Thomas Mann, *Tagebücher 1944–1.4.1946*, ed. Inge Jens (Frankfurt am Main: Fischer, 1986), pp. 4f.

2 The essay 'Spätstil Beethovens', first published in 1937 in the journal *Der Auftakt* (see Adorno, 'Late Style in Beethoven', in *Essays on Music*, ed. Richard Leppert [Berkeley and Los Angeles: University of California Press, 2002], pp. 564–9).

3 A nephew on his father's side.

4 Adorno's draft for the 'Address to a Meeting of the Jewish Labor Committee, January 20th, 1944' has survived in the Horkheimer-Archiv.

29 January 1944

My dears,

a thousand thanks for your sweet letters and the wonderful hippo gathering. Please do not be cross, I would have written to you at length about my illness long ago, if only I knew where I stood. During the last weeks – up to Max's departure – yesterday the 28th – my motto has been: to muddle through[1] and lie down as much as possible. We had so unbelievably much to do, and I also had to assist the healing of my jaw bone with the help of vitamins. I have an appointment with a new doctor on Monday, Dr Kling, recommended by all sorts of friends, and I shall tell you what he thinks. My general condition has improved most remarkably. If I were in New York I would no doubt have followed all WK's advice, but here, like everything, it is a little difficult. Could I get the sodium iodide solution without a prescription, for I cannot really ask the doctors here? Max will be arriving in New York on Monday, and will give five lectures[2] there at Columbia. He was very sad at having to interrupt the work here with Teddie. Archie will meanwhile relax a little, and even though we cannot hold any parties and I still find it very difficult to drive, we are still having more visitors than usual – Liesel Maaskoff will be coming to make some music this afternoon – tomorrow afternoon we will be at Salka Viertel's place – where I can also lie down. On Tuesday evening we will be hosting Mady Christians,[3] whom Archie met the other night and took a great liking to. Norah Andreae will probably be coming back from Mexico today, as her mother's 75th birthday is tomorrow.

Teddie's lecture was a success, though whether or not the study will genuinely be carried out with the Jewish workers must still be decided in New York.

I do not know if you found out through Aufbau, which apparently printed a notice, that Hans Lothar,[4] Anita Seligmann's husband, died in London of a heart attack. We do not know any more than that either. – Today we can finally send you photos of Ali Baba which the old postman took for us. But we would be very grateful if you could return them, as we naturally live in fear of the day that he leaves us, even if it will hopefully be some time yet. –

My brother-in-law[5] will probably be coming overseas[6] in the near future, though he is still unsure whether to the East or the West. And now the most important thing: how is our good Marinumba, is her face all right again?

The very fondest regards ever your
old hobbler
Giraffe Gazelle

My dears, a thousand thanks for your letter. My lack of attention to details is no callous disregard, but rather a very old defect of mine that Giraffe too always used to complain about. In this particular case I can claim extenuating circumstances on account of my complete ignorance in medical matters – especially as we have *truly* told you everything we know ourselves about Gretel's illness – and that is rather *little*, as the doctors clearly do not know anything either, and the therapy therefore consists of lying down, taking sodium salicylate and ironing with a hot steam-iron.

As far as your relationship to my work is concerned, incidentally, I am *not* thinking of the studies on music, but rather numerous others, such as:

1) the Benjamin issue (including the big piece on George, among others)

2) the essay on Spengler,[7] which treats an extremely non-specialist topic

3) the Veblen essay,[8] which should be of particular interest to WK on account of its subject-matter (critique of technocracy).

4) turning down the big essay on Thomas.

Those are all things that would pose no problems for you. – The comparison with mechanical interest = modelling and my efforts, which do not carry out predefined tasks, but are rather genuinely intended to put forward something new, is somewhat – mechanical. For that, one would really have to find nuclear fragmentation, and not know something that is being carried out by specialists – and what specialists! – all the time.

However, it was not my intention to reproach you, only to give voice to a certain sadness and the feeling that WK values all sorts of philistines, going as far down as the Villingers, more highly than his own child – that he does not duly appreciate the wondrous animal he himself produced, so to speak, and I wanted to help this appreciation along somewhat. That does not mean I love you any less. On the contrary – how much you must need my love if you do not even know what a beast I am. Apropos beast: the reason for my anger was a remark about Lore Villinger[9] in connection with Berlin.

Max, who left with the greatest reluctance (and rightfully so!), will give you a call – please receive him *with affection*, not inquisition. He is *touching* in every respect, and no one is more deserving of your love, for our sake, than he!

The speech to the workers went very well. I apologized for not speaking Yiddish, the language of the meeting. Admittedly I did not write that to Luli. – Now I am curious as to whether the workers will finance the project[10] that Max and I worked out (in place of a pitiful exposé from N.Y.).

I am taking a holiday of sorts: and have already composed a song.[11]

Did you know that Ali's tail has a name of its own: Dr Fenichel![12]

I hope the Hippo Sow will be rid of her neuralgia soon – I had it too during the summer, it is ghastly.

So: up with all animals that have tusks, horns, thick skins and trunks, and down with the Black Forest menace. Hearty kisses from your child Teddie

We have answered *every* letter. As far as I can tell, none have been lost.

Archibald m.p.

Original: handwritten letter.

1 *to muddle through*: EO.

2 These were published in revised form by Oxford University Press in 1947; see Horkheimer, *Eclipse of Reason* (New York: Continuum, 1974).

3 The Vienna-born actress Mady Christians (1892–1951), who had studied with Max Reinhardt, worked primarily at the theatre, but also acted in both silent and sound films. In 1933 she emigrated to the USA, where she performed in and directed Broadway productions.

4 Lothar's obituary states: 'Dr Hans Lothar, editor of the anti-Nazi *German-language* weekly paper "Die Zeitung", died in London, where the paper has been published since 1941. Lothar was a son of the author and theatre critic Rudolf Lothar, who died some years ago, and was formerly one of the leading editors of the business section of the "Frankfurter Zeitung" ' (*Aufbau* 14, January 1944, p. 6 [vol. 10, no. 2]).

5 Nothing is known about Egon Wissing's military post in the Pacific.

6 *overseas*: EO.

7 Adorno's essay 'Spengler nach dem Untergang' [Spengler After the Decline], which appeared in English in *Studies in Philosophy and Social Science* in 1941; see *GS* 10 [1], pp. 47–71.

8 See letter no. 44, note 7.

9 The teacher Leonore A. Villinger, born 1901, the daughter of Adorno's aunt Jenny Wiesengrund and Arnold Villinger.

10 The American Jewish Labor Committee did not finance the research project 'Anti-Semitism among Labor'. The four-volume hectographed research report, of which one copy has survived in the Max-Horkheimer-Archiv, was produced entirely by the Institute of Social Research. The Jewish Labor Committee had only supplied funds in 1942.

11 Adorno had started work on his final song cycle, *Vier Lieder nach Gedichten von Stefan George für Singstimme und Klavier*, op. 7; see Adorno, *Compositions*, ed. Heinz-Klaus Metzger and Rainer Riehn, vol. 1: *Songs for Voice and Piano* (Munich, 1980), pp. 76–85.

12 An allusion to the doctor and psychoanalyst Otto Fenichel (1897–1946), who had worked with Freud since 1915. Like Wilhelm Reich, Fenichel belonged to the Marxist faction of psychoanalysts. In 1938, following emigration stays in Oslo and Prague, he had gone to Los Angeles, where he worked as a doctor and analysis teacher.

Los Angeles, 8 February 1944

My dears,
a thousand thanks for your letter. Gretel herself told you about her condition: my impression is that she is now recovering slowly but surely; no comparison between her current state and before Christmas. The new doctor strikes me as the most sensible so far – instead of treating far-flung and problematic causes, he is concentrating on what seems more obvious, namely Gretel's inadequate blood circulation, and is curing her where it hurts. I hope she will be mobile again in 1–2 months – she is now already up to most activities once more.

I am taking a break with a little work on the book with Eisler and a draft for Max and myself.[1] Miss Christians was here, stayed until 2 o'clock in the morning, and it was especially pleasant; she is a charming and astute person. Her mother, Berta Klein (?),[2] was apparently at the Frankfurt Opera with Schröder Hanfstängel,[3] and often heard her mention the Hippo Cow's name – i.e. not Hippo Sow or Marinumba, but Calvelli-Adorno.

On Sunday at Salka's for tea. Aside from the family (with old Frau Steuermann) there was only a sportily dressed woman who was vaguely familiar. I had only noticed that Salka told her our names, but not vice versa, from which I inferred that she must be so famous that she expected us to know who she was anyway. It was only after having this thought that I recognized her as Garbo. She was pleasant and friendly, and stayed for a long time – whereas she normally leaves, out of an almost pathological shyness, any social gathering at which she encounters new faces. She is beautiful, but not as beautiful as Luli, very affected and probably not especially intellectual, to put it discreetly – comes across as someone who makes a great effort to live up, at least somewhat, to her own nimbus. Ali Baba waited in the car. He cropped up in the conversation, and Miss Garbo, who loves Afghans, requested that he be brought in. Now, Salka has three dogs of her own, two highly nervous setters and an enormous German shepherd that had just bitten Miss Garbo (it bites everyone). But the three monsters were locked away. So Ali was then allowed in. He smelled his colleagues, stormed about like mad – I had never seen him so beside himself – and suddenly, before we knew it, he had lifted his little leg by a bookshelf and made his mark upon a book by Osa Johnson[4] – in the presence of the supposedly most beautiful woman in the world. Probably Salka's dogs had done that before in the same place and he wanted to leave them his card. At any rate, one certainly cannot accuse

170

him of excessive inhibitions or lack of temperament after that. He was born here in California, incidentally, while Luli still had her ranch.

He became very sad when I told him that you had not taken much of a liking to him. He is the most beautiful and well-behaved animal in the world – does not eat his dog biscuit in the evening unless I sing him to sleep. To console him, I promised him the last of my German relatives roasted (he does not touch anything raw). Our reserves are used up now, and if the slightest trifle comes up I shall have to resort to the English ones, which I would prefer to spare him.

The Steinberg review[5] also struck me as rather racket-like, though his Beethoven has never much impressed me. On Sunday we heard Schönberg's latest work, a piano concerto, broadcast from New York, with Eduard playing and Stokowski conducting. It is a quite extraordinary, indescribably convincing and mature work that can only be compared to Beethoven's late style. The performance and transmission excellent. I called the old man afterwards and he was very happy.

I shall send you the Spengler separately; that essay was written during the worst period, when a German victory seemed certain. If only things would turn out well this year. Italy is simply inexplicable.

I consider our other controversy settled, and no longer intend to torment you with my things. One new song is finished, another almost done.

I expect WK will also hear the other lectures by Max, and I shall be very curious as to his opinion. I do not know the first, incidentally, but the others – except the last one – all the better.

Kisses from your old child

Teddie

I am glad with all my heart that the Hippo Creature no longer has any pains – regarding Herr Bohm's review: there is no *transition* to the Adagietto in the 7th – that begins with the famous second-inversion chord – but only in the 1st movement between the introduction and the main movement, which is not marked Allegretto, of course, but Vivace. B. does not know what he is talking about.

Original: typewritten letter with handwritten postscript.

1 This is Adorno's draft for a critical engagement with Paul Tillich's essay 'Man and Society in Religious Socialism', which had appeared in 1943 in the journal *Christianity and Society*. The critique was conceived as a joint letter from Adorno and Horkheimer. The draft, which has been preserved in the Theodor W. Adorno Archiv (Ts 52148–52173) and is twenty-six pages long, bears the date 16 February 1944. There does not seem to have been any joint working-out of the draft.

2 Unknown.

3 The singer Marie Schröder-Hanfstängel (1847–1917) worked at the Frankfurt Opera from 1882 to 1897; she sang, among others, the roles of Aida, Lucia, Norma, Senta and Salome. From 1897 onwards she also taught at the Hoch'sches Konservatorium in Frankfurt.

4 Osa Johnson (1894–1953) had published her autobiography *I Married an Adventure* in 1940; in it she writes about her filming trips to the South Pacific and Africa with her husband Martin Johnson.

5 The concert review of a performance of Beethoven's Seventh Symphony, as is clear from the postscript, under William Steinberg (1899–1978), a conductor of German descent who was musical director at the Frankfurt Opera from 1929 to 1933, has not been traced.

28 February 1944

My dears,
a thousand thanks for your sweet letter of the 22nd, which actually only arrived today. – Yes, I am getting better, albeit slowly. I took the sodium iodide without asking a doctor, and have now stopped that on Dr WK's advice, but have not yet felt any effects. I do not know what the primary cause of my condition is, whether it is the climate, overexertion etc., but I am taking life decidedly more enthusiastically again, if still with great caution. – Meanwhile, we had a terrible shock: Alibaba came home one evening bleeding profusely and limping; he seemed to have stepped in some glass and sustained a very deep cut to his right front paw. He had to receive stitches and spent a week in hospital. Our house was completely deserted without him. But his return was all the more touching. – Horkheimer was also sick in New York in the meantime, an irritation of the kidney; he is supposed to leave there on the 6th and come here on the 9th. – Tonight we shall be eating in town with Maidon, for it is her birthday. – Lottchen gave us the book about Stubby the little hippo, and the giraffes are there on almost all the illustrations. – Archie has completed his song cycle and two fine chapters for the Eisler book (i.e. in collaboration with Eisler), he is well rested and lively. Very many kisses your old Giraffe
A very speedy complete recovery for the dear Hippo Sow

My dears, this time the long delay is no fault of ours, for your letter only arrived today, and if there had been nothing in the mail I would have cabled. The words you both wrote were quite especially sweet and made me extremely happy, as did the fact that the Hippo Cow enjoyed the Schönberg concerto and our good and *astute* WK the

172

Spengler. – Gretel *much* better, should be back to normal in just a few weeks. I am very pleased with my 4 new songs, which you will naturally receive once I have had them duplicated. Aside from that I wrote a long draft[1] for a collaboration with Max and 3 chapters of the book on film and music with Eisler, which should soon be finished. *Despite* all that I have had quite a good rest. We are glad that our little hoof-paw, alias Reverend Trotter (because he trots so venerably), is back home and well again.

Kurt Weill and Lotte Lenya were here for quite a while; we all only heard about it by chance and shortly before their departure, but met up several times. Personally we got on superbly, though artistically we have little to talk about these days. He has become a big Broadway earner (One Touch of Venus,[2] among others).

Tonight we are going out with Maidon, whose birthday it is. Tomorrow Mady Christians is coming again before her departure. On Sunday I *might* be going to San Francisco for a few days in connection with the project.*

Did Max visit you? He wrote that he would come as soon as he found a spare moment; he is under terrible pressure. I am glad that WK liked the 3rd lecture.[3] Max was not feeling very well (kidney stones).

I agree with the Hippo Sow's judgement on Stokowski's Schubert, as I usually do in such cases – but he studied the Schönberg with great care. Which Mozart symphony is called the *'Fourth'*? (there are over 100!!). Walter is an indescribable conducting virtuoso, but in his sentiment no more than a cultivated slushmonger.

The war could still go on *forever*, as risks are being avoided at all costs. I feel like Ludwig Reis[4] in the last. What does WK think about the danger of inflation? Norah gave us quite a scare about that yesterday, but I cannot see what one should do about it.

We are fine, we are in good spirits and glad that you are well. Hopefully the Hippo Cow's knee will soon be in shape again and the swelling is genuinely only a local matter.

Heartiest kisses to you both from your old child
Teddie

Original: handwritten letter on the reverse of the title page of *The Happy Hippopotamus* by Anne Heyneman and Hugh Kappel (see fig. 3).

1 Probably that of the previous letter.

2 The Broadway premiere of the 'musical comedy' by S. J. Perelman and Ogden Nash had been on 7 October 1943, conducted by Maurice Abravanel.

* [Marginal note:] please do not mention this!

173

3 It bears the title 'The Revolt of Nature'.

4 Unknown.

Los Angeles, 12 March 1944

My dears, a thousand thanks for your very sweet letter of 4 March. We have meanwhile also heard good things about you from Max, who arrived well, albeit very rushed and still with some pains. He enthused greatly about the hour with you; is taking a few more days off, we are only starting up properly again on Thursday. We are naturally very concerned about the Hippo Cow's knee, especially the fact that it is dragging on for so long, and that the treatment from Liefmann, who is after all a competent man, proved fruitless. We too are absolutely against a puncture, unless it is truly necessary – too much of a strain on the Hippo Cow's heart. What else does L. have to say about the latter?

Regarding the reading of philosophical writings such as my little Spengler, I have only one piece of advice: not to worry so much about the *words*, look them up etc. The 'layman' greatly overestimates the importance of terminology. If one reads with a certain largesse and pays attention to the overall sense, then the individual meanings, even of unfamiliar expressions, will transpire of their own accord. Probatum. The terms are not some magical code, but in most cases rather a means of developing more *specifically* ideas that, in everyday language, are used so vaguely that they no longer really mean anything.

Luli is in Reno to get divorced – we had another very sad letter from her. Not out of the question that she might come here briefly. Sadly we are unable to take her in, as a) there is too little space and b) Max would have a fit and chase her away.

We agree with you about inflation – one can do very little at present. The war is more unclear than ever – could equally well drag on for years or end very quickly with a catastrophe for the Germans. Many things suggest that they are in fact weaker than they seem; though in the East it looks as if they had settled into the defensive and thus grown stronger.

I have not heard from Ilse[1] since the letter in which she denied having any notebook with a draft of mine. I do not hold it against her, as her mental health is still very fragile. Our current project assistant[2] reminds me of her, incidentally. Forgive the quill – all the typewriters are full of manuscripts, and now the ink is showing through this ghastly paper. Hopefully you can still read it.

174

A thousand kind wishes and a good recovery for the Wondrous Hippo Cow.
Heartiest kisses from
Your old child Teddie

My dears,
please let us know immediately how the Hippo Cow is feeling. I am struggling again – also thin and without a salt cellar, but in quite good spirits. I had a decent rest in the '6-week' holidays.
Very fondest regards
a hasty complete recovery

ever

your old

Giraffe

Original: handwritten letter.

1 Ilse Mayer.

2 Jane Constance Reinheimer.

102   LOS ANGELES, 28.3.1944

Los Angeles, 28 March 1944

My dears,
I was sick for a few days, which is why I am only answering your sweet letter today. Had a sort of stomach influenza with fever and diarrhoea, but it passed after 2 quiet days spent in bed, only with Aspirin, no doctor, so that last night we were able to dine on abalone and sea trout in our favourite inn far out by the sea, in an enchantingly beautiful spot. Incidentally, I donated blood again 2 weeks ago, the 5th time, I took it very well again and intend to do it eight times in order to join the gallon club.[1]
Touching how our good WK is looking after our good Hippo – we are so relieved that it is a nuisance but nothing more serious, above all nothing to do with her enormous heart. If the weather there is even half as lovely and warm as it is here, she should make a complete recovery very soon.
Otherwise there is nothing new here, we have resumed our own work very intensively, between that the usual contacts for the project. Actually no, we were invited to tea at the Feuchtwangers, together with Scholem Asch[2] (the most famous Jewish poet), but he did not appeal to us at all. Brecht back since Sunday, he had not written his wife a single

175

word in the 4 months of his absence in New York, not even when they made a real killing through the sale of some film rights, an amount that will give them security and independence for the next few years. But Helli is so accustomed to such treatment that it does not bother her; on the contrary, it only seems to increase her devotion to her poet-prince.

Luli's divorce is entirely on her own initiative; her husband, who has no independence at all, is resisting it, and is in no enviable situation.

Today we enclose a considerable number of pictures featuring Ali Baba in the leading and accompanying roles, and would ask you to keep them. Taken with my old camera – you will say that one can tell, but they are well meant.

Churchill's speech[3] was pathetic, and I am particularly gloomy about the course of world events, despite the Russian victories.

We would have to talk properly about the matter of experience and history; even touching on the question would completely exceed the scale of a letter. On the other hand, I still recommend liberality in the reading of philosophical texts, not getting bogged down in expressions or even individual sentences, but rather seeking to grasp the overall conceptual structure first, after which the details will become largely self-explanatory. Even I often find myself not understanding details in the texts that are most important to us, the two principal works by Hegel, and in the case of Kant I have actually made a rule of always reading forwards and backwards at the same time, so to speak. In Kant, for example, one often stumbles over some incomprehensible sentence that one thinks is about God knows what, but in truth contains no more than some pedantic observation on the disposition of the book. Incidentally, the most difficult passages in Hegel are almost entirely lacking in special terms, simply German words, and yet in a fashion that would make poor WK's head spin. Highly terminological writers such as Husserl are much easier to follow – in fact terminology is generally a means of facilitation, in the sense that it serves to fix the meanings of words, to capture them identically, whereas the greatest difficulties – admittedly also the most profound insights – are found where thought-movements take place within the words themselves, i.e. where (in a highly specific sense) the demand for 'clarity' in our *conventional* understanding of the word is suspended.

But such reflections on philosophical language are not remotely applicable to my little Spengler. It was a lecture I gave to the teachers at Columbia, and is therefore rather elementary, even in the few passages I added later. The whole thing, entre nous sois dit, was dictated on the side in three afternoons, precisely to keep it simple, while working at the same time – as my main project – on the Philosophy of New Music (unpublished and unknown to you). But enough of my stuff. Take care of yourselves, have the most beautiful Easter to be

176

found outside of Amorbach, and think of us as we shall be thinking quite especially of you.
Heartiest kisses from your old child
Teddie

My dears,
please forgive my weakness for thin little writing paper, but it is only of use for writing single-sided letters.
Hopefully the Hippo Cow's knee is already so much better that she is not even considering the possibility of consulting another doctor (Bucky, the one praised by Julie).
The two horses weighed themselves: Archie 150 in clothes, I 120, which without clothes corresponds to 143 and my European 52 kg, which I was always very happy with.
Have a very enjoyable Easter, with hoofed hugs from
Your Giraffe Gazelle

Original: handwritten letter.

1 *in order to join the gallon club*: EO.

2 The Yiddish writer Scholem Asch (1880–1957).

3 Adorno is probably thinking of Winston Churchill's radio address of 26 March 1944.

103   LOS ANGELES, 9.4.1944

Los Angeles, 9 April, Easter Sunday, 1944

My dears,
we tried to call New York as soon as we received your letter and Julie's, but did not get through. We were told at 7 in the evening to wait another 3–4 hours, which would have been between 10 and 11, but for you between 1 and 2 at night, and naturally we did not want to wake you so late. Hence I sent another cable.
I need hardly tell you how I am feeling. If only our good old WK could pull through and still see things change for the better again. I send him all my love and good wishes. As you have not cabled for the last few days and 3 days have passed since your express letter, I hope that – if each further day is indeed a step towards recovery – the worst immediate danger has passed. I so hope that the attack has not weakened him too much so that he can make a proper recovery. Is he dozing of his own accord, or is Liefmann keeping him unconscious? And are

177

the many injections etc. not too great a strain on him? But naturally we cannot judge all that from here, and so we must leave it to you and your own judgement. I am happy that Julie is there, who no doubt has a good grasp of the situation, and makes up her own mind rather than blindly following the doctor – all too often the doctors only see the specific illness, not the overall condition. Please do tell us in particular about his strength, breathing, diet etc. 3000 miles are just so terribly far – one really cannot imagine some things at that distance. Was Liefmann not on friendly terms with Thomas Mann? Perhaps it would give him additional motivation if you told him that I know Th. M. very well. My poor old Hippo, what terrible things – a hippo that has to care for its own hippo warden. What fear you must be going through, my creature. I love you terribly, am ever with you in my thoughts and kiss you on your kind huge Mother Hippo cheeks.

Your old faithful child
Teddie

My dear Hippo Cow, if only we still lived on our good old Rwanda Drive, right around the corner from you. Then we could always be with you and help you to care for our good WK. Just when you need us we cannot be with you. We think of you all the time and hope with you. Dear, dear Maria. Ever your old Gretel

Original: handwritten letter.

104   LOS ANGELES, 11.4.1944

Tuesday

My dearest Hippo Cow,

   how happy we were to learn from the telegram this morning that our good WK is feeling better at last. We are also very glad that E and Lottchen came to see you, I am sure E explained everything to you and you know that he is a good doctor. And who is Prof. Kirk?[1] Did Liefmann recommend him? A heart specialist? Did he give different instructions? How long will dear Oscar still have to remain in bed? And how is your knee? I hope you have now recovered a little from the terrible strain. I was just glad that you could at least keep Oscar at home, rather than having to put him into a hospital with all its 'business'. – Here everything is quietly taking its course; Max had an attack of gout, so Teddie is working upstairs at the Horkheimers. Please let us know if there is anything we can send WK. A thousand kisses

Your old Giraffe

178

My dears, I truly cannot tell you how happy I was yesterday
(continues overleaf so that you can read it – I really am very stupid!)

My dears, I truly cannot tell you how happy I was yesterday upon the arrival of your telegram. As we had not had any urgent messages from you, only the letter of the 6th, we had already assumed that there had been an improvement, but were still very nervous. But now I think we can hope that the worst is behind us. How these days must have been for you. WK must see to it that he does not over-exert himself, above all not do too much business to save sisters etc. – that is not what counts, nor can it be allowed to count. Do you have any idea at all what might have caused the attack, so that you can avoid such situations in future? I daresay he will still have to stay lying down for a long time – but then one must be doubly careful that he breathes deeply whenever he feels greatly weakened and gets enough fresh air. Fortunately the current weeks are among the finest in N.Y.

We really have nothing to report otherwise, except that Max topped his kidney pains by having an attack of gout too; but we are working together nonetheless, just as hard as usual. Naturally everyone is asking after WK and sending him their best wishes, in particular Max and Maidon, Norah, (who was here on Easter Sunday) and the Eislers. I refrained from writing anything to N.Y. about WK's sickness in order to spare you bothersome telephone calls, which after all cannot help anything.

It might interest you to know that we often see the Palfis, Lotte Mosbacher's first husband (much nicer than her present one) and his enchanting, quarter-Malaysian wife. She is, incidentally, a direct niece of Julius Meschaert.[2]

So, let me say this time, even more than usual: just carry on like that, and you might make something decent of yourself. Heartiest kisses from your old and once more relieved child

Teddie

Original: hand- and typewritten letter.

1 Unknown.

2 Unknown.

105   LOS ANGELES, 16.4.1944

16 April 1944

My dears:

I fear that you will have to direct your complaints at the postal service, not us, for we have been writing at least every other day, and often to Julie too.

179

Our work is going ahead at full steam again, and at the moment a lady from San Francisco[1] and the analyst Simmel[2] are here to speak about the project with Horkheimer and Teddie. Please do tell Julie that, in case things do not work out with Frau Gabriel, I also know an American woman in 114th St. – an acquaintance of Fräulein von Mendelssohn – who would be worth considering for small duties and trips etc. Hopefully WK will have his appetite back soon. Hugs

ever your
Giraffe Gazelle

My dears, hopefully WK is continuing to make such good progress, eating well and regaining his strength. Aside from work, we have little to report. No: we went bride-hunting for Ali Baba today, at the place of a doctor who lives very far out, who breeds Afghans and has 10, but none of them as magnificent as our Magic Baboon. Negotiations are still underway regarding marriage to a lady who has just become available. WK must take care, for I know how easily one overestimates one's own powers during convalescence. I wonder if he is already going for a sit on one of our benches by the Hudson? Then he must think of us as we think of him.
Heartiest kisses

from your old Hippo King
Archibald Stumpfnase Kant v.
Bauchschleifer

Original: handwritten letter.

1 Probably the psychologist and psychoanalyst Else Frenkel-Brunswik (1908–58), who had studied in Vienna with Karl and Charlotte Bühler and completed her PhD in 1930. She emigrated to the USA in 1938. From 1939 she worked at the Institute of Child Welfare in Berkeley. Else Frenkel-Brunswik worked on the institute's anti-Semitism project from 1943 onwards, in particular *The Authoritarian Personality*. In 1944 she gained a post at Berkeley.

2 The doctor and psychoanalyst Ernst Simmel (1882–1947) had been a co-founder of the Psychoanalytical Institute in Berlin in 1920 and was president of the German Psychoanalytical Society. After being imprisoned by the Nazis in 1933, but managing to escape, Simmel fled to Switzerland and emigrated to the USA in 1934, founding a centre in Los Angeles providing psychoanalytical training for doctors. From 1942 to 1944 he was president of the San Francisco Psychoanalytical Society. In 1946 he edited the book *Anti-Semitism: A Social Disease*, with contributions from Adorno, Bernhard Berliner, Else Frenkel-Brunswik and R. Nevitt Sanford, Otto Fenichel, Horkheimer, Douglass W. Orr and Simmel himself.

Los Angeles, 19 April 1944

My dears,
a thousand thanks for your message of the 16th, which just arrived here, so relatively quickly. We are very happy that the recovery is continuing, but naturally still very uneasy. The great Hippo Cow's description made it all too clear how weak he must still be. I do not know if it is a good idea, with his general bodily condition, to give him so harsh a substance (at least it never agreed with me at all) as snuff. I suppose that in the entire situation one has to choose between all possible evils. In my layman's opinion, the biggest problem is that, on the one hand, the heart should be subjected to as little strain as possible, while on the other hand he has to regain his strength, which will inevitably – through the necessarily solid diet – involve a certain effort for the weak heart. I cannot, of course, judge what decisions have to be made at each moment, but perhaps it would at least be sensible to be aware of these alternatives and discuss them with Dr L. My instinct tells me that now of all times one must counteract the loss of his powers, once the attack itself has been overcome to some degree.

Hopefully now the beloved old Giant Hippo Cow can herself rest up a little.

We hardly have any news – the Brechts were here yesterday with old Karin Michaelis,[1] who lives with them; tomorrow is old Hahn's birthday. I gave the young v. Marx an affidavit, the first since Hermann's[2] immigration. – Otherwise, we are constantly working. Max is feeling better at the moment, but he has a tendency to over-exert himself and put off a truly thorough treatment. – A marriage project for Ali Baba fell through because we do not have his papers, family tree etc.

Hopefully dear WK's recovery is finally making more energetic progress. Continue to be so reliable with your writing – every favourable message lessens the burden on our hearts.

Heartiest kisses
from your old Hippo King   Teddie

If I were an Afghan bitch, I am certain I would marry Alibaba, even without papers. It will still take a long time before I am back to normal, but my current condition is not so much painful as simply a hindrance. Fond regards
ever your Giraffe Gazelle

Original: typewritten letter with additional handwritten note by Gretel Adorno.

1 The Danish writer Karin Michaelis (1872–1950) had emigrated to the USA during the Second World War.

2 Hermann Grab.

107 LOS ANGELES, 23.4.1944

Los Angeles, 23 April 1944

My dears,
we are very happy to infer from a letter Julie sent us that our good WK is now finally feeling genuinely better, that he is eating once more and beginning to reproduce himself. I think the worst has now truly passed, and look forward with yearning to the next letter bearing his signature. In the world, the most decisive of events should truly be imminent at last, and there is nothing I long for more than for you to experience them together and still to experience together, however weak you might be, the coming of better times.

Max is also feeling better; his two kidney stones came out of their own accord, probably the other day when he was here in the evening and suddenly felt sick. We are working feverishly to wrap up a mimeo-graphed publication[1] containing much of our work in L.A.

Otherwise very little news, tonight going to a reading by our friend Granach, one of the dearest people we have met since emigrating. Hippo Cow, please write which Frau v. Marx[2] was your friend, the *mother* of Norah's son-in-law (née Goldschmidt-Rothschild) or his *grandmother*.* For we got this relationship rather mixed up in a letter for his immigration.

Heartiest kisses – and a continued good, quick and thorough recovery! Your old child

Teddie

I am eagerly proof-reading the book and otherwise letting Ali Baba tyrannize me. Hugs
Greetings [?] from your Giraffe Gazelle

Original: typewritten letter with additional handwritten note by Gretel Adorno.

1 The first issue of the *Dialectic of Enlightenment*.

2 Unknown.

* [Marginal note in Adorno's hand:] (a classic Hippo Cow situation! 'Yes ma'am, Frau v. Bauchschleifer')

Friday[1]

My dears,
we are quite over the moon that WK is feeling so much better. Hopefully it will not be so long now before he can get up and sit in the sun. Has it meanwhile worked out with the sisters or do you in fact no longer need any. I know very well that we owe Julie a vast debt of gratitude. Do you know of some gift that would bring a smile to her face?

Nothing new in Brentwood. My doctor found a quick solution to Max's attack of gout from a distance. Sadly, my case is somewhat more difficult and protracted. – The colour of Ali Baba's eyes is not blue, even though he really does look like a big tomcat sometimes, but amber. Old Hahn will be turning 86 next week, you should both take him as an example.

Continue your good recovery with hugs
ever your Giraffe Gazelle

Hail to the recovering Giant Tusker! May he soon slit open the brood's bodies with his mighty tusks, and wild snorts (even the very *last* relatives, the ones in England, will be sacrificed to him!), to the joy of his child! I am so stupid and sadistic from so much happiness, and bare my teeth for joy! Thank God you are feeling better. Kisses from your little tyrant, the young boar
Teddie

Original: handwritten letter.

1 *Friday*: EO.

2 May 1944

My dears,
hooray WK can get up again, all the hippos and giraffes are coming running to share your joy and and are letting out terrifying war-cries. Archie was a little off-colour for a few days, probably a little cold from the terrible fog. Otherwise only stubborn work to complete the book, as Max has to go to New York for two weeks for the project, at the Jews' expense. Give Julie my warm regards, with hugs from
your Giraffe Gazelle

183

My dears, so the end of the tunnel is finally in sight, and we are very happy about it. I am up again, albeit a little wobbly, but, as Kaiser Franz Joseph said, 'I do not have time to be tired', or, as Pallenberg[1] varied it: 'have no time. Am tired'. We are all working like mad on completing our big publication and hope it will turn out well. Is WK allowed to read yet, and how is his schedule[2] anyway now?

Heartiest kisses from your old child
Teddie

Original: handwritten letter.

1 The theatre actor and comedian Max Pallenberg (1877–1934).

2 *schedule*: EO.

110   LOS ANGELES, 10.5.1944

10 May 1944

My dears,

we were overjoyed to read the lines from WK, overjoyed that he can finally write himself again. But he must be very careful and not put himself out, he knows all about these things himself and will no doubt be sensible.

Meanwhile Teddie accompanied me to the doctor, and all three of us concluded that I should continue the current treatment for another few months. Then one may still have to take a special x-ray that seems to be quite unpleasant, one even has to spend a day in hospital and then decide whether an operation is advisable. But for now I am in good spirits and struggling away to pick all the burrs that Alibaba constantly gathers out of his paw.

Hugs and kisses from your
Giraffe Gazelle

My dears, never before in my life has the written word made me as happy as those lines written in pencil by WK, who has now been restored to us. Now he must only be *extremely* careful, and avoid every effort. I am not hysterical – E wrote to us especially regarding that.

Max and I are adding the finishing touches to our mimeographed book, which now bears the title 'Philosophical Fragments'. Gretel is going through it for corrections – also political ones. This is a great step forward; Max is going to N.Y. for a conference on Tuesday at the latest at the Jews' expense, and will naturally see you and tell you about it. We are in very good, raised spirits, only a few more days of

184

mad rush.[1] We will write at great length as soon as Max has gone. Heartiest kisses

from your old child
Teddie

Original: handwritten letter.

1 *rush*: EO.

111   LOS ANGELES, 5.6.1944

LA, June 5, 1944

My dear animals, very many thanks for your letter. I hope the trip[1] went well and good WK is recovering quickly and complete so that he can fully enjoy Hitler's downfall which may happen any time now. We are vacationing and utterly lazy, for that matter. Were Sunday at a big party at Thomas Mann's, with Ali Baba who danced. The day before yesterday we had unexpected visitors: Klemperers. Very nice though still in pretty poor condition, but much better. That's about all. Have a good time and think of us. Love yours ever Teddie
Many kisses the long necked Giraffe

Love from Miedecke[2]

Original: photo postcard: Santa Fe's 'Super Chief traveling thru the Orange Groves, California. One of the Santa Fe's great fleet of streamliners with gleaming stainless steel coaches, drawn by 1800 H.P. Diesel-electric locomotives, passing through the Orange Groves of California, 39¾ hours from Chicago; stamp: LOS ANGELES, JUL 5, 1944. Manuscript. Translator's note: written in English.

1 Maria and Oscar Wiesengrund had gone to Rhinebeck by the Hudson River to rest up.
2 Difficult to read; unknown.

112   LOS ANGELES, 5.6.1944

THE SUPER CHIEF

5 June 44
riding on the train

My two animals,
    I only wish to send you these wobbly greetings directly before I arrive in LA, to say that I have had a good and pleasant trip, how nice it was with you, how grateful I am for it. Hopefully again soon.

185

Before I left I still sent Julie one of '*those* Boxes' of chocolates, hopefully they arrived in good shape.

In Chicago, where I still had some project business to sort out, I saw the wonderful French film Mayerling[1] (Rudolf – Vetsera) with Boyer and Miss Darrieux. – The early morning here in southern California is paradisiacal.

Kisses from the old child

Teddie

Original: handwritten letter with printed letterhead.

1 This film from 1936 (directed by Anatole Litvak) with Charles Boyer and Danielle Darrieux in the leading roles is based on the suicides of the Austrian crown prince Rudolf von Habsburg and Baroness Maria Vetsera.

113   LOS ANGELES, 12.6.1944

Los Angeles, 12 June 1944

My dears,

a thousand thanks for all your letters, which we received this morning. I arrived here well, and happy to have put the bustle of New York behind me to return to my humane quiet atmosphere – the only thing that really made the New York trip worthwhile was seeing you, after all, and if it made you even a fraction as happy as it made me, then I can be entirely satisfied. Now I – and Max even more so – am thoroughly tired and very much ripe for a holiday, but it is no use, for we both have to go to San Francisco on Friday and give lectures on anti-Semitism there in a meeting[1] of the Psychoanalytical Society. We are going back again on Monday, and you can write to me at: Hotel Mark Hopkins, San Francisco, Calif. (incidentally one of the nicest hotels I know – the view of the city and the bays from the rooftop restaurant is a true wonder of the world, and accordingly famous). As the only speakers aside from us are the most famous living analysts (Bernfeld[2] and Fenichel, the same one after whom Ali Baba's tail is named . . .), it is a great honour, and all expenses will be covered. Now we still have to prepare the papers, but then: sleep, nothing but sleep. Never in my life have I been as tired as I have been these last few days, despite constant pill-popping. Perhaps also a first sign of ageing. Our generation is simply not as durable as yours. The sheer expenditure of nerves is too great even in the best of all possible worlds.

Last Monday I went to bed very early, and from a distance heard – at half past midnight – the telephone entering my confused dreams. It was Lu Eisler, informing us of the invasion (as she had previously reported

186

the fall of Mussolini); she had just caught the very first announcement on the radio. Naturally we still listened for a long time. So far everything has gone well. Hopefully the Allies, lacking any proper ports, will be able to land enough of the heaviest tanks and artillery to stand up to the likely attacks of the German strategic reserves. If they succeed, the worst part of the war should be over, and we can still hope for it to end this year. Things are not looking bad. I am particularly glad that you two, after the terrible heart attack, you now have every chance of experiencing the coming of better times, however gradual.

Luli was the last person I managed to see in N.Y. – she cried bitterly, the farewell was very, very sad. If I had to choose between your existence and hers at the Ambassador I would prefer yours – and watch utterly helplessly.

We celebrated Giraffe's birthday enjoyably with very few people over a few bottles of outstanding WK wine (for the first time in many months). Only Max and Maidon, the Hahns and Lu Eisler, and Norah. The wine was received with complete enthusiasm, and we drank WK's health. May it do him some good.

We saw Mietze once at Norah's place, and yesterday we were invited to the Brechts, otherwise our usual quiet and orderly life.

Nice to hear that WK now also has one of those razor-whetting devices. Interesting, incidentally, that such things are already being produced again.

Everything is a sea of blossoms here, in the most intense colours. Ali Baba has acclaimed me joyfully, but has made a habit of barking at night – and tonight, when Gretel let him out, he barked angrily at his own echo. But is the dearest and most beautiful of all animals.

WK should continue to take things slowly and recover well. Heartiest kisses from your old child

Teddie

My dears, a thousand thanks for the magnificent shawl[3] and the meat-extract, the lace no doubt looks enchanting in black too. I am happy that Archie was able to give me good news about you. When are you going to the farm? Is Julie going with you? Please give her my warmest greetings. Hugs and kisses from

your old long-necked
Giraffe Gazelle

Original: typewritten letter with additional handwritten note by Gretel Adorno.

1 *meeting*: EO. It was held on the invitation of Ernst Simmel; some of the lectures were published in 1946 in the volume *Anti-Semitism: A Social Disease*.

Horkheimer spoke on 'The Sociological Background of the Psychoanalytical Research Approach', Adorno on 'Anti-Semitism and Fascist Propaganda'.
2 The pedagogue and psychoanalyst Siegfried Bernfeld (1892–1953) had emigrated to San Francisco in 1937. He did not contribute to the aforementioned volume.
3 *shawl*: EO.

114   SAN FRANCISCO, 16.6.1944

June 16, 1944
San Francisco

My beloved, this is just to tell you that we have safely arrived, occupy marvellous rooms with a gorgeous view over the Pacific, and in elated spirits, looking forward to our papers – and I think of you. Love yours ever
Teddie

Here we are again – together. I think we make a good team.
Heartful greetings yours
Max.

Original: photo postcard: Hotel Mark Hopkins; stamp: SAN FRANCISCO, JUN 17, 1944. Manuscript. Translator's note: written in English.

115   LOS ANGELES, 22.6.1944

429 WEST 117TH STREET
NEW YORK, N.Y.

Los Angeles, 22 June 1944

My dears, a thousand thanks for your letter, which I received just now. I was naturally very shocked to learn that WK had 'fallen apart' during a little walk, as we would have said in Frankfurt. It shows just how careful he must still be, though according to Pollock, who arrived here on Monday, the weather in New York seems to have been so unbearable that even a young madcap would find it very difficult to endure. At least, I would on no account embark on the journey up the Hudson, which after all demands a certain adjustment of established living habits, without having first asked the doctor very seriously whether he considers it dangerous, or rather whether that strain strikes him as the lesser evil compared to the inhuman climate in

188

New York. It would perhaps be wise to postpone the trip a little, especially if things cool down somewhat in New York. I would also consider it questionable to travel in any way other than by car.

We returned from San Francisco thoroughly tired, but in good spirits. My lecture was the greatest success that I have ever had as a speaker in emigration. All the big names in psychoanalysis, Bernfeld, Fenichel, a number of high-ranking psychiatrists from the fleet and God knows who[1] were there, and they were actually enthusiastic – I received by far the most applause of all the speakers. You know that I am not boastful, and that objectively speaking I am entirely indifferent to popular success, but at that moment it was a pleasant sensation, and beyond that shows that I am, when it is my intention, able to communicate – which is reassuring.

Max and I have always been interested in psychoanalysis, without committing ourselves to it as a philosophy – which it is not. Nothing has changed in this respect, except that today we feel we have a deeper understanding of the connections between the unconscious processes within individual persons and the social ones between them. Max supplied the sociological 'frame of reference' in his introductory remarks, and I presented the clichés of fascist propaganda as a 'ritual'. I enclose the programme. Our lectures, together with those of the analysts, are to be published as a 'symposium'.

In the first night here I slept – with brief interruptions – from half past eight until quarter past nine the next morning. Now I am already quite well rested again. We are taking our holiday slowly – all I am doing now is going through the Eisler book, for which the rough draft was completed last week, before San Francisco. It is still unclear whether we will go to the mountains a little in August. The air would be good for us, but at the moment I dread the prospect of even the smallest journey.

Kisses, my two dear animals, from your
old child
Teddie

It is the general opinion, also among serious and well-oriented people, that Germany will be out of the war before the year is over. Let us hope so. We entirely agree with WK, incidentally. The most dangerous ones, by the way, are not the openly fascistic Reynolds and Wheeler,[2] but people like Gerald K. Smith[3] and especially McCormick[4] at the Chicago Tribune, backed with money from Ford.

Please let us know about WK's progress. We wish you all the best for the farm: pleasant hosts, friendly co-guests, good food and above all lots of peace and quiet. Many kisses from your
big faithful Giraffe

Original: typewritten letter with additional handwritten note by Gretel Adorno.

1 *God knows who*: EO.

2 Robert Rice Reynolds (1884–1963) was Democratic Senator for North Carolina from 1932 to 1945. Burton Kendall Wheeler (1882–1975), also a Democrat, was a member of Congress and founded the American First Committee with Charles A. Lindbergh in 1940. Both had shown clear fascist sympathies.

3 Gerald Lyman Kenneth Smith (1889–1975) was, like Martin Luther Thomas, an anti-Semitic radio agitator.

4 Robert Rutherford McCormick (1880–1955), owner and editor of the *Chicago Tribune*, was the model – together with Randolph Hearst – for Orson Welles's *Citizen Kane*.

116 LOS ANGELES, 24.7.1944

Los Angeles, 24 July 1944

My dears,
this is to send our very best, heartiest wishes to WK on the occasion of his birthday – above all the wish that his heart should behave well with the strength of a young boar, and that Hitler's defeat will now finally be realized. I think you have good chances of celebrating WK's 75th birthday, and then even the 80th of the Wondrous Giant Hippo Sow, in the knowledge that the Nazis, who are really the worst thing the world has ever produced, have lost power. I do not wish to over-estimate the importance of the generals' crisis,[1] although something like that cannot be very easy to bear during such an unstable phase of the war. But I think the fact that they have not succeeded in prevent-ing the invasion after 7 weeks will seal their fate. For the only truly great advantage the Germans still had was the geographical one that the Allies were unable to make the most of their numerical and mate-rial superiority. It would surely have been in the interests of the Germans to prevent the growth of a large front in France at all costs – even with the greatest losses. The fact that they were unable to do this, knowing very well that they would soon be unable to resist an enormous Allied army, proves that they are no longer free, no longer able to act reasonably, instead operating compulsively like bankrupts, stuffing one hole while being forced to open another. If one adds the evidently quite overwhelming power of the Russians, it hardly shows inappropriate optimism to expect the end to come within a year – probably sooner. It is now really more or less a matter of adding up

190

the figures for production and military resources. So the silver lining is an entire sash, and the thought of experiencing the change of fortune should give you both plenty of pep and joy.

One part of our present – the big mimeographed book by Max and myself, which is now finished, looks good and will be for sale from the autumn – will be sent once you are back and WK is fortified, in order to be up to such reading. For now he still has a period of grace. But he should at least find the parts on the culture industry and anti-Semitism directly appreciable. – As for the rest of the present, Giraffe will take care of that as soon as she has been informed as to your wishes and needs.

As for me, I have been having daily medical treatment for my neuralgia, which had actually become extremely unpleasant, not only because of the frequently ghastly pains, but above all because of my general state of exhaustion. As I had exactly the same problems last year after my trip to the East (with even stronger symptoms, though less persistence), there is reason to assume that it is connected to the climatic change, and probably specifically to breathing artificial air for days on end, which often results in such ailments. I am relaxing completely until sometime in September – and have not in fact been especially overworked by any means. And I receive extremely large doses of Vitamin B1 via injections, with clear results – yesterday in bed, today I genuinely feel much better for the first time. And the wife of an acquaintance is also giving me massages, also with considerable success. I will be back to normal soon enough. The only unpleasant thing is that the slightest decision – reaching for the telephone or walking the dog – costs me an entirely disproportionate amount of resolve. That is why I have also written more sparingly than I should or would like.

Otherwise there is little to report. We are receiving monstrous numbers of invitations, but have turned them all down. Ali Baba, our little Jesus, was prophylactically vaccinated against rabies – but a few days later there was a general dog ban, which has affected him very strongly, as he is accustomed to jumping about like mad and we cannot possibly keep up with him if we have him on a leash (he can run faster than the fastest car when he wants to). Gretel bought an endlessly long rope with a keylock, which we use to tether him outside, so that he at least has the illusion of freedom. He puts up with everything like a lamb, only casting us an occasional sad, questioning look with his indescribably beautiful eyes, and runs about whining[2] as he dreams. I do not know if I shall ever be able to keep the promises I am making him now – I am just gambling.[3] One of the more modest ones is that Aunt Jenny's[4] legs will be cooked for him in the beard of Uncle Louis (in sauerkraut fashion). Aside from that we also sing him

191

the four-verse song 'Afghan Hound, why do you cuddle' to the melody of 'Mariechen sat upon a stone'. It is immensely comforting.

Look after yourselves and enjoy the birthday celebrations. If I were with you I would take our good WK aside and tell him a few juicy atrocity stories, which he could feast upon with outrage while the Hippo Sow looks around the table silently.[5] But I am certain that your imagination does not fall short of mine. And aside from that: 'the most important thing for a hippo is peace and quiet'.

Heartiest kisses from your old daft child
Teddie

My doctor, a Berlin man by the name of Abraham, had the same trouble as WK 3 years ago – very suddenly, without any external cause. He is around my age, only a little older. Recovered completely and practises very widely; evidently very hard-working. Says that thrombosis is much more common here than in Europe, but evidently less severe – very often found e.g. among army recruits. A possible cause is the change of diet.

Q: Afghan Hound, why do you cuddle . . .?
A: I cuddle because I needs must cuddle . . .–
Q: Who tells you that you needs must cuddle? . . .
A: It is my own black nose that tells me . . .
Q: How is it that your own nose knows? . . .
A: It heard it from the ground . . .
Closing line: Now you know that I must cuddle . . .

My dears, you can tell that we are not letting the poor holiday weather – not really warm, mostly fog – get us down. For WK's birthday I wish him above all many antibodies, so that he can rejoice with us at the Hitler gang's downfall. Since things started looking more favourable on that front we are taking everything else more lightly. I wish I could fly over to you on the 30th to aid you in your rejoicing. Please let me know as soon as possible what WK would like. A great many kisses and hearty hugs from your

old Giraffe Gazelle

Original: typewritten letter with additional handwritten note by Gretel Adorno.

1 The assassination attempt on 20 July.

2 Translator's note: the translation of this word is conjectured, as the meaning of the original *gilpsen* proved impossible to find.

3 *I am just gambling*: EO.

4 Jenny Villinger.

5 Translator's note: this is an allusion to the famous book of cautionary children's tales *Der Struwwelpeter* by Heinrich Hoffmann (1809–84). One of these, entitled 'Die Geschichte vom Zappel-Philipp' [The Tale of Fidgety Philipp], tells of a boy who cannot sit still at the table, instead rocking back and forth in his chair. While his father scolds him, his mother remains passive: 'Und die Mutter blickte stumm / auf dem ganzen Tisch herum' [And his mother looked around / across the table without a sound]. This continues until Philipp falls backwards while clinging to the tablecloth, thus pulling everything on the table with him onto the ground. The formula used earlier to describe the mother is repeated (albeit in the present tense), showing her silently helpless while her husband fumes and her son lies buried under the tablecloth and dinner items.

117   LOS ANGELES, 15.8.1944

Los Angeles, 15 August 1944

My dears,
this is just to tell you that I have been feeling truly and decidedly better for the last few days. The headache is almost gone, only a sort of recollection of the ones I had – and without having to take Empyrin or Gelonida. Abraham cured me, albeit with a true kill-or-cure remedy; it was Ephedrin, taken through the nose, that made the most difference, admittedly with the side effect that I was incredibly hyper, spent a sleepless night and was as wide awake as during the daytime. Now I am beginning to recover both from the cure and the illness. I was in very poor shape – in an indescribably reduced condition that also had very strong physical effects on me.

Otherwise there is little to report – I am hardly working any more, aside from a Jewish memorandum[1] of a very urgent nature that I am hastily dictating. Max is incidentally going to New York again on the invitation of the AJC at the end of the week. As you will presumably be back by early September, you will definitely see him. The entire situation – today the invasion of southern France – is so much in flux that it is quite conceivable that I too might appear again in the foreseeable future. The whole question of Europe should become acute for us all in a few months, if not weeks.

Otherwise, the only thing to report is that we have developed quite an intense and pleasing relationship with the film actress Luise Rainer,[2] whom I had been wanting to meet for years (WK should remember her; she played – and masterfully so – the leading role in the China film The good earth, which, as I recall, he saw). Sadly she is heading east the day after tomorrow after selling her house here (she went to North Africa and Italy from a war tour, saw Naples and

193

Ravello again –). She is as pleasant as she is beautiful and talented – she is the exact opposite of Luli in that she achieves the utmost modesty through great artfulness. Our Lulilein, meanwhile, seems genuinely to be marrying her multimillionaire;[3] we had a triumphant and happy, though at the same time slightly down-hearted, letter from her that dealt mostly with her property in Long Island.

Luise Rainer also introduced us to her parents; her father was evidently a very wealthy businessman in Germany. It truly made me realize what kind, cultivated, dignified and humane parents I have. I normally take that much too much for granted[4] and must tell you quite frankly that you are not only my two dear animals, but in fact the nicest parents that ever walked the earth. Compared to the Hippo Cow, old Frau Rainer is a bridge Jewess from Café Wien, and compared to WK Herr Rainer is a joker from the Rhenish Herzberger sphere – vous comprenez. As he also had thrombosis a few years ago and is now extremely lively, this somehow seems to be a part of life here and thus seems less horrible. – Luise, admittedly, is a different matter. Who knows if Julius Herzberger[5] or Salomon Kahn[6] could not also have had a brilliant child. And she is that child, the apotheosis of that sphere. Apotheosis in the fullest sense of the word, for she looks as if she were the offspring of the god and the bayadere.[7] Though admittedly instead of mounting the pyre she has dinner[8] with Feuchtwanger (everyone is always having dinner with Feuchtwanger, who is incidentally a very amusing and pleasant person) – such is life.[9]

As you can see, I am beginning to be my old self again.

Take care, my two beautiful showpieces, look after yourselves, grow, flourish and prosper, so that I can continue to show you off, with heartiest kisses from your convalescent old child

Teddie

My dears,

I consider Archie's declarations the crassest understatements,[10] you are above all the most honoured attractions in our zoo. Queen Mother Marinumba and the only living tusk-goblin WK. Hugs

Your old

Giraffe,

who is now diligently bathing her leg
and her back
in the sun.

Original: typewritten letter with additional handwritten note by Gretel Adorno.

1 Probably the eleven-page 'Intern Memorandum on Progress of Project on Antisemitism within Labor', whose New York copy is dated 4 September 1944.

194

2 The actress Luise Rainer, born in Vienna in 1910, had moved to Hollywood in 1935 and won her second Oscar in 1937 for her role in the film *The Good Earth* (based on the novel by Pearl S. Buck). Her last Hollywood role – in *Hostages* – had been in 1943. Nothing is known about her parents.

3 The German-born engineer and inventor Paul Kollsman (1900–?), who constructed the barometric altimeter in 1928.

4 *for granted*: EO.

5 The merchant Julius Herzberger (1866–1934); no further information could be found.

6 Unknown.

7 See Goethe's ballad of the same name from 1797.

8 *dinner*: EO.

9 *such is life*: EO.

10 *understatements*: EO.

28 August 1944

My dears,
a thousand thanks for your sweet letter, we are very glad that WK is feeling so much better, that he can even stop taking his medication, hopefully the dear Hippo Cow will soon also have recovered sufficiently to forget her pains. – I have further good news about my own health: I even had to have two dresses made wider.

But today I must request WK's advice: as it seems that we can finally expect the Germans to be totally defeated in the not-too-distant future, the question of Melly's fortune is also becoming acute for us. Do you think that as an heir and present American I could stake a claim to the fortune so that it does not all disappear again? Do you know where I could take the matter? There are probably countless Americans who have property in Germany and do not want it to be buried under Germany's aggregate liabilities. On the other hand, one could perhaps also construct the argument that it was Jewish money which Melly only had up to her death, but which should then be returned to her children, i.e. Jews. We have quite reliable information that people are seriously considering compensating the Jews for their losses. Please dear WK help us, I am sure you will have better ideas than we foolish horses.

Continue your good recovery and be sensible. Alex Granach is now in New York too, perhaps he can find a way of looking you up sometime.

Hugs and kisses from your
old Giraffe Gazelle

My dears, as happy as I was to read your sweet letter, I do still worry that our good WK, under the weak protection of little Kohn, will become wild and take on *much* too *much*. 1 hour strikes me as *excessive*. *Every* sensible doctor says: rest, rest, rest. Especially as with this disposition there is often an extraordinary difference between one's subjective well-being and one's objective condition. So: I beg you *urgently* to be careful.

I am feeling much better, especially when I expose myself to the sun, but still not *entirely* well. But I can work again – and am now involved in a particularly interesting matter (anti-Semitism among labourers).[1] Also: final editing of the little book on film + music, and on 18 Sept. a lecture[2] at the university on music & fascism.

Heartiest kisses from your old child
Teddie

Original: typewritten letter with additional handwritten note by Adorno.

1 See letter no. 98, note 10.

2 Probably 'The Musical Climate for Fascism in Germany' (see *GS* 20.2, pp. 430–40).

119   LOS ANGELES, 9.9.1944

My dear ones, this is only to tell you that we had no news about Melly. If anything would have happened we certainly had heard *via* Sweden where some relatives of mine live. But I think it is also our interest to save her money. Yesterday it was already seven [years] that we all were together in Oxford.[1] We did not celebrate but only enjoyed the marvelous[2] heat of 104°. Many kisses

yours ever
Giraffe Gazelle

My dear ones, our friend Alex Granach, the famous actor, will probably visit you and I am sure you'll like him

Yours ever
Teddie

196

Original: picture postcard: Yucca in Bloom in California. The Yucca with its beautiful panicle of waxen bells is a familiar sight in the foothills of California. 'God's Candle', as it was named by the early Californians, grows from six to ten feet tall and the unique wood is often used for novelties; stamp: LOS ANGELES, SEP 9, 1944. Manuscript. Translator's note: written in English.

1 The Adornos had married there on the same day in 1937.

2 *marvelous*: sic.

Los Angeles, 26 September 1944

My faithful, dear old Wondrous Hippo Cow,
I had actually hoped that you would be able to celebrate this birthday, the seventy-ninth, in the wake of Hitler's overthrow and the liberation of Europe. But world history evidently has a sense for big dates and wishes to reserve those festivities for your eightieth birthday, upon which you will be elevated to the status of Wondrous Old Ancient Hippo Cow Lady. So today, one little year before then, all I can do is to send you the best possible wishes and the hope that you will celebrate that occasion not only in good, lively shape, but also in the knowledge that the ill-fated old world has been given a chance to see better days after all. But let me add to all that the very special wish that your health will improve, your blood pressure will drop and that you – with all due respect, insofar as one can wish a hippo cow such a thing – will not remain too fat and simply roll about in the mud, but become mobile enough to stroll comfortably along Riverside Drive again. If you do, you will no doubt always cast a glance at our old skyscraper and think of me and wish me back there again. Today I can at least tell you that there are good chances of seeing each other again in the not-too-distant future. As you will have heard by now, Max – after considering the matter together, and for a number of very sound reasons – has accepted a post as scientific consultant, in fact: Research Director of the American Jewish Committee. He is going to N.Y. for a considerable time at the end of October, but will keep his residence here. As the projects that have been planned are to be carried out primarily by the institute (which, as the old Jews say, is 'getting into the business' in this manner), it is very likely that in a number of months I shall also turn up in N.Y. for a few weeks, or even months, and join in. None of this is certain, and I ask you to maintain complete discretion (except regarding Max's post, which is public), to avoid any frightful

197

Jew-babble,[1] and I do not want to make your mouths water for nothing, but I think there is a decent chance. And the more frequently we see each other, of course, the happier I shall be. Now, meanwhile, I have more than enough to do, with the conclusion of our part of the Labor Project, and then with the studies that we have going on at Berkeley, where I shall probably have to go quite often (i.e. so to San Francisco).

I am in much better health now, though still not entirely in shape, but at least I have not had any headaches for days, and the last ones were much weaker, especially since catching a morning cold in Hippo Cow fashion.

It goes without saying that our New York plans are very much connected to the considerations regarding Europe – one is simply much closer to the action there, or rather the end of the action. In this context I would ask WK once more to give some thought to the question raised by Gretel regarding our claims to assets. As far as your claims over there are concerned, one should perhaps consider that we are already Americans, while you are not. It is a whole can of worms that I simply do not have enough time to pursue, but which our good WK can reflect upon quietly in his armchair.

Just one more thing: what would you like for your birthday? We do not, after all, want to give you something that is not really of use to you, and at such a distance it is so difficult to see what you could do with most. So, my good giant animal, do not write: I do not need anything, but make your royal wishes known to us unashamedly and with due authority.

I would only like to append the egoistic wish that you should be able to sniff at me with your own nose soon.

Ali Baba, our little Christ child, appends his warmest regards. He is as good a dog as he is a beautiful one. If only you could see him sometime.

Heartiest kisses to you both, my two dear animals, from your faithful and old child

Teddie

I had a long letter from Carl Dreyfuss, the first in many years. His business is going fairly well, but he is very concerned about fascism in Argentina.

Original: typewritten letter with handwritten postscript.

1 Translator's note: the original expression *Judde-Gediwwer* is in Hessian dialect.

12 October 1944

My dears,
great tragedy: a telegram from Luli that her wedding with the nabob has taken place; at the same time, it calls for Ali Baba to be returned to her on her luxury ranch in Long Island. The news knocked us both out; we have grown so indescribably fond of the animal, literally considered it our child, and he has also attached himself to us to such a degree that he would not even let our landlady walk him, and starts howling frightfully the minute we leave the house. For now we shall await the letter Luli promised, and will then attempt to negotiate somehow – but I do not under any circumstances want to have any other dog than a black Afghan hound, and if at all possible our little Jesus – the notion that one dog is interchangeable, one as good as any other, sickens me to the very depths of my soul.

A thousand thanks for your letter – we were already concerned at not having heard from you for so long. As far as Max's position is concerned, he will remain director of the institute, but his salary will be paid by the American Jewish Committee. They have meanwhile accepted the first of the research projects we sent them, and I am co-director of this part-project with a certain Professor Sanford from Berkeley University (in San Francisco). Maidon will be going to New York at the end of November and stay there until spring, but then return here – we are all retaining our residences here. Although the whole development is a great personal success for Max, and I may say also for me, he is by no means leaving happily, but genuinely out of a certain sense of responsibility. The interruption of our big study is equally painful to both of us and we are quite determined not to drop it, even if the world does God knows what to support us. Max will probably leave next week, and I will go to San Francisco for a week directly after that to organize the new project there. One of our female assistants[1] was just here. Aside from that I still have to wrap up the Labor Project here and write two substantial memoranda for that. Then I will have to conduct endless negotiations with all sorts of authorities (including non-Jewish ones) interested in minority protection. In other words, the immediate future holds substantially more practical tasks in store for me than the last few years, but as the next year will be quite full of activity in any case, and little suited to contemplation, that does not bother me at all.

Like WK, I also believe that the war with Germany will extend well into next year. In that regard I would also like to say that, in my opinion, it would be best if WK already transferred the German claims to me by notary *now*, for the reason that his state of health does not permit him to deal with the matter himself as energetically as necessary. I do not doubt that American claims will be given priority over German (or 'stateless') ones, and the transfer will be much more convincing if it takes place before any such regulation is made public. I need hardly tell you that I view the entire transaction as a pure formality for the purpose of salvaging as much as humanly possible. Max, whom I recently asked about the matter, also advises you to transfer the claim soon at all costs. It would at least be sensible, perhaps, for Julie to discuss it with Leo Frenkel, who might be able to obtain a good tip from his legal adviser.[2] As far as Gretel's claims are concerned, we will probably only be able to sort that out once we are in contact with Melly again. Do not forget, incidentally, to get hold of your naturalization papers now if possible. You will have been in the country for five years in January, and it is possible to submit a month earlier. The most important thing is to find witnesses for the time you spent in Florida, and I would sort that out now, as in my experience the bureaucratic search for witnesses for the time spent in other states often wastes several months. It may also help to speed up the procedure if you mention the Wondrous Hippo Cow's great age and her urgent wish to become an American citizen.

We are receiving many invitations, more than we would like with Gretel's current migraine condition, and I am already seeking to spare her as much as possible, e.g. a dinner with the heads of the Jewish community in LA that Max and I subjected ourselves to a few days ago. Yesterday we and the Dieterles went to the Horkheimers for a farewell turkey. Ali Baba is lying next to us, and has made a little nest with his paws and his tail and inserted his dear head into it, and he has no idea what is happening to him. I am sure he will not be as well off in the dog house[3] of the giant estate with however many other Afghans and cold-hearted servants as here with us, in emigration with liver sausage.

Heartiest kisses from your old child
Teddie

My dears, please be sure to buy yourselves some lovely waistcoats and clothes as birthday presents from us, and then let us know what it costs so that we can send the cheque. What would you enjoy for Christmas?
Many hugs and strokes with the little horns
from your old
Giraffe Gazelle

Original: typewritten letter with additional handwritten note by Gretel Adorno.

1 Presumably Else Frenkel-Brunswik.

2 *legal adviser*: EO.

3 *dog house*: EO.

LA, Oct. 15, 1944

My dear ones, this is just to let you know that I shall go tomorrow (Monday) to San Francisco and stay exactly one week. I shall have to meet my 'co-director', to take over things with him, and to organize the whole Project there. We planned this trip originally for the week after Max has left but the whole task is so urgent that we do not want to postpone it. If anything urgent should turn up you can reach me
c/o Prof. N. Sanford
Department of Psychology
University of California
Berkeley, Calif.
But normal mail will reach me better at home in LA than in SF. I had a few lines from Fred that he is going to lunch with you. Max will probably leave around the 20th.
　　Love from both of us
　　　　　　　Yours ever
　　　　　　　Teddie

Original: picture postcard; stamp: LOS ANGELES, OCT 16, 1944. Manuscript. Translator's note: written in English.

San Francisco, Oct. 19, 1944

My dear ones, this is just to tell you that I am o.k., enjoying this city of which I am particularly fond (unfortunately I do not live in town but in Berkeley, on the other side of the bay, but today I am here talking to some 'key people'). My negotiations, which are delicate and highly responsible, are going well; I think I managed my 'co-director', a psychology professor who became jealous, thus endangering the whole setup. I spent last evening at the S.F. Labor School, quite interesting; tonight I am going with a colleague from Berkeley (who is actually a Count Brunswik[1] of the Austrian family) and his wife, who is our ablest assistant, to 'Salome', the first time I see an Opera for many

years. I hope you are both well; take good care of yourselves. – I had
not even time to see Seligmans and Anita – acting like a member of the
managerial bureaucracy. Love yours ever
Teddie

Original: postcard; stamp: SAN FRANCISCO, OCT 19, 1944. Manuscript.
Translator's note: written in English.

1 This probably refers to the Budapest-born psychologist Egon Brunswik
(1903–1955), who was assistant professor at Berkeley. Nothing is known
about his membership of the aristocratic house of Brunswik.

124 LOS ANGELES, 30.10.1944

30 October 1944

My dears,
I returned from San Francisco safe and sound after a successful trip,
and to my great joy found the liqueur and the Hippo Cow's present
awaiting me. But: these wondrous products of the Ancient Lady's diligence are much too fine to be used as flannels. Flannels lead much too
ephemeral an existence for me to subject these delicate and lovingly
fashioned creations to such a fate. We will use them as pouches and
little cloths, and hold them in high esteem. We shall drink your health
with the schnapps.
    Thank you also for your very sweet letter. Above all, I wish to tell
you not to worry in the least about what might happen in four years.
I do not doubt that a satisfactory solution will be found then, especially as we seem to be gradually – to use the vulgar expression –
getting into the business. I consider it out of the question that we might
find ourselves in a predicament where we would be compelled to
pawn our German property claims, and would make the decision
regarding the transferral of the German claims quite independently of
that; on the other hand, however, I do think that you too will have
been naturalized by the time the matter becomes ripe for decision. For
my part, I continue to be in favour of a speedy transferral, but do not
by any means wish to force you into it.
    It should interest you to know that I had the opportunity in San
Francisco to speak to Robert Alexander,[1] an extraordinarily respected
German heart specialist from Hamburg, about our good WK. Dr
Alexander says that the chances of complete regeneration are especially
good if one contracts coronary thrombosis at a relatively advanced age,
because arterial sclerosis, paradoxical though it sounds,[2] has a tendency
to develop subsidiary arteries. Though you will no doubt understand

202

that better than I do, but at any rate: carry on like that and you could go far in life. I was especially pleased by the information, as I have far greater confidence in Alexander than in Liefmann.

Incidentally, I also had a long meeting with the vice-president of the University of California,[3] who is showing a lively interest in our project, which has the official approval of that university.

We had a delightful letter from Luli, and can keep Ali Baba for now. She wants to take him with her when she comes here with her husband, but is already hinting that she fears he would rather stay with us. He has also been a little unwell these last few days, and I gave him some sulfanilamide by mouth, which was not at all to his taste. Nonetheless, he did not even think of applying his terrible teeth to my hand, which I repeatedly inserted deep into his mouth, but rather kept spitting out the tablet with touching patience until I finally held his mouth shut so that most of the tablet did enter the organism after all.

Max has meanwhile arrived in New York, and is staying at the Oliver Cromwell.

Heartiest kisses
from your old child
Teddie

My dears,

a thousand thanks for buying the presents yourselves. It is only a shame that I can admire neither the Hippo Cow in her new dress nor WK in his smoking jacket. I enclose the cheque. But please make sure not to forget our Christmas presents for you. Our poor dog-child had a mishap at the beauty parlor[4] for dogs, i.e. his good doctor and obstetrician: while drying his long and copious fur, he got caught in the dryer and injured his leg. It cannot have hurt him at all, for he made no sound, but we had to give him large amounts of sympathy and stroking. Abominably enough, a permanent regulation has been issued that dogs have to be kept on a leash in Los Angeles. It had already been introduced once on a trial basis for 90 days, and now it has been perpetuated. We are now constantly writing fan mail to the city council to achieve at least some easing or other, e.g. letting him run freely for at least a few hours daily. Teddie has meanwhile become a very big and significant 'key people',[5] and is conducting his negotiations wonderfully. Yesterday, in that celebrity context, we frittered away our Sunday with a lecture[6] by a female student of Mr Spier[7] from Frankfurt who intends to turn palmistry into a science. We were rewarded for our enthusiasm, however, by meeting some very nice Americans who then took us to their place.

Many hugs from your old
Giraffe Gazelle

Original: typewritten letter.

1 No further information could be found regarding this Hamburg-born doctor, who died in 1959.

2 *paradoxical though it sounds*: EO.

3 Monroe E. Deutsch (1879–1955).

4 *beauty parlor*: EO.

5 *'key people'*: EO.

6 On 9 November, Adorno wrote the following to Horkheimer about the event: 'A week ago last Sunday there was an enormous gathering at the house of Simmel, with a lecture from a palmist – an abhorrent potpourri of tea-leaf superstition, fascistoid expression theory and pseudo-scientific nomenclature. She was assisted, incidentally, by Renée [Nell], who passed around the photographs of the palm lines, very much in the manner of the pretty girl who accompanies a ventriloquist. In the discussion, which was at a pathetically low level, it was only Fenichel and I who protested against this humbug, while Simmel and the deeply repugnant Eindholz glowingly defended the interpretation of palm lines.'

7 The psychoanalytically trained palmist Julius Spier, whose book *The Hands of Children* had been published posthumously in 1944; the dates of his life could not be discovered.

125 LOS ANGELES, 22.11.1944

Los Angeles, 22 November 1944

My dears,
a thousand thanks for your very sweet letter of the 10th, and forgive our silence, which was rather long this time. There was no particular reason, except that we were working quite especially intensively, among other things a long memorandum[1] evaluating our results from the survey on anti-Semitism among labourers – perhaps Fritz or Max have told you a little about it in the meantime. But we are having a long weekend[2] now, from Thanksgiving until Monday, and I am using the eve to write to you.

Ali, who feels more at home than ever here, has meanwhile started making himself comfortable on the couch and the bed in our absence, whenever we leave the doors open by accident, and casts us reproachful looks if we ask him gently to come down (sometimes he grumbles quietly, as if to say: 'And you claim to be so fond of me'). He is particularly keen on the large woollen blanket knitted by the Hippo Cow. I can certainly understand that, but not approve, on account of his claws. Aside from that he now has his last few weeks of freedom before he can only go out on a leash, but we hope that he can let off some steam on the enormous property of the people opposite, whose dog is quite a good friend of his, if the gate is kept shut.

What Fritz told you about Gretel was without any substance – she is by no means entirely cured, and above all still lacks any feeling in the one leg, but is entirely fit for action again and most importantly: she acts like someone who is fit for action. The joint work with Max has now settled into a very comfortable routine. Sometimes, after talking through the matter in depth, each of us sketches his ideas separately, but normally we discuss, agree on something and then formulate it together, often in such a manner that one of us begins a sentence and the other concludes it, which is possible because what we plan to write has always been precisely determined beforehand. There is always a unification of our opinions before anything is written down. There is not a single line in the Dialektik der Aufklärung, the Culture Industry and 'Elements of Anti-Semitism' that we did not formulate together, often many times over.

The re-election of FDR[3] is a greater blessing than one can say, especially as a guarantee that the Nazis will truly be broken. I was quite nervous beforehand. Listened to the election results until 3 o'clock during a big gathering at the Kortners. The wife (she is the actress Johanna Hofer,[4] whom the Hippo Cow may recall from Frankfurt), Salka, old Frau Steuermann, Ruth Berlau[5] (Brecht's new partner – which is why the Brechts are not here tonight) and the charming Palfis (Lotte Mosbacher's ex-husband and his beautiful new wife) are our guests tonight.

Otherwise there is quite simply nothing to report, we are living very quietly and certainly with a view to getting as much decent work done as possible. Good news from Max; his work there is starting well, but he would already like to be here again.

Heartiest kisses, my two good animals, from your old child
Teddie

Today just a brief greeting, as we still want to send off the letter. I have plenty of sugar, can I not at least send you 5 lb? Fond regards ever your
old Giraffe Gazelle

Original: typewritten letter with additional handwritten note by Gretel Adorno.

1 Probably the memorandum of 1 December 1944 headed 'Write-up of final report'; see Theodor W. Adorno Archiv, Ts 52660–52672.

2 *weekend*: EO.

3 Franklin Delano Roosevelt had won the presidential election for a second time on 7 November.

4 Adorno had seen Johanna Hofer (1896–1988) playing the role of Dina Dorn in *The Pillars of Society* by Henrik Ibsen in April 1917, as he noted in an early diary; his comments indicate that he had already seen and heard her in other roles before then.

5 The Danish writer, actress, director and photographer Ruth Berlau (1904–74) had met Brecht in Denmark; she followed him and his family to the USA in 1940 and later to East Berlin. See Ruth Berlau, *Brecht's Lai Tu. Erinnerungen und Notate* [Recollections and Notes], ed. Hans Bunge, 2nd edn (Darmstadt and Neuwied, 1985).

8 December 1944

My dears,
a thousand thanks for your letters. I am naturally a little anxious about the Hippo Cow. She has always had an inclination towards enteritis, I believe in connection with her operation, and I urgently hope that it is only the old and more or less established tendency that is now making its presence known. The most important thing: to keep up her strength. And, to offer at least my modest contribution to that: there is a good chance, albeit no certainty, that I will be turning up in New York for a few weeks sometime around February. Let us keep our fingers crossed.

We have practically nothing to report; our work is progressing intensively and is making us very happy. At the moment I am primarily occupied with finishing the basic questionnaire for the new Berkeley project.[1] It is a particularly interesting and delightful matter. My assistant is coming here for two days next week to continue working on it with me, and in January I will probably be at Berkeley again.

I had an idea regarding Else.[2] The occupation of the Saar region is surely only a matter of weeks now. The occupation troops will then no doubt require people who are intimately familiar with the situation there, far-sighted in economic matters and politically reliable. Else would be the perfect choice as economic adviser for the administration of the Saar region, and I would urgently advise her, if she intends to gain such a post, to contact either the French embassy in Buenos Aires (who is responsible for her as a Frenchwoman) or the American embassy (which will determine the administration of the Saar region). The question of which is better is a difficult one that cannot be answered from here, so she must decide that for herself. For certain reasons, I am currently unable to write to her

206

about my own idea. It would be very kind of WK if he could sort the matter out soon. She could genuinely do something useful in such a function, and at the same time it would be the given solution for her. Perhaps it would be wisest if she let the French embassy refer her to the American one, with documents relating to her earlier status as Saarland financial director and her early option for France. The actual decision will most likely depend on the Americans, but if the French 'back' her and present her history in the appropriate terms, she will doubtless be put into a higher administrative category[3] than if she were to contact the Americans relying on pot luck.

Did WK know a building or real-estate firm named Cohn und Kreh in Frankfurt? What sort of people were the owners (Cohn lived in the Zeppelinallee)?

Did you read the essay on the book Max and I wrote[4] in the November 10th issue of Aufbau, entitled 'Why are we still barbarians'? Nice enough, not exactly profound; the reviewer is an acquaintance of ours; what was he supposed to do in that paper, which should – my friend Eisler had the idea – bear the motto: Now it is time to act.

On Saturday I played chamber music again for the first time in quite a while, Mozart and a wonderful, rather intricate Bach sonata that I had practised beforehand – it went so well that the Wondrous Hippo Cow would have been delighted if she had heard it.

From the 14th onwards poor Baba will have to be kept on a leash again, but we have added our signatures to a petition demanding the abolition of this inhumane restriction of dogs' freedom of movement out here in the middle of the country.

Heartiest kisses and above all, dear Wondrous Hippo Cow, return soon and fully to your usual mild state

Your old and faithful child
Teddie

My dears,

I am quite desperate (disparate* is a heightening of desperate) because you did not write anything to me about your Christmas wishes. Today, in order not to be too late in the end, I enclose a small cheque for some nice Hippo Cow stockings if you still want them, and equally something nice that WK could use. While we were downtown the other day, I saw once again what real shops actually look like, but we were in such a hurry that we drove back home to

---

* The word *verzweifelt* had been erroneously spelled *verzwifelt* and subsequently corrected.

the country as soon as possible. Did Julie receive my parcel? With all my current projects I am hardly getting around to writing any personal letters at all.

I wish you a very very good recovery and hope to hear from you soon

Your old Giraffe Gazelle
Gretel

Original: typewritten letter.

1 This refers to the famous F-Scale.

2 Else Herzberger.

3 Translator's note: in the original, the German word *Verwaltungskategorie* had been misspelled, instead reading *Veraltungskategorie*, which would mean 'category of obsolescence'. Adorno corrected it, however, adding in the margin: 'note the typing error!! T.'

4 See Ludwig Marcuse, 'Weshalb sind wir immer noch Barbaren?', in *Aufbau* 10, November 1944, p. 22 (vol. 10, no. 45).

127 LOS ANGELES, 24.12.1944

24 December 1944

My dears,

a thousand thanks for your *very* sweet letters and the presents, which are simply much too much! I was especially pleased to receive the fountain pen. I will hold it in high esteem – for the moment I am saving it, as the one I have (also from the Hippo Cow) is still excellent.

I am especially glad that the Wondrous Hippo Cow has *completely* recovered from her gastric trouble, and equally that WK – as Julie was kind enough to tell us – is also back in shape. Then sail well, happily and carefully into the jubilee year 1945, which will bring the Hippo Cow's 80th and WK's 75th birthday. And let us hope that it will also, in spite of everything, bring the final victory over Germany.

We are continuing to work at an easy pace. Tonight only the very pleasant Palfis (the ex-husband of Lotte Mosbacher) will be here, tomorrow the Eislers, on New Year's Eve we will be at Salka's for a big party.

Max called a few days ago with Maidon, both would like to be back here, which I can understand only too well.

208

May you have enjoyable New Year's Eve celebrations, and think of us as we shall think of you. I send you the best imaginable wishes with all my heart.

Heartiest kisses

from your old child
Teddie

Original: handwritten letter.

1945

Los Angeles, 12 January 1945

My dears,

a thousand thanks for your letters and the alcohol parcel, as large and heavy as an unshapely hippo, which arrived today in the best condition, without any breakage, only a few minutes after the letter. It had been packaged with a love and care that would already have been touching in itself, even if the parcel had been empty – and it is anything but empty – considering the miserliness with which we guard all the alcohol you have ever sent us, it will be a long-lasting supply (guests are normally only served Californian booze or at the very most rum or whisky and your wine and schnapps are only opened on the most special of occasions). I really cannot tell you how happy we were. I am especially eager to sample the Bénedictine. Incidentally, we only discovered the giraffes on Gretel's belt upon closer inspection, and hold the ornamental animals in particular esteem.

It is nothing short of a scandal that the Horkheimers did not drop in on you, an outrage for which there can be no excuse. Certainly Fritz is ill, with exactly the same thing – except for the most specific symptoms – that Gretel had, and is bedridden; and Max is kept busy by the Jews until late at night, and is evidently not at all content with his lot. But considering the relationship, all this is insufficient as an explanation, and Maidon should at least have found her way to you despite all hindrances. It is not out of ill will, simply stubborn self-centredness, the inability to deviate from one's own path. I was on the point of writing a furious letter, and only refrained for the most basic material reasons. Such things are much better said than written, and also sharper, yet without becoming as objectified as they would in a letter. But you can believe me that I will give Max a thorough talking-to as soon as I am in New York. That is precisely why I would ask you not to let on when Maidon comes – vengeance is mine,[1] spake Archibald. But there is more culture in the knots of the string wrapped around the wine package than in Maidon's entire existence, and it is a mystery to me why Max lets her have her way. Our wine package from the Horkheimers has still not arrived, incidentally, despite having been announced countless times.

My current plans are – sauf imprévu, as a Louische would say – as follows: I will leave for Berkeley on 2 February, stay there for a week, go to New York on the 9th, should arrive there on the 13th. Pray that it works out and nothing gets in the way. –*

I need hardly tell you what satanic delight I derived from the news that you had terminated all relations with the brood, any more than I will divulge my reflections on Louis that followed your letter. You will see soon enough what a brood the brood is.

Allow me to pose my question about the Frankfurt building firm Cohn and Kreh (or vice versa) once more, for it is one that interests me a great deal. And, to give the dear Wondrous Hippo Sow something to do too: can you recall the name of a bank manager – possibly of a bank in Amorbach, or also one who lived there but worked at a different bank (Deutsche Bank?) – who hunted near Weckbach? And also: what is the name of the composer who wrote the Prayer of a Virgin?[2] I argued over it with Brecht, during a very pleasant and ani-mated evening here with a few very pleasant people.

New Year's Eve at Salka's place was rather lovely, a few truly beau-tiful film actresses were there and a few pleasant men and outstanding food; it was a picnic, and all the more or less Austrian ladies brought the best dishes they could cook. We stayed until almost 2 o'clock.

Do you recall, my Hippo Cow, the detective novel 'The Key to Power', which I (and the tigress) devoured voraciously in 'Das Blättchen' as a child? I made the acquaintance of its author, Georg Fröschel,[3] who writes very successful scripts for MGM here, and he gave me a proper book copy of that novel. It is very strange to see a piece of one's childhood move up in the world like that, and I was no less pleasing to him as his 'first reader' than the story, which has now become rather flimsy, was to me.

Ali Baba, of whom we enclose the latest photograph, was denounced by someone in the neighbourhood for roaming freely, and if we do not wish to pay a considerable fine we shall have to put him – the poor,

* [Marginal note in Adorno's hand along the edge of six crossed-out lines:] there was nothing bad written here, simply more outrage at your being left out, and I should not curse too much, as things are going well enough otherwise.

211

good-hearted darling, our little Grecoesque Jesus – on a leash again, despite the act of mercy at Christmas, which does not offer any complete legal protection. We are naturally very sad about this.

I believe I wrote to you that I had completed a major philosophical text,[4] but this is top secret, especially as far as Max is concerned, as it is to be a surprise for his 50th birthday.

Gretel will accompany me to San Francisco, though she will not be staying at Berkeley, but rather in town with the Alexanders,[5] who were so charming as to invite her over for a week (we are on very good terms with them, especially the enchanting wife). Dr A., who phoned us especially for that reason, says that he could cure Gretel of her rheumatic troubles, which are still not entirely gone, and we would naturally be overjoyed if it worked. We will only be seeing each other in the evenings, as I will be rushed off my feet at the university during the day.

This has now turned into a frightfully long letter, but there was so much to tell. I hope it will not do the Wondrous Hippo Cow any harm to sit around indoors for so long – but do be careful – according to Maidon's letter of yesterday, the weather in New York seems to be genuinely ghastly.

Heartiest kisses from your faithful and old
child

Teddie

My dears,

a thousand thanks for the splendid parcel. I am especially proud of the crème de cacao, but all 6 bottles are magnificent, you good man. I had better not even start complaining about Maidon, or you might no longer want anything to do with me. We take matters concerning us very lightly, as she would never find out and even means well, by her standards. But with you it is a different matter, you can be sure Archie will make that clear. Many hugs and kisses from your
old Giraffe Gazelle

Original: typewritten letter with additional handwritten note by Gretel Adorno.

1 Romans 12: 19.

2 It was, as Maria Wiesengrund noted in the margin, the Polish composer Tekla Badarzewska-Baranowska (1834–61).

3 The Vienna-born writer and scriptwriter George Froeschel (1891–1979), as he wrote his name in America. Froeschel, who worked first for the UFA and then, in the 1920s, the Ullstein-Verlag, emigrated to the USA in 1936 and went to Hollywood in 1937. He enjoyed particular success as an author of anti-Nazi films (*Mortal Storm*, 1940; *Mrs Miniver*, 1942). The novel mentioned in the letter was first published in Vienna in 1919.

4 This refers to *Minima Moralia*.
5 Robert and Charlotte Alexander.

29 Jan. 45

My dears,
  here is a sweet little farewell greeting. You can reach Teddie at Berkeley at:
  Suite 402
  2131 University Ave.
  Berkeley, Calif.
Hopefully our good Hippo Cow will soon grow nice and fat again through the cod-liver oil. I am sad that Archie is going away, but it is a comfort that he is coming to you; I would truly frightfully have liked to visit you in Westend Ave. again. The hippo boy will bring his fur and a blue winter coat to make sure he stays warm.
  Fond regards
                    your old
                    Giraffe

The very fondest regards, I am looking forward incredibly to seeing you and am keeping warm so as to arrive in good shape.[1]
                    Kisses from your child
                    Teddie

Original: handwritten letter.

1 *good shape*: EO.

21 March 1945

My dears,
  I arrived here well after a pleasant journey, with a roomette the whole way, am looking after myself and have all but got rid of my stomach neuralgia. The few days in Chicago were quite interesting, and I achieved everything there that I had intended. Here, admittedly, I was met by exceedingly sad news: our dear friend Alex Granach, whom WK recently met at Max's lecture, died suddenly in a

213

completely senseless fashion, an embolism following an appendix operation. We are indescribably sad about it.

I returned to find Giraffe looking good and generally in better shape and am full of hope that Robert Alexander will help her with thorough treatment.

I was infinitely happy to be close to you those four weeks, and only hope that it will be less hectic next time.

How did Maidon's visit go? My energetic appeal to Max seems to have helped after all. He called me again in Chicago, incidentally.

Ali Baba is sweeter and more beautiful than ever.

We just heard on the radio that there is fighting in Mainz, and that there has been a mass exodus from Frankfurt and Mannheim.

Kisses, my two dear old animals,
from your old
Hippo King
Archibald

A thousand greetings Giraffe, who is very happy with her dear Archibald.

Original: typewritten letter with a handwritten greeting from Gretel Adorno.

131   LOS ANGELES, 7.4.1945

INSTITUTE OF SOCIAL RESEARCH
429 WEST 117TH STREET
NEW YORK, N.Y.

Tel. UNiversity 4-3200
(Columbia University)
Ext. 376
7 April 1945

My dears,

a thousand thanks for your Easter letter, which remained unanswered for a few days, as I suddenly had a pile of Jewish matters to take care of.

I am glad that old Hahn, who will be 87 this month, has done something for Hermann Levi. I discussed his entire case in detail with Norah, and learned such exceedingly peculiar things that I cannot refrain from sharing them with you – naturally with the utmost discretion – i.e. absolutely no one but you and the Hippo Cow must

214

know anything about it. Neither the old Hahns nor Norah are willing to take on a serious material responsibility for Hermann. The official and entirely convincing reason is that Hermann was only a member of the investment bank for a very short time, around three years, and that they have extensive obligations to countless former employees. In reality, however, it is because of what happened when the association bank took over the investment bank. Messrs Kramer and Rosenstein,[1] who represented the Wertheimbers'[2] interests in the association bank, falsified the balance sheets when they handed over the bank. In reality the association bank was broke. Big Albert probably smelt a rat immediately, but still went in for the deal, and it was only after the bank had been taken over with those two gentlemen as directors that he fired them with reference to their manipulations. He kept Hermann, who was admittedly a friend of Kramer, but surely did not really understand the storms and atrocities at the top, because he represented the interests of the Michaelis firm in the bank and brought his own old clients with him. On the other hand, these goings-on explain why Albert demoted Hermann. The whole thing sounds like one of my made-up Louische stories, but is true. The situation is too confused to examine the moral aspects, but I cannot hold it against Norah if she does not show any great gusto over the whole business. She thinks, however, that the Michaelis firm might be willing to do something. The old South African nabob Michaelis[3] has joined his forefathers. The general assignee of his heirs is: Frederick G. Chart, London E.C.2, London Wall 4910, Building 4. Chart has countless millions at his disposal. I would write to him on fine paper in excellent British English as an old friend of Hermann that the latter worked for the association bank for years, was taken over by the investment bank in connection with the Michaelis interests and is now in a tight spot, and ask him if it would be possible, giving particular consideration to his advanced age, to pay him a pension. The way things are in Belgium, one could already achieve a great deal with modest sums (rich people always like to hear that).

Meanwhile, our wishes are starting to be fulfilled. In Germany a general commotion has broken out that I am following with unmitigated joy. I was strangely moved by the sudden appearance of names that I had not heard since childhood, such as Idstein and Camberg, where two armies have joined forces.

I have resumed medical treatment due to my neuralgia, after the pains had wandered back to the head from the body. There is a centre of inflammation in the throat–nose system. I have noticed a decisive improvement in the last two days. Gretel is looking better than she has in years, and I entertain the hope that we shall truly be able to get her back to normal again (hold your horses, Giraffe).

215

We are very happy that spring has finally come to New York and that you are getting regular doses of fresh air. That, together with the news from Germany, should do your old heads some good.
Heartiest kisses

from your old Hippo King
Teddie

A thousand congratulations on your naturalization! The sweet and well-meant poem by WK does not make it clear, however, whether you had your examination or your final hearing,[4] i.e. whether you are thus formally naturalized. If the latter were the case, you would already have had the examination before I was in N.Y. But if it was only the examination, then the actual naturalization could still take a long time – with us it took from June till November. At any rate, I am extremely happy that it worked out. The Hippo Cow as an American –

A thousand congratulations on the citizenship.[5] How nice that you kept the whole procedure secret from us. You must have had your examination long ago if you have already been sworn in now. The papers are lovely. I am happy for you and would dearly like to celebrate it.

Many kisses from your
Giraffe Gretel

Original: typewritten letter with handwritten postscript and additional hand-written note by Gretel Adorno.

1 Unknown.

2 A Frankfurt banking family; no further information found.

3 Unknown. According to a different source, the bank was taken over by the firm of Jakob Michael.

4 *final hearing*: EO.

5 *citizenship*: EO.

132   LOS ANGELES, 1.5.1945

1 May 1945

My dears,
    we have just heard the news of Hitler's death. Hopefully it is true – part of the horror of this world is that the truth always sounds like a lie and lies sound like the truth,[1] and the fascist big shots[2] are so much merely functions of their own propaganda machinery that even

whether they live or die cannot be taken in itself, but only in the context of all the publicity politics. Nonetheless, there can no longer be any doubt as to the genuine defeat of the Boches – after I had still thought, until a few days ago, that they were drawing back in order to strain the Allied connecting lines and then, as in December, further postpone the end through a counter-offensive. But no, they could not go on any longer, and everything one has been wishing for all these years has taken place: the country reduced to rubble, millions of Hansjürgens and Utes dead, the neck of the German people probably broken in such a way that it will disappear from history as the Carthaginians did after the Second Punic War. Only one cannot be nearly as happy about it as one would think. I at least cannot shake off the feeling of 'too late' – in truth, the Germans have pulled the whole of civilization down with them, and what we are now witnessing is precisely that downfall which could have been prevented if Germany's defeat had been 10 years ago. It is as if that yearning had consumed itself, and now that it has been fulfilled it lacks the ability to feel any joy. All the more so because there is every reason to believe that the principle upheld by the Nazis will outlast them – on a broader economic basis, and therefore all the more horrifically. In the face of the historical tendency, I do not feel able to hope for any more than breathing spaces and loopholes. I am nonetheless deeply grateful that you can experience this moment – for you in particular there is an element of that justice which cannot bring us nearly as much joy, and ultimately one has to say that, in reality, Hitler is the most dreadful thing there ever was, in relation to which everything else was a form of fear and expectation, but not yet real – so one can certainly be happy that it has ended. There will surely be a good few decisions facing us all soon – we shall keep you informed about everything, and would ask you to do the same. I still tend towards Europe (Austria? South of France? Italy?), not because I imagine it is ideal over there, on the contrary – but because I believe that, after what happened, there will be a greater chance of survival there. But perhaps that is also completely wrong – should there genuinely be a war between Russia and the Anglo-Saxons, that will be the end and the individual will be completely lost.

Robert Alexander was here (with Anita)[3] and gave Gretel a thorough examination. And here I can truly give you good news: in the space of less than three months' treatment her condition has improved *decisively*, subjectively and objectively – so much so that our good horse, in her own words, feels as if she has been reborn. The basal metabolism has increased from -22 to $+5$, i.e. to the normal level, her blood pressure is normal again, she has warm hands and feet, and above all her pulse has returned in her ankles – its absence was the most distressing symptom. She looks superb, 10 years younger, red-cheeked

217

without any rouge, and is in better shape than she has been in 15 years. Robert said that, if there had not been any decisive intervention, one would have had to fear the severest of complications within 2 years (Burger's disease and similar very threatening circulatory afflictions). I cannot tell you how grateful I am to him. Gretel does, incidentally, still have certain symptoms, such as headaches and lack of feeling in one lower leg, but they are certainly bearable, compensated for by her overall condition, and we hope that she will also shake those off completely. Robert is the first doctor in my life in whom I have truly had unlimited faith on account of the positive results. I think it would make him very happy if you wrote him a few lines regarding his heroic deed for Giraffe* – I can also act as 'director'. Address: Dr. and Mrs. Robert Alexander, 54 Seventh Avenue, San Francisco, Calif.

I myself am feeling much better – today without headache pills for the first time. I am taking a very long time to recover, still feel shattered in the morning and by no means in full possession of my powers, but at least a human being capable of working once more. I am going to Berkeley again for a week on the 14th to direct my project, after my co-director was here two weeks ago. I will take the opportunity to let Robert give me a thorough makeover too. He thinks I have been suffering from a sort of overall poisoning.

Look after yourselves my two dear old animals. I can imagine how WK must be hanging on the radio – even I am doing so – and the Hippo Sow will be cursing, yet still rejoicing. Repulsive, incidentally, how the mob pounced on Mussolini's mistress.[4] The people's revenge always seems to be directed less towards its oppressors than against beautiful actresses – out of sexual envy. The true revolution will succeed at the moment when this element is disabled.

Robert knew Villinger well, incidentally, Jenny too, whose youth movement clothes and flat-heeled shoes he recalled, but above all the lady friend of old Arnold, who is 20 years younger, called Hüpeden,[5] supposedly a real beauty (believe it or not) and very pleasant. The world is amazingly small. Villinger used to play the music expert . . .

Heartiest kisses

from your old and faithful hippo
Teddie

Hugs and kisses from

your old Giraffe

Original: typewritten letter.

* [Marginal note in Gretel Adorno's hand:] I think that will only be necessary once he has also brought Archie into such splendid shape.

1 See the aphorism 'Pseudomenos' from *Minima Moralia*.

2 *big shots*: EO.

3 Anita Lothar, who married Robert Alexander following his divorce.

4 Clara Petacci and Mussolini had been captured while fleeing to France on 27 April, and shot the following day; their bodies were hung up on 29 April – the day of Hitler's death.

5 Jenny L. Wiesengrund (1874–1963) had married Arnold Villinger in 1898. Their son is Franz Villinger (b. 1907). Nothing further is known about Frau Hüpeden.

133 LOS ANGELES, 10.5.1945

Los Angeles, 10 May 1945

My faithful dear old Wondrous Hippo Cow,
    a thousand thanks for your very sweet letter. My silence has been purely a result of an extremely tense week in Berkeley and San Francisco and the hectic work following it. The state of stagnation you describe is dreadful – this continuation of a condition one can barely call living is almost more frightening than the catastrophe itself was. The only remaining comfort is that he is evidently not going through any subjective suffering, but rather existing as if beneath a veil.
    I must tell you – and this is no empty phrase – how much I admire your bearing in the situation. Max, who is incidentally feeling better, was equally impressed by it. And I am quite especially touched that you continue to highlight and cut out the articles on Germany from the Times with your eighty-one-year-old Hippo Cow hooves (or paws) like poor WK. I send you my most heartfelt thanks.
    I am *much* better; I am truly feeling back to normal for the first time in a long while. Max and I will go to San Francisco at the end of the month.
    It might interest you to know that our 'Philosophical Fragments' are being published as a book, in German, by Querido in Amsterdam. The translation of the film book I wrote with Eisler is also finished, and is very worthy; that book is also supposed to be published this year. Ever more news is reaching us from Europe, especially Paris. One is no longer cut off from the world.
    Who is now to look after our interests in Germany? I enclose the very loyal letter from Alois.[1] Do you know if Schöne Aussicht 7 is still standing, and whether the firm BW[2] still exists? Alois seems to presuppose a knowledge of these matters. How dearly I would have wished for WK to have the satisfaction of at least a formal

restitution – but I daresay he is hardly aware of all this at the moment. Give him my heartiest greetings; he will no doubt understand.
And kisses to you, my old wondrous animal, from your faithful child
Teddie

Dear Hippo Cow, a surprise will be making its way to you in the coming week, and will hopefully give you some joy, but I shall not yet reveal what it is. I could put together another package of clothes if you had any use for it in Germany: a suit, a dress of mine, 2 blouses, 1 shirt. Many hugs and kisses from the old Giraffe.
We have given up our house-building efforts for the moment; it is impossible to get a permit[3] if one did not serve in the war.
Tell Oscar that we are thinking of him a great deal

Original: typewritten letter with additional handwritten note by Gretel Adorno.

1 Alois Günther, whose address in Sachsenhausen [an area in southern Frankfurt] in the famous Klappergasse (no. 28) was included in Adorno's address book, had worked as cellarer in the Wiesengrunds' wine wholesale shop.

2 The headquarters of his father's firm Bernhard Wiesengrund, whose liquidation – begun by Oscar Wiesengrund directly before his emigration in May 1939 – was completed in spring 1940.

3 *permit*: EO.

134   LOS ANGELES, 31.5.1945

31 May 1945

My dears,
many thanks for your lengthy letter. I have meanwhile returned from Berkeley – or rather San Francisco, as I was living with the Alexanders and came over each morning. I was unable to attend the conference[1] through lack of time, but I do not think I missed much; it was almost only the representatives of the South American states that were speaking during my stay. Molotoff and Eden were already gone, and Manuilski,[2] who would have interested me most (he is acting as Ukrainian representative!), is evidently very inconspicuous there. My project is making lively progress and has spawned new offspring, a project dealing with the inception of anti-Semitism in early childhood[3] (one of the central questions in my opinion), which I am carrying out there with money from the AJC together with the Child Welfare Institute. I get on very well with its director, Jones, one of the most pow-

erful psychologists in the country. Things are also going extremely well with my closest staff members. I am currently working on a funda-mental theoretical study for the project, as well as a new questionnaire.

Robert Alexander examined me thoroughly, and I also went through a considerable part of the tests, which are extremely advanced nowa-days. The diagnosis is neuralgia on a rheumatic-infectious basis, the centres of inflammation probably the teeth (my wisdom teeth have been somehow inflamed for years) and throat, whether inflammatory due to the teeth or the tonsils themselves. Both are now being thoroughly examined, and I am determined to take the necessary steps to get rid of the stuff. My head is all but clear now and my overall condition is good, but the heart is affected, as the electrocardiogram also showed. For a number of weeks now I have been sensing my heart for the first time in my life, often a very strong pulse; one time in S.F., on a Sunday, I was outside with Robert, Charlotte and Anita, a real attack, so I can join the club too. Robert is quite convinced that it is nothing severe, but it does require attention, for though it is surely related to the infection it may also be due to my constitution, this absurd and inflated stomach on a body that is itself by no means fat. I am adhering to an exceedingly strict diet, and, as unpleasant as it is to abstain from potatoes, sauce and any kind of chocolate, I do as a result already feel much better on the whole. The neuralgia, however, is wandering across my whole body, even the most delicate parts, where it is asserting itself in a rather depressing fashion. But I am not seriously ill, as I had feared for some weeks, and think that I should definitely be back to normal soon. I am in good spirits, and will take things easy for the summer.

Fritz and Maidon arrived today, joyful to be back, and Max is hardly likely to be back before mid-July, perhaps only in August. But the overall situation of the institute and the Jewish things is more favourable than it has been in years, which also helps me get back in shape. The institute had two reports on Frankfurt. The institute build-ing there was hit spot on, and is now rubble. There are still three large buildings standing in the city: the central train station, the IG adminis-trative building (that is precision bombing)[4] and the synagogue in Westend. Otherwise thousands of houses, but completely random. The university is totally burned out. I was unable to find out anything about Schöne Aussicht, but it seems that the whole of the old town centre was destroyed, including the Römer and the Goethe House. Apparently there is still such an abominable stench from the countless bodies buried under the ruins that it is impossible to take a walk through the streets.

Direct contact with German civilians is quite out of the question; even for such influential people as Norah, who is in Kitzbühl. We are not even trying it with poor Melly, who must be in Russian territory, regardless of whether she stayed in Berlin or fled to Vienna. I would advise you against seeking contact with anyone in Germany until you are naturalized. The only way to find anything out is through American friends in the occupation. This situation is expected to continue for another 6–8 months. The report on Frankfurt by Herr Rothschild[5] would greatly interest me. In the case of some acquaintances, I learned that they are still living through the newspaper, like Radbruch,[6] with whom I spent much time in Oxford, and also the loathsome Beutler from the Goethe Museum, who has yet again made a nationalistic appeal[7] and should be hung.

One is now only gradually getting around to being glad that the worst thing in the world no longer exists. The death of Himmler was a symbol of that. After that, I am also starting to believe in Hitler's death: if he had escaped in a submarine, there would also have been room for Goebbels and Himmler. I have not given up the hope that I shall one day write down the things that occupy me most in a little house in Amorbach.

You must make sure that the soon 80-year-old keeps up her strength. How happy Agathe would have been to witness the end of the Nazis, quand même!

But something has happened that does in fact symbolize the demise of the world of my experience: the Würzburg residence has been destroyed.

Heartiest kisses

from your old, now truly old child
Teddie

Many hugs and kisses from your
Giraffe

Original: typewritten letter with a handwritten greeting by Gretel Adorno.

1 The founding conference of the United Nations was held in San Francisco during that time; the UN Charter was signed there by fifty-one nations on 26 June.

2 Dimitri Manuilski (1883–1959[?]) had been first secretary of the Komintern from 1929 to 1934.

3 The psychologist Harold E. Jones (1894–1960) was professor at Berkeley from 1931 onwards, and from 1935 also director of the Institute of Child Welfare. The planned 'Study of Antisemitism among Children', which formed one of what were originally nine part-projects of the study on anti-Semitism, was not concluded.

4 *precision bombing*: EO.

5 'The letter from young Rothschild', as it is referred to in the following letter, does not seem to have survived. It is unknown whether it was written to Maria Wiesengrund or circulated in New York.

6 Gustav Radbruch (1878–1949), who lost his post – the first professor to do so – at the start of May 1933, went on study trips to Oxford in 1935 and 1936.

7 Ernst Beutler (1885–1960), director of the Freier Deutscher Hochstift from 1925 and of the Goethe Museum from 1931, had lost his honorary professorship at Frankfurt University in 1937 due to lack of political reliability and his wife's Jewish descent. The 'appeal' is presumably the following notice signed by Johann Georg Hartmann and Ernst Beutler: 'Appeal to our members! The 22 March 1944, the anniversary of Goethe's death, also marked the death of the city of his youth.' Adorno was probably sent this appeal in 1945 after the Allies' victory. The phrase 'yet again' in Adorno's letter refers to Beutler's 'Appeal' of March 1931: 'Deutsche Volksspende für Goethes Geburtsstätte – Ehrenschirmherr Reichspräsident von Hindenburg' [German people's donation for Goethe's place of birth – honorary patron Reichspräsident von Hindenburg].

135   LOS ANGELES, 21.6.1945

21 June 1945

My dears,

a thousand thanks for your cheque, which I used to buy myself a lovely playsuit.[1] We spent my birthday very quietly – on Saturday afternoon Maidon, Pollock and Norah Andreae came for tea, on Sunday just the two horses to dinner with old Hahn and Norah.

On Monday (18th) Archie had his wisdom teeth on the right side pulled, which was quite a tough job – the lower tooth had to be chiselled out – and he had severe pains for the first two days after that. Thanks to Sulfen, however, there were no complications, and today he is still a little swollen, but is working energetically again. –

I am still feeling well – without any particular efforts –, and I am receiving compliments from all sides about how well I am looking, a very nice change for me. – The left side of our little house has now finally been rented again, and the people will be moving in around the first of July; hopefully the relationship will be pleasant this time too. –

Today Archie was at the Federal Court to register as a potential juror, as his name was drawn. The time of his possible jurorship would only be from February 46–47, however. –

When are you going on holiday? – I read in the newspaper that it is already very hot in New York. Hopefully it is not causing you too many problems.

The very fondest regards and kisses

Your old Giraffe

(please turn over! Archie!)

223

My dears,

so one half – the right – of the dental orgy is behind me; there was a great and unexpected commotion, as the x-ray did not show that the tooth was not in its pulp cavity, but had rather grown deep into the jawbone and had to be broken before the root could be removed. But the local anaesthetic helped, and whenever he was labouring too wildly inside my mouth I imagined I was Lujche,[2] which made me feel better immediately. Sulpha is truly a miracle: today, the 3rd day after what the doctor termed an exceptionally difficult matter, almost no pains, except for feeling as if someone had smacked me in the gob, on the outside also coloured as after a blow. On 9 July there will be the same procedure on the left – but I am happy to go through it all if it gets rid of my neuralgia once and for all. My overall condition is *incomparably* better since following Robert's instructions.

I am at work again – all sorts of work, am making good progress and feel fully capable of action again for the first time in half a year – not such a troubled animal as in New York. Am also making music once more. I am having to spend a lot of time assisting the translation of the book I wrote with Eisler ('Music for the Movies').[3] It is coming along well, and the translator, Prof. MacManus[4] from the university here, is a charming fellow and is making an enormous effort, but calls me about every trifle. Next time I shall write in English to begin with, the only reason for not doing so this time was the collaboration with Eisler, whose English is too poor.

The letter from young Rothschild is very interesting in its factual part, and I would have a burning interest in anything similar you might read or hear. The same goes for reports on Germany in your major newspapers. The ones here are pathetic, and so far out of the way that they hardly print anything about Europe.

I hope you are well and will soon have a pleasantly cool holiday. Heartiest kisses from your faithful hippo

Teddie

Original: handwritten letter.

1 *playsuit*: EO.

2 Translator's note: a different spelling of 'Louische'.

3 The title of the English edition published in 1947 was *Composing for the Films*.

4 George MacManus.

DR. T.W. ADORNO
316 So. Kenter Avenue
Los Angeles 24, Calif.

2 July 1945

My dears,
    I was sent the newspaper cutting[1] from the 'Frankfurter Presse'
enclosed here by Robert de Neufville, who is over there as a lieutenant
in the American Army. It transpires that Helene (Louis's wife) was
deported to (the supposedly bearable) Theresienstadt, but was saved,
so both good and bad news.
    Robert was in Frankfurt and writes that it is horrific.
    We are well enough, up to our necks in work. Holidays are sup-
posed to start around 1 August.
    Heartiest kisses
                              from your old child
                              Teddie

Original: handwritten letter with printed letterhead.

1 On 14 June 1945, the newspaper *Frankfurter Presse* – published by the
American 12th Army Group – printed a list of survivors, under the title:
'Lebendig in Theresienstadt: Frankfurter wurden befreit' [Alive in
Theresienstadt: Citizens of Frankfurt Were Freed], which included the name
of Helene Calvelli-Adorno. Helene Calvelli-Adorno (née Katz; 1883–1945)
was the second wife of Louis Prosper Calvelli-Adorno; she had been deported
to Theresienstadt at the end of February 1945 and died in December of the
same year, a mere six months after being freed.

Los Angeles, 27 July 1945

My dear faithful old WK,
    this is to send you the heartiest, best possible wishes on this solemn
occasion, that of the three-quarter century. Even if, after the crisis of last
year, we have every reason to be grateful that you can celebrate it in such
good spirits and health, and in the knowledge that the worst thing imaginable has left the world for now, I still view it merely as the threshold
to the next notable date, the eightieth, and wish for you and for us that

your condition will continue to improve, and that you will carry on being as sensible and careful as you have been this last year. And I cannot refrain from hoping that precisely the next five years will continue the change for the better, also objectively. The English elections are a good omen – they show, as Max put it, that fascism did not triumph *after all*, and the days of the Francos, Umbertos e tutti quanti should now be numbered.[1] At the same time, it means an era of undreamed-of social reforms in England.[2] And although I do not overlook the danger that, faced with a more or less socialist world, American capitalism will be pushed in the direction of fascism, with the conflict with the Soviet Union in the background it is still difficult, on the other hand, to imagine that the masses here will stand for the madness if there is full employment in the Europe that has been bled dry, yet 9 million unemployed people in the richest of all countries. – Incidentally, the question of a return to Europe strikes me as more relevant than ever. –

I was in San Francisco from the 17th to the 24th, and stayed with the Alexanders, as there was no hotel room available either in S.F. or over in Berkeley. I now have two big projects running there, the old one with Berkeley University, on which the first report has just been finished, and the new project about children (examining the inception of anti-Semitism in children), with the Child Welfare Institute, the largest such research centre in America, with whose director, Jones, I work for hours every day.

Meanwhile Max has returned, and we had meetings all day on Wednesday and Thursday, together with his assistant from New York and mine from Berkeley. He is in good spirits and achieved a great deal, but is totally overworked and more than ripe for a holiday. I am hardly any less so. Following my dental business I contracted tonsillitis, which I managed to keep temporarily at bay with Sulpha etc. to avoid having to postpone the trip to Berkeley; suffered a relapse there, was patched together by Robert, and feel much better now, after three nights of decent sleep. The neuralgia has disappeared, except for some very slight traces. The remaining wisdom teeth will be slaughtered on 1 August, and then I will get on the case of my tonsils, a chronic centre of inflammation, to finally get rid of all this stuff.

Luli is here with husband – and has taken our child, Ali Baba Fenichel de Goertz zu Onkelsmülle, with her for the duration of her stay (2½ months), swearing a sacred oath to restore him to us before her return to New York – but we doubt whether she will part with our little Jesus again once she has got used to him. Gretel is naturally dreadfully sad about it, for the animal is as dear to us as if it were truly our child. Aside from that, Giraffe is still feeling splendid.

I have a peculiar feeling about your 75th birthday – namely that, at both our ages, the feeling of an age difference, with all that accompanies it – almost the difference between parents and children[3] – is no longer present – even less so if one considers that, in the face of today's infantile collectivist world, we have long become *one* generation. There is something deeply comforting in that.

Hopefully you will both enjoy a good, thorough rest, so that the Wondrous Hippo Cow will be able to celebrate her 80th birthday in all good cheer. We shall be on holiday from 1 August.

I embrace you, my dear WK – 'abundant well-being and blessings'[4] – and many, many yet to come. With hearty and fond regards from your meanwhile almost equally old child

Teddie

Hugs and kisses from

Your old Giraffe

Original: typewritten letter with handwritten ending.

1 Umberto II had become general governor of the kingdom in 1944, following the abdication of his father Vittorio Emanuele; he was crowned king of Italy in May 1946, but left the country after a referendum in favour of the republic. The political reign of Franco only ended with his death over thirty years later.

2 The Labour Party had won the general election, and in the following years placed the coal-mining industry, the railways, and the iron and steel industries under state control – as well as the Bank of England; in addition, the Labour government under Clement Richard Attlee (1883–1967) introduced a uniform national insurance system and the National Health Service.

3 See the aphorism 'Rasenbank' [Lawn-bench] from *Minima Moralia*.

4 The original ['lauter Heil und Segen'] is the closing line of the second stanza of 'Frühlingslied' [Spring Song] by Heinrich Hoffmann von Fallersleben.

138   LOS ANGELES, 19.8.1945

19 August 1945

My dears,

I feel very guilty for not writing to you for so long. Meanwhile we have some peace and quiet. From Tuesday on we were no longer amid the bustle of Hollywood, but rather alone in our little house, and thought of you a great deal. On Wednesday – a public holiday in California – we made immediate use of the petrol derationing and drove 43 miles south along the ocean to Oxnard for a stroll. (We went on the same outing on 7 December 1941.) Aside from that, the last weeks in particular have been rather full of work; next to some quite important meetings with Max also a seminar and work on the anti-Semitism project. Last Friday we had a big victory party with the Thomas Manns, the whole institute, Palfis, Hanns Eisler (Lou was in San Francisco at the time), Lily Latté[1] (it turned out that she went to the same school as I did, and that all of us there fancied the young Latin teacher Rommel (!)). – I still miss Ali Baba as much as on the first day. He was here the other day with Luli, and when we said goodbye – she had just taken us to her new estate[2] – he absolutely wanted to get out of her white Cadillac into our modest Baldchen. The estate is a dream, high up in the hills of Beverly Hills and with an inde-scribable view, and despite the Spanish style it has a slight air of a German fairytale castle. She is having it modernized, and they want to move here in the spring and spend at least eight months of the year over here. The separation from us has not done Ali Baba any good; he has heart attacks, coughs and generally seems rather sad. Luli is ill herself at the moment, apparently poison oak poisoning.

Hopefully you are finding it pleasant in Rhinebeck again and can take your walks. It truly would be so very lovely if we could show you the West Coast next year.

Hugs and kisses from

your

long-necked Giraffe

My dears, today just these few words before the holidays start in a few days. The 2nd dental operation went very smoothly and painlessly, except that it bled like mad for 5 hours, and I am somewhat weakened and generally worn-out as a result. The last weeks have been all right; except for correcting the 2nd part of a big philosophical study I have almost only been at meetings with Max – we both have more on our plates than ever, and are trying to do it as well as possible. The day before yesterday we had a big peace party in honour of Lix (who had thrown one for us before that), with Thomas Mann e tutti quanti – Giraffe had ordered an incredible amount of meat, and it proved a succès fou both for the belly and for the spirit. – No headache etc. *at all*; I think I am truly cured. Thanks to the diet I weigh only 59 kg – am as thin as I was 15 years ago, and feel good for it; only badly in need of a holiday. Hopefully you are having a good rest. I shall write to you properly soon. My assessment of the Japanese war as a colon-ial one has proved as accurate as my verdict about Germany. We are thinking of Europe because of the danger *here!* Speaking of which: what do you think about the atomic bomb?

Heartiest kisses from your old and faithful child

Teddie

Original: handwritten letter.

1 Elisabeth Lily Latté (1901–84), née Schaul, came from Berlin and had been together with Fritz Lang since the mid-1920s. She emigrated to Paris in 1933 and went to the USA in 1935. Latté and Lang bought a house together in Beverly Hills in 1945. She worked as Lang's assistant and secretary.

2 *estate*: EO.

139 LOS ANGELES, 30.8.1945

30 August 1945

My dears,
    your sweet letter gave me an acutely guilty conscience, and I can do no more than ask you to forgive me. I was not actually ill during my weeks of silence, but nonetheless so exhausted and worn-out[1] that something as simple as writing a letter or even picking up the telephone cost me an entirely disproportionate effort. That sounds like a very pathetic excuse, but perhaps you can indeed imagine such a state. There was absolutely no other reason. My dear Giraffe Gazelle is still feeling well, looks splendid and can even drive for long stretches once more with the help of the now freely available petrol. Yesterday we went on a big driving tour to the South, to Laguna Beach, a bathing resort situated in truly enchanting surroundings that one can only compare to the most beautiful spots on the French Riviera, and during the holidays, which have just started with a vengeance, we intend to take advantage of our car and the now radiantly fine weather to the fullest extent. Max is away, was in Berkeley for a few days and is now going to the mountains, but will be back here around the 20th. As all the hotels are outrageously full, however, we find it more comfortable to spend our holidays here. I also have to play director a little for our projects on the side. Meanwhile, incidentally, I have advanced to the position of official director of all scientific activities[2] of the American Jewish Committee on the West Coast, and can already hear WK saying that that is worth about as much as tuppence ha'penny, but tuppence ha'penny is certainly nothing to sneeze at for a half-descendant of the Colonna family,[3] after all.
    Luli was quite ill, had contracted streptococcus poisoning through an insect bite, but is more or less back to normal. We were at the beach with her yesterday (without husband). She has aged peculiarly, and although she constantly declares how happy she is, and throws her money away generously in small amounts, one has the feeling that

229

something is amiss, without being able to say exactly what it is. At any rate, she has lost a considerable amount of the radiance she had as a princess in the mouse-fortress since becoming the wife of her precision engineer nabob.

Ali Baba is healthy again, and we shall get him back in approximately four weeks when Luli goes back to New York, until she moves to her estate here once and for all, which will supposedly happen in the spring. She wants to have him back then, but will give us a little Afghan puppy as compensation. Ali Baba, our little Jesus, is decidedly happier with us than with his mistress, where he has to play the wild Afghan hound, which he is not at all, just as she frantically plays the lively young baroness, which she no longer is either.

Aside from that we are seeing a lot of Fritz Pollock and Felix Weil, who has been showing a touchingly trusting nature. We are being invited a little too much for our ideal of horse-peace, but it is difficult to avoid if one is to stay here.

I am genuinely worried about the Wondrous Hippo Cow, both because of what WK wrote and because of her own somewhat resigned words. I demand energetically that my most royal mother, by her Bauchschleifer honour, not entertain such foolish thoughts as 'a rich life lies behind her' and continues to live life with the same energy that got her through fascism, emigration and war.

Purely out of egotism, because I have the greatest yearning to see her again in good health and spirits. Unfortunately I cannot yet fix a date for it this time either, because I have so many things on my plate at the moment, above all the responsibility for my two big projects, so I cannot simply go away in the middle of everything. But it goes without saying that I shall come as soon as I can find some pretext, and Max knows that.

September is generally a very pleasant month in New York, not so oppressively hot any more, and I hope that Marinumba is sensible enough to avoid going on any par force tours and instead take a sit as peacefully as possible on Riverside Drive.

I have been spared any headaches at all for weeks now, and have every reason to assume that the dental operation genuinely fulfilled its purpose. One will have to see about the tonsils.

Heartiest kisses from your old child, who is rolling in the mud as the massive Hippo King.

Ever your child
Teddie

Fond regards ever your Giraffe Gazelle. What are Marinumba's birthday wishes?

Original: typewritten letter with additional handwritten note by Gretel Adorno.

1 *worn-out*: EO.

2 *activities*: EO.

3 The details of Adorno's complicated lineage are not entirely clear. There were unquestionably members of the Genoese family Colonna in Corsica; it was impossible, however, to ascertain when these encountered the Calvellis and Adornos.

140   LOS ANGELES, 13.9.1945

Los Angeles, 13 September 1945

My dears, a thousand thanks for your lengthy birthday letter and the munificent cheque, which my cousin Franz Villinger would unquestionably term a 'noble present'. Speaking of which, I am glad with all my heart that Jenny survived the Nazi disaster, but I am also somewhat glad that family contact came about through Fritz[1] in particular. One could almost call it a national community – one from which I am glad to be excluded.

The main thing: there is a good chance, albeit *no certainty*, that I will be coming to New York soon. Max should be there at the start of October, and I will join him about four weeks later; he would then go back again earlier, while I plan to stay approximately until Christmas.* The plan is entirely confidential for now. Naturally I would rather have been there for the Hippo Cow's 80th birthday, but with the enormous distance and the complicated arrangements I simply cannot fix it so precisely – you will understand that. I need hardly tell you that I will do my utmost.

Max put in a surprise appearance on the evening of my birthday: he had ended his holiday prematurely, as the burden of the current responsibilities left him no peace. Incidentally, he is now also being treated by Robert Alexander, who cured Gretel and also helped me a great deal, though I have had some traces of neuralgia again these last few days. The dental operation seems to have offered my body great relief. (Heart!)

* [Marginal note:] The whole thing only if Max goes *at all*; if he decides not to return, which is not out of the question, I would also stay here. This is just to make quite sure that you are not disappointed! Nobody must know that Max might *not* come, because of the Jews.

231

I had to smile at your remark about Lix – the only problem is how to avoid his sitting around all day and preventing any decent work, not his 'reserve'.[2] He had somehow found out that it was my birthday and immediately came to us with all sorts of wine. He takes a touching part in the work, unfortunately with more zeal than understanding.

As I hardly got around to any holidays – I urgently had to write a new typology of the anti-Semites for Berkeley – I do intend to relax genuinely and radically, though only once Max is gone. But we at least went on a few very nice driving tours; but Gretel does find it exhausting to drive for very long (we once drove 180 miles, i.e. around 300 kilometres, in a single day), and I also have the feeling that the train does not do my neuralgic disposition any good. There should be an article coming out within the next few days in the journal 'Commentary' by James Rorty;[3] it is essentially (without naming names, with good reason) a report on a big unpublished study of mine. Besides that, my Theses on Art and Religion[4] will also be appearing in the autumn issue of the Kenyon Review.

Our house has been sold; after the very unpleasant, xenophobic previous owner, the new one is a friendly Sicilian by the name of Vita (I have given him the name 'Mr Landlord-life'), and there is a chance that we can stay here in peace, at least until we have bought or built something with the help of the institute. The feeling of not being exposed to any housing shortage is exceedingly reassuring and a moral uplifting.[5]

I am glad you are both well rested. The pictures are a great joy, WK truly looks excellent; the Hippo Cow a little sad – but perhaps I can soon put her in good spirits.

Heartiest kisses from your old Hippo King
Archibald

Many hugs and kisses from
Your old Giraffe Gazelle

Original: typewritten letter with additional handwritten note by Gretel Adorno.

1 The historian Fritz T. Epstein (1898–1979), who had obtained his post-doctoral qualification [*Habilitation*] in 1924 with a dissertation on Russia and world politics 1917–20, and emigrated first in 1933 to England then in 1937 to the USA, where he acted as research assistant and belonged to the faculty until 1943; he worked for the US State Department until the end of the war. Epstein returned to Germany in 1969. He was the older son of the mathematics professor Paul Epstein and Alice Epstein (née Wiesengrund).

2 *'reserve'*: EO.

3 See James Rorty, 'American Fuehrer in Dress Rehearsal', *Commentary: A Jewish Review*, vol. 1, no. 1, November 1945, pp. 13–20. Rorty refers to Adorno's 1943 study 'The Psychological Technique of Martin Luther Thomas' Radio Addresses'.

4 See now *GS* 11, pp. 647–53.

5 *moral uplifting*: EO.

141 LOS ANGELES, 27.9.1945

27 September 1945

My dear faithful old Wondrous Hippo Cow,
    so Monday is the big day, and I am already writing today, to make quite sure that my congratulations reach you, even at the risk of arriving one day too early. I need hardly tell you how infinitely sad I am that I cannot spend the day with you both. Initially I could have come by a hair's breadth, but then Max had to go to New York after all and I did not, and aside from the fact that I would now be superfluous for the work in New York, I have so many commitments here that I cannot possibly leave everything as it is, especially as Fritz has gone to Berkeley for a few weeks and I thus have to look after Lix all by myself. So there is no alternative but to hope that it happens somehow later on in the year, although all the arrangements are still so uncertain that I cannot with the best will in the world promise anything.
    So I wish you, my now eighty-year-old Wondrous Hippo Cow, as much good and fair fortune as anyone could ever wish another person, let alone their own dearest mother. And that you continue to retain your intellectual faculties, remain healthy and still experience as much joy as this life could possibly yield. It is not *only* out of egotism that my foremost concern is to see you, for I know that it is as important to you as it is to me. If I look at the lives of almost all the other people I know, it seems to me that yours, despite the ghastly emigration, has altogether been one of the most fulfilled, untroubled and happy ones, and I hope with all my heart that it will also continue in this fashion, now that you are a true old hippo lady, which I never recognized before this eightieth birthday, essentially because I could never imagine that you have meanwhile become an old woman. Sometimes I envy you for your eighty years and for everything they encompass – not for the number of years, but rather, I mean to say, for all the suffering you have been *spared* during so long a life, despite Agathe's death and the exile. Yet it is only due to *you*, however, that you were spared it, you of whom no truer claim could be made, in the language

233

of astrologers, than that you were born under a lucky star. May it light your evenings long and faithfully, while my own landscape is already beginning to resemble that of Baudelaire:[1] 'sans ces étoiles dont la lumière parle un langage connu'.

I was very pleased to hear of Franz Adorno's appointment[2] – he is thus the first of us all to be in an exalted position once more, and perhaps he owes it to the ponderousness with which he stayed, and which I can understand only too well. Incidentally, I may be not entirely innocent in the matter, as I was asked about reliable people in Frankfurt a few months ago, and named him as my first choice. I already knew about Lanskoronski (the husband of Maus Wertheimber)[3] through Norah.

Commentary is the new journal of the American Jewish Committee, replacing the previous one, Jewish Record. My name and that of Leo[4] (it deals with both our studies) are not mentioned because these are analyses of highly dangerous agitators on the West Coast who could otherwise cause us great personal strife – c'est tout. Typology literally means the study of types, and refers to the division of a subject or group of people into dominant types. My one, then, lists the basic psychological types among anti-Semites.

Our good WK's concerns regarding Lix are entirely unfounded – on the contrary, he has attached himself to us very strongly, and is a deeply good-natured and friendly, but weak, person with a horrible wife. He comes to me for advice about everything, even the most private matters.

Tonight we shall be at the house of Thomas Mann,[5] who asked me to read to him from the manuscript of my book of aphorisms; tomorrow evening is the farewell party for Lix, who is going back via San Francisco at the start of next week. Next week we plan to take a trip to the mountains with the very pleasant illustrator Eva Hermann,[6] a friend of the Manns.

And now, my dear faithful old mother-animal, accept these unshapely embraces, sniffs, kisses and congratulations
from your
infinitely loving child
Teddie, alias Archibald, m.p.

My dear good Wondrous Hippo Cow,
as an honorary hippo I would like once again to thank you for beating time to the passing of the ages with your tail so selflessly (together with the other hippo cows at the Nile sources). Sadly I cannot fill in for you with my giraffe nature. But I am doing my best with my little horns. I send you all my best and fond regards, and hope that you will continue to be the jewel of the hippos for at least another

234

twenty years, that you are feeling well and that we will see each other again as soon as possible. Due to the three hours' time difference and the frequently poor connection we will not call, unfortunately. With eighty hugs and kisses from

from your old tall-legged Giraffe Gazelle

Our birthday present, a cheque for a hundred dollars, is enclosed. Use it to buy yourself something that you can genuinely have fun with.

Original: typewritten letter with additional handwritten note by Gretel Adorno and handwritten postscript by Adorno.

1 The quotation is from the first trio of the sonnet 'Obsession', which reads: 'Comme tu me plairais, ô nuit! sans ces étoiles/Dont la lumière parle un langage connu!/Car je cherche le vide, et le noir, et le nu!'

2 Franz Calvelli-Adorno had been appointed chairman of the Reparations Committee.

3 Unknown.

4 Leo Löwenthal's study was entitled 'Prophets of Deceit: A Study of the Techniques of the American Agitator', the fourth part of *Studies in Prejudice*.

5 Mann wrote about the reading from *Minima Moralia* in his diary entry of 26 September.

6 The illustrator Eva Hermann (1901–78), a friend of Erika and Klaus Mann, lived in Santa Barbara.

142   LOS ANGELES, 31.10.1945

31 October 1945

My dears,
   a thousand thanks for your sweet letter. I am so infinitely sorry that poor WK is having unexpected trouble with his eyes. I can empathize with his mood all too well – it is a particular blow, after the treatment had helped for decades, that it is suddenly no longer working properly. Hopefully, with today's extremely advanced methods, they can be restored to normal working order again. We sent you a little book by Huxley that Gretel had bought me for my own use.
   There is nothing mysterious about my workload here; sometimes it is simply difficult at this distance, if one is not spending every day together, to convey an impression of everyday events. It is simply that I have to devote myself very energetically to the two Berkeley projects, at the same time as having spent all my energy keeping the theoretical

235

work going that was interrupted for a year through Max's departure to New York, so that not only can we pick up where we left off, but also I will have made serious progress during that year. I think I have succeeded on that count, in the form of a very long manuscript written in the Nietzschean aphoristic form, relating to a relatively wide range of philosophical objects, but above all the question of what has fundamentally become of 'life' under the conditions of monopoly capitalism.

Max returned on Monday after an evidently very successful stay in New York, but is horribly exhausted. The institute continues to exist unchanged,[1] and I do not understand at all why you thought it might no longer exist. The Jewish matters are continuing, but we are determined to organize them so that we do not spend our most productive years on things that, after all, are only of peripheral interest to us.

I am not in especially good health; after three months' rest the neuralgia has returned, no longer as bad as it was, but still irksome enough, and above all with additional drowsiness. I am now fairly determined to have my tonsils out too, after all sorts of people have told me that they got rid of similar complaints entirely by doing so. It is only a question of time, as I may have to go to Berkeley now, and certainly will in December.

I expect you know that Norah Andreae's husband died in Germany. A few days ago we received word that Anton von Webern was murdered in the street about four weeks ago by his son-in-law,[2] a fanatical Nazi. I am so ineffably sorry – the artistic loss, together with that of Bartok, is a blow to the music I stand by, the greatest imaginable loss.

I hope to hear good news from you soon, and am glad that the Hippo Cow is swimming so cheerfully into her 81st year.

Heartiest kisses

from your old child
Teddie.

Many hugs from your old Giraffe and your old Ali Baba. What would you like for Christmas?

Frau Herz[3] called, we will be meeting her once. A thousand thanks for the newspaper cuttings – I was just about to repeat my request for such news when they came. The newspapers here are of a pitiful standard; even as far as pure news is concerned – a cross between the Miltenberger Anzeiger and Filmkurier.

The New School advertisement[4] is wonderful – a veritable trouvaille. We can indeed be *very* grateful to be spared such sell-offs of the intellect.

Fond regards again!
Archibald

236

Original: typewritten letter with handwritten postscript.

1 Surely not 'unchanged'!

2 Webern had in fact been shot dead on 15 September by an American soldier who had mistaken him for an armed black marketeer.

3 Unknown.

4 Its place of publication could not be ascertained.

143 LOS ANGELES, 18.11.1945

18 November 1945

My dears,
a thousand thanks for your letter and the news about Louis and his loved ones. I enclose the letters. It must be terrible in Europe, the reports one hears are gruesome – the only oasis seems to be Monte Carlo.

Pollock went back again today; I am sure he will call you, perhaps also find you and tell you about us.

Your Christmas wishes will be fulfilled, I am very proud already to have acquired the presents despite the great material scarcity, especially here in California.

We are in the following situation: we naturally value WK's apricot brandy extremely highly, but with the ban on sending alcohol from one state to another we do not want to encourage you to do so, though nothing has ever happened so far, or perhaps Pollock could bring it with him. Otherwise something like a nice big bar of bath soap (a few years ago it was one with a magnificent sandalwood fragrance) would be most welcome. – Archie is not in particularly good shape, but is soon going to San Francisco to have Robert Alexander check and fix him.

Many hugs from your
old lanky Giraffe

My dears, your letter made me unspeakably happy, and I am equally grateful for the newspaper cuttings. Ley's will,[1] for example, which is extremely interesting, was not printed in its original wording in any of the papers here. And the poor Hahns![2] What a horrific world! When one hears such things one can only regret that the atomic bomb was not tried out on Germany. Nonetheless, I did not prove entirely well behaved with the lines written by Franz, which I could have made up myself. I expect you know that all the Adelaers[3] in Holland are dead. Also Ludwig v. Gans.[4]

237

I am feeling so shaky that I can hardly postpone the tonsil operation any longer, but you should not worry.

> Heartiest kisses from your old child
> Teddie,
> and cuddles from Ali Baba!

Original: handwritten letter.

1 From 1933 to 1945, Robert Ley (1890–1945) had been director of the Deutsche Arbeitsfront [German Workers' Front] (DAF), which forced all free and independent trade unions to conform to the party line. Ley, a furious anti-Semite who had been a party member since 1924, was captured by American troops in 1945 and was to be put on trial in Nuremberg. He committed suicide on 25 October 1945 and left behind his 'Political Testament', which he had written in his prison cell. 'In his political testament Ley admitted, for example, that anti-Semitism had been wrong, that Germans and Jews had to be reconciled – yet stated in the same breath that anti-Semitism is legitimate as long as it is purely defensive, and that now the Jew has won the war. His image of an enemy was evidently unshaken. Ley prophesied that anti-Semitism would erupt more strongly than ever if the Jew sought retribution, and the occupying soldiers would come up against the "Jewish problem"; the coming "show trials" would bring this problem to the world's attention. If the Jews refrained from seeking retribution, however, then Germany would become their homeland. Ley even recommended the founding of a committee of Jews and anti-Semites to work out the necessary conditions for Jews and Germans to live together, as well as an organization for "schooling and propaganda" in order to disseminate these ideas' (Ronald Smelser, *Robert Ley – Hitlers Mann an der 'Arbeitsfront'. Eine Biographie* [Robert Ley – Hitler's Man at the 'Workers' Front': A Biography], [Paderborn, 1989], p. 288).

2 It could not be ascertained what happened to the Hahns.

3 Unknown.

4 It could not be ascertained whether this refers to the major industrialist Ludwig von Gans (b. 1869), who, according to other accounts, died only in 1946.

144   LOS ANGELES, 1.12.1945

1 December 1945

My dears,

my very warmest congratulations on your citizenship;[1] it is really a very pleasant feeling. But I would almost congratulate WK even more on his enterprising spirit, for which I have unlimited admiration. We and Ali Baba will cross our fingers and paws that his efforts succeed.[2]

On Thursday Archie had his tonsils out. The doctor, Dr Kully, was extremely deft, the whole thing took only just over half an hour with a local anaesthetic. In that time, Teddie spoke to the doctor and the nurses. He was in hospital for one day, has been back in his own bed since, felt no pain during the operation, now feels as if he had a severe throat infection, cannot speak and swallows only with difficulty, but he has no temperature and is entirely satisfied. They have allowed him to get up a little on Monday and eat more solid food.

We have meanwhile heard through my cousin Gertrud Bohm[3] in Poughkeepsie that Melly is alive. She went to Vienna in 1943 and later to her brother in Krems.[4] Unfortunately I do not know which zone Krems is in.

My brother-in-law[5] is still in Manila and is hardly likely to be released before the spring. Lottchen has a very unpleasant bowel complaint and has to mind her health very carefully.

Please forgive my brevity, but I have to go and make Archie's lunch. Hugs and kisses from

Your old Giraffe Gazelle

My dears, your letter made me incredibly happy. I got through the operation in good shape, and it was not terrible at all, except that one already had to be at the clinic at 7 in the morning (an hour's drive from here!), and that I received a penicillin injection every 3 hours for 24 hours, even at night, which was very irksome with all that codeine. But it would be a lie for me to call it an affair – it is amazing, after all, what things one can do nowadays. I now feel quite well – hardly any more sore throat or trouble speaking and swallowing – and am enjoying lying in bed in joyful anticipation of the butter soup.

Congratulations on your naturalization – it is one of those things that mean little once one has them, and are very unpleasant if (like numerous acquaintances of ours) one does *not*!

I am very happy that Melly was saved. We know about the Adelaers' deaths from Viktor Palfi, the ex-husband of Lotte Mosbacher.

Our good WK must not overdo it!

Heartiest kisses from your old child
Teddie

Original: typewritten letter with additional handwritten note by Adorno.

1 *citizenship*: EO.

2 Unknown.

3 No further information.

4 A town in Lower Austria, where the river of the same name joins the Danube.

5 Egon Wissing.

7 December 1945

My dears,
a thousand thanks for your letter. You really need not worry about Archie, as I am looking after him very carefully. He is already eating normally again and has recovered his voice. – Otherwise, we have been having quite an exciting few days, as our new landlord has now also told us that we should seek housing elsewhere. Old houses have disappeared almost entirely from the market, and after putting our heads together with Max and Fred at great length we all decided that it would be best, despite the high prices, to build a new stable for the horses. The location is in Pacific Palisades, about 5 miles further outside than we are living now, so 2½ miles west of Max, whereas we are currently living to the east of the Horkheimers. It will be a little house, divided roughly the same as now, 2-storey: downstairs a little forecourt, garage, kitchen, savic [?][1] porch,[2] living room, upstairs 2 bedrooms, den[3] (study) and sunporch.[4] We have a splendid view of the mountains and the ocean from there. It could be magnificent, and we are extremely happy and grateful that the institute is enabling us to finance it. – Father Christmas is equally welcome with different soap (lavender or lily of the valley or Gilly [?] fleurs or violets). Many hugs and kisses from your old Giraffe, who is well (touch wood)[5] despite a great deal of work.
The very fondest regards from your convalescent, proud – as a future house-owner – slightly ashamed and self-amazed child
Teddie

Original: handwritten letter.

1 Difficult to read; unfortunately, the consultation of reference books and dictionaries did not produce any better result.

2 *porch*: EO.

3 *den*: EO.

4 *sunporch*: EO.

5 *touch wood*: EO.

23 December 1945

My dears,
a thousand thanks for your lovingly prepared package, the soap, the perfume, the calendar, the meat-extract, and the little blanket. Today I enclose the photo of Giraffe so that you can see she is truly well. Two days of frightful rain here, and as poor Ali Baba, with his long coat, was no longer getting dry at all, I made him a green rain cape from an old oil-cloth and some curtains, which he now takes proudly on his walks. – Archie has a quiet disturbance of the cardiac muscle, is resting a great deal and working mostly in bed, and has already made a very good recovery during the week following his return from Berkeley. – The house contract will probably be signed next week, and I will give you all the details then.
A happy New Year kisses from your lanky Giraffe
Warm regards from dear Julie

My dears, do not worry about me at all – I am in the best hands, and Robert says my heart will get entirely back to normal. Ad Elisabeth: Franz, as I learned *positively* in San Francisco, received his appointment because of my recommendation to one of the primary bodies concerned, and there would be no harm in his knowing that he owes it to me. Best wishes for the New Year. Kisses from your Teddie

Original: handwritten letter on the reverse of a giraffe card (see fig. 4).

1946

7 January 1946

My dears,
a thousand thanks for the newspaper cuttings with the Low caricatures and the little animals. We are living an even more solitary life
than usual, as Archie has not been feeling at all well. The radiocar-
diogram showed that the coronary vessels are not in good condition,
so for the next while he must be very careful that nothing chronic
develops, but the current business can be entirely cured. It is good that
Archie's medication took immediate effect and his overall condition is
also much better already. We shall keep you informed
                    A kiss
                            Your old Giraffe

My dears, do not worry, I will be back to normal soon enough. Hearty
kisses from your old child
                            Teddie

Original: handwritten letter.

13 January 1946

My dears,
today I have good news for you: Teddie is feeling much better, he
still has to take it easy, but he is out of danger and the cardiogram is

almost normal, not quite as good as it was in May. I wanted to telegraph you via Julie to avoid your getting a shock while still informing you right away, but sadly it is impossible on account of the strikes. – Thomas Mann is here at the moment, and Teddie is giving him musical advice for his new novel (about a musician). – My cousin Gertrud[1] received word directly from Melly, and we will try to correspond normally, as the post office has just opened – I do not know whether the committee and Vatican embassies ever reached her. She writes that it is much worse than 1918, and that the Gestapo interrogated her a number of times about Teddie. My cousin Kurt[2] (who was negotiating with Oscar's brother[3] back then) fell in France.

Many hugs and kisses from your
lanky Giraffe

My dears, Robert just called from S.F. – the new cardiogram is *much* better, I am out of danger, must still lie down a great deal for another few weeks (and can therefore *not* go to Berkeley on the 19th) to recover completely, and definitely did *not* have thrombosis. I am naturally in very good spirits, and know that you will also be reassured. A few days in S.F. and here were rather disconcerting; many things came together. I can still feel something I never knew: that I have a heart; but my basic feeling is that of the convalescent. Max is also better; the parallels between our respective illnesses really are too peculiar. Thomas Mann just left here. Heartiest kisses

from your son
Teddie, who is still very much alive.

Original: handwritten letter.

1 Gertrud Bohm.

2 No further information.

3 The engineer and manufacturer Bernhard Robert Wiesengrund (1872–1935), who changed his name to Bernard Wingfield after acquiring British citizenship.

149 LOS ANGELES, 30.1.1946

30.I.46.

My dears,

I am feeling *much* better, so much better that I will be going to Berkeley next week, which also has the advantage that Robert can have a look at me.

243

I received the sweet Hippo Cow Christmas present and it made me infinitely happy, especially the passages about Louische, which were like balsam for me – and that, after all, is why you wrote them. The fact that he outlived poor Helene, to top it all, is something I could have made up. I feel very sorry for her – everyone always derided her because of her somewhat unpleasant nature, but actually she never did any of us any harm, in fact did many people some good, and this end erases her faults once and for all. I do not want to change places with Louis. I have no sympathy at all for Helenchen Mommsen[1] – she belongs to the Nazi mob, and her brother is one, so let *him* help her. Do you think Franz is still convinced that the world is just?

Rudi[2] was here, to our greatest joy; unfortunately he was staying with the Schönbergs, who more or less held him prisoner.

I am working in bed a great deal, which very much agrees with me. Now too I am writing while lying down, hence my scrawl. But – I am over the worst. Look after yourselves my two dear old animals – thank God you are sitting peacefully in N.Y. The Germans will now have to pay terribly. Do you have anyone looking after our interests at home?

Heartiest kisses from your old Teddie

Original: handwritten letter.

1 Franz Calvelli-Adorno's wife. Nothing is known about her brother Helmut.

2 Rudolf Kolisch.

30 January 1946

My dears,

so, our dear animal (Archie) is feeling much better. He is still taking things easy, but one really cannot compare his current condition to before, and you would be as happy as I am about it. – My cousin Gertrud Bohm, née Pie, was brought up by Frau Seele.[1] She told you about it herself once, as she is very attached to her two surviving children Gertrud and Hans. We have not yet received any direct response from her. Melly did not even know our California address. – We received word from Egon Wissing yesterday that he is on the direct journey home eastwards via the Panama Canal. The date of his release is not yet fixed. I assume he will turn up here somehow during the summer. – We are awaiting the start of our house-building with the greatest suspense; it is supposed to happen by 10 February. Until then

244

we shall still have to take Ali Baba for walks on the empty property. It really is especially lovely there. And the name of the street will also appeal to you: Via de la Paz. – We enclose a cheque and are very grateful to you for taking the recovery and forwarding of the Adornos' things off our hands.*

In opposition to your reports, Norah Andreae has been receiving – to our horror – letters from Frankfurt saying that things are very well there, that people are having parties until 5 in the morning and that the two Heymanns[2] (Pussy's first husband) have founded a private bank again. It all seems completely incomprehensible to us. We had a very sweet letter from Luli, who will probably be coming here in April. My only fear is that little Baba (Affo Schwanzo)[3] will no longer be around to see the new house.

Many hugs from

Your old Giraffe
Gretel

Original: handwritten letter.

1 See letter no. 11, note 4.

2 Unknown.

3 Translator's note: this nickname is presumably based on *Affe* (monkey) and *Schwanz* (tail).

151   LOS ANGELES, 22.2.1946

22 February 1946

My dears,

our patient is feeling much better again, he returned from San Francisco in good spirits, and the doctor here, Dr Friedgood,[1] believes that Archie will get entirely back to normal, especially if he avoids excitement as far as possible. – Yesterday he received a letter from Benjamin's sister Dora,[2] reporting that Benjamin's notes for the Arcades project have been saved in the Bibliothèque Nationale in Paris. – A thousand thanks for the lovely box, which will make it much easier for us to keep the desk tidy. – Many hugs from

Your old Giraffe

My dears, Berkeley proved fine, despite piles of work and difficult negotiations. Overall much better; today my heart played up properly again

* [Marginal note by Adorno:] (NB Giraffe – not the bad old Hippo!)

245

for the first time. It needs time; but Max and I are both *very* careful and are taking things slowly; have not started the big piece yet, as we should both be fully in shape again first. Thomas Mann just left here, and has been most charming – he visited me every Sunday during the worst time. I wish I no longer had to tell you about my stupid health and could only ask after you. Just think of all the Louische atrocities I could write *with impunity* now, as I must not get worked up, after all. But I shall refrain, for I am noble, helpful and good. Heartiest kisses from your
old child   Teddie.

Original: handwritten letter.

1 There is no further information on the doctor Harry Friedgood.

2 Dora Benjamin (1901–46) [translator's note: not to be confused with his wife of the same name], who had studied national economics and psychology and worked as a psychologist in the field of social welfare following her studies, and then emigrated to Paris, like her brother. She was incarcerated in the camp in Gurs in 1940, but was soon able to escape and meet with Walter Benjamin in Lourdes. She was to be deported in August 1942, but was saved by a medical officer's report stating that she was unfit for transport, and in December 1942 managed to flee to Switzerland, where she died in July 1946. Her letter dates from 13 February 1946.

152   LOS ANGELES, 25.2.1946

25 February 1946

My dears,
a thousand thanks for your sweet letter. I am sending you a small package with a few old things: a pair of trousers, a skirt, 2 blouses, 2 sports shirts. – Naturally our little house has steps, doors and windows, but I merely wanted to give you a general idea of the matter. – On the other hand: no, we do not know the new Frau Pollock,[1] and would like to know exactly what you thought of her. – How was it with Lottchen? We have not heard from E since his return. Archie will write to Louis; you can no doubt imagine the sort of letters he is always dreaming up, but which are of course never sent.
    Look after yourselves
with hugs from your old
Giraffe

All my fondest regards! Did you see E too? We would all *very much* like to know *in detail* about your impression of the new Frau Pollock!

246

Do not always speak so badly of Luli, she brings us more joy than all the Louischers and Villingers put together, she behaves delightfully towards us in every respect – e.g. by guessing one of my secret Christmas wishes – and it is understandable that her heart clings to the angelic dog as much as ours do.

Heartiest kisses from your child Teddie

Original: handwritten letter.

1 Pollock had married Carlota Bernecker (1905–83) at the start of the year.

11 March 1946

My dears,

a thousand thanks to you both for such sweet and lengthy letters. I laughed myself silly about the Hippo Cow's tale of E's visit – je vois ça d'ici. This silence of his is by no means new to me; it probably just means that he simply has nothing more to say (seriously, it probably stems from a neurosis, but it is not meant personally at all, and he is especially fond of you). Hopefully things will remain fine with Lottchen.

I am glad that Frau Pollock made a good impression on you; it was only your emphasis on how 'natural' she is that startled me somewhat, as those people who are known as natural generally have nothing more to offer than dressing sloppily and behaving unpleasantly. But that is not what you meant in the case of Lotte, or Carlota, whatever she is called. We had long known that Fritz was on the lookout, of course, only not quite in which direction, and he does not seem to have been entirely sure about it himself. But that is a different matter.

As far as my own precious health is concerned, the tonsil operation has indeed rid me entirely of my neuralgia (fingers crossed), but my heart is still playing up, albeit much less. I cannot easily say to what extent – as Robert thinks – it is really to be attributed to coronary insufficiency,[1] or to what extent it is rather neurotic – probably, as always in such cases, the neurosis combines with something organic. I have now also found a genuinely sensible doctor here, and will be going to San Francisco again on the 20th, so Robert can give me a check then.

It is a mistake to think that I am fundamentally unwilling to engage with our good WK's political ideas, and on many points, alas, we are

247

of the same opinion. Only I am reluctant to correspond with you about the Jews,[2] as that is not good for both our more or less broken hearts. After 6 million have been murdered, it goes against my instincts to dwell on the manners of those few who survived, whom I incidentally do not need to like. In addition to that, the 50% goy in me feels somehow responsible for the Jewish persecution, so I am therefore quite especially allergic to everything that is said against the chosen people, e.g. also by Max, whose anti-Semitism more or less matches that of WK, though he has the excuse of having spent a year working for the American Jewish Committee. Commentary, the journal of 'our' (anti-Zionist) committee, is a revolting, lying gutter-rag, and I only sent you the issue because of the passage about Bavaria.[3]

What WK wrote about the measures regarding our German property is extremely interesting. He will no doubt do the right thing; only I think that, in this case, *too* patient and careful an approach is not unproblematic *either*, for I suspect that the little there still is in Germany will go to those who are already there and make energetic efforts. (Giraffe's theory is that old 87-year-old Hahn will get everything.) It would really be best if one of us could go there. But at the moment this is barely possible because of the aforementioned hearts. Please keep me up to date with your measures, which we shall naturally keep entirely to ourselves. I am only fairly positive about one thing, namely that one should somehow get a reliable man to take care of the matter (and perhaps give Franz a hint that there would be something in it for him). Incidentally, similar problems should also be coming up in the foreseeable future regarding Melly – from whom we have still not heard anything – and I would then ask you for your wise advice. I too am convinced that Alois is reliable, but this would only have a bearing in the case of witness testimonies etc., and he has no right of disposal whatsoever.

It is indescribably beautiful here at the moment, and we did not do any work on Saturday, but simply warmed ourselves and enjoyed the southern ocean. The business of our house is entirely within the realm of theology at present.

I enclose a delightful and touching letter to Louische.

Heartiest hugs and kisses

from your old child
Teddie

Original: typewritten letter.

1 *coronary insufficiency*: EO.

2 In his letter of 9 February, Oscar Wiesengrund had written: 'Is your work on the Jewish project making any progress? There is a man dining at the Fischers' who has been reporting disturbing things lately from the camp of the

248

truly "religious" Jewry in Brooklyn. Practically mediaeval. These people are openly hostile to those outside of their own circles. They are mostly eastern Jews. [Paragraph] Knowledge of these things in gentile circles might well be contributing to the clearly growing tide of anti-Semitism. The number of public houses etc. who do not admit Jews is apparently increasing throughout America. That shows a much greater hostility than in pre-Hitler Germany.'

3 This was presumably important to Adorno on account of the property in Seeheim: 'The Bavarian government announced that property seized from Bavarian Jews under the Nazis would be returned to them, and where the property had been destroyed the government would pay compensation to the former Jewish owners. It has also announced that persons in Bavaria who had been fined by the Nazi administration under the Nuremberg laws would have the money refunded to them, and 500,000 marks were to be available for long-term loans to Jews who resided in Bavaria before March 1933, when the Nazis came to power, and who wished to resettle there' ('The Month in History', *Commentary*, February 1946, p. 49).

154   LOS ANGELES, 29.3.1946

29 March 1946

My dears,
    a thousand thanks for your sweet letter and the little picture. – Has our little package of clothes arrived in the meantime? – According to Helenchen's letter it must be ghastly in Germany, compared to that we really are in paradise, as incredible as that may seem.
    Archie will probably be admitted to the Catholic Hospital tomorrow (or early next week at the latest) to be put on a tailor-made diet. Because his heart business seems to be no more than a consequence of his diabetes. Now that he has stopped eating carbohydrates and sweets, his heart is much better. I hope that after 10 days, once everything has been determined, Archie will go back to being the old warthippo again. I shall be working with Archie tomorrow morning, and in the afternoon he is to receive guests; the hospital is only a few minutes' drive from here.
    Many hugs and kisses from your
                        Giraffe Gazelle
                        Gretel

The next time you write to the Adornos, please tell Helenchen that we would very much like to see an issue of Sternberger's magazine 'Wandlung'.[1]

I still have a stable full of work to take care of, and I am dreading the clinic – am generally rather down, although the possibility that it could be the diabetes rather than any serious heart trouble is also comforting. Hopefully I will soon no longer have to bore you with this pitiful stuff. Forgive the brevity today with heartiest kisses from your old child Teddie

Original: handwritten letter.

1 From 1945 to 1949, Dolf Sternberger (1907–89) was editor of the monthly journal *Die Wandlung* [Change], published in Heidelberg; its contributors included Karl Jaspers, Marie Luise Kaschnitz and Alfred Weber.

155 SANTA MONICA, 5.4.1946

The Santa Monica Hospital
Owned and Operated by Lutheran Hospital Society of So. Calif.
1250 SIXTEENTH STREET
Santa Monica, California

5 April 1946

My faithful old Hippo Cow,
    the letter from Julie with the dreadful news reached me here in the clinic, where I am receiving treatment for my diabetes and having my diet 'set up'. At present I am unable to tell you more than that all my love and hope, even against reason, are with you. Perhaps there will be a miracle and he will pull through – and be back to his old self again. Otherwise we can do nothing from here – I cabled Leo Löwenthal that he should contact Julie.
    And you will show all your unfathomable courage once more – I wish I were like you.
    Give Julie a thousand thanks
    with heartiest kisses
                        from your old
                        Teddie

Dear Hippo Cow,
    if only I could be with you in these terrible days. Poor Oscar! Teddie is in good hands here, and I hope that, aside from the diet, he will soon no longer notice that he was ever unwell.
    Hugs and kisses from
                        Your old Gretel

Original: handwritten letter with printed letterhead.

250

The Santa Monica Hospital
Owned and Operated by Lutheran Hospital Society of So. Calif.
1250 SIXTEENTH STREET
Santa Monica, California

9 April 1946

My dear faithful old Hippo Cow,
    this is just a small sign – we are sitting, waiting and hoping, that is all we can do at the moment. Naturally we are clinging to any hope of the slightest improvement, but I know all too well from 1935[1] how serious it is – especially at this age, and 2 years after such a heart attack. It is infinitely comforting to know that you and dear Julie are with him at a time when I myself am tied down.
    I have good news regarding myself, incidentally. My diabetes is 'under control'[2] following the most careful of diets, and *without* requiring any insulin. Now the dietician[3] and Gretel have to calculate precisely and organize my *long-term* diet, and then I can go home – tomorrow or the day after. The most important thing is that the heart complaints and other neuritic symptoms have reduced *noticeably*, and the cardiogram is also good – so there is *every* reason to assume that I do *not* have a serious heart condition and that the heart business is indeed only secondary, so that there is a good chance that I will soon be in full possession of my faculties again.
    Max just called; he has made a very abrupt decision to go to N.Y. regarding Jewish affairs – he is leaving now. Will only stay a few days, will naturally get in touch with you. I would like to have gone in his place, but I am simply not yet in shape for it, and it is also business that can only be seen to by Max.
    Give my father the heartiest possible greetings from his child – I am sure he will understand, and wish him all the very best. Warm regards and a thousand thanks to Julie, without whom we would be lost, and no one knows that better than I do – and do tell her that.
    Heartiest kisses
                                        from your old child
                                        Teddie

Dear Hippo Cow,
    I shall now diligently do some sums – the trick with Archie's diet is that he has to take in more or less the same amount of nutrients at breakfast, lunch and dinner. Not only sugar and starch (the carbohydrates) but also fat and protein are being precisely monitored, so that

251

he does not lose his strength and feel constant hunger. But we will no doubt have found out a routine soon.

Hugs and kisses from your old Giraffe

Gretel

Tell Oscar how much we are thinking of him.

Original: handwritten letter with printed letterhead.

1 Adorno's aunt Agathe had died that year following a stroke.

2 *'under control'*: EO.

3 *dietician*: EO.

157 LOS ANGELES, 12.4.1946

12 April 1946

My dear Wondrous Hippo Cow,

a thousand thanks for your lengthy letter. It is not only touching, but indeed heroic that you can manage to give us so composed a report under the circumstances. Can Oscar see at all, or does he only recognize you by your voices? Is he in full possession of his mental faculties, or is it the same as it was with Agathe when I returned from England? I assume from your mention of glucose etc. that he is receiving artificial nourishment, a terrible drudgery. We really have little choice but to hope for a miracle and stand by you with all our love and thoughts.

The letter from Louis[1] is extraordinary in every respect, and made a great impression on both of us. I would like to reply to him. Would you be able to forward a letter of mine to him? Do please let me know.

My health is continuing to improve. I already went home on Wednesday. I am taking to the diet very well, and it is after all a mental relief to know that the heart symptoms are not signs of a severe heart condition, but neuritic in nature. Today I have to go to the doctor once again, after which this sector will at least hopefully be taken care of.

It is as if the full force of the emigrant's fate had struck us only now, after the end of the Nazi regime, and in every respect. And yet, reading the letter from Louis, one has the feeling that we ourselves are still fortunate in our misfortune compared to those who were caught in the hell of Germany. It is a comfort to know that my poor, dear father at

252

least had a few peaceful and relatively untroubled years – seven years; for I think it was in April 1939 that you went to Cuba.

Heartiest kisses, my faithful old mother-animal

from your old child

Teddie

and from Giraffe Gazelle, who is diligently feeding the hippo with fruit and vegetables and studying diabetic cookbooks.

Original: typewritten letter.

1 Not preserved.

158 LOS ANGELES, 20.4.1946

DR. T.W. ADORNO
316 So. Kenter Avenue
Los Angeles 24, Calif.

20 April 1946

My dearest faithful old Wondrous Hippo Cow,

thank you for your letter – it is all indescribably sad, and yet, under the circumstances, one still has to be grateful that it is not getting any *worse* – and that subjectively – as your letter seems to state – he is not suffering. Perhaps, in the face of this awful helplessness, his half-conscious state is actually a blessing. And as, after all, he has held out for almost 3 weeks now, one can still hope for a miracle. I know that your nerves have never failed you when it mattered, and this is the hardest test of endurance they have ever been subjected to. There is nothing I desire more than to be able to help you, but I am ultimately just as helpless as you and Julie.

My health is improving all the time. On Wednesday I have to go to Berkeley regarding my research projects and then attend the psycho-analysts' meeting[1] in San Francisco over the weekend,[2] where I shall be giving a lecture.

I can be cabled:

on the 24th in the evening, all day on the 25th & 26th, on the 27th in the morning:

Hotel Shattuck, Berkeley, Calif.

on the 27th from noon onwards and on the 28th: Palace Hotel, San Francisco, Calif.

On the 29th (Monday) I return home.

Thomas Mann is seriously ill: is having an operation on Monday in Chicago because of a lung tumour. Hopefully it is nothing malignant

253

and he will pull through. He has become especially attached to me these last six months, and I am also *very* fond of him.

Give W.K. my thousandfold best wishes – perhaps they will reach him! And heartiest greetings to dear Julie.

Kisses to you, my Marinumba
from your old child

Teddie

Dear Maria,

it is Easter tomorrow. If only I could be with you and sit at Oscar's bedside with you. – Archie is taking to the diet exceedingly well; he is feeling better than he has in months.

Kisses, dear Hippo Cow, from the

old Giraffe

Original: handwritten letter.

1 At the 'meeting' on 27–8 April, Adorno gave a lecture entitled 'Social Science and Sociological Tendencies in Psychoanalysis', which initially remained unpublished. A German translation by Rainer Koehne appeared in 1962 in *Sociologica II* under the title 'Die revidierte Psychoanalyse' [The Revised Psychoanalysis] (see GS 8, pp. 20–41).

2 *weekend*: EO.

159 LOS ANGELES, 6.6.1946

6 June 1946

My dear faithful old Wondrous Hippo Cow,

I returned from San Francisco fresh in body and mind, and was overjoyed to learn that you had fun with the pictures.

I hardly dare ask after WK anymore, only to request that you extend him my greetings, which will perhaps reach him in a lucid moment. What is the situation with your holidays? Will you and Julie see to it that you can at least go away for two weeks in the summer? The New York heat, which seems already to have set in at the end of May, is surely nothing for an 81-year-old hippo. I am sure you and Julie will solve the problem together.

We have been seeing an incredible number of people in the last few days, including some very peculiar ones: on Sunday afternoon I had a long conversation with Chaplin and yesterday we went to have tea with Thomas Mann,[1] who survived the operation miraculously well and is in amazingly good shape. He incorporated all my suggestions into his new novel.

Anita Lothar, who accompanied us to Norah's place on Sunday

254

(together with Luli and a load of other people), also flew to New York yesterday and intends to get in touch with you.

I would ask that you or Julie forward the letter I have enclosed to Franz Adorno. Please read it and discuss with Julie what detailed information you can and wish to give him about our German claims. (If he is to represent our claims, we cannot keep them from him, and he may be a bureaucrat, but still a decent person.) As far as I know, you had a large balance under your name at the Dresdner Bank that may possibly have escaped confiscation. I have the feeling that you, as you are now an American, could get it released relatively easily. In the light of WK's illness that would naturally be extremely important. Therefore, please give Franz instructions and authorization if necessary.

Alibaba is supposed to go back up to Luli's castle during the summer months and try to produce offspring, though we all doubt that he will be willing. We will receive him back in the autumn. Luli, who is more delightful than ever, was in Europe and brought her mother[2] to Switzerland. The old Hahns, incidentally, plan to return to their property in Ascona in September – he is 88 years old.

Fare thee well, my animal – I shall keep my fingers crossed for you. A thousand kisses

your old
Archibald, Hippo King
m.p.

My dearest Wondrous Hippo Cow,

the day before yesterday we received our first direct letter from Melly by completely ordinary mail, as if nothing had happened. She seems to be well enough; she did not write anything about food, and even seems to be looking for an apartment in Vienna. – We found your description of Hermann Grab and Leo very amusing, especially as Archie is now very slim and does not look middle-aged[3] at all. I enclose all the letters from Germany you sent us, and hopefully Franz will genuinely do something about the matter. Can you think of some way to get him properly moving?

Many hugs and kisses

from your lanky Giraffe
Gazelle

Original: typewritten letter.

1 In his diary, Thomas Mann noted down the date of the visit as 4 June.

2 Baroness Dorothea von Bodenhausen, née Countess von Degenfeld-Schonburg (1877–1969).

3 *middle-aged*: EO.

18 June 1946

My dear good Hippo Cow,
a thousand thanks for your letter and for copying out the lines from Franz. Hopefully he will undertake something sooner rather than later. – The pictures of Archie were genuinely taken by Franz Roehn,[1] and naturally *only* for our dear mother-animal. – The newspaper cutting[2] I enclose today shows two very important scholars being interviewed in San Francisco. The two pachyderms look incredibly funny together. Max still seems to be in Chicago, but is expected to return within the next few days. – Pollock spent a week at Lake Arrowhead with his wife. – I used your $5 to buy myself some magnificent yellow pyjamas with little coloured flowers, a thousand thanks. – Give dear WK our heartiest regards, perhaps he will understand after all. Is he suffering a great deal under the heat? We are now seeing quite a lot of Lily Latté, with whom we share – shared – many friends in Berlin. It has meanwhile turned out that she even went to the same school as I did for a few years, except that back then she was black as night (and now blonde). She is an oasis for me – a real piece of the best Kurfürstendamm[3] (with a mild air of North Berlin) in all-too-beautiful California.
Many hugs and kisses from
Your lanky Giraffe
Gretel

My dear Wondrous Hippo Cow animal, today just the heartiest regards! What can one say about poor WK! The only comfort is that you and Julie are with him. Naturally I understand that you do not want to leave now. Hopefully the heat is not getting to *you* so much. It seems already to have been very severe around the end of May.
Have you seen Anita?
On Sunday we were up at Luli's place – I cannot describe Ali Baba's behaviour there – like a child. I am working a great deal – at the moment only my own things.
I send you all my wishes – perhaps the miracle will still occur *after all*. At least it seems that he does not have to suffer.
Kisses from your old
Hippo King Archibald, m.p.

Original: handwritten letter.

1 The actor and voice teacher Franz Roehn (1896–1989).
2 Not preserved.
3 Translator's note: one of Berlin's largest (and best-known) streets.

L.A., 30 June 1946

My dear faithful old Wondrous Hippo Cow,
a thousand thanks for your letter – what can I say about it, my animal. As far as anyone can tell there is no hope – according to your letter, his condition has not only not improved but in fact deteriorated – Liefmann's statement tends in the same direction – so there is nothing to be done except stand by him and inwardly prepare to cope with the worst.

You asked me about my voice a few weeks ago, and in so doing gave me an idea. An acquaintance of ours, Thora d'Oporto[1] (formerly Countess Boxberg), owns a machine with which one can make recordings, and yesterday I made a record of myself speaking for you, which I enclose here. It contains (on both sides) a series of German and French poems, the latter from memory.

On the one side are:
   Ilse   } by
   Erdgeist } Wedekind
   Green, by Verlaine
On the other side:
   Les Ingénues, by Verlaine
   Im Windes-Weben
   Im Morgen-Taun   } by
   Es lacht in dem steigenden Jahr } George

I think 'Erdgeist' and 'Les Ingénues' came out well, the George poems *not* very well, curiously enough, but perhaps the whole thing will bring you some joy – at least that is its *sole* purpose; the record makes *no* artistic claims. Have it played on a decent gramophone, best of all with an amplifier (electric) 'the better to hear me with'.[2]

Otherwise we are very well, apart from fearing once more that we shall be driven out of our little house due to the dissolution of the OPA.[3] On verra.

Hopefully the heat is still not bothering you too much.

We paid another visit to Thomas Mann,[4] who gave me a further large portion of his novel. One of the new chapters was worked out entirely according to my suggestions. I told him you had recently read Buddenbrooks, which made him very happy.

Ali Baba almost bit his fellow Afghan, Syrian, to death; the poor victim's jaw is in a plaster cast. The wedding plans for Ali Baba have been abandoned, as his bride, Ulila, – has breast cancer. One learns something new every day.

257

Keep your chin up, my great Hippo Cow, as we shall too – that is all we can do in the situation.
Heartiest kisses from your old child
Teddie

Is everything being done to ensure that WK *definitely* feels no pain? It is terrible that the last remnant of a human being is their pain.

Original: handwritten letter.

1 Theodora Elisabeth von Boxberg, born in 1907 in Rehnsdorf, near Kamenz, probably emigrated to the United States with her first – Jewish – husband in 1936. Following her divorce, she married the Vienna-born visual artist Dario Rappa d'Oporto in 1940. She died in Hawaii in 1976.

2 An allusion to the fairytale *Snow White*, transcribed by the Brothers Grimm.

3 Office of Price Administration.

4 On 27 June Mann noted down: 'Had a lively conversation. Gave him the chapter-complex from the outbreak of war until the apocalypse' (Thomas Mann, *Tagebücher 28.5.1946–31.12.1948*, ed. Inge Jens [Frankfurt am Main: Fischer, 1989], p. 14).

162   LOS ANGELES, 9.7.1946

L.A., 9 July 1946

My dear faithful good Maria animal,
it was around 7 o'clock yesterday evening, Max had just left and Gretel and I were playing our evening round of sixty-six when the telegram came – unexpectedly, for when one has been expecting the worst for a considerable time, and gradually become familiar with the idea, then that same readiness has deprived it of a part of its reality, and the blow ultimately comes from out of the blue, as it were. I can hardly describe to you how I am feeling. There are two thoughts that I cannot shake off. The first: that I find a death in exile, even though it was certainly a blessing compared to an existence over there, particularly dreadful – that the continuity of a person's life is senselessly broken in two, that he cannot live his own life to its natural conclusion, as it were, but instead ultimately has the entirely external identity of the 'emigrant' forced upon him, a representative of a category rather than an individual. Even though he never once complained about it, any more than you have, I know how it must have eaten away at him, especially with his profound sense of personal independence; and it is genuinely almost the only consolation

258

that his foresight enabled him to remain at least materially independent, his own master, to the end. – The other thought: that when one's father dies, one's own life feels like theft, an outrage, something that has been taken away from the older person – the injustice of continuing to live, as if one were cheating the dead man of his light and breath. The sense of this guilt is ineffably strong in me. Perhaps it sounds confused and high-flown to you – it indeed has nothing to do with genuine guilt, for how could I have changed anything! – and yet I cannot escape it. Do you think he would even have recognized me if I had been there? What was his state of consciousness (which does not entirely correspond to the capacity for verbal expression)? And: was he at least free of pain at the end? Write me as much about it as your inner feelings permit – there is something therapeutic in knowing how things really were.

I think of him with infinite love, and with him also of you. I know that you will also bear up in the face of this extreme situation, that you will not surrender, and am proud of you for it. But I do think that you should soon travel somewhere cool where you are well looked after and can relax a little. Do not relinquish your will to live, and think of me as you persevere. Naturally I plan to come, perhaps in August or September, but I cannot make any firm promises yet, as it does not depend on me alone, but also e.g. the American Jewish Committee. And then we shall discuss the whole situation. Fortunately you are free of external worries as far as possible, and so your own problems can essentially be overcome – except for the decisive one, that of irretrievability. And that is as present for me as it is for you.

Yesterday evening Norah was there, this morning Max and in the afternoon Eduard, who flew here yesterday. He extends his sincere apologies to you for not visiting during the illness. But he was genuinely unable. He had to admit his daughter to a mental home a few days ago. I cannot describe what he has been through.

I had drafted the obituary notice,[1] and also suggested music – hopefully these external matters will take a dignified form.

No one knows better than I do how you are feeling, and I would rather say nothing about it except that all my love and all my thoughts are with you, more than ever, and that I am already looking forward to seeing you, quand même!

Heartiest kisses from your old child
Teddie

My dear Hippo Cow, Teddie has expressed everything we are feeling so well that all I can do now is to embrace you. I am comforting him as best I can.

Kisses from the old Giraffe Gretel

Original: typewritten letter with additional handwritten note by Gretel Adorno.

1 It appeared in *Aufbau* as follows: 'Our faithful Oscar A. Wiesengrund died at the age of 76 from the consequences of a stroke. We will keep him in loving memory. The bereaved/Maria Wiesengrund, née Calvelli-Adorno/Dr. Theodore W. Adorno/Dr. Margarete Adorno, née Karplus/Julie Rautenberg/ New York – Los Angeles, 8 July 1946'.

163   LOS ANGELES, 15.7.1946

15 July 1946

My dear faithful old Wondrous Hippo Cow,
your express letter came on Saturday evening, and I cannot tell you how much we both admire you for your truly unprecedented composure and bearing, which Leo has meanwhile also written to me about.[1] I understand every emotion expressed in your letter, and I also know how comforting it must have been for you that you were alone with him at the end, even if he barely realized it anymore.
Even after all your reports, I can still not quite assess to what extent he was conscious during the last few months, i.e. whether the speech disorder genuinely related only to the vocal cords, or also the *mental* functions of speech; the latter seems more likely, as he would otherwise have found other forms of expression besides the vocal. Evidently he only had sporadic flashes of consciousness in which he became aware of his condition, and it must have been in such moments that he then made those terribly sad utterances. I did not know that the tumour caused him such unbearable pains, and hope that at least the doctors did not delay for a second before administering the morphine. Was the tumour the cause or an effect of the stroke? All our friends attempted to comfort me in the most touching fashion, Luli even with her spiritism, to which she unfortunately seems entirely devoted. When I told Thomas Mann – who just escaped death narrowly himself, and of whom nobody knows whether his recovery will really last – about the last weeks on morphine, he said with an indescribable expression that he hopes that, when his own time comes, he too will not be denied the relief of morphine, and in the same context he spoke of his grandmother, who suffocated through an affliction of the lungs, and in whom he sees the image of his own illness. But he is working on the novel once more, and we have resumed our meetings relating to that.
I hope I will soon be able to tell you more about my plan to come to New York. Will you not take a little trip somewhere? I have to go to San Francisco again on Wednesday. Has Anita been to see you, by the way?

Did they play the Schubert piece*[2]

at the funeral in the end, or was it replaced with 'Es ist bestimmt in Gottes Rat'?[3] Where did the ceremony take place, and where was he buried? Did you think of having the ashes transferred to the grave in Frankfurt? The thought of it would have something extraordinarily comforting about it, but I do not wish to force it upon you.

I am profoundly sad, and think of you constantly.

Heartiest kisses from

your old child
Teddie

Many hugs and kisses from the lanky Giraffe Gazelle

Original: typewritten letter with additional handwritten note by Gretel Adorno.

1 On 10 July, Leo Löwenthal had written the following to Adorno: 'I have just returned from your father's funeral. Your mother bore up wonderfully. [Paragraph] I have the impression that the few words I spoke were quite good for her. [. . .] It should interest you to know that I began my speech with Hölderlin's late poem 'Höhere Menschheit' [Higher Humanity] and closed with his poem 'Die Entschlafenen' [Those Who Have Passed Away]. [Paragraph] The wreath was hung on the coffin and looked wonderful.'

2 The second – Allegretto – of the Four Impromptus from 1827 (D 935).

3 The first verse of the poem 'Auf Wiedersehen – Gottes Rath und Scheiden' [Farewell – God's Council and Parting] by Ernst von Feuchtersleben (1806–49), which was set by Felix Mendelssohn-Bartholdy.

164 LOS ANGELES, 26.7.1946

DR. T.W. ADORNO
316 So. Kenter Avenue
Los Angeles 24, Calif.

26 July 1946

Mumma, my dearest animal,

back from San Francisco safe and sound.

If everything goes smoothly, I will be in New York during the first days of September and stay for 8–10 days. Then we shall take our

* [Marginal note:] (he was especially fond of it!!)

break in the mountains, which we are both in considerable need of, Gretel no less than myself.

I cannot tell you how much I look forward to seeing you – the Hippo Cow with the Hippo King she spawned. In the meantime you can go on holiday with full peace of mind, and I *ask* that you do – alone out of egotism, so that my Giant Cow is healthy and in good shape when I come.

In S.F. the young Baron Bissing,[1] who was still in Frankfurt 5 weeks ago and got out with the help of a Jewish relief organization, told me the agency where one can already register property claims. Its name is:
Civilian Property Control Agency
Frankfurt Main, Germany.

As the house in Schöne Aussicht was only sold after your escape, it can be written down in the land register under our name without any complications and managed for you, or rather for us, and the *property* is still there. Please tell dear Julie. (The management of the institute building's remains has already been taken over by the American authorities.)

One small request: please keep the little razorblade-sharpener for me as a keepsake. It is the last thing of his that I know made him happy!

Everyone is full of admiration for you, from Anita to Golde, and I am more proud of you than ever.

So: have a good and proper rest!

Heartiest kisses from your old child
Teddie

Fond regards from Giraffe, who has to finish something urgent just now.

Original: handwritten letter with printed letterhead.

1 Uncertain; possibly Hans-Ulrich von Bissing (b. 1910).

165   LOS ANGELES, 14.9.1946

DR. T.W. ADORNO
316 So. Kenter Avenue
Los Angeles 24, Calif.
14 September 1946

Mumma my Wondrous Hippo Cow, this is just to tell you that I arrived here in good shape after a smooth and entirely uneventful journey, except for having terrible hay fever. I was so tired that I slept through from half past nine in the evening until quarter to nine in the morning.

I cannot tell you just how happy our 10 days together made me. I called Max last night at his holiday retreat, told him about the conversation with Slawson and the plan[1] to go to N.Y. with him again, and he was very enthusiastic. So, the chances are good. You just carry on like that, my animal, and you could still go far in life, and think of your child. Heartiest kisses from your old

Teddie

Warmest regards to Julie

Of the suits you sent, is 1 or 2 from Iwens, and what is the second one? The two small suitcases from you arrived safely, a thousand thanks once again!!!

My dear Hippo Cow, I am in a frightful hurry, so just very quickly a thousand thanks, I was incredibly happy about the brooch. I shall write properly this evening.

Giraffe

Original: postcard with printed letterhead; stamp: Los Angeles, SEP 15, 1946. Manuscript with additional note by Gretel Adorno.

1 The social psychologist John Slawson (1896–?) had been vice-president of the American Jewish Committee since 1943.

166 ARROWHEAD, 16.9.1946

Arrowhead Alpine Club (Calif) Twin Peaks, P.O.B. 24

16 September 1946

My dearest Wondrous Hippo Cow, we arrived here safely – although Baldchen found it somewhat difficult to climb to a height of 2000 metres – find it very beautiful and infinitely peaceful after N.Y., and are thinking of Mumma.

A thousand kisses your child Teddie

Dear Hippo Cow,

our pale Archie already gained some colour today – we are taking walks eagerly, sleeping a great deal and letting Baldchen work now and again. I am happy that Teddie has such good news to report about you. Just carry on like that, my animal.

Hugs and kisses from your old Giraffe Gazelle.

Original: picture postcard: Lake Arrowhead California; stamp: illegible. Manuscript.

263

Arrowhead Alpine Club
Alpine Glens Park near Lake Arrowhead
25 September 1946

My dear old veritable Wondrous Hippo Cow,
on the occasion of your 81st birthday – what an impressive date! – I send you the very heartiest congratulations, in the very largest letters that my micrological script can offer, so that your good round, golden Hippo Cow eyes do not have to wear themselves out – and the type-writer is at home. I know that this birthday will not be easy for you; it is probably the saddest you have ever had, and at your mythical age doubly hard. On the other hand, I found you so admirably composed and, now that you are responsible only for yourself, in a certain sense so much younger and more mobile that I am certain you will overcome the feeling of loneliness that must take hold of you, and draw as much enjoyment from this festive occasion as you are able. And after all, as long as I, the other hippo, am still here, you are in fact *not* alone, and there is nothing I yearn for more than to warm you with all my love, just as you have warmed me with yours all my life. So think of us as we shall think of you when you go to Luchow[1] with Julie to eat Haspelchen[2] (or do they already have rabbit now?) and drink some decent beer with it.

I need hardly add that I shall do everything in my power to visit you again as soon as possible.

We have had a superbly refreshing time in the mountain air; some-times going for a drive, sometimes for long walks. My heart stands the altitude *effortlessly*. We are both tanned and rosy-cheeked. Lily Latté stayed here for 4 days (it is only 3 hours' drive from Los Angeles), most delightful. We return on Monday; the hotel – charm-ingly built as a log cabin – will be closing that same day. We are almost the only guests. Even though it is late in the year to be high up in the mountains, we are having beautiful weather, not a cloud in sight, very hot around noon, with a fresher undertone from 4 onwards. Darkness falls at 6; I am now sitting in the giant hall (like Hunding's hut in Die Walküre) under an appropriately large black bear, and write to the even bigger Hippo King Mother Marinumba von Bauchschleifer.

A thousand of the heartiest kisses my Mumma
from your faithful child
Teddie

Original: handwritten letter with printed letterhead.

1 Luchow's Restaurant, 110 East 14th Street, between Third and Fourth Avenue, had been established by Guido August Luchow in 1882; this famous German restaurant did not survive the decline of Union Square in the 1970s, and the building was pulled down in 1995.

2 Translator's note: this is a Frankfurt speciality. It consists of a cured leg of pork that is roasted in the oven and eaten off the bone (also referred to as *Haxe* or *Schweinshaxe*).

168 LOS ANGELES, 12.10.1946

12 October 1946

My dear Wondrous Hippo Cow,
   your pictures arrived here a few days ago. Archie and I have decided unanimously that II is by far the best of them. They made us very happy, and it made me yearn to see you again, hopefully we can arrange that next year. – I have now made good friends with WK's typewriter, so Julie does not need to send me her instructions. – Annachen's letter is actually very touching; should we send her a food package too? Last night at the Horkheimers we met Pollock's new mother-in-law, Frau Bernekker, the epitome of all mothers-in-law. We are still having splendid summer weather here, though the nights are already very cool. When we are finished with our daily workload we regularly take a walk in memory of Ali Baba. Of the two books I would read the Granach[1] first, if only because it is shorter. The first part is much more interesting than what comes later; it was naturally best of all when he read it aloud himself with his warm voice. – In a certain corner of my heart I envy Else for going to Europe soon; despite the conditions, which are surely still ghastly, we simply yearn for it with all our heart. But I am not very optimistic that my wish will be fulfilled in the foreseeable future.
   Eat good things at Luchow's, my animal, and once you have eaten your fill, go to sleep.
                    Your old
                    Giraffe

My dear Wondrous Hippo Cow, naturally your previous letter arrived here without incident, but at that point we had already sent off the books we had chosen to help you through the long, lonely

265

winter hours when you cannot sit down by the river and stare at the Nile, and also because books really are something for you – both very specific – and cannot be converted into sacrifices to any characters in Europe. I would have liked for Thomas Mann to write something in a copy of Der Zauberberg, but he was somewhat unwell – plagued by itching –, and I did not want to pester him, but did not want any useless delay in the delivery. That is why!

I found the idiotess's letter entirely humane, alone because it contains something about us instead of scrounging, unlike the pronouncements of soit-disant educated persons. Even if it were calculated, it would at least show an element of thinking of other people. I know well enough that Annachen behaved terribly in the end, but still find myself unable to become genuinely angry about it – such a one-off change of character cannot simply erase the pleasant recollection of many years, and, after all, she is my Françoise[2] (the name of the old maidservant in Proust, about whom Gabi already said that she was very similar to Annachen).

I find Else's letter artificial, not sympathetic. Conspicuous that she does not even mention me. How much she must resent me.

We shall write to Julie within the next few days.

Max and I have finally resumed work on our big dialectics study. The editing of the film book is complete, and it will go to press as soon as I have looked through it again for corrections.

I am glad that you are still well. Just be careful, my animal, during this transitional weather.

Heartiest kisses

from your child
Teddie

Original: type- and handwritten letter.

1 Alexander Granach's autobiographical novel *Da geht ein Mensch* (see letter no. 75, note 3).

2 The cook of the narrator's parents in *A la recherche du temps perdu*.

169   LOS ANGELES, 28.10.1946

My Hippo Cow,
   this election announcement, which was sent to me by an acquaintance from here, an American professor who happens to be staying in Middletown, will perhaps amuse you.
   On Wednesday I have to go to Berkeley/San Francisco, but hope to be back by Sunday. Max will also be there for 2 days.

I am well, though Giraffe unfortunately had a migraine attack. I am working a great deal.

I completed the final manuscript of the film book yesterday; it is going to press now.

Your long letter was particularly sweet; and the *unspoken* reservations about the book of our poor Alex Granach are right.

He was a thousand times more than he wrote down; and yet it does seem worth the effort of reading it.

You can imagine how I am looking forward to Louis's offspring. What a rabble!

But you are the best, kindest and cleverest of all Hippo Cows.

Lily Latté gave me a *splendid* red hippo with wide-open mouth (the hippo, not Lily!).

I wish I were already back from S.F. –

Heartiest kisses

from your child Teddie

L.A., 28 October 1946

A thousand thanks for the typewriter instructions. The horse is dictating at such a lively pace that I would normally be unable to keep up, and will now be using the days of his absence to copy everything with the typewriter. Ali Baba (with Luli) paid us a visit, we even saw the husband again. She is as lonely as ever, and we are both giving her jester's licence – that way things work out fine.

Many hugs and kisses from your

lanky Giraffe

Original: handwritten letter on the back of Joseph Adorno's election announcement (see fig. 5).

170   LOS ANGELES, 20.11.1946

DR. T.W. ADORNO
316 So. Kenter Avenue
Los Angeles 24, Calif.
20 November 1946

My Hippo Cow animal,

I have a very guilty conscience for remaining silent. But I had an incredible amount to do, and besides that also a block, as I must disappoint you: I now *cannot* come to N.Y. Max has to go because of the committee, and the Jews would not pay my travel expenses too; so we must be patient; but not for too long, I hope.

You were very right to think that I went to San Francisco reluctantly; that does not prevent me from already having to go there again in 2 weeks to see to it that the book is finished; another reason for being unable to go to N.Y., which would be a thousand times more to my taste. I am *at least* as sorry about my not coming as you are, if not even more.

I am entirely free of diabetes, but I had a few days of neuritic pains moving about through my entire upper torso (as in February 1945 at your place); since today nothing more. We are receiving more invitations than we would like. Tomorrow Thomas Mann here, on Saturday we shall visit him. Did you finish Der Zauberberg? Incidentally, the book is *not* identified with Settembrini; he is only one aspect – the (human, not philosophical) model for Naphta is Georg Lukács.

Main news: Ali Baba has fathered 11 little Afghans. Luli as proud as if she had produced the big litter herself. One of them belongs to us, but unfortunately we cannot take it at the moment because our house-owners do not tolerate any dogs.

I am very glad that you can stay in your apartment.[1] Be very careful not to catch cold. The weather in N.Y. apparently leaps from one extreme to the next.

Giraffe had a lot of headaches, but we are both now having vitamin injections, which are doing us a lot of good.

Milton Seligmann will also turn 80 at the start of December. Wrote to Louis at length.

It should interest you to know that the institute has received an official invitation[2] to return to Frankfurt University. We are negotiating for the long term; it is still undecided whether anything will come of it; but we certainly did enjoy it.

I expect you know that the name Eisler has been all over the newspapers.[3] It is a problem for me; coming at the very moment when a book that I wrote with Hanns E 2 years ago is finally being printed. But it will still be a few months before it appears, and then we shall see. Do not mention it.

Heartiest kisses, my animal, from your old
Hippo King
Archibald

Original: handwritten letter with printed letterhead.

1 Adorno's mother and Julie Rautenberg, who had been staying with her since Oscar Wiesengrund's death.

2 The letter from the president of Frankfurt University, Walter Hallstein, dates from 17 October 1946; see Horkheimer, *Briefwechsel 1941–48*, pp. 765f.

3 Hanns Eisler's brother Gerhart Eisler (1897–1968), who, as a communist, had been forced to flee Germany in 1933, arrived in the USA in 1940. He was targeted by the senate committee set up to investigate 'un-American activities'. Eisler's sister Ruth Fischer (1895–1961), who, like her brother, had belonged to the KPD and Komintern in the 1920s but was expelled for her radical leftism, had published a series of six articles in mid-November – 'The Komintern's American Agent' – in *Journal America*, in which she denounced Gerhart Eisler as a spy, also mentioning Hanns Eisler and warning of his influence in Hollywood.

171   LOS ANGELES, 17.12.1946

17 Dec. 1946

My dear Wondrous Hippo Cow,
a thousand thanks for your sweet letter and the cheque. I hope you have meanwhile received my package and eaten the stollen[1] – it is at least a small reminder of the old days. I even wanted to get you a pair of warm fur-lined gloves, but I could not find them anywhere here.

I enclose a cheque, and perhaps Julie will be so kind as to get them for you. But if you would prefer something else, that would naturally also be fine. I am constantly sending Frau Seele packages, and, as she no doubt also receives some from my relatives in the East, I would ask you not to send her anything. – On the evening of the 23rd we shall celebrate Christmas at the Horkheimers, and we have been invited by Fritz Lang and Lily Latté for the 24th. Aside from that we do not have any plans.

Many hugs and kisses from the old
Giraffe

Have an enjoyable Christmas – we shall be thinking of you. We have not heard from Franz Adorno and family in such a long time – have you? I have already accumulated a few clothes for them too.

My dear faithful old Wondrous Hippo Cow,
a thousand thanks for the letter and the cheque – which is *much too* munificent and aristocratic. Hopefully our little present will also bring you a little joy.

I returned from S.F. in good health and spirits, in a much better mood than the previous times. The work there is progressing well. Max had to go there the Tuesday after I did; is also back; with him and Lix today.

I had a truly astonishing thank-you card from Lujche. Amazing how he is keeping himself together. Also news from Pfeiffer Belli[2] and Juliette Rumpf.[3] I probably wrote that I had a letter from Margot.[4]

We shall be at Norah's place for a truffle supper on Christmas Day. This Christmas will be hard for you. One is completely over-whelmed by memories on such days, and the happier things used to be, the more painful it is now. I hope so very much that you will get through it, that you will have a lovely time with dear Julie in spite of everything and turn your remembrance of the past into a source of consolation. We send you all our love and concern. How dearly I hope we shall soon see each other.

Max also thought you were in admirable form. Just carry on like that, said the mother to her hopeful offspring – and head bravely for the year 1947, my best and only Mumma.

Heartiest kisses from your old child
Teddie

Original: handwritten letter.

1 Translator's note: also known as *Christstollen*, this is a variety of Christmas cake made with raisins and almonds and coated with icing sugar. Though eaten throughout Germany, it is associated most strongly with Dresden, where it is customarily sold at Christmas markets.

2 The writer and journalist Erich Pfeiffer-Belli (1901–89) was feature editor of the *Berliner Tageblatt* in 1933, and in 1938 switched to the *Frankfurter Zeitung*. After liberation he moved to the *Süddeutsche Zeitung*. In 1986 he published his memoirs, entitled *Junge Jahre im alten Frankfurt und eines langen Lebens Reise* [Early Years in Old Frankfurt and a Long Life's Travels].

3 Josefine Rumpf (1901–83), who called herself Juliette, worked at the Freies Deutsches Hochstift [translator's note: a cultural institute in Frankfurt that owns the Goethe-Haus and the Goethe Museum] from 1928 to 1974, and was director of the library there. She had studied together with Adorno, who was a friend of hers. Her 1925 dissertation bore the title 'Die Beziehungen der auf Goethe, Kant, Fichte folgenden Generation zu Italien' [The Relationship of the Generation Following Goethe, Kant and Fichte to Italy]. Juliette Rumpf had written to Adorno on 7 October 1946.

4 Margot Rocholl, the daughter of Bernhard Salomon, general director of the former Lahmeyer works (which had built electrical machines and power stations). Margot, whose mother was murdered by the Nazis, was a friend from Adorno's youth.

26 Dec. 1946

My dearest Wondrous Hippo Cow,
thank you so much for your sweet letter. I hope that you not only had peaceful holidays, but will also begin the new year well. – We were at the Horkheimers on the 23rd, at Norah's on the 25th, and on Christmas Eve proper Lily Latté (the child from my school) had us over for a quite lovely evening up at Fritz Lang's place. – Otherwise, I am afraid I do not have such good news today: Teddie suddenly had the severest stomach pains, had an x-ray and was found to have stomach ulcers. Now he first of all has to stay in bed for 2 weeks and eat even more carefully, and then we shall see. I am telling you immediately so that you know how things are here. There is no cause for concern, and Archie is quite comfortable in bed and is working. I hope we shall soon have everything 'under control'[1] again, as one says here.
many hugs and kisses from your
Giraffe Gazelle

My dear faithful wondrous animal,
your letter was *so* sweet, it made me incredibly happy. You should not worry on my account; I am recovering well and enjoying having a rest. No pains at all at the moment.
Christmas Eve with Lily Latté and Lang was especially nice; less exciting at Norah's place.
What Liefmann said is all stuff and nonsense; I had a charming evening with Milton in S.F.
My stomach business is ulcers,[2] i.e. *harmless*, but rather unpleasant. We are doing everything to get rid of them. Working in bed is quite pleasant.
Meanwhile a book on anti-Semitism[3] has come out with the first of our pieces on the subject.
Enjoy your New Year's festivities, and you should *really* not fret on my account.
And heartiest kisses
from your old child
Teddie

Original: handwritten letter.

1 *'under control'*: EO.

2 *ulcers*: EO.

3 This is *Anti-Semitism: A Social Disease*, ed. Ernst Simmel (New York: International Universities Press, 1946), with contributions from Theodor W. Adorno, Bernhard Berliner, Otto Fenichel, Else Frenkel-Brunswik and R. Nevitt Sanford, Max Horkheimer, Douglass W. Orr and Simmel himself.

1947

6 Jan 1947

My dear Hippo Cow,
   the two pleasant horses have caught a ghastly cold, I even more severely than Archie, who will be in bed until Thursday anyway. Aside from that, the doctor said that he was already much better. There is a flu epidemic here at the moment; I am dripping all day and we both have sore throats, but no fever, only a slight temperature. There is no cause for concern, really, one only feels lethargic and drowsy. Archie is sitting in bed quite cheerfully, while my own senses are only up to playing 66 and draughts or nine men's morris. What a pain. – Hopefully the cold weather is not giving you so hard a time. – The Löwenthals plan to come here by car around the middle of the month. – Did the Pollocks call you after their return? Take care of yourself, and make sure not to imitate us. Hugs and kisses from your
lanky Giraffe

My dear faithful old Wondrous Hippo Cow, I have a heavy cold, which is already subsiding, but otherwise I am feeling *much* better – subjectively speaking, I can no longer notice any stomach trouble, and will already be getting up in a few days. Incidentally, the pains I had in N.Y. 2 years ago, which you perhaps recall, were probably the same thing.
   I am working with wild energy and much joy.
   Begin the new year well, my animal. I would be *infinitely* happy to see you soon.
   Heartiest kisses
from your faithful child
Teddie

Original: handwritten letter.

12 Jan 1947

My dear Wondrous Hippo Cow,
   a thousand thanks for the splendidly warm blanket. Are you quite
sure you can spare it? Archie is very much afraid that you will now be
cold. – He has been up again since Friday, and is feeling quite well on
the whole. At the moment he is up at Thomas Mann's place. I am still
not quite back to normal, and just now I am having a rather irksome
bout of conjunctivitis. – I have meanwhile sent a package with clothes
to Franz Adorno and family with an additional 3 lb of chocolate. – The
Dieterles came back from Europe recently, and have been telling us
some very interesting things; life in Germany must still be horribly
difficult.
   Many hugs and kisses from your long-necked
                                        Giraffe

My dear faithful old Wondrous Hippo Cow animal,
   I cannot tell you how happy I was to receive the blanket – as a child
I had always envied my father for it! – but at the same time I have a
terribly guilty conscience, and imagine you lying there and shivering,
whereas you could cover your dear old motherly bones with this good
warm blanket, my animal. After all, it is madness for me to have the
blanket here in the warm South while you, in the grisly New York
winter, do not! If you catch pneumonia, I will tear out my – not hair,
for I hardly have any, but rather my last bristles.
   And *yet* I was *incredibly* happy, perhaps more happy than I have
ever been in my whole life upon receiving a gift. But: let me know if
you are properly warm, whether you genuinely do not need the
blanket.
   I am rid of my ghastly cold and, thanks to the medicine, I hardly
notice my ulcers after spending 2 weeks in bed.
   Thomas Mann, whom I visited today, has written the new chapter
of his novel,[1] following my suggestions to the letter. It is a *very* peculiar relationship.
   Tomorrow is a solemn day: Max and I are starting a big piece of
work together.[2]
   I myself have completed another big text[3] I had been working on
feverishly in bed. I am in the most productive condition possible,
and extremely happy despite my laughable stomach business. It is
probably a result of psychological factors, by the way, like all ulcers.
In my case, these go by the name of Charlotte Alexander[4] (*completely*

entre nous). Perhaps more on that another time. But do not worry; that has nothing to do with the horses.

I kiss you upon your rosy hippo snout
                        Your old Archibald

Original: handwritten letter.

1 The chapter dealing with Adrian Leverkühn's composition *Doktor Fausti Weheklag*.

2 The close theoretical collaboration between Horkheimer and Adorno, as in the case of the *Dialectic of Enlightenment*, was not continued. At the time, both were still considering writing the book on dialectical logic.

3 Adorno was working on the third part of *Minima Moralia* at the time.

4 No further information.

175   LOS ANGELES, 19.1.1947

T. W. ADORNO

19 Jan 1947

My dear faithful Wondrous Hippo Cow,
    today I come to you with a request.
    Felix Weil has separated from his ghastly wife, thank God, and went back to New York today. This circumstance is very favourable in every way – also for the institute. It was a great tragedy; he went through the most atrocious time, remained *extremely* loyal to all of us; and became incredibly attached to me.
    I have now asked him to look after you in N.Y.; not only because I know you enjoy hearing directly from us, but *above all* for his sake. He really has no idea what to do with himself, and the mere fact of having a task to fulfil would do him a world of good.
    So, please invite him *at once* when he calls, be particularly cordial and friendly towards him (he thirsts for it), speak well of the institute, and let him come again soon, even if you find it is a little boring. He is a profoundly unhappy person in great need of love; and for all his bad manners and strange character traits he is a loyal, dead reliable good fellow. You only need to let him talk, and he will already be happy.
    You would really be doing me a huge favour.
    I am feeling much better; I am lively and in very good spirits. At the start of February I shall be going to S.F.
    Heartiest kisses
                        from the old child
                        Teddie

275

The lovely writing paper was a Christmas present from Lily Latté.
Many hugs and kisses from your lanky
Giraffe

Original: handwritten letter with printed letterhead.

176   LOS ANGELES, 30.1.1947

30 Jan 1947

My dear Wondrous Hippo Cow,
I am very sad that your dear eyes are unwell. What did the doctor
say? Can one do anything to prevent rapid fatigue? My eyes got back
to normal very quickly with some penicillin cream. – We just received
the letter enclosed from Franz and Helenchen; I am sure it will interest Julie to know that one can now correspond about business matters
once more. – Have you meanwhile heard from Felix Weil already? The
wife has just flown to New York after him.
Many hugs and kisses
from your
lanky Giraffe

My Hippo Cow animal, today just this quick greeting – I have an
incredible amount of work to do, have to complete a chapter of the
Berkeley book before I go to S.F. (on 5 February).
Tonight at Max's for a party. Leo and Golde arrived in good shape.
I am feeling fine; the little ulcer is still making its presence felt, but
the pills prevent any real pain. Otherwise I am very lively and in good
spirits.
Are you being treated by an ophthalmologist? I am naturally very
concerned about your eyes, my animal.
As it is freezing cold here at present, I am sleeping with the new
blanket every night; it warms me quite wonderfully.
According to the letter from Franz, we can now send him lists etc.
Heartiest kisses from your old child
Teddie

Original: handwritten letter.

276

20 February 1947

My dear Wondrous Hippo Cow,
but of course you sent me the lovely violet Madonna pendant, and I could have sworn I thanked you right away. Please forgive your foolish Giraffe. – We are working at full throttle here once again. The project team in Berkeley is now writing the manuscript, and Teddie is up to his neck in work. Unfortunately I cannot help him with it as much as I would like, as I have been rather unwell these last few weeks; I have a migraine attack almost every week, and otherwise also many headaches. – On Saturday we were on the set at Lang's studio (I for the first time in my life, Archie had already visited sets in Neubabelsberg and with the Dieterles). Crowd scenes were being shot, and for me – I almost never go to the cinema – it was quite interesting to see something like that for once. The whole thing reminded Archie very strongly of an opera rehearsal with conductor. I am sure you would have had fun too.

Yesterday we visited Norah's mother for the first time since old Hahn died. She genuinely intends to go to Switzerland in May; her energy is amazing. – The Pollocks and Lix Weil are expected to return on Sunday; hopefully the institute will not be so busy.

Many hugs and kisses from your
Giraffe Gazelle

(If you look properly, you will notice that the letter is written in the finest Giraffa (the real language of giraffes).)

My dear Hippo Cow animal, I am back from S.F. and have completed a long chapter for the Berkeley book (about 100 pages of type), almost finished a big German manuscript, and also finally the proofs for the film book with Eisler, which looks very decent. So an inhuman heap of work. The Berkeley manuscript has to be finished by 1 May (I still have to write 2 chapters!); then Max and I will finally get around to ourselves again.

Charlotte and I have been reconciled since December (after a 9-month break), and we were recently invited there together 3 evenings in a row. But I very much doubt that it will still be as good as it was – there is too much that stands between us, her reasons being anger that I did not marry her, and in my case profound bitterness about many things she did to me. In spite of everything I am still incredibly attached to her, and it seems that she, in her curious fashion, is equally attached to me. She is still not divorced, and Robert not yet naturalized; it was because of the extremely delicate situation between us that I did not stay for the Seligmans' golden wedding anniversary, even though everyone pestered me half to death.

277

I often told myself that I should not tell you anything about this business, which shook me to the very depths of my soul, but what is the point of having a mother if one cannot talk to her about everything. One day I will tell you the whole story my animal. Incidentally, C. was marriage-hunting in N.Y. in September, at the same time that I was there, and at that point we were entirely separate – I did not see her at all, and did not even know her address. I would so like you to meet her. Well, perhaps another time. Her marriage-hunts (our reason for breaking up) have all been fruitless. Objectively, she is deeply pitiable; but it is she who destroys everything for herself and for others.

But I am now much more in control of myself, and also in much better health. I do not doubt that all my ailments have been connected to C., and neither does Robert. Forgive the letter of confession; I had an irresistible need to write it.

Heartiest kisses from your old child
Teddie

Original: handwritten letter.

6 March 1947

My dear Hippo Cow,
a thousand thanks for your dear long letter. At the moment there is nothing special here apart from a great deal of work. – I am glad that Golde is checking up on you so well, even though I do not especially like her, as I find her too subservient and too much lacking a mind of her own. But then I am a horrible Giraffe and generally very big-headed. – The letter I have enclosed from Frau Seele may interest you; she is certainly a poor soul, but her view of the world is really very narrow. –

How are your dear eyes? I am terribly worried about them. If I could at least keep you company and read to you and have conversations with you, oh those stupid 3000 miles!

Many hugs and kisses from your lanky
Giraffe

My dear old Hippo Cow,
today just these lines – I am most terribly worried about your eyes. I hope it is nothing serious. The most important thing is to follow your doctor's advice closely, and do not read and write too much, my animal.

Nothing new at all here, only dreadful amounts of work, but matters will improve after 1 May.

Fortunately I am still getting around to my own projects. My relationship with C has hit rock bottom again; I have not answered her last two letters. But it is all much more complicated than one could comprehend from a distance, especially as far as the 'blame' is concerned. But we shall talk about all that one day

Keep me in your heart as I think of you
with kisses

from the old child
Teddie

Original: handwritten letter.

179 LOS ANGELES, 26.3.1947

26 March 1947

My dear Wondrous Hippo Cow,

you are quite right to be very angry with the two horses for not writing to you for so long. And yet there are a great many things to tell that will interest you. Last week we went to the cinema on two occasions – albeit both private showings. First to Lang to see his 11-year-old film 'Fury' (with Spencer Tracy, who was discovered around that time), an anti-lynching film, very exciting and much better than the things being shown today. The second was Chaplin's new film Mr Verdoux, which is coming out in New York between 1 and 5 April. Although the film is 2 hours long, it is extremely exciting, very funny in parts, and definitely Chaplin's best since Gold Rush, despite laying on the ideology too thick. It is about a petty bourgeois Bluebeard who, after being fired from his job as a banker, earns a hard living by marrying older women for their money, quickly murdering them and then hurrying on to the next one. Please do let us know if you would enjoy it, and whether it would be too much of a strain on your eyes if you were to watch the film with Julie. The two horses would like to treat you (both) to it.

Last night visited Thomas Mann, who read us his Nietzsche lecture;[1] at the end of April they are going first to Washington and New York, and then to Europe – England, Switzerland, Holland, Scandinavia. Hopefully the whole thing will not be too strenuous for him. – The Löwenthals are going back again next week, while Archie has to go to San Francisco once again.

Please give Julie my very best, and tell her that we have already received confirmation from the lawyer that the signatures arrived without incident. Have you sold any securities in the meantime?

Many hugs and kisses

from your old Giraffe

279

My dear old Hippo animal, Giraffe forgot to tell you that we were *invited* to Chaplin's 'Monsieur Verdoux' with only about 15 other people, then afterwards to a private dinner at his place – with Gretel as his dinner partner. It continued late into the night. For a laugh, he, an American parodist and myself invented operas by Verdi, Wagner and Mozart. He is fantastically musical, acted and sang everything, I was at the piano and also sang. I think it was truly lovely. All sorts of celebrities such as Clifford Odets,[2] one of the Vanderbilts etc. also there. Mrs Chaplin is enchanting, as kind and modest as she is beautiful (she is the daughter of Eugene O'Neill). The Chaplins have now gone to N.Y., but should be back in about 6 weeks. His way of turning *everything* into theatre (he acts incessantly!) reminds me very much of you, my animal.

I now have the bulk of my study for Berkeley done; now only 1 long chapter to finish by 1 May so that I can breathe more easily again. Unfortunately I *have to* go to S.F. again next week; I wish I were back already. You really cannot imagine the amount of work I have had during the last 8 weeks. But I also got a great deal of enjoyment out of it, and I am in fairly good health.

Thomas Mann's novel is finished; we received the last bundle of pages yesterday.

Max is feeling better; we hope finally to start properly again on 1 May, for then I will have put the 'big' Berkeley project behind me.

I hope you are well, my animal, and that those heavy hippo eyes are not giving you too much trouble after serving you loyally for so long.

My address from 2–7 April: Hotel Mark Hopkins, San Francisco, Cal.

Heartiest kisses from your old

Teddie

Original: handwritten letter.

1 'Nietzsche's Philosophie im Lichte unserer Erfahrung' [Nietzsche's Philosophy in the Light of our Experience].

2 The dramatist and scriptwriter Clifford Odets (1906–63), who was temporarily married to the actress Luise Rainer.

180   LOS ANGELES, 11.4.1947

11 April 1947

My dear Wondrous Hippo Cow,

the newspaper cutting enclosed[1] shows you, once again, what strange children you have. – I had ghastly toothache – an abscess, then had the villain pulled and it simply would not heal, the nerve-ends were exposed, then a migraine, but now everything is back to normal. Robert Alexander is here, first stayed with Max for a few days, now with Lix. Anita lives in Los Angeles. – Early yesterday morning there was a little earthquake, the table wobbled and all the little animals I have standing around here rattled. Today it is almost unbearably hot.

Many hugs and kisses from your lanky
Giraffe

Archie postponed his trip to San Francisco, is only leaving on the 20th for a week.

11 April 1947

My dear faithful old Hippo Cow animal,
how are you? How are those good motherly eyes faring? I am so worried – how touching the end of your last letter was, where you wrote that your eyes have got cold feet. Hopefully your doctor will help you (– that makes me think of Tristan:[2] 'Unless the healing lady' etc.)

I have postponed my trip to S.F. for 2 weeks, as my colleagues' manuscripts were not yet finished. Meanwhile they have arrived, and are very decent (I am still waiting for one part). I will leave on Sunday the 20th, and this time will stay for at least a week; wish I were already back here.

Broken up completely with C., I did not write to her any more. Incidentally, Robert and Anita are here; he is staying with Lix, we had all three of them over two nights ago.

Tonight we are having Lisa Minghetti here who is delightful.

I am glad I shall soon be done with the work on the project so that we can get around to our own things again. I am simply a little tired, have not been sleeping well. Incredibly hot since yesterday.

Golde will tell you about us at length.

Get well very soon with heartiest kisses from your old child
Teddie

Original: handwritten letter.

1 Not preserved.

2 Adorno quotes the words spoken by Kurvenal, who is keeping watch over the sleeping Tristan, at the start of Act Three: 'Were he to awake, it would be only to leave us forever, unless the healing lady, she who alone can help us, first appears.'

1 May 1947

My dear good Hippo Cow,
as I had forwarded your letter to Archie, I did not manage to reply to you; so, Luli is in New York, we have not heard from her in a long time, her husband was apparently very ill. – I went up to see Ali Baba, he was very happy to see me, sadly he looks thin and somewhat neglected. The children are indescribably funny, they look even more ape-like than Baba. – Archie is still taking his medication, though he does sometimes interrupt his diet when tempted by particularly good cocktails or sweets, but his diabetes is nonetheless absolutely under control. He is in very good spirits. – On Sunday at Norah's for a farewell party; on the 10th she and her mother are going first to New York, then to Europe. – Further good recovery for your dear eyes.
Many hugs from your lanky
Giraffe

My dear faithful old Wondrous Hippo Cow,
I returned from San Francisco safe and sound and in good spirits, after a trip that was in every sense very successful and pleasant. The big collective Berkeley book is almost finished (I only have about 20 pages left to write for my own contribution, and my associates are also making haste). I think it will be as decent as one can expect with such research stuff. I only have to go there once more concerning the book and the 'Adult Project';[1] the child project will be continuing.
To my great joy, I discovered upon my return the first 80 pages of proofs for the big German book I wrote with Max, printed in Amsterdam. Completely European – my first *real* communication with our homeland.
Norah Andreae is going to Switzerland with her mother for 3 months, also to Frankfurt. I will ask them to see Franz.
In S.F. there was a great surprise. Charlotte called me (after I had been completely silent for 3 months), insisted upon seeing me, and explained – not inhumanly, in fact even touchingly – that our estrangement had resulted from the fear that her relationship with me would prevent her, both inwardly and outwardly, from achieving the marriage she so desires (which would be a refuge for her) – and occasioned a complete reconciliation. There is no telling how long it will last, with her marriage obsession (and her anger that I will not leave Gretel), but it was certainly a great triumph, though dampened slightly by pity – for I think it is more a case of her being determined not to *lose* me than her loving me as much as she once did. Her situation is indeed a grisly

one, with endless wrangles about her divorce. I still consider her the most delightful and enchanting creature in the world (– a creature: not a human), but now that she has returned the matter has lost its power over me. I am entirely engrossed in my work and happy with Giraffe.

Went to see some ice dance with the Horkheimers last night, rather nice. Tonight we are having a meeting here.

I am glad that you are sensing an improvement with your eyes. Hopefully it will last. – Today Mietze is coming to L.A. for 2 weeks. You should have seen her face when Charlotte and I turned up there. Robert and Anita were still here at the same time.

Heartiest kisses from your old child
Teddie

Original: handwritten letter.

1 This refers to *The Authoritarian Personality*.

182 LOS ANGELES, 14.5.1947

14 May 1947

My dear Hippo Cow,

Archie is downtown in Los Angeles with Max and Fritz, so I have a little time to write. No, good Hippo Cow, you really need not worry about Charlotte. She has many negative and some positive aspects,* but in essence Archie was simply tormenting himself; the object was not so important. Perhaps his depression was also related to the emigration and the disappointment at the false peace. But after the reconciliation he realized that the whole business really only came about because Charlotte simply wants to marry at all costs, and I hope that he is now safe from any further anguish. Giraffe will make sure to look after the hippo, you can rely on that. – Lotte and E. are thinking of coming here in August. Oh, if only you could visit us sometime. – Luli was just here for four days, very sweet, but crazier than ever, and yet it is always a joy and a surprise to be with her. – At the moment I am not taking in any of Ali Baba's children – the dogs finally have to be house-trained. But I reserve the right to a male descendant of Ali Baba. Afghans are simply wild animals and a certain risk, so one at least has to be sure that the landlord will not make any trouble. And – just between you and me – Ali Baba is still the only one for the two horses. – Max's health is very erratic; he has a predisposition towards angina pectoris and should simply avoid strain, which he is not really doing.

* [Marginal note:] she is very pretty and sympathetic, but terribly stupid

283

We shall keep our fingers crossed that your poor eyes will soon get better; unfortunately the stupid doctors are not such a great help.
Many hugs and kisses from your lanky
Giraffe

Redvers Opie will be turning up here next week

After just returning home with Max and Fritz dead tired, but in the *best* of spirits, I shall today only cuddle you in authentic Afghan style and kiss you heartily.
Your faithful child
Teddie

Original: handwritten letter.

183   LOS ANGELES, 23.5.1947

23 May 1947

My dear Hippo Cow,
thank you for your sweet letter and the newspaper cuttings. Archie has just borrowed the Kracauer book[1] from Lang and has been getting very worked up about it. – A few days ago we were treated to the pleasant surprise of having Redvers Opie over for dinner. It was enjoyable, a reminder of the old days. He had divorced Kathrin[2] fairly soon, given up his fellowship[3] at Oxford and also his post at the embassy. Aside from that he is still his old self, only broader, full of youthful adventurousness.
Today I am finally sending you the letter from Dr Knöll,[4] our former chemist, who then took over K+H.[5] Perhaps you could be so kind as to forward the letter to Lottchen in Boston too, it should also be interesting for her. – Archie cannot remember the Heinlanger (Zuber) affair at all, what is that about? – I am glad that you are going to Rhinebeck in the summer, we also kept slinking off to Bar Harbor. If we manage to get away at all this year, it will probably only be in September, when it is no longer so crowded and cheaper. – Our landlady is tormenting us once again with a new threat, namely that she will sell half the house. There is still a massive housing shortage here, there may be apartments, but the prices are too high for horses to afford. – We are more and more tempted to see Europe again, perhaps someone from the institute will go there next year to get an idea. An acquaintance (the writer Thorberg)[6] said something amusing: that the thought of Europe does not make him homesick, but rather go-sick. – Hopefully Julie will see many a lovely sight on her trip to Canada.
Many hugs and kisses from your lanky
Giraffe

284

My dear faithful old Hippo animal,

a thousand thanks for the letter, hopefully those poor eyes truly are getting better. I have no news apart from work. I have proof-read the book I wrote with Max and the one with Eisler; in the latter case I shall, for very sound reasons, probably give up my co-authorship. Work on the project is decreasing; I hope Max and I will finally get around to our things. I am putting the finishing touches to the 3rd part of the book of aphorisms. A shorter piece of mine[7] is appearing in the yearbook Psychoanalysis and Social Science.

The man who wrote the review of the (atrocious!!) book by Friedel is a good acquaintance of mine.[8]

Norah, who is just about to leave for Europe, will call you (if she has not already done so), as also will Redvers in a few weeks. Today a highly talented young Englishman[9] is speaking to a small group of us about his sociological theory of the novel.

I am well, am lively and in good condition, and hope that the depressive phase has been entirely overcome; am also taking the housing crisis calmly. I shall probably have to go to S.F. again in mid-June, but that is rather welcome now.

Would it not make things easier for you if we typed our letters? Look after yourself, my animal, and have a fine thorough holiday.

Heartiest kisses from your old child

Teddie

Original: handwritten letter.

1 Siegfried Kracauer's book *From Caligari to Hitler: A Psychological History of the German Film* had been published in April by Princeton University Press.

2 Redvers Opie's wife, née Taussig.

3 *fellowship*: EO.

4 Unknown.

5 Karplus und Herzberger, the company owned by Gretel Adorno's father.

6 The Austrian writer Friedrich Torberg (1908–1979), who became known in 1930 through his novel *Der Schüler Gerber hat absolviert* [The Pupil Gerber has Graduated], lived as an emigrant first in Los Angeles, then later in New York.

7 It had presumably been planned that Adorno's lecture 'Social Science and Sociological Tendencies in Psychoanalysis', given in San Francisco in 1946 (see letter no. 158, note 1), would be published; this did not happen.

8 Eric Bentley (b. 1916), a student of Brecht and Eisler, whose review had appeared in the *New York Times Book Review* on 18 May; no further information was found regarding Adorno's contact with Bentley.

9 Ian Watt (1917–99), who had studied in Cambridge and, of his seven years as a soldier in the Second World War, was forced to spend three in a Japanese camp on the River Kwai, held a fellowship at the University of California in Los Angeles from 1946 to 1948. From 1952 to 1962 he taught at Berkeley, then – following some years in England – in Stanford. – His 'theory of the novel' appeared in 1957 under the title *The Rise of the Novel*.

13 June 1947

My dear Wondrous Hippo Cow,
naturally we shall type our letters from now on, so that you will not have to strain your eyes so much in attempting to decipher our scribblings. As for you, however, please write in pencil.

A thousand thanks for the cheque, I will use it to buy myself a nice black belt. My birthday this year was the nicest in a long time. I also received magnificent gifts, in particular from Archie: a new carriage, as he calls it, a real automobile, a dark blue four door[1] sedan with 8 cylinders. We are both incredibly proud of it. The night before we had the Horkheimers and Lily Latté here for dinner, and ate farmed pheasant (I cannot find any wild ones here, sadly). On Tuesday we ate out with Lang and Lily. Giraffe was also given a giraffe-shawl, a fountain pen and a pretty black snakeskin bag.

Otherwise a great deal of work again, and Archie's associates from Berkeley are coming here for a day. It would be unwise to buy our half of the house, much too expensive and difficult to resell. We will just have to wait and see how the situation develops.

Many hugs and kisses
from your old
Giraffe

Marinumba my animal,
The car is a brand-new, very pretty and powerful Ford, and very difficult to get hold of; we only managed to acquire it through our good connections in the almighty film industry. We are having a lovely time with it, driving a great deal and far – lately in San Pedro, for example, the very remote outside port of Los Angeles. Are cheerful and in good shape, also in our work. Max and I have finally got back our own things properly, though we are still not free of our Jewish project and the accompanying administration. I will probably have to go to S.F. again in July, but that has now lost its sting. C. will probably go to Reno in August, and we expect to meet with her in September during our holiday near Lake Tahoe. I am afraid the chance of coming to N.Y.

286

is slim at the moment, as the whole Jewish project is coming to an end, but this could change at any time. This week the whole Berkeley gang is coming here for a meeting of the Social Science Research Council (Rockefeller), to which Max and I have also been invited: for its West Coast director, Harold Jones, is my co-director from the children's project. But we (Max and I) are occupying ourselves with it primarily to clear the decks, so that we can devote ourselves to our big new project as far as possible. I have gone through the proofs of our book, which is in the process of being published, with the untiring assistance of Lix (he has separated from his wife once and for all and is very happy about it). As for the film book, the Oxford press was very understanding: I will be mentioned very emphatically in the foreword, but not as the official co-author. It is a shame, as I in fact not only wrote, but also *conceived*, 90% of it; but it is still better this way. If my 'co-author' had been a little more loyal, *he* would have been the one to step down in the light of the true situation. But he is too vain for that, and on the other hand I can understand that, in his position, the publication of a purely scientific book under his name must be very important to him; and, after all, it was he who originally had the contract. So, let us leave it at that. You will receive it as soon as it is in print; it looks thoroughly decent in every respect. Except that film music is ultimately too limited and indifferent a subject to warrant an entire book. I did, however, incorporate various more peripheral matters that interested me.

Hopefully your good round hippo eyes are remaining somewhat stable! Heartiest kisses from your old child
Teddie

Original: handwritten letter.

1 *four door*: EO.

185   LOS ANGELES, 6.7.1947

6 July 1947

My dear Hippo Cow,
you must not be angry at us for taking a little longer to write this time. There were such piles of work – the big Berkeley manuscript has finally gone off to New York, almost a thousand pages – and after that I had an especially heavy migraine attack as a result of the over-whelming strain. The only thing that can help then is complete rest, lying in the open as much as possible, but today I am sufficiently better at least to imagine lively horse-jumps again. We have no news, Archie

and Max are having the preliminary meetings for their next book and are both very happy about it. You are going away soon now; I hope you have a lovely summer in Rhinebeck. It has now been one year since poor Oscar departed from us, dear, dear Hippo Cow.

Many hugs and kisses

from your lanky Giraffe

My dear old faithful Wondrous Hippo Cow,

this is just a little sign to tell you that I am thinking of it – of 8 July. In fact, I can still not quite believe that it is truly and irrevocably the case – and how this day must feel for you after a whole lifetime together. All my thoughts are with you, and I dearly hope that the sorrowful memory turns into a happy one of all that once was. – I have nothing new to report except what Giraffe wrote. The more the external (Berkeley) projects recede the more I enjoy the things that really matter to us. We spent the evening of the 4th of July[1] at the Kortners; he has become rather attached to me. Giraffe is gradually getting back to normal. Max got through a very unpleasant attack of gout in good spirits. At the Eislers yesterday; I am very sorry for him, although the manner in which he draws profit from his misfortune, so to speak, is not exactly to my taste.

How are your dear golden Hippo Cow eyes faring? Hopefully you can escape the New York heat, which is presumably quite terrible now, and enjoy a decent recovery at your familiar location. Our car is running nicely; we are having a great deal of fun with it.

Heartiest kisses from your old child

Teddie

Original: typewritten letter.

1 *4th of July*: EO.

186   LOS ANGELES, 11.7.1947

11 July 1947

My dear Hippo Cow,

here are just a few lines to greet you in Rhinebeck. I hope you had a good journey. I am glad that you are out of the New York heat, have a proper rest, my animal.

Archie is in good health, he is obediently devouring his tablets and vitamins, but otherwise gives little thought to his stomach. It is especially nice that he and Max are eagerly conducting the preliminary meetings for their new study; it is doing both of them a world of good.

Today I enclose a letter from Helenchen that might interest you, as well as a few envelopes with our address. I am sending the Adornos everything I can, and have also asked Lottchen to help with some clothes; she is a little smaller than myself, so her things will probably fit little Agathe better than mine. Lix's divorce is proceeding in the style of an operetta, he appears in the newspapers now and again, initially even with his picture, and is very proud of it.

Lotte and E plan to come here on 8 August and stay for a week – I am looking forward with great suspense to the arrival of my little sister, whom I have now not seen in almost 6 years.

Many hugs and kisses from

your lanky
Giraffe

My dear Hippo Cow animal,

welcome to Rhinebeck. Today just this brief but doubly warm greeting upon your arrival.

I do, at least, have some news. As additional work alongside my duties at the institute, I have taken on a teaching post[1] at a newly founded college in La Habra (roughly 35 miles from here) in all composition subjects, i.e. harmony, counterpoint with fugue, musical form and free composition – have to teach there for one day a week. I find it very enjoyable to take on some musical responsibility again in this manner, and to teach young people. I do not have to restrict my activities to music, incidentally, but can also teach sociology and philosophy there. Max will also take on an analogous appointment[2] there, assuming his health, which is still erratic, permits it. I have already signed the contract.

Rudi turned up here a few days ago; he is spending (together with his wife) the summer in the area – i.e. about 70 miles from here – at his sister Mitzi's place.[3] We were very happy to see each other. Sadly the distance, which in relative terms is actually very great, 4 hours there and back, makes it impossible for us to see as much of each other as we would like, unless he manages to find something suitable in Hollywood or out here. He is in better shape than he was last time, only strangely gaunt. His wife appeals to me less and less, but it is generally a problem with the new wives of old friends, and it is difficult to remain fair.

Enjoy a good rest, my animal, and above all make sure you do not expose yourself to the sun without some protection. Do you wear tinted glasses to protect those good Hippo Cow eyes?

Heartiest kisses from your old child

Teddie

Original: typewritten letter.

1 In its *Bulletin* no. 1 of September 1947, Los Angeles University of Applied Education, La Habra, California, does indeed list Adorno as a teacher of music theory and composition. The college, however, or at least its music department, closed soon afterwards.

2 *appointment*: EO.

3 Lorna Kolisch was Rudolf Kolisch's second wife; his sister Mitzi was Gertrud Schoenberg (1898–1967), the second wife of the composer Arnold Schoenberg.

21 July 1947

My dearest Hippo Sow,
   how nice that you are enjoying yourself in Rhinebeck, you just make sure to rest up well, my animal. I am very gradually feeling better, after having another migraine attack that was even stronger than the first; we all get older.
   Luli suddenly appeared with four dogs, two Afghans and two puppies; sadly, Baba is already getting a little stiff – I try to tell myself that he is missing our love.
   Today I enclose a letter Norah sent from Switzerland that might interest you; I wish I (or rather we) were in Engadin in her stead.
   I am very stupid and can think of nothing to tell you, which is also a result of my genuinely not seeing anybody and lying out in the open as much as possible, forgive your stupid Giraffe.
   Many hugs and kisses
                                        from your Gretel

                    My Wondrous Sow,
I too, owing to a complete lack of anything worth telling, can only wish you the very finest of holidays and send you a thousand greetings. I am well, currently working at a slightly more relaxed pace, and Giraffe is also taking things easy, and is already feeling well rested. I was in downtown Los Angeles with Fritz today (about 1 hour's drive from here!!), incredibly hot. Hopefully it is pleasantly cool and friendly where you are. Heartiest kisses
                                   from your old child
                                        Teddie

Original: typewritten letter.

290

7 August 1947

My dear Hippo Cow,

so, on Friday Lottchen and E. are to arrive here, after six years I am certainly very excited about seeing her. They want to spend a week in Santa Monica, I am sure it will be quite lovely, and then they can also tell you a little about our life. As it has meanwhile become genuinely hot, I suddenly decided to work a little less for a while and take a daily swim in the sea. It is doing me a world of good: my appetite has increased, I look quite brown and feel much fresher, and sometimes I even get Archie to accompany me. We see quite a lot of the Kolischs, Rudi is in very good shape, and he and Teddie have resumed proper contact again; the wife does not get in the way too much, at least, it is only bothersome that we always have to speak English. On Sunday we took a slow stroll along the sea with Aladdadinchen (the new car) and ended up in San Diego (137 miles from our house). So I can drive 250 miles a day without any trouble, which is very important for our planned holiday trip to Lake Tahoe in up state[1] California, not so very far from San Francisco, though we are unlikely to pass through there. We will leave after Labor Day and only return at the end of the month, as we are both in need of a rest, and above all some fresh air and walking. We shall pick up the Horkheimers in half an hour to take them to dinner at a particularly good fish restaurant situated in the middle of the sea.

How are you taking to Rhinebeck, are you resting well, my animal? How are those dear eyes faring?

Hugs and kisses

from your old Giraffe
Gretel

My dear little Wondrous Hippo Sow,

Giraffe has already taken all the 'news'[2] away from me, so there is nothing left for me to do but express my love. I completed the draft for another theoretical chapter for the Berkeley project. Yesterday evening with Kolisch at the Maaskoffs late into the night, a very interesting discussion. I go to the sea with Giraffe whenever I can, and it is very good for me. The long tour on Sunday was especially nice – we got as far as the Mexican border and drank good coffee in a bathing resort called Karlsbad.

Hopefully you are as well as I am right now – then I would be very happy. And are you not too lonely? And how are you faring with your English? (There are times when I am full to the back teeth of that language.)

291

Have a thorough rest and take care of yourself, my dear animal, I love you so very much. Heartiest kisses from your old child
Teddie

Original: typewritten letter.

1 *up state*: EO.
2 *'news'*: EO.

189 LOS ANGELES, 26.8.1947

26 August 1947

My dear Wondrous Hippo Cow,
so, Lottchen and E were here – you will have received our card[1] by now – and we had a very enjoyable time together. I think Lotte has developed in truly excellent fashion, she has become much more independent and mature, and I am very proud of my little sister. They are both very enterprising and thus appear very young, not like us settled folk. Sadly they only stayed for a week, as they still planned to visit some friends in the Rockies. – We are finally going on holiday too at the start of next week, the address is: Tahoe Cedars Lodge, Tahoma P.O. Lake Tahoe, Calif. It is our first more substantial car journey, and I am very curious to see how I will cope. We will drive there in two days, so as to reach that other kind of air as soon as possible, but on the way back we shall take a little more time, and also plan to have a look at a few especially attractive places along the coast. – Tomorrow we shall have the opportunity to watch a very old Lang film, 'Der müde Tod'; I wonder how one will like it after 26 years?
But how are you, my animal? What do you do all day? How is the weather? Do the people there treat you well, and what sort of summer guests are there these days?
You take good care of yourself, with many hugs and kisses
from your old Giraffe
Gretel

My dear faithful old Hippo Cow beast,
this little greeting amid heaps of work – finishing off lots of trivial matters before the holidays. Tout va bien. Among other things, I had a very cordial letter from the publisher Siebeck,[2] who had published the Kierkegaard book: it continued to be sold, even under the Nazis, and in the last few years actually very well, a strange feeling. The film music book has come out, without my name on the title page, but with all 'credit'[3] in the foreword I myself formulated,[4] and looks very decent.

292

A foolish letter from Helene de Bary.[5] Otherwise I cannot think of any other news at all, except that Max's and my joint project is proceeding very well once more, and are very sorry to have to interrupt it.

We heard from Julie, to our joy, that you are resting well and being duly spoilt. If only we could join you. Make sure to stay long enough, my animal, that you do not still get caught in the New York heat – there is apparently a heat wave moving towards there from the Midwest precisely now.

Heartiest kisses
from your old child
                    Teddie

Original: typewritten letter.

1 Not preserved.

2 The letter was not preserved among Adorno's belongings. Adorno replied to the publisher on the same day he wrote to his mother:

> Dear Herr Doktor,
>   your friendly words of 5 August were a great joy to me. It is difficult to describe the feeling that came over me upon hearing something about the fate of my book again after all these years, let alone that this hardly very accessible text had peacefully continued its existence during the downfall of the world to which it belonged, while I myself was living 6000 miles away. I feel a sincere need to thank you for looking after my ideas so faithfully. Did the Nazis really never make any official efforts to prevent the distribution of the Kierkegaard book?
>   Please accept my deepest thanks for your information regarding future publications. Under the circumstances you refer to, I hardly think that now would be a favourable time for the very large book of aphorisms I mentioned to you. I could, however, make a different suggestion.
>   A few years ago I wrote a treatise entitled 'Zur Philosophie der neuen Musik'. This study concludes, in a certain sense, my efforts regarding the aesthetics of modern music, and at the same time is very closely connected to my philosophical intentions. It would yield a booklet of under 100 printed pages, for which the paper should be easily obtainable; I recall that you previously also published philosophical booklets such as the one by Tillich on Goethe and Hegel. The treatise, though decidedly philosophical in nature, is not as extravagantly difficult as the Kierkegaard. It is unimaginable that a board of censors might have any objections.
>   If there were a genuine chance of printing the booklet, I would – after returning from my holidays at the start of October – make a series of additions that I now consider absolutely necessary. I would then like to send you two finished copies. But first I would like to know whether the sending of printed manuscripts to the French zone from abroad is now allowed, and whether there would be a good chance of publication, as I

would not like to expose the two copies to the risks of such a journey in vain. I am sure you will understand that.
With the most cordial regards
your devoted (typescript copy in the Theodor W. Adorno Archiv)

3 *'credit'*: EO.

4 In the German version, the passage in question reads: 'As far as the present book is concerned, my thanks are due above all to T. W. Adorno, who directed the musical part of a different Rockefeller study, the Princeton Radio Research Project. The questions he examined are closely connected to those of film in social, musical and even technological terms. The theories and for-mulations presented here came about through collaboration in general aes-thetic areas, as well as sociological and purely musical ones' (quoted from Theodor W. Adorno and Hanns Eisler, *Komposition für den Film*, critical edition by Eberhardt Klemm [Leipzig, 1977], pp. 27f.).

5 She was a member of a family of Calvinists who had originally moved to Frankfurt from Bari, near Tournai, in 1555, and worked as merchants and bankers. The de Bary family founded the Vereinigung von Welschen zur Regelung der Geldkurse [Francophone Union for the Regulation of Buying Rates] with the de Neufvilles and the du Fays. Translator's note: the term *Welsche* is broad, referring to peoples such as the French Swiss and the ori-ginally Celtic (as in 'Welsh') inhabitants of Alpine regions in Switzerland, France, Germany and Austria, as well as some in other Romance countries. While its meaning thus varies between a number of Romance and Celtic ethno-lingual contexts, its application here to the aforementioned families would seem to make 'Francophone' the least misleading equivalent.

190   LAKE TAHOE, 4.9.1947

Tahoe Cedars Lodge, Lake Tahoe
4 Sept. 1947.

My Wondrous Hippo Cow,
   arrived and settled in well after a smooth journey, mostly through the desert. It is *truly beautiful* here, as blue as Italy and infinitely peace-ful. A shame that you were not able to take the boat around the whole lake with us today. Forgive the writing, I do not have the typewriter here. Heartiest kisses from your child Teddie
   Dear Hippo Cow, the typewriter might have seduced Archie into working – that had to be prevented. Here we are having our first real holiday in 6 years. Hugs from your old Giraffe

Original: picture postcard: Scenic Drive – Lake Tahoe; stamp: TAHOMA, SEP 5. Manuscript.

294

Lake Tahoe, 11 Sept. 1947

My gigantic Hippo Cow, we are celebrating my birthday in the
restaurant 'Sportsman' in Truckee, where they serve *real* game, are
awaiting our wild duck, enjoying ourselves immeasurably and thinking of you with all our love. Heartiest kisses from your child Teddie.
   This is the loveliest birthday in years. We are having a good rest,
taking many walks and thinking a great deal of our dear Wondrous
Hippo Cow. Hugs and kisses from your Giraffe

Original: picture postcard: Donner Lake, Calif. and Highway U.S. 40; stamp:
TAHOMA, SEP 12. Manuscript.

Tahoe Cedars Lodge
Tahoma, P.O.
LAKE TAHOE, CALIFORNIA

My dear Hippo Cow,
   today I shall do my best to write in big letters so that you can read
better. I am glad that you returned to New York without any problems; hopefully the heat will soon let up over there. – On Friday
evening – we were already in bed – we suddenly received a telephone
call that Mr Kolisch was 18 miles away, and indeed Rudi and Lorna
were there in ½ an hour. We had a delightful day with them, even went
swimming in the clear, cold lake, ate at the good game restaurant in
the evening, then they drove on to Reno and we went home. Rudi saw
Anita in San Francisco, the old Seligmanns have already gone to
Switzerland. – If the weather stays fine (fingers crossed) and nothing
else gets in the way, we will stay here until the 25th and should be back
in Los Angeles on the 29th.
   Many hugs and kisses from your old
Giraffe

My Wondrous Animal, I am glad that you arrived at home safe and
sound! Take good care with the heat and get used to things again.
We are having our most relaxing time since Bar Harbor – today
a four-hour journey high into the mountains. We had the greatest fun
with Rudi, as you can imagine. Take care of yourself my Mumma with
heartiest kisses from your old Hippo King Archie

Original: handwritten letter with printed letterhead.

On the dating: according to a note, Maria Wiesengrund received this letter on 17 September.

Virginia City, 17 Sept. 47

My Hippo Cow, this unspeakable opera house[1] that we are visiting at the moment is located in a completely deserted and dilapidated yet once famous gold-diggers' nest – but Jenny Lind[2] and *Patti*[3] sang there, and we imagined you standing amid the scenery.[4] The men had to hand in their revolvers at the cloakroom. Heartiest kisses from your child Teddie

Today is the first fresh day, the air is even better than usual. Kisses from your Giraffe

Original: picture postcard: HISTORIC OLD PIPER OPERA HOUSE BUILT DURING 1880's, VIRGINIA CITY, NEVADA; stamp: VIRGINIA CITY, SEP 17, 1947 (see fig. 6). Manuscript.

1 Piper's Opera House had its heyday in the 1870s and 1880s, when Virginia City was a rich town, primarily through the silver mines. The building, erected by John Piper, has been undergoing restoration since the 1960s; today it is in use again. Nothing is known about the guest performances of Lind and Patti.

2 The Swedish soprano Jenny Lind (1820–87) went on triumphant tours through Europe and America between 1844 and 1858.

3 The Italian soprano Adelina Patti (1843–1919) had gone to America early on with her parents and her sister. She received her musical training from her sister Carlota, also a singer and a pianist – as with the sisters Agathe Calvelli-Adorno and Maria Wiesengrund – and gave her first concert performance in New York in 1850; her debut was as Lucia in Donizetti's opera in 1859. Adelina Patti sang the title role in the premiere of Verdi's *Aida*. She was extremely famous, and received considerable sums for her appearances.

4 During the 1884–5 season, from 3 November to 15 January, Maria Calvelli-Adorno guested with Adelina Patti's ensemble in North America; Adorno is alluding to that tour, which took her as far as San Francisco.

Tahoe Cedars Lodge
Chambers P.O.
LAKE TAHOE, CALIFORNIA
24 September 47

My dear faithful old Wondrous Hippo Cow,
a thousand thanks for your letter – we were already concerned not to have heard from you so long after your return, and are all the happier to hear that you are well. The heat should finally have exhausted itself by now – the coming days are usually the finest in N.Y. Enjoy the autumn sitting down by the Hudson, my animal.

My last letter was already the reply to the one you sent for my birthday, and I am truly sorry if that was not absolutely clear. En tout cas I thank you once more for all your wishes.

When we return from our trip it will be your 82nd birthday – Goethe's age. Our best possible wishes on that occasion, and continue to burrow your way through the mass of years as courageously as you have so far, so that you become an

ANCIENT WONDROUS HIPPO COW LADY

And above all, make sure you remain in good health, especially without any trouble with those good mother eyes. That is what I wish you more than anything else. And myself: that I might see you again very soon.

Our holidays were the loveliest since Bar Harbor, in fact since Europe. You cannot imagine the beauty of the Sierras, and especially that of this very large, deep blue and green mountain lake. We enjoyed it in every way: very long hikes in the mountains (including one to a pasture with cows with bells like in the Alps), very big car tours (sometimes 200 miles in one day), much lying about in the open, playing ping-pong, sleeping our fill. We are both very well rested.

Charlotte did not appear, although she must (if she genuinely went away to get divorced, in Nevada) be fairly close. Et si déjà. Tomorrow we are going back home at a very leisurely pace, in 4 days, via Sacramento and later along the ocean. We want to spend a whole day on the famous Monterey peninsula (Carmel etc.). We expect to reach Los Angeles sometime on Monday. Max, who was in Oregon, is coming on Tuesday. La Habra only starts in mid-October.

Lily Latté, who is *truly* a very close friend of ours, is thinking of going to N.Y. in the first days of October. If she does, it goes without saying that she will call you. She is one of the very few friends in the true sense that we have found in America. An enchantingly graceful

297

and personally *absolutely* reliable person whom you are sure to like a great deal. Gretel and Lily are inseparable; I am *not* involved with her, so you need not get any silly ideas. The best of company, very elegant; and yet totally unpretentious. You must only know that she is the partner – virtually the wife – of Fritz Lang, the most famous German film director, who is also incredibly successful here. So receive her kindly, you will enjoy yourself.

And now farewell, my animal, and remember that I will be with you with all my soul on 1 October.

Heartiest kisses

from your old child

Teddie

My dear Wondrous Hippo Cow,

let me send you, with all my heart, the best and fondest wishes on your 82nd birthday, may you remain in good health and your poor eyes improve. – Everything is already packed here, and we are just about to get an early night so that we are fit for the long drive tomorrow. Leaving here is incredibly hard for both of us.

Many hugs and kisses from your lanky

Giraffe Gazelle

Original: handwritten letter with printed letterhead.

195   SANTA MARIA, 28.9.1947

28 September 1947

My Giant Hippo Cow, this is the final stage of our return journey, which has been extremely pleasant – named in honour of you. Among other things, we saw some healthy 5000-year-old giant trees near Santa Cruz that reminded me very much of you. Get your 83rd off to a good start. Tomorrow we will be home again, in the evening at Lang's place for Lily's farewell. A thousand kisses from your child Teddie

Only another 160 miles to Los Angeles. Many kisses from your lanky Giraffe

Original: photo postcard: Santa Maria Inn / Santa Maria, California / On the Mission Trail / 'It is always blossom time at the Santa Maria Inn'; stamp: SANTA MARIA, SEP 29, 1947. Manuscript.

18 October 1947

My dearest Hippo Cow,
    it is terrible, we have once again not written for a considerable time,
but only because there is nothing to tell. Archie has truly made a good
recovery and also seems to have saved up his strength to a degree,
whereas I am finding it incredibly difficult to readjust to the mild
climate and have almost constant headaches, more or less severely.
– Herbert Marcuse from the institute, who is currently in the State
Department in Washington, however, was here, and there were some
quite interesting discussions. Norah – who has meanwhile gone back
to her daughter in Mexico, whose restaurant is apparently doing
superbly, by the way –, Thomas Mann, Charlotte Dieterle spoke a great
deal about the European impressions, how Switzerland is so eerily
unchanged, that the Germans are saying the Jews were crafty once
again and got out in time – it has already been forgotten that they were
driven out and murdered – that England is essentially unchanged, but
in the positive sense. – I enclose a letter from Franz that should interest you, and which I would also ask Julie to read. Archie still has to
reply to it, so please send it back.
    Many hugs and kisses from
                        Your old Giraffe
                             Gretel
My little Hippo Sow,
    today just a thousand greetings and hearty kisses amid piles of work
for the institute. Take care of yourself, my animal. Absolutely nothing
new. Lily is quite ill, otherwise she would have called you!
    The very fondest regards
                        ever your Teddie

Original: typewritten letter with additional handwritten note by Adorno.

Los Angeles, 28 October 1947

My dear faithful old Wondrous Hippo Cow Marinumba,
    last night we were at Lang's place for dinner when Lily called us from
New York and told us about her visit with you (apparently with Lotte
and E!). As happy as I am that you had a pleasant afternoon together,
I was distressed by what she told me about your eyes and above all your

hearing. If you can neither read for long nor even listen to the radio – then what do you do the livelong day, my animal? I must *urgently* advise you to get yourself one of those modern, outstanding 'hearing aids'.[1] It was a great help to old Frau Steuermann, for example. The price is not an issue, need not be an issue, must not be an issue. I will not have a peaceful moment until I know that your contact with the outside world is restored in a manner that allows you the necessary comforts. Please discuss it immediately with Julie, and do not make excuses. Otherwise, Lily thought that you were in good shape, mobile, and not fat, and I am glad. But how much does that count for compared to the severe impairment of the most important senses.

Lily also told me that you were living, as it were, from one letter of mine to the next. My animal, if I sometimes refrain from writing, it is neither because I wish to keep anything terrible from you (for neither is there anything terrible in my life nor do I keep anything from you – I even informed you about Charlotte), nor because I have forgotten you out of egotism. But quite simply – because there is often nothing, truly nothing at all to report. I always have long weeks that are entirely full of work, with Max and alone; sometimes I hardly see anyone, nothing worth reporting occurs – and I do not really wish to feed you with my partly extremely difficult theoretical matters. So understand my silence, then – and I will greet you with hippo grunts as often as I possibly can, even if there is no other content (though I will hardly be able to compete with Charlotte's letters as regards lack of content).

Yesterday up at Lang's place the servant suddenly came in – a stag that devours the most delicate flowers in the garden and tramples over everything each night had ventured as far as the lawn. We immediately rushed out to see it, but naturally it was faster than we were – all we found were the giant, entirely fresh hoof-prints. It was an especially pleasant evening.

Now for your questions. Luli: I enclose her last letter, which is very characteristic, and would ask you to send it back. The poor girl – evidently she never truly recovered from the encephalitis she had a few years ago. Norah's mother is back in her villa in Ronco, near Ascona, supposedly for good, but she is already travelling through Europe with her royal household, and it is very possible that she might return here – she kept her insanely expensive apartment here. She is quite remarkable – a shame you do not know her. A member of the Wertheimber family. I received a letter from Helene de Bary, incidentally, but did not respond, as her father turned out to be a rabid Nazi. – The old Seligmans have also definitely gone back to Switzerland. Mietze fell out completely with Norah, is also a little peeved at us because we are on good terms with Norah (and deeper down – because she was unable to reshuffle and remarry all of us); but still friendly with old

Frau Hahn; took her to the train in Zurich. Charlotte has been at Pyramid Lake in Nevada since 20 September, not at all far from Lake Tahoe, we did not see each other – but I did receive a highly unexpected letter a few days ago. She will be divorced in a few days, will be back in S.F. on 2 November and Robert can marry Anita if he wants (he does not especially want to). So, my animal, now you know everything. Krenek is here, very pleasant. They asked me about Else – but I did not have anything definite to tell them. Do you know anything? He has written a new symphony² that I intensely dislike.

Mumma, I am *not* planning to return to Germany in the long run, for brief visits at the most – so you need not worry about that. But it would be unwise to tell Franz that. The threat of my return exerts a certain pressure in our business matters. – There is no risk of war *whatsoever* – it is all a war of nerves.³ I am making great efforts to ensure that I can turn up in N.Y. in the not too distant future, but do not yet know when or whether it will be possible. So keep your fingers crossed for us, my animal.

I started in La Habra; there are only a few students, but as the college has now been acknowledged by the Veterans Administration, that should change very soon. I am there every Wednesday.

Heartiest kisses from your

old Teddie

Original: typewritten letter.

1 *'hearing aids'*: EO.

2 The Fourth Symphony, op. 113.

3 *war of nerves*: EO.

198 LOS ANGELES, 4.11.1947

Los Angeles, 4 November 1947

My dear faithful old Wondrous Hippo Cow,

a thousand thanks for your lengthy letter. It would have made me very happy if – if Lily had not told me some things you said to her, and especially to Lotte, which do not at all correspond to the picture you paint in your letter, such as the gravest problems of eyesight. Restriction to 20 minutes' reading time per day and in particular also such a decline in your hearing that you can no longer really listen to the radio. Lily thought that you deny these things in order 'not to burden me with them'. If that is the case, then it is certainly infinitely heroic and well meant, but really very foolish. For one thing, I cannot have a moment's peace until you have sworn me a solemn oath (on the

301

life of the great Luiche!) to tell me truly how you are; but then we can only discuss what can reasonably be done if you lay your cards on the table. So: the truth, the whole truth and nothing but the truth! The Galsworthy[1] is superior trash; save your eyes for something better, my animal. Golde is very good-natured, but dreadfully stupid. – From Luli a second letter that possibly even exceeds the fears you voiced. Her manner of first making all sorts of gifts, then taking them back, is itself a highly disconcerting symptom. You are an astute old Hippo Sow to tell that from the letter.

The start in La Habra (where I have to go for the whole day tomorrow) is extremely modest, as are the students, who do not even know the different keys properly, but as the college has meanwhile been officially acknowledged by the Veterans Administration, things should get moving properly after Christmas. For the meantime I only have 2 lessons per week.

Tonight at the preview of Lang's new film[2] with Lily (we celebrated her return at L's on Saturday). Otherwise nothing new. Max and I are incredibly tied up with piles of technical work for the institute. But tout va bien, even my newest invention, the hyena[3] Jean-François,[4] who can speak.

Heartiest kisses from your old child
Teddie

Original: typewritten letter.

1 It is unknown which novel by the English writer John Galsworthy (1867–1933) Maria Wiesengrund was reading.

2 This is *Secret Beyond the Doors*.

3 Translator's note: in the original, Adorno writes '*der* Hyäne' (masculine), deliberately contradicting the correct form '*die* Hyäne' (feminine), evidently for humorous purposes.

4 The name of Adorno's maternal grandfather.

199 LOS ANGELES, 10.11.1947

Los Angeles, 10 November 1947

My dear faithful old Hippo Cow animal,
a thousand thanks for your very sweet letter. It is, through its solemn oath, a great reassurance to me. Have your eyes improved as a result of the treatment or by themselves? Eyesight is often connected to blood pressure, incidentally.

We are living and working quietly. Max and I wrote a substantial essay[1] within a week, which was made possible by dividing it up between us. Aside from that, I have also nearly finished a 'manual'[2] on the tricks of anti-Semitic agitators.[3]

Only Fritz and I have officially taken jobs in La Habra, but Max also wants to read there.

The other night, Kortner took us along to see the 'young', in fact already 50-year-old, Schildkraut,[4] the son of the actor you so esteemed. On Saturday I played him and Kortner the second part – the Faust scene – of Mahler's 8th Symphony.

Charlotte is now divorced, but also from me – – – I did not respond to her last letter.

Otherwise I can really not think of anything to tell. Hopefully the transition to the cold season in New York is not too abrupt, so that the gigantic Hippo Cow organism can adjust in good time. Do be very careful – these weeks are always risky on 'Pneumonia Hill'.

Heartiest kisses my animal
from your old child
Teddie

Original: typewritten letter.

1 Presumably 'Authoritarianism and the Family Today', which appeared in 1949 in the volume *The Family: Its Function and Destiny*, ed. Ruth Nanda Anshen.

2 *'manual'*: EO.

3 This does not appear to have survived.

4 The actor Joseph Schildkraut (1894/5–1964) was the son of Rudolf Schildkraut (1862–1930), who had started his career as a 14-year-old working for a touring company, appearing on stage in Vienna – where Maria Wiesengrund would have seen and heard him – and Berlin. Rudolf Schildkraut had already gone to America early on; he took on film roles there, but worked mostly in the theatre.

200   LOS ANGELES, 20.11.1947

LOS ANGELES UNIVERSITY
OF APPLIED EDUCATION
LA HABRA, CALIFORNIA

20 November 1947

Marinumba, my Hippo Cow-Sow,
a thousand thanks for your lengthy letter of the 15th. Your writing looks much better – I am so happy that you genuinely seem

303

to be better. Regarding Kreisler, I agree entirely with you. After all, his success revolved more around the charm of his violinist's diction than a truly meaningful capacity for musical representation. Now that he has lost that charm, like an aged actor, it is particularly clear. Incidentally, Kreisler showed very little loyalty during Hitler's reign.

I am writing to you today on La Habra paper – I received the first instalment of my salary yesterday (they are still very short on money). But it is a lot of fun, and my students are making noticeable progress.

We spent a long time at Luli's place, for the first time since her severe illness. She still looks wretched, but was otherwise in good shape and more delightful than ever. I am sure that Lily, who is incredibly jealous of her, gave you an entirely false impression of her – for all her flaws, there are very few people who are as close to me as she is. – Baba has grown terribly old and lethargic – only recognized us after quite some time. I fear his spine is paralysed, as our old Wölfchen's also was in the end. But still an angel. Luli *carries* him into the car.

Thomas Mann's novel has come out. In the copy he sent me he wrote: 'For Theodor Adorno, the High Privy Councillor'. Charming, don't you think?

On Sunday Robert called from S.F., spoke for almost an hour, quite desperate. He is divorced, but does not know if he should marry Anita. This is *absolutely* between the two of us, my animal!!!

As far as the business partner is concerned, only you can decide that – I for my part can understand it only too well if you would rather remain alone than have someone completely indifferent brought in from without purely for that purpose, but naturally the problems with your eyesight do create special circumstances.

Kortner remembers the Kampen anecdote[1] very well. I cannot judge the young Schildkraut's ability as an actor; in private I find him a little too chatty.

Keep your fingers crossed, my animal. How I would love to visit you soon.

Heartiest kisses from your old child
Teddie

If you can manage it *at all* – go and see the Chaplin film Monsieur Verdoux. It is just your sort of film!!
Many kisses
Giraffe

Original: typewritten letter with handwritten postscript and additional handwritten greeting from Gretel Adorno.

1 For a private publication on the occasion of Fritz Kortner's seventy-fifth birthday, Adorno wrote:

Dear Herr Kortner
allow me to extend my most heartfelt congratulations to you on your 75th birthday. The admiration I feel towards your art, which unifies unruliness and intelligence in a manner that is so exceedingly rare in the German world, is accompanied by a personal relationship that, to this day, has always shown itself in the most unexpected circumstances. From that summer of 1921, when you were acting in the film Das rote Kliff [The Red Cliff] in Kampen and I played you piano pieces by Schönberg, to the period in which we were neighbours in Los Angeles and our dogs growled at each other, without our own contact ever mirroring their inexplicable behaviour, to that night in the bar of the Sacher Hotel in Vienna, when you found me in a not entirely responsible state, but did not hold the presumably highly irrational stuff I was spouting against me. Things seem to be continuing in the same manner, and I wish not only for you that it should thus continue into 'the pianissimo of the oldest age', in Max Weber's words, but also at least as much for myself. But above all, I wish that you might retain that explosive force through which you, standing in the middle of the German and Austrian theatre industry, ensure that it does not become an industry (cited from the typescript copy among Adorno's belongings)

201   LOS ANGELES, AFTER 30.11.1947

INSTITUTE OF SOCIAL RESEARCH
429 WEST 117TH STREET
NEW YORK, N.Y.

Tel. UNiversity 4–3200
(Columbia University)
Ext. 276

My dear Hippo Cow,
thank you kindly for your sweet letter. We would rather not say anything to Luli about Ali Baba, for we are, after all, glad for every day he goes on living, and for now he may be indolent, but apparently without pain* – Today letter from England from the Adornos – you will probably have heard from them too. – Meanwhile we ordered some Mahler records from New York for Archie's birthday and Christmas, the 4th Symphony and Das Lied von der Erde. They are both of moderate quality, but we still have a great deal of fun with them and play them almost daily. – Last week we had two

---

* [Addition in Adorno's hand:] and is well off up there.

turkey dinners,[1] one on Wednesday on the hill at Lang's place with the Schildkrauts – who are really quite stupid people – then later we were joined by Kortner, who is on the way to Switzerland right now (he is married to Hanna Hofer). The second one on Saturday at Lix's with forty people – on Sunday there again to eat leftovers with bones and sweet-and-sour beans. Tomorrow evening to Norah's place to have a nice quiet evening with her before Christmas, when the Rauschnings[2] will be moving in with her. So, that is all the news from our industrious but quiet life. You must excuse my true Berlin daftness.

> Hugs and kisses
>
> from your lanky
> Giraffe

Marinumba my animal,

today just a few lines. We had two pleasant Thanksgiving celebrations, the first at Lang's with Lily, the Schildkrauts and Kortner, until 3 a.m.; then Saturday at Lix's with an enormous company of 42 people, the most of them like ourselves from the Jewish Club.[3] You can pretty much imagine it.

Keep your fingers crossed, as you promised so dearly. It will still take a while, but I am hopeful.

Did you read Virgil Thomson's review[4] in the Herald of Eisler's film music book (which I in fact wrote)? You would have enjoyed it. Unfortunately the translation of the book is very modest. I have meanwhile received offers for Italian and Dutch editions,[5] and there will be more. We will be seeing Lou Eisler for the first time in a while on Saturday. Hanns is in N.Y.

Did you hear the Philharmonic play the 4th Symphony by Krenek[6] on Sunday, and what is your impression? I do not wish to bias you.

For Christmas, Giraffe gave me the Bruno Walter recordings of Mahler's 4th Symphony and Das Lied von der Erde. The performances are very bad – upon closer listening, Walter is exactly what I always took him to be, namely a skilled, but smudgy, unmusical and essentially quite inferior conductor. But everything is set so wonderfully that he cannot entirely lay waste to it, and I am glad to have it, and listen to it a great deal. The singer in Das Lied von der Erde, Kullmann[7] by name, is admittedly dreadful. As if you were trying to imitate him. E.g. 'ist merr wärt, ist merr wärt, ist merr wärt' etc.[8] Why does music always have to be made by such brutes?

We had a sweet letter from Franz and Helenchen from England, where they are visiting the brood. We are feeding them amply with packages, a classic case of sausage and a side of bacon.

> Heartiest kisses from your old child
> Teddie

Original: typewritten letter.

On the dating: Thanksgiving Day was on 27 November 1947.

1 *turkey dinners*: EO.

2 Hermann Rauschning (1887–1982), who was politically initially a follower of the Nazis and a confidant of Hitler, had resigned from his post as senate president of Danzig, which he had gained in 1933, in November 1934 and gone into exile in 1936; he published two books, which were widely read as internal views of the Nazi dictatorship: *Die Revolution des Nihilismus* (1938) and above all *Gespräche mit Hitler* [Conversations with Hitler] (1939). Rauschning had gone to the USA in 1941, following stays in Switzerland, France and England.

3 *Jewish Club*: EO.

4 It was not possible to view a copy of this article.

5 It is rather peculiar that the offers were made to Adorno, who had withdrawn his name as co-author.

6 The premiere was conducted by Dimitri Mitropoulos (1896–1960), who was still director of the Minneapolis Symphony Orchestra at the time, but went to the New York Philharmonic in 1949.

7 The New Haven-born tenor Charles Kullmann (1903–83), who since 1931 had also sung in Berlin, Vienna and Salzburg, was a celebrated singer at the Metropolitan Opera in New York.

8 In the first song – 'Das Trinklied vom Jammer der Erde' [The Drinking-Song of the Earth's Moaning] – the line goes: 'Ein voller Becher Weins zur rechten Zeit ist mehr wert, ist mehr wert, ist mehr wert, als alle Reiche dieser Erde' [A full cup of wine at the right time is worth more, is worth more, is worth more than all the kingdoms of this earth].

202   LOS ANGELES, 11.12.1947

11 December 1947

My dear Hippo Cow,
    it is so sweet of you that you always reply to our letters so promptly, and we can read them quite superbly, hopefully you are not straining your poor eyes too much. – We do not own a copy of the Thomson review either, only read through it quickly, so unfortunately we cannot send it to you. – As Norah's dog, a terrier, died here during her trip to Europe, she has now got hold of a new one, four months old, which she showed me yesterday; it is very cute, but naturally no comparison to a little Afghan. – If we do not write anything about our stupid health that

simply means that we are feeling fine, touch wood. The Pollocks have meanwhile bought themselves an old house, as they had some trouble here with their master builder from New York, and aside from that are also afraid of being evacuated from their current provisional apartment. We have not seen it yet, but it is situated in a nice area where we often used to take Baba for walks; they hope to move in in January.

Keep taking care of yourself, my animal, with hugs and kisses
from your old
Giraffe

Marinumba my animal,

we are having a somewhat hectic time at the moment, as Max is going to San Francisco on business tomorrow, then on to New York from there, likewise regarding the projects, and there has still been endless stuff to sort out. Max will no doubt give you a call, although his time in N.Y. will be a dreadful rush, but it cannot be avoided. A common acquaintance of ours, the psychoanalyst Simmel (not to be confused with the famous philosopher who has been dead for 30 years), has died, and Max and I have come up with a eulogy[1] for him together, among other things. Also much La Habra – it is more than questionable whether the university will be able to keep going, and that has necessitated many meetings, which admittedly look uncannily like creditors' assemblies.

Rauschning, whom you asked me about, was a Nazi and senate president in Danzig, and became famous for parting ways with Hitler early on and publishing his conversations with him, the most interesting document for an understanding of Hitler's true thinking. Rauschning is a very pleasant, albeit arch-reactionary, but privately decent and educated man – it is impossible, of course, to forget what he was.

A few days ago I went with Fritz and Carlota to a concert for the premiere of a wind sextet by the young Rebner,[2] not bad at all, written with a good ear and good instrumentation; admittedly nothing independent, à la Stravinsky. Outside, a gentleman unknown to me asked me if I was Adorno. It was René Leibowitz,[3] from Paris, one of the most talented young composers (Webern pupil), who had sent me some things of his a few years ago in exchange for some of mine – he is now having some of my songs performed in England. An exceedingly pleasant, artistically extremely radical man. He is coming for lunch on Saturday.

Otherwise nothing new. I am adding some nice verses to Mendelssohn's songs without words, e.g.: 'Go not into the night, my-hy child, for in thi-his night it is cold' etc. Do you like that?

Heartiest kisses from your old, old child
Teddie

308

Original: typewritten letter.

1 Horkheimer gave the speech 'Ernst Simmel and Freudian Philosophy' on 13 December at the 'Memorial Meeting for Ernst Simmel'.

2 Wolfgang Edward Rebner (1910–93) was from Frankfurt; his father was the string quartet leader Adolf Rebner. Wolfgang Rebner had studied with Paul Hindemith at the Hochsches Konservatorium and then in Berlin with Artur Schnabel. He went to England and moved to the USA in 1937, where he worked as an accompanist. From 1940 onwards Rebner worked for the film industry in Hollywood. In 1955 he returned to Germany. The composition Adorno refers to is most likely his *Suite für Bläser 1942* [Suite for Wind Instruments 1942] (see *Verdrängte Musik. Berliner Komponisten im Exil* [Suppressed Music: Berlin Composers in Exile], ed. Habakuk Traber and Elmar Weingarten, Berlin, 1987, p. 316).

3 The composer René Leibowitz (1913–72), who was born in Warsaw and had lived in Paris with his family since 1926, was a highly talented violinist before he turned to composition and conducting. Leibowitz studied first with Schoenberg in Berlin and then with Anton Webern in Vienna. After the Second World War he was the primary advocate of the Schoenberg school in France. Leibowitz wrote several books and conducted on many recordings.

203   LOS ANGELES, 22.12.1947

Los Angeles, 22 December 1947

Marinumba my dearest Hippo Cow animal,

a thousand thanks for your dear letter and all the presents – all of them so lovingly chosen, and apropos presents: a thousand thanks also to Julie for everything. – From now on I shall always be good and write on a separate sheet, not on the back, so that those good Hippo Cow eyes do not have such a hard time.

Our Christmas plans are as follows: Hanna Kortner and Maidon were supposed to come here for duck tomorrow (Tuesday), but Maidon was very suddenly struck with bursitis in the knee and also in the diaphragm, has to lie completely still, and can unfortunately not come; it is still uncertain whether we shall find anyone to replace her. Christmas Eve up with Lang and Lily with quite a large company for a 'gala dinner'. On Boxing Day at the Palfis. New Year's Eve two parties, one at Norah's and one at Fritz's, whose mother-in-law arrived by aeroplane from Argentina last night. As you see, we are very much in demand. I have a styful of work, but mostly of an editorial nature, and will take things a little easy now.

Robert had a serious car accident, and a few days later his son also did. Charlotte called *Maidon* on the telephone about it!!!

Otherwise little to report except for a new princess, by the name of Radziwill,[1] née Baroness Brentano, who was also invited when I went up to Luli's place for lunch on Saturday, pretty and pleasant: a sort of lady-secretary for Luli, who thus finally has a serious and not likewise half-crazed person around her. A few lines from Max; you are sure to hear from him.

Unfortunately I did not hear Mahler's 6th; and you? Though I doubt that Mitropoulos is up to it. Yesterday at the Eislers, who, despite constant threat of deportation, are extremely well. He is composing a (very pretty) score to be added to Chaplin's circus film. Our book appears to be selling well. Aside from that, you simply have to imagine me as a sort of living correction pencil. Heartiest kisses, my animal, and once again a thousand thanks, and the very best wishes for the New Year, in case I do not write again before then, from your stupid old child

Teddie

Original: typewritten letter.

1 See letter no. 209, where she is referred to as an impostor.

31 December 1947

Marinumba my animal,

a thousand thanks for your very sweet letter and the long one from Else,[1] which we enclose here. I am glad that you had a pleasant Christmas; here it was also nice, an exceedingly elegant party chez Lang and Lily, prepared by her with the most touching care, exceptionally good food and drink. Up there for a quiet visit the day after.

As far as Else is concerned, I am sincerely happy that things are bearable for her and that she will evidently soon be able to walk properly again. But my joy at that, as well as at the rekindling of contact with one of your oldest and closest friends, cannot prevent me from detecting the hostile intent with which Gretel and I are demonstratively not mentioned, except for my one appearance as 'your son'. She is evidently angry that we did not give her any material help – unjustly angry, for we really could not have helped, and I am utterly convinced that even during that time, with the French fortune in the background, she was better off than we were. When you write to her, I think a hint from you would be called for – it can hardly be possible, after all, for her to rekindle her friendship with you and be at war with us. She, who did not even bring her own sister to safety in time and also, aside from that, never showed particular generosity towards myself or Gretel, even in better times, should at least refrain from feigning outrage (naturally you should *not* mention the latter; I do not want there to be any ill will between you – simply a few words of regret at her behaviour towards us, which is evidently based on an entirely mistaken perception of the circumstances).

And now, my animal, celebrate a merry farewell to the old year and roll forcefully, as the massive Hippo Cow, into the new, which has the mythological 83rd birthday in store for you. I need hardly tell you all my hearty wishes for you – and also myself – least of all what I wish for most. Give dear Julie a thousand greetings from us, and tell her that Else's wondrous hymns of praise have not made me any less fond of her – in this case at least, Else would be right, factually speaking.

Heartiest kisses from your old child
Teddie

Original: typewritten letter.

1 Maria Wiesengrund's correspondence has not survived.

1948

15 January 1948

Marinumba my animal,
we were so happy to hear from you – why were you silent for so long? Imagine if we had done the same!!

Giraffe has already given you most of our news.[1] All I have to add is that I have just finished, *definitively* and in agreement with my American colleagues, the first of my chapters for the big Berkeley book; that the faculty meetings in La Habra increasingly resemble creditors' assemblies; that we heard quite a fine recording of Mahler's 5th Symphony under Bruno Walter. Toni Maaskoff, an excellent violinist, is *very* ill, a malignant glandular business; supposedly, however, he is reacting well to a new kind of treatment. You are quite right, I did already know Lisa Minghetti in Frankfurt, we are meanwhile very good friends, she has made great progress musically and is otherwise also delightful. Last night we worked on a Beethoven trio together.

Robert had called Gretel the evening before the wedding (I was at the Chevalier with Lily Latté); we have not heard from him since then. Charlotte cancelled her visit because she 'did not want to leave Robert alone' – while he married Anita. This was her version, at least – the true reason is that her trip to LA would not have been a triumph. I am glad she did not come. We are not writing at all any more.

Hippo Cow, my animal, was the formulation about the decline of the friendship in your letter to Else not a little too pointed – i.e. are we not thus making it very difficult for her to write to me, for example? But it is not important – if we ever see her again, we shall get around to it, and as things are now we are certainly out of contact.

312

Thomas Mann responded to the 3rd part of my book of aphorisms in a manner so positive that I truly cannot reproduce it. You would have enjoyed yourself. – Maidon is better again; the Pollocks are moving into their new house in a few weeks.

Hopefully Liefmann is not seriously ill; I would find it quite terrible for you.

Write soon, my animal, and look after yourself. Here we are having the most unnatural midsummer weather.

Heartiest kisses from your old child
                                    Teddie

Original: typewritten letter.

1 Gretel Adorno's letter has not survived.

27 January 1948

Marinumba my animal,

we were so happy to receive your letter, finally, after we had already started to worry. Admittedly Max, who has been back for a week, had given us a very satisfied account of his visit with you – he found it particularly pleasant and said that he had had a much more stimulating conversation with you than with most 'young people'. He found you generally cheerful and in good condition.

The name of Luli's husband is, as we have already written a number of times, Paul Kollsmann – a selfmade man[1] who amassed a great fortune through an aeronautical invention in the war, and is now working on further inventions, though without much success, it seems – evidently more of a one-off 'bullseye' – an aeronautical Cavalleria,[2] so to speak. He is a fairly simple man who attempts somewhat awkwardly, in the manner of a Raimund folk play, to play the grand gentleman, incidentally quite harmless. Luli herself is in a much better state, now much more the way she was in the first years of our friendship.

We also listened to the broadcast of Das Lied von der Erde, and it is a lovely feeling to know that we were all immersed in the same phenomenon for hours. I too was glad once more to hear this work that is so ineffably close to my heart. In our assessment of the performance, however, we differ. The woman certainly has a wonderful voice, but is primitive and carefree in a manner that makes a parody of the whole as far as the expression is concerned. The tenor too is essentially quite clueless (he was best in Der Trunkene im Frühling). But worst of all

313

was Herr Walter, that old goose-dripping gourmet, the Korngold[3] of conducting, who would be better off doing Lehar than performing Mahler. None, absolutely none of the musical characters were captured – he really has only two basic types at his disposal,[4] the exaggerated cantilena and a manner of sour, brash brio. And imprecise to boot, with the musical context completely incomprehensible in some passages. A symptom of the general decline in musical presentation. Otherwise nothing new here, a great deal of work on the final editing of my portion of the Berkeley project. Tomorrow probably at La Habra for the last time.

Heartiest kisses from your daft old child
Teddie
Hearty kisses
Giraffe

Original: typewritten letter with handwritten closing greetings.

1 *selfmade man*: EO.

2 An allusion to the opera *Cavalleria rusticana* by Pietro Mascagni (1863–1945), which remained his only success.

3 The composer Erich Wolfgang Korngold (1897–1957), son of the music critic of the Vienna newspaper *Neue Freie Presse*, had composed almost exclusively for the cinema since 1938.

4 See Adorno's posthumous work *Towards a Theory of Musical Reproduction* (trans. Wieland Hoban [Cambridge: Polity, 2006], p. 147), where Adorno writes about a recording of *Das Lied von der Erde* under Bruno Walter featuring the tenor Julius Patzak and the contralto Kathleen Ferrier. On Walter, see also pp. 78 and 83f.

207   LOS ANGELES, 10.2.1948

10 February 1948

Mumma my little Hippo Sow,
so, we are d'accord about Herr Schlesinger[1] von der Vogelweide.[2] Incidentally, he – quite good friends with Thomas Mann from Munich days – is angry about the cultural bolshevism in some of the Faust novel's musical elements, and thus about me, so everything is as it should be. – Meanwhile I heard the famous Herr Münch with Berlioz' Phantastique, but the purely musical quality of that piece is simply so poor that one cannot have any fun, not even with Herr Münch, if one cannot see his dinner jacket, which is admittedly reported to be extraordinary.

Little news; good progress with the Berkeley book, which it seems will be printed by one of the most respected publishers.[3] Meanwhile I am making certain additions to my 'Philosophie der neuen Musik' of 1941, which will make a little book of it.

How I would like to see Helenchen's letter (we have not had any news from Auerbach for ages) – I imagine wee Frau Pastern getting into a dispute with the wife of the local bank manager and the two of them hurling abuse at each other, a true petty bourgeois idyll with murder in the air. Could I see the document? Gretel recalled our situation when he had to return Baba, which I rejected as insulting Baba.

On Saturday there was a housewarming party[4] at Eva Herrman's place with the Manns, the Feuchtwangers etc., in her delightfully tasteful little new house. Sunday evening Lix's 50th birthday, celebrated with a good goose and champagne in a very small group, only the Horkheimers, the Pollocks plus mother-in-law and ourselves, with a strong feeling of kinship. Tonight after supper Max and Maidon will be here together with Lang and Lily for the first time. On Friday dinner with Thomas Mann. That is more or less everything, but you can see that your horses are not exactly living in the deepest solitude, although they, and Max too, would often prefer it. Keep looking after yourself my Wondrous Hippo Cow with heartiest kisses from your old child
Teddie

Hugs and kisses from the stupid Giraffe

Original: typewritten letter with handwritten greeting by Gretel Adorno.

1 Bruno Walter's real name, Bruno Walter Schlesinger, which he gave up in 1896 in favour of his stage name.

2 Translator's note: this is a reference to the poet and Minnesinger Walter von der Vogelweide (*c*.1170–*c*.1230), chosen for his nominal resemblance to Bruno Walter. It is conceivable that Adorno may also have intended a mock-pastoral tone through the meaning of *Vogelweide* ('bird pasture').

3 Harpers & Brothers.

4 *housewarming party*: EO.

208   LOS ANGELES, 24.2.1948

L.A., 24 February 1948

Mumma my Hippo Cow Animal,
    thank you most kindly for your letter. A shame you were unable to hear Eduard's concert. He is quite successful in his profession, but has to pay a doctor (whom I consider highly problematic) 1000 dollars

every month for the unfortunate Mausi's[1] treatment – and how can the poor man afford that.

A pleasant letter from Franz that was also quite optimistic as regards our German claims. He said that Louis'che had not heard from you in an age. – The letter from Helenchen is sadly not as nice as I had hoped; I herewith return it.

An extremely high-spirited letter from Anita from her 'young marriage'; evidently it is a load off both their shoulders. No word from Charlotte. Incidentally, Max is in S.F. for a few days.

Last week we brought quite a few of our records such as Kainz, Moissi, Pallenberg, Yvette[2] etc. to Lang, who was a little down, and they proved a quite incredible success. The famous (but unsympathetic) dancer Mattray[3] recorded some of them with his tape recorder[4] afterwards, which had been arranged with the help of the young Schildkraut, who was also at Lang's.

I expect I have already told you that I am writing a whole new part on Stravinsky for 'Philosophie der neuen Musik'. It is now, along with some other additions, to become a book.

I gave one of my chapters for the big Berkeley book to a professor at UCLA[5] (the major state university here, the sister of Berkeley) for the first time, and he was most impressed.

Last night at a boring concert with Norah, Walter Lehmann and his wife[6] (Giraffe skived). Afterwards with the truly enchanting Lisa Minghetti and the party.[7] Her husband's condition has improved just a touch.

That's about all,[8] my animal. Hopefully you are well. How are those Hippo Cow eyes? Your writing seemed less clear again – do tell me how things stand. With heartiest kisses from your old child

Teddie

Original: typewritten letter.

1 Eduard Steuermann's daughter.

2 The gramophone records of the actors Josef Kainz (1858–1910), Alexander Moissi (1879–1935), Max Pallenberg (1877–1934) and the chansonnière Yvette Guilbert (1865–1944) have not been identified.

3 The Budapest-born Ernst Matray (1891–1978) worked for years as an actor and dancer of grotesques at the Deutsches Theater under Max Reinhardt; his successful film career began with his debut in Reinhardt's silent film *Das Mirakel* (1913). In 1927 he married the actress Maria Solveg, with whom he emigrated to the USA via England in 1933. In Hollywood, Matray was active as a choreographer and director of well-known film productions until 1955.

4 *tape recorder*: EO.

5 Unidentified.

6 Uncertain; possibly the former Frankfurt surgeon Walter Lehmann (1888–1960) and his wife Wera von Kuszowski, who had lived in emigration in California since 1939.

7 *party*: EO.

8 *That's about all*: EO.

209 LOS ANGELES, 4.3.1948

4 March 1948

Marinumba, my best Hippo Cow,
    a thousand thanks for your letter. It is difficult to gain a precise impression of the illness of Eduard's little daughter; the diagnosis is schizophrenia, but at least it seems a slightly less severe case than that of Gretel Herzberger,[1] and her private medical treatment seems to have led to a certain improvement, but it is of course horrible. I voiced a suspicion of mental illness to Eduard years ago; he dismissed the idea back then; if he had subjected the child to analysis sufficiently early, as I wanted, one might perhaps have been able to save her.
    The first big book written together with Max is coming out now; the next is in its infancy, delayed through the Jewish projects, regarding which Max will probably have to go to N.Y. again soon – but in the meantime I have finished, as well as the Berkeley things, my big book of aphorisms, and 'Philosophie der neuen Musik' has made great progress. – La Habra is finished.
    Else is still ignoring my existence, it seems. Or not? You did not believe it, but it does seem to be the case. I would be grateful to receive all the letters, and will return them promptly. Regarding poor Hermann,[2] I tried once to gain the rich Norah's help in the matter, but entirely in vain – she hardly knew him, and there are no claims upon the family. It would naturally be easy for her to help, but unfortunately she is 'tight',[3] and also irritable about anything relating to the association bank's take-over of the investment bank, and rightly so.
    You should keep the Cronberg picture – it gives you pleasure, and with our constantly insecure housing situation one should really not send it over here – but a thousand thanks nonetheless.
    Naturally we do still have the old gramophone, and it is still serving us well, though we would like to have a more modern one, but this too shall have to wait until we have secure housing. Today, incidentally,

317

I received a few nice lines from Hilda Crevenna[4] in New York – Pace mio Dio[5] . . . I think she is in quite a bad way, she has no money, and her lover, a singer and conductor by the name of Wolf,[6] on whose account she had left Germany under the Nazis, has left her in the lurch.

On Saturday Luli introduced us to her sister Christa,[7] very pleasant and pretty, but not a patch on the real Luli. But we struck up an immediate rapport as if we had known each other for years. We then took a substantial walk through the park, with whole packs of Afghan hounds leaping about around us. Though Ali Baba is like an old spinal patient and hardly gets up from his warm bed by the heater (when he is not lying on Luli's bed), he still did us the honours – tried to get into our car and followed us with a long gaze from the archway as we left. Touching. On Sunday Gretel went across country with Lang and Lily to an artificial 'Pioneer Town';[8] there are such things here, rather like the artificial hermitage at the Favres' in Weilnau; I had to stay home to see young Rebner, who discussed his by no means untalented compositions with me. In the evening we went to Norah's with the writer Willi Speyer,[9] with whom we were also at Luli's on Saturday (he is a childhood friend of her brother, who was murdered by the Nazis). – Did I already tell you that Baroness Brentano turned out to be an impostor? Luli's accounts alone were a theatre performance.

Poor Giraffe has a terrible but entirely innocent cold, and yet she is accompanying me tonight to the Horkheimers, where there will be a few people.

The rough dictation of my Stravinsky is approaching completion – that is when the work really starts.

Would it not be lovely if we could get the houses back again, and you ended up moving into the Seeheim[10] house as an old queen mother and Ancient Hippo Sow?

Poor Thomas Mann has broken his shoulder – at the Horkheimers, incidentally – but it is a 'smooth' break, he is almost better already, I saw him at length on Monday.

Heartiest kisses from your old child
Teddie

A kiss, not infectious at this distance, from the stupid lanky
Giraffe

Original: typewritten letter with handwritten greeting from Gretel Adorno.

1 No further information could be found concerning Gretel Herzberger, who had lived in Berlin during the 1920s.

2 This refers to Hermann Levi.

3 *'tight'*: EO.

4 Hilda Viktoria Plieninger, from a family of merchants and industrialists, had been married to Alfred Bolongaro-Crevenna (1881–1962) from 1913 to 1932; no further information could be found.

5 An aria from Verdi's *La forza del destino*.

6 Unknown.

7 Christa von Bodenhausen (1909–86).

8 *'Pioneer Town'*: EO.

9 The writer Wilhelm Speyer (1887–1952), who had collaborated with Walter Benjamin on occasion, lived in Beverly Hills during his American exile; in 1947 he published the novel *Das Glück der Andernachs* [The Good Fortune of the Andernachs].

10 Adorno's parents owned a villa on the Bergstraße in Seeheim, where they had intended to spend their retirement. They had been forced to sell the house and the property on 7 July 1938.

210   LOS ANGELES, 15.3.1948

15 March 1948

My dear good Hippo Cow,
   Norah Andreae just dropped in to entrust us with her papers once again, for tonight she will be flying to Mexico again for her sixtieth birthday, and spending Easter there with her children. The Marxes will be opening another restaurant there, as the first one is running so superbly. A few days ago we were up with Luli and Baba, Teddie tried out a Steinway for her, and, just imagine, Baba jumped on his daughter Dusky and she is now expecting offspring from him. I am quite amazed that he manages it with his slow movements. – Max is leaving in a week, and this week there is much activity here, meetings about the Jewish things, university matters etc. – Today Archie finished dictating the second part of his 'Philosophie der neuen Musik', the part on Stravinsky, and in high spirits as a result. Even if there is still much to do, it at least exists now. – Yesterday we had a nice, peaceful Sunday up with Lang and Lily with fresh sausages, sauerkraut and beer, with which we drank your health. It is nicest completely improvised, without any party.[1]
   Many hugs and kisses
                                        from your lanky Giraffe

Has Hermann Levi gone mad or is Herbert[2] really a monster, or both? Else is systematically ignoring my existence. I do think you should

319

then mention me again; it is unclear to me, incidentally, what she really expected from me.

Heartiest kisses from your old child

Teddie

Original: typewritten letter.

1 *party*: EO.

2 Herbert Levi.

211 LOS ANGELES, 24.3.1948

24 March 1948

Marinumba, my Hippo Sow,

a thousand Easter wishes and thanks for your letter. In a few days it will be your 82½th birthday, a date that I shall honour with the appropriate solemnity. Hopefully you are well and your dear hippo heart is not having too much trouble coping with the rapid change of temperature that is customary in New York at this time of year. Here the rainy season has started again, enough to make one melancholy. Max and Pollock are in New York, but are under incredible pressure, and you must not be angry if you do not hear from him. I have the whole Jewish business on my shoulders here, and I hardly know if I am coming or going, but 'Philosophie der neuen Musik' is more or less finished. I went to a Stravinsky concert under his excellent direction, exclusively with recent works, incredibly well done, but rather standardized and hollow, also the new symphony, despite presenting itself as more demanding and modern. But next to our good Virgil Thomson he is of course a true Beethoven, although he struck me as a cross between a clown and an executive, and his music also has an element of that. Also a concert of Krenek's music, rather uneven, very weak new songs, but a delightful clarinet trio. I am glad that Julie is coming here, though she will not have much fun in downtown Los Angeles; Gretel already wrote to her about that. I think you should simply write to Else asking why she is ignoring my existence, tell her that I am very sad about it, that it is evidently due to a completely mistaken assessment of the situation, and that such friction is quite ridiculous. That the whole thing is inexplicable to you and she should spit it out. Forgive my haste, with heartiest kisses from

your old child
Teddie

320

An especially sweet Easter kiss
                    your lanky Giraffe

Original: typewritten letter with handwritten greeting from Gretel Adorno.

212 LOS ANGELES, 1.4.1948

                                    1.IV.1948

Marinumba, my animal,
   a thousand thanks for your letter. We had a pleasant, peaceful
Easter with Maidon and listened to the 5th Symphony, Giraffe's
present to me. Lily got through her rather complicated appendix operation well, and is back home.
   I am up to my neck in Jewish negotiations, and having a great deal
of fun. As well as that I am trying, as far as I possibly can, to advance
the final editing of Philosophie der neuen Musik, looking after Lix and
seeing all sorts of professors about institute matters. On Easter
Saturday I played some sonatas with the dangerously ill violinist Toni
Maaskoff, including the last, very difficult one in C minor by
Beethoven, and he, whose condition has temporarily improved,
played more beautifully and vigorously than ever.
   I can well imagine the Violin Concerto by Kreisler[1] and its interpretation, and am glad that nowadays such stuff gets on your nerves
just as much as those of your cultural bolshevist child.
   Ilse Mayer has arrived in New York, even though we all advised
against such an undertaking. I assume that she will look you up
together with Carlota Pollock, who flew to New York for 2 weeks.
Max called me yesterday from N.Y.; he is under incredible pressure,
but in good spirits.
   The offspring of Ali Baba's incest all died at once.
   On Monday we shall have some theatre here: Luli with the Thomas
Manns[2] and perhaps Lang for tea. Tomorrow evening we are at Lix's
for dinner with a few film people. We are both well despite all the
work.
   Heartiest kisses from
                    your old child
                    Teddie

The hippo pinched all my news, many kisses
                    your old Giraffe

Original: typewritten letter with handwritten greeting from Gretel Adorno.

                    321

1 Presumably Fritz Kreisler's C major Violin Concerto 'In the Style of Vivaldi', assuming that Adorno is not simply referring to a concert by Kreisler including a violin concerto (the Beethoven?).

2 Thomas Mann's diary contains the following entry for 5 April: 'In the afternoon at the Adornos for tea with his pride and joy, the rich baroness, who had little to offer' (Thomas Mann, *Tagebücher 28.5.1946–31.12.1948* [Frankfurt am Main: Fischer, 1989], p. 245).

213   LOS ANGELES, 15.4.1948

15 April 1948

Mumma, my animal,
the only reason that we have now gone for longer than usual without writing is our unimaginable workload. The whole of the Jewish negotiations, with the heads of all organizations, all carrying a relative responsibility, are entirely down to me here. I have gone through the entire book of aphorisms thoroughly once more before sending it to a publisher[1] who has shown interest. 'Philosophie der neuen Musik' is finished, except for a series of additions that I am continuing to dictate. There will not be a final draft for months yet. But you will receive a copy of the book I wrote with Max as soon as I have one myself. – Also, the longest of my chapters for the anti-Semitism project has come back from Berkeley, edited by Sanford, and I have to go through the whole thing again, a small book in itself, with the utmost precision before the fair copy is made. Lix is being a very good helper.
You can imagine that I can barely get around to writing amid all the work, and at the moment I have next to no private life worthy of report. Maidon returned today from New York, where she had been for four days. Reason: there is a considerable chance that Max will be taking a trip to Europe without coming back here. That will probably be decided within the next week.
The afternoon with Luli and Thomas Mann provided less theatre than we had hoped – she was a little inhibited and reserved, and he spoke mostly with Ali Baba and me. Norah is back from Mexico, very pleasant.
We are very well despite all the commotion, and are thinking of you.
Heartiest kisses from
your old child
Teddie

Our pretty friend Lisa Minghetti (Maaskoff) is in N.Y. for a few days, and will call on you if she can, my Hippo Cow.
Many hugs from Giraffe

Original: typewritten letter with handwritten postscript and hand-written greeting from Gretel Adorno.

1 This was Fritz H. Landshoff at the Querido Verlag, who had published the *Dialectic of Enlightenment* the previous year. Adorno had offered Landshoff *Minima Moralia* in his letter of 25 March 1948. No direct response to the letter from the publisher has survived among Adorno's belongings. On 9 July, however, Landshoff wrote that he had only recently started reading the book.

214 LOS ANGELES, 23.4.1948

Los Angeles, 23 April 1948

Mumma my dearest Wondrous Hippo Cow,
    a thousand thanks for your very sweet letter, and for not getting in a huff about my not writing. Max suddenly decided to go to Europe with a mission and money from the Rockefeller Foundation, and will be reading in Frankfurt, among other things – very interesting, but horribly exhausting. Yesterday evening for dinner at Maidon's with Lix and the Pollocks; Carlota spoke extremely highly of you and said what great presence of mind you had shown; but she also says that Ilse is in very good shape at the moment.
    Main event: today our lovely cupboard arrived, delivered in the Pollocks' lift. Fritz and Lix will install it together next week, in the den;[1] it was no mean feat to find a spot for the giant thing in our limited space, but I am very happy to have it. A sign of the Hippo Cow.
    Stiedry conducted the Metropolitan here and gave me a call, was here on Tuesday and will probably come again tomorrow, very pleasant and stimulating. My part in the novel by Th. M. is apparently common knowledge in N.Y. Tomorrow evening at the Kreneks with Stiedry, at Norah's in the afternoon of the following day. All this, together with our incredible amounts of work, is a little too much for Gretel, who is on the edge of a migraine. But the work will now be reducing somewhat. I still have one part of Philosophie der neuen Musik to dictate and a few additions to sort out; my Berkeley chapters are also nearly finished. Lix gave me some very useful help with them. Next week I have to speak in a highly official capacity, together with a professor[2] from the university here, at an executive dinner[3] held by the local branch of the American Jewish Committee; in general a great deal of Jewish stuff.
    I remember Otto Kömff[4] quite well; what has he done wrong that he should have such a guilty conscience – I have no idea any more. I shall write to him on my next 'correspondence day'; at the moment

323

I have not even been able to reply to Franz's last, lengthy letter, it is only the Giant Sow who is being flooded with letters!!!
Heartiest kisses from your old child
Teddie

Has Liesl got in touch?

Original: typewritten letter with handwritten greeting.

1 *den*: EO.

2 Presumably the sociologist Leonard Bloom, who taught in Los Angeles.

3 This took place on 28 April with the purpose of inaugurating a new project towards the 'Re-education of the Germans'. Translator's note: EO.

4 Maria Wiesengrund wrote the following response on 29 April: 'The Kömpf boys had stolen some of your things. Willi Röckl was *not* there during the afternoon in question. And he would *never* have stolen even a bun from *you*. While clearing up your things, we immediately noticed that some toys, little notebooks with good, rare stamps, stones, in particular a very large and beautiful amethyst, unprocessed of course, were missing. So, as no one had been there except the Kömpf boys, we knew what was what. Dädd [Agathe Calvelli-Adorno] went to the people at once and said that the children had taken this and that 'by mistake'. The children had hidden themselves. The mother said she would have a look and after a few hours brought the toys, a 'teddy bear' etc. She did not find the stamps and the amethyst, but in fact a few other stones. The woman was most agitated. The boys did not come any more! So be careful and do not mention it. I remember *very* well. –' (See also the following letter.)

215   LOS ANGELES, 6.5.1948

Dr. T.W. Adorno   6 May 1948
316 So. Kenter Ave.
Los Angeles 24, Calif.

Mumma, my animal,
    a thousand thanks for your sweet letter. Max has meanwhile arrived in Paris. He was especially sorry that he was not able to look you up, but he truly was under the most unbelievable pressure.
    The most important thing I have to report is that 'Philosophie der neuen Musik' has been accepted by my old publisher (Siebeck) in Tübingen, and in fact without even seeing the manuscript. I have meanwhile written a theoretical introduction for it, and am now putting the finishing touches on that. I am quite happy about it. But please do not talk to anyone about it; I only want it to become public once I have signed the contract.

Last week we were invited to Lang's with Miss Massary,[1] who now looks exactly like what she has been for the last twenty years: an old Jewess, very uneducated, she evidently climbed up from the petty bourgeoisie, but talented and intelligent. The point of the evening was for us to play her our Massary records, which she does not have. She was very moved by it and is having them copied.

The day before yesterday we had an especially pleasant evening with Luli and Baba. They are thinking of going to Europe for a few weeks.

My speech[2] at the Jewish dinner was, as far as all those involved were concerned, a great success, but it is highly doubtful whether it will have any practical consequences.

I now have a lot of work to do on the final editing of the Labor Project for the institute. – I will not rush my response to Kömff. Incidentally, he was not the boy with the amethysts, it was Beuschel.[3]

Heartiest kisses from your old child
Teddie

Hugs and kisses from your lanky Giraffe

Original: typewritten letter with handwritten greeting from Gretel Adorno.

1 The operetta star Fritzi Massary (1882–1969) lived in Beverly Hills; she had emigrated to the USA in 1938. She was married to Max Pallenberg and was the mother of Liesl Frank.

2 Nothing has remained of Adorno's speech – which was presumably unscripted – among his belongings.

3 No information could be gained about this friend from Adorno's childhood or youth.

216 LOS ANGELES, 22.5.1948

Los Angeles, 22 May 1948

Mumma my Hippo Cow,
there has been an uncommonly long interval between my last letter and this one. But nothing is amiss, nor am I guilty of neglect – my work had simply piled up to such a degree in the last 2 weeks that I literally could not find a minute for myself. My two last Berkeley chapters arrived in the version edited by Sanford, which I had to work through thoroughly once more before they can be copied, and at the same time I also (leaving aside my own editorship for the Labor Study) had to prepare my lectures[1] for the budding psychoanalysts

here (lots of young doctors) on Freud's sociological and anthropological writings. The last lecture was yesterday, and was an extraordinarily great success – they want me to collaborate on a larger scale. And my part for Berkeley is now entirely finished, after long, long birthing pains, in good shape. The final chapter of the book will now also be based on a roughly 40-page text I wrote last year. At that time, my colleagues at Berkeley showed great resistance to it; but now, as the water of the deadline is reaching their necks and they are too lazy to do it themselves, they are falling back on it – a small victory.

Aside from these professional matters I can hardly think of anything to report, for, as you will understand, we have hardly seen anyone. From next week onwards things will be much quieter here, peaceful constant work on the Labor Study and the last check through Philosophie der neuen Musik before the fair copy is made and sent to the publisher. This morning we took a breather by the sea. – Max was in Switzerland and is going to Frankfurt tomorrow.

Milton Seligman died – entirely peacefully of a stroke, returning home from a bridge session with Willi Dreyfuss.[2] I am very sorry, for I truly liked him and we had become particularly close in the last, rather complicated years. He was 81 years old, but seemed much younger. – It appears that Norah will be going to Europe to see her mother. Are you well? Is it not yet too hot for your good Hippo Cow head? I asked Norah through an acquaintance at the Frankfurt zoo to inquire about Lieschen[3] the hippo cow!

Heartiest kisses my animal from your old child
Teddie

Original: typewritten letter.

1 Among Adorno's belongings there are two English texts marked '1st lecture, 5/22/48' and '2nd lecture' (undated); they both bear the title 'Psychoanalysis and Sociology'. It is possible that both texts were only typed out by Gretel Adorno from the shorthand after the final lecture on 21 May.

2 The Frankfurt banker Willy Dreyfus (1885–1977) had been vice-president of the Hilfsverein der deutschen Juden [Relief Organization of German Jews]. He emigrated to Switzerland.

3 A picture postcard from the Tiergarten der Stadt Frankfurt am Main, depicting the hippo cow Lieschen (Hippopotamus amphibius), had last been sent to Adorno by Maria Wiesengrund in 1936.

10 June 1948

Marinumba, my animal,
a thousand thanks for your letter. The last week was rather rough, as I wanted to force the definitive completion of Philosophie der neuen Musik at all costs. The manuscript was finished today, on Gretel's birthday, and Fräulein v. Mendelssohn will be collecting it later to produce the fair copy. It is a great load off my shoulders. I am also approaching the end of my part of the editing for the Labor Project, and my last Berkeley chapter has gone out as well. So I can finally breathe again; though admittedly I still have to give a very important lecture[1] for the heads of the Jewish organization here. But then I can divide it up as I please, and above all deal with Benjamin's remaining works, which is for me an intellectual and moral duty of the highest order. I would like to afford my own production a small hiatus.

It should amuse you to know that a German magazine[2] asked me to write an essay about the music in Thomas Mann's Faust novel. Naturally I declined.

We had a very sweet telegram from Max today; he hardly has the time to write, and the results of his journey cannot yet be fully judged. –

We shall be celebrating Giraffe's birthday tonight at Lang and Lily's with good fodder; Maidon is in Lake Arrowhead and had constant nosebleeds, and Fritz and Carlota had to drive up there to check up on her. We have not heard from Else either, but from Charlotte, who is hunting in New York.

Max is giving lectures at the universities in Frankfurt and a few other cities.

According to a charming letter Lix received from old Frau Drevermann,[3] there does seem to be more left of the institute building than the first photograph of the ruins suggested.

On account of a remark in a letter from Franz that Julie mentioned to me, I am enclosing a statement that I would ask you to date, sign *in the presence of a notary public*[4] and send to Franz please. *Very important.*

Our health is good, though understandably we are also both somewhat tired.

Heartiest kisses
from your old child
Teddie

My dear Hippo Cow,
a thousand thanks for the greatly excessive cheque, which I shall use to buy myself some nice dark stockings. I am happy that your eyes and

blood pressure are in good shape; we shall soon hear at length about you from Julie. When is she planning to turn up here?

I enclose a letter from Melly that may interest you; please have Julie read it to you. I have not heard any more from Helenchen, although packages, even an insured one, are en route with winter overcoats and a great deal of writing paper etc. One rather solid one was lost last year, unfortunately, with shoes and a handbag and the like. – Norah is genuinely going to Switzerland again at the end of the month, as her mother could ultimately not bring herself to come here. She has let out her house. Luli is also in Europe.

Quite especially hearty kisses from
your old stupid
Giraffe

Original: typewritten letter.

1 No further information.

2 Unknown.

3 Ria Drevermann was a friend of Max Horkheimer; her son, the architect Wolf Drevermann, planned the rebuilding of the institute in Frankfurt.

4 *notary public*: EO.

218 LOS ANGELES, 21.6.1948

21 June 1948

Mumma, my animal,
thank you most kindly for your letter of the 15th.

Today I enclose something that might entertain you: the letter Thomas Mann wrote me back in 1945[1] regarding the Faust novel. Naturally *utmost* discretion: do not show the letter to anyone under any circumstances, and send it back once you have read it. I should add that the document is from a time when my collaboration was still in its earliest stages: my main contribution, the detailed descriptions of Leverkühn's works, which fill entire chapters, only came about in a later phase. Thomas Mann told me a few days ago that he is interrupting his present work, a novella, to write an autobiographical essay[2] in which he plans to reveal the whole business to the public, and I naturally have no intention of preventing that in any way, not least because the significance of such an essay for me can hardly be overestimated. We are having the Manns over on Wednesday evening. Otherwise I would also add that the passage on the op. 111 sonata

328

and the enthusiasm of Herr Walter is written with a smile, as that very passage is a 'montage', i.e. taken directly from an essay of mine[3] that appeared many years ago in the Prague journal 'Auftakt'.

Quite a number of interesting people have crossed my path, for example a truly quite extraordinary pianist by the name of Pesha Kagan,[4] a student of Schnabel and both musically and pianistically a phenomenon the like of which I have heard only very rarely – far above Josie.[5] And yesterday, at the Pollocks, a son of Carl Friedberg[6] who told me all there is to know about Fred and Céline Goldbeck. Fred has now finally married Yvonne Lefébure,[7] who is now also in her late forties. They waited for so long because of an inheritance they were expecting from Céline's family, but which naturally never materialized. Céline spent the war in New York, but did not get in touch with anyone due to a general state of anger. The Friedbergs had arranged the immigration to America for Fred and provided him with a very good position, but, with the indolence that is particular to him, he chose instead to stay over there and fled to Spain during the German occupation, where he began a sort of urbane career through Sir Samuel Hoare,[8] as something between a private tutor and a dandy.

Anita and Robert seem, judging by a letter he wrote, to be very happy, but they have not been here for over a year, nor I in San Francisco. Yes, I had a letter from Charlotte, and gave a very brief response, c'est tout. You need not fear that she will visit you, but if she did, it would only be a friendly gesture, and the old Hippo Cow Queen Mother would no doubt have enough savoir vivre to receive her courteously.

I am now in the thick of working through Benjamin's remaining writings, which I have at my disposal – an extremely gripping task. Max will, I hope, be back here by August.

Melly is not planning to emigrate, as far as we know. Lotte and E are very well. Sperber[9] is a pleasant and friendly wire-haired fox terrier.

Heartiest kisses

from your old Hippo King
Teddie

Many kisses   Giraffe

Original: typewritten letter with handwritten greeting from Gretel Adorno.

1 Thomas Mann's letter of 30 December 1945; see Theodor W. Adorno and Thomas Mann, *Correspondence 1943–55* (Cambridge: Polity, 2006), pp. 11–14.

2 Thomas Mann interrupted his work on *Der Erwählte* [published in English as *The Holy Sinner*] to write *Die Entstehung des Doktor Faustus. Roman eines Romans* [published in English as *The Genesis of a Novel*].

3 See letter no. 97, note 2.

4 No further information could be found regarding this pianist, who played at the Adornos on 23 June 1948 in the presence of Katia and Thomas Mann. Pescha Kagan (as she signed her letters) still wrote to Adorno a number of times during the 1950s, and Adorno replied at least once.

5 Concerning Josefa Rosanska, see letter no. 4, note 14.

6 The pianist Carl Friedberg (1872–1955), born in Bingen am Rhein, had studied with Clara Schumann at the Hoch'sches Konservatorium; he taught there himself from 1893 to 1904. He also taught at the Juilliard School of Music in New York from 1924 onwards. The name of his son is unknown.

7 See letter no. 38, note 7; no further information could be gained regarding Céline Goldbeck.

8 The British Conservative politician Viscount Samuel Hoare (1880–1959) was special envoy in Madrid from 1940 to 1944, and succeeded in counteracting German attempts to persuade Spain to enter the war.

9 Maidon Horkheimer's new dog.

219   LOS ANGELES, 14.7.1948

14 July 1948

Mumma, my Hippo Cow,
 a thousand thanks for your letter of the 10th with the one from Else, which latter I enclose. I have, in spite of everything, made a further attempt to reach some understanding with her, and also enclose that letter. If she behaves like a human being, then no one shall be gladder than myself. If not, then my response will be the same as it has been in other cases that meant more to me: just too bad.[1]
 We were deeply happy to receive the plain red tie (I have an old preference for plain colours, perhaps due to lack of visual imagination) and the handkerchiefs, and send you our heartiest thanks.
 It was wonderful to see Julie again, harmonious and peaceful for all concerned. We spent a great deal of time together. On Sunday we collected her as soon as she arrived at her hotel in Hollywood and dragged her to our cave. On Monday Gretel picked her up from Hollywood again, and she spent the evening with us once more, and today we still went to her for lunch before her departure. She had a superbly relaxing time, looks marvellous and is in good spirits. We admire her for her enterprising spirit. I think we would barely have the élan vital to spend our holidays on such a strenuous and arduous trip.

330

She will give you all the details about our time together, including the big cupboard.

Otherwise nothing new here, I am correcting the fair copy of 'Philosophie der neuen Musik'. We are both very well, only a little tired. We went to the beach for the first time this season.

Heartiest kisses

from your old child
Teddie

Please send me back my letter to Else![2]

Fond regards   your old Giraffe

Original: typewritten letter with handwritten postscript and handwritten greeting from Gretel Adorno.

1 *just too bad*: EO.

2 On 12 July Adorno wrote Else Herzberger the following letter:

> My dear Else, you old sourpuss,
>
> so you finally came out with it and told my mother that you cannot write to me. Well, I can; and I shall; and I ask you if we should really, after a friendship that has shaped our whole lives and left its indelible traces, however you might behave – if we should really be cross with each other like children, and whether it would not be a thousand times better and more humane, for every possible reason, for Agathe's sake, but equally for our own, to resume contact at once. As if we could afford to lose each other in this ravaged world.
>
> I really have no idea how I have disappointed you. If it is about material matters (and I can hardly imagine anything else), then you probably had fundamentally mistaken expectations. I would like to explain the situation, but before you hold a grudge against me, you must definitely tell me what is the matter and give me a chance to speak. Firstly, because one always – except under fascism – gives the accused a chance to be heard; but secondly because I am convinced that what stands between us will prove to be as light as a feather if we get hold of it and get it out of the way.
>
> I shall tell you about us as soon as I receive word from you. I expect you know that a big book I wrote together with Max was recently published by Querido. But above all, write to me about yourself, and about the very pressing matter of repatriation.
>
> Do I still have to tell you how atrocious I find the state of things between us and how it saddens me? No: we are not so far apart that you could fail to know that.
>
> Fond regards from your old
>
> (typescript copy in the Theodor W. Adorno Archiv).

> Else Herzberger did not reply to Adorno.

24 July 1948

Mumma, my animal,

one of those sayings that have lost their validity is that lightning never strikes twice in the same place. After sending us the eviction notice,[1] as you know, in order to move into our apartment himself, our landlord sent us a second eviction notice a fortnight later. The house is sold; the new owner intends to move into our apartment, and the present owner will stay in his old one for now. We are attempting to defend ourselves against this latest attack, but there is little hope. I am convinced that we shall have to leave this time, and the matter of finding even a remotely suitable apartment is, for the most basic financial reasons, a problem of the highest order.

In connection with this concern, however, your own housing question also arises. Julie told us that things are becoming increasingly embarrassing, uncomfortable and expensive for you, not to mention that she thinks the whole business will not continue much longer in any case due to the landlady's plans. Julie herself would like to find an apartment of her own, so that she can finally have a home of her own – an intention that I can well understand in the light of the difficult work she has to carry out, and after all the touching solidarity she has shown. The three of us together have had the idea of finding something else for you, and if possible sharing with others, so that you are not isolated, and where the practical matters that are starting to become a burden for you can be taken off your hands. A solution such as this would also give us all a greater feeling of material security, as then things would become more comfortable for you than they are at present, and at the same time our finances – which are limited, after all – would last considerably longer. The most logical and natural option of simply coming to live with us can be ruled out due to the housing crisis and the uncertainty of our whole plans. I know how hard it is for you to leave the apartment, after sharing it with my father to the end, but I do advocate it on the basis of a sense of reason that he would have been the first to promote, and above all for your sake and that of your own inner peace. Julie wants to take some time to look for something suitable, and it goes without saying that nothing will be undertaken before she has found the right place, one that also appeals to you. No decision in this matter will be made without you, but I do mean *together with* you, and I would first of all like to know your initial reaction to my suggestion.

I just received your letter of the 20th, a thousand thanks. I am happy with all my heart that you are well in spite of the atrocious heat. We have little to report, except for terrible amounts of work. Max is embarking today, but will probably come here directly without any stopovers. I shall write to you concerning Herr Grau[2] within the next few days.

Heartiest kisses, my little sow,

from your old child
Teddie

Hugs and kisses from your lanky

Giraffe

Original: typewritten letter with handwritten greeting from Gretel Adorno.

1 *eviction notice*: EO.

2 Unknown.

221 LOS ANGELES, 30.7.1948

30 July 1948

Mumma, my mother-animal,

a thousand thanks for your very sweet letter. I am glad that you mastered the Julie-less time so well and with such bearing, and glad too that we are d'accord regarding the problem of your 'lodgings'. I am quite sure that Julie will find the best solution, and in good time, before the situation in the guesthouse and with Miss Young gets truly out of hand. Please keep us informed. As for ourselves, and the uncertainty of the plans you asked about, it is quite possible that I shall have to go to Europe to give some guest lectures. It also looks very much as if the institute in Frankfurt is being rebuilt. A committee has already been formed for this purpose. If it does work out, then we would all have to see to it temporarily. Max, who did not even spend two days in New York, will be here again on Tuesday, and then all these possibilities will be discussed. There is nothing alarming about it, simply that no decision can be made in this tiresome housing business until our common intentions are entirely clear. The housing situation as such is unchanged and a great strain on our nerves.

Else has *not* replied to my letter, but Charlotte, on the other hand, wrote to me once more, and a pleasant letter at that. Are you sure you do not want me to send her to you sometime after all? I would be so very curious to hear what you think of her. She wrote, incidentally, that after San Francisco she 'shook the dust off her feathers' – as if she had suspected that we call her the Christmas goose.

333

My impression is that she is quite lonely, even if she would naturally never admit it.

Ilse is staying with the Pollocks for a few weeks. We saw her at length the day before yesterday, and both had a very good impression. The business with the mental illness is all based on a truly malicious manoeuvre by the rightfully deceased Clara Plaut.[1] Ilse had by no means made her famous costly acquisitions out of recklessness, but – highly rationally – to get larger material amounts out of Germany; old Aunt Louise would only have had to hand over the equivalent sums to the Nazis, and the ghastly Clara was so afraid of losing any money as a result that she had Ilse locked up in an asylum for five months under observation, without her idiotic and egotistical mother, who was living in Berlin at the time, doing anything to prevent it. Please also inform Julie about the matter. Until now we all knew only the distorted version from Clara. A miracle that Ilse did not genuinely go mad in the course of the affair, which also coincided with the November pogroms. But she makes a much more balanced impression now than she did upon her New York visit ten years ago.

Yesterday, at Thomas Mann's, spoke at length about 'Felix Krull', which – to my pleasure – he plans to finish. This afternoon a long walk by the sea, tomorrow probably to the beach with Ilse; as we are not taking any proper holidays, we at least plan to relax a little that way.

Heartiest kisses

from your old child
Teddie

Fond regards from your lanky

Giraffe

Original: typewritten letter with handwritten greeting from Gretel Adorno.

1 No further information could be found concerning the private music tutor Clara Plaut (née Mayer, 1886–?) or the circumstances mentioned in the letter.

222 LOS ANGELES, 12.8.1948

12 August 1948

Mumma, my animal, a thousand thanks for your very sweet letter. Here there is still nothing decisively new regarding either the housing question or the greater plans lying ahead of us. Europe did Max a great deal of good, both physically and mentally – he looked 10 years younger when he returned, but is now struggling once more with the Californian climate, which, the longer I stay here, I increasingly consider much worse than its reputation. We are spending quite a lot of time by the sea, where the heat of summer has now finally arrived, a modest substitute for a holiday trip. Tonight we are having Ilse over for supper.

Eduard is here; we are seeing him a great deal, and he is leading a truly heroic life by not only paying the incredibly high costs of his insane daughter's treatment, but even living with her. After two years' interruption we are closer and more intimate with him than ever.

We had a very sweet card from Clem[1] with the requested addresses, without a word or a greeting from Else. Her behaviour disappoints me; there will be no further efforts in the matter from my side.

Charlotte is still called Charlotte Alexander, and I shall write to her in the next few days to give you a call – receive her cordially.

Otherwise we have nothing to report, we are both in very good shape.

Heartiest kisses

from your old child
Teddie

Many kisses

Your Giraffe

Original: typewritten letter with handwritten greeting from Gretel Adorno.

1 Presumably short for Clementine; she was a relative or friend of Else Herzberger.

223   LOS ANGELES, 1.9.1948

1 September 1948

Mumma, my animal,

a thousand thanks for your very sweet letter. We were glad to learn from it, and one from dear Julie, that the question of your housing has been solved in a satisfactory manner, and that, above all, the new landlords are pleasant and familiar. You really are a heroic Hippo Cow Queen, departing from your routine and resettling. But life in 808[1] strikes me as becoming so problematic in the long run that the move is also worthwhile for the sake of your own well-being.

Hopefully the abominable heat will soon be over. Here too it is meanwhile making itself greatly felt, and both our nerves are rather frayed due to the housing matter. But, thanks to the sea, Giraffe is feeling better again.

If you really want to make me very happy on my birthday, then send me the Storm that you have, unless you like reading it yourself. (That reminds me: as a child I always confused the writings of Storm with Storm's railway timetable, but associated both of them with my father.) And then tell me what you would like to have for your 83rd birthday. Do you know that you have now surpassed Goethe, who was renowned for his size and age, my Wondrous Animal?

Max has travelled north for a few days. Today and tomorrow we are spending much time with Eduard again, we went to a party with him on Saturday and played Mahler's 6th Symphony, which I enjoyed more than ever. Aside from that I quite simply cannot think of any news.

Heartiest kisses

from your old child
Teddie

Original: typewritten letter.

1 The house number in West End Avenue.

224 LOS ANGELES, 14.9.1948

14 September 1948

Mumma, my animal,

a thousand thanks for the letter, the cheque and your very sweet birthday wishes, of which we are in quite particular need this year. From this day forward we are living here as outlaws,[1] so to speak, i.e. despite the eviction, which would have taken effect yesterday, and are now waiting to be taken to court – a delightful state of affairs. We spent my birthday alone with Lily and Lang; Max is only coming within the next few days, and now Lix's divorce case is also starting, which the press is sure to meddle in. In short, it is a peaceful life . . .

You have still not written what you would like for your own birthday, so please be so good and tell us, so that we can get you something in time. Incidentally, my animal, it is your 83rd birthday, not your 84th – do not make yourself older than you are.

I enclose a letter from Franz, and would also ask you to show it to Julie. I have replied to him, saying that he should focus on the concrete facts for now, the ownership of the property and the house, and

336

also attempt to calculate the value of the total assets, as represented by the business, on the basis of my father's and Julie's statements in combination with whatever he finds out in Frankfurt.

A rather nice chamber music evening at Thomas Mann's house,[2] including quite an interesting piano trio by Weber and an indescribably beautiful quartet for flute and string trio by Mozart. Excellent flautist. Menuhin's youngest sister, who is really no genius, was pussyfooting about at the piano. My big manuscript arrived safely in Tübingen, and the preliminary censorship of the French military authority has been cancelled; I hope there will be no further difficulties.

It is a great shame for you that Liefmann is going; I would certainly think about whether you want to take his 'successor' or a different doctor, one you know *personally*. Perhaps you could discuss that with the Löwenthals! – Liefmann's return to F., admittedly, is very interesting as a symptom. Heartiest kisses from your middle-aged (no longer obliged to do military service!) child

Teddie

Many kisses the old Giraffe. What is the new address?

Original: typewritten letter with handwritten ending.

1 *outlaws*: EO.

2 In Thomas Mann's diary there is mention of 'the big musical soirée' in the entry of 6 September: 'Works for quintet and quartet, 2 cellos, one flute. Dinner and "cold duck" in between. Dahl, a good pianist. Vandenburg with wife and sister. Satisfaction all round.' Neither the G minor Trio for piano, flute and violin, op. 63, by Carl Maria von Weber nor the Flute Quartet by Mozart are mentioned. It is known, at least, that the pianist Hephzibah Menuhin (1920–81) was staying in California during July.

225   LOS ANGELES, 28.9.1948

28 September 1948

Mumma, my animal,

a thousand, a thousand congratulations! So, on this 1st of October, your 83rd birthday, you begin to move towards the legendary, as it were mythical, like Archinumba, the mother of Marinumba, who is the source of all those wise sayings such as 'The most important thing for a hippo is peace and quiet'. May you fare well in your palaeontological dignity, and may you also continue to live in it peacefully and happily in your new apartment. I am glad that the move will take place gently and without great shocks, and that Julie has taken the unpleasant side of things off your hands.

Need I still tell you how much I hope to turn up in New York in the coming year?

Everything is still unclear and in limbo here, but we are getting through it as well as we can with work. Our court case will probably take place in mid-October. At the moment I am elaborating a study on Huxley[1] that I conceived long ago, and preparing two older pieces for German publication.

Tonight we are going to a semi-private performance of Mahler's Fifth Symphony[2] under Thomas Mann's brother-in-law Pringsheim; the Manns asked us to do so. Thomas Mann has written a large part of his autobiographical representation of the genesis of the Faust novel, and told me yesterday 'you come off very well in it'.

I shall be with you in spirit on Friday and join you in your celebration with all my heart.

Heartiest kisses

from your old child
Teddie

Original: typewritten letter.

1 See 'Aldous Huxley and Utopia', and presumably also the essays 'Spengler after the Decline' and 'Veblen's Attack on Culture', in *Prisms*, trans. Samuel Weber and Shierry Weber [Cambridge, MA: MIT Press, 1981], pp. 95–118, 51–72 and 73–94 respectively.

2 Thomas Mann made a note of this performance, conducted by Katia Mann's twin brother Klaus Pringsheim (1883–1972) – a conducting student of Mahler – on 27 September.

226   LOS ANGELES, 6.10.1948

6 October 1948

Mumma, my animal,

a thousand thanks for your very sweet and eagerly awaited letter, for the book package and above all also for the folder with my manuscripts, which is most welcome, as it contains some material I do not have here. I am very happy that your move went so smoothly and unproblematically, and that you had an enjoyable birthday celebration. I hope you will continue to feel so comfortable in your new Hippo Cow stable, and not be too lonely. Norah Andreae will probably call on you within the next few days, incidentally, as she is arriving in New York from Europe today. And please be so good as to give us your new telephone number – not only for us, but also so that we can pass it on to our friends in New York. To be honest, it is very reassuring to me that you are no longer living at 808. I ultimately found that beehive-like house and its inhabitants, to say nothing of the lift boys,[1] rather unsettling, and Frau Young did not exactly inspire confidence either. Do tell us more about the conditions there.

We have no news; we are working consistently and greatly enjoying it. The house business has still not been decided. Hopefully you will continue to feel just as much at ease in your new home as you did during the first few days. Give dear Julie a thousand thanks from us for everything she has done in this matter, above all the masterful organization of the move. Has she already found something suitable?

Heartiest kisses from both of us
Your old
Hippo King
Archibald

Original: typewritten letter.

1 *lift boys*: EO.

227   LOS ANGELES, 1.11.1948

1 November 1948

Mumma, my animal,

a thousand thanks for your letter. You can naturally keep Ilse's pictures. There is quite a commotion here, as the Pollocks are flying to New York today and then on to Argentina, and we all have a hundred things to discuss. I also finished dictating an English text[1] today that represents the first practical step in drawing on the results of the anti-Semitism study. There was a very pleasant large farewell party at the Pollocks yesterday. Lix's divorce went much better than we had all expected, and he is in high spirits as a result.

Charlotte will get in touch soon enough; she may be waiting for my reply to her last letter, in which she told me she had arranged something with you. Carlota Pollock will also be getting in touch, although she is in great haste.

Reading the German will Julie sent me a few days ago, I saw for the first time that my father also included her as heir to 3/10 of the German assets, not, as you once told me, 1/16. (Naturally you should not mention the complex to Julie.)

339

Aside from that, I cannot think of any news to report. We are completely involved in work, and are very well. We were glad to receive so favourable a report about you from Norah.
Tell Julie that I hope her sciatica improves soon.
Heartiest kisses

from your old child
Teddie

Many kisses Giraffe

Original: typewritten letter with handwritten greeting from Gretel Adorno.

1 Probably 'Democratic Leadership and Mass Manipulation', published in 1950 in *Studies in Leadership: Leadership and Democratic Action*, ed. Alvin W. Gouldner, New York, 1950; see *GS* 20.1, pp. 267–86.

228 LOS ANGELES, 12.11.1948

Los Angeles, 12 November 1948

Mumma my animal,
a thousand thanks for your very sweet letter. I have meanwhile completed an essay 'Huxley und die Utopie' for a German essay collection entitled 'Kulturkritik und Gesellschaft', which, if all goes well, is to be published over there; and an English text for a collection; a second, psychoanalytical one[1] has to be finished by the end of the year. As you see, I am not being idle. Unfortunately, Giraffe has had a very heavy migraine attack during the last few days, the first time in 8 weeks, and is recovering only slowly. But on Saturday we went on a lovely, very long drive (almost 400 miles in all) with Lily Latté and an acquaintance, to the desert around Palm Springs, where we released a tortoise that had not been very comfortable up at Lang's place. The view from the mountains across the landscape of sand and rocks shimmering in all colours is indescribable, and I know you would also have enjoyed it.
Thomas Mann has finished that autobiographical essay on the Faust novel, and I am naturally very curious to see it. I enclose an American review;[2] it should interest you to read what it says about the music. Meanwhile the first German reviews of 'Dialektik der Aufklärung' (the book I wrote with Max) are starting to appear, including an especially nice one by my former student Raudszus.[3]
The result of the election[4] is very pleasing, and suggests a chance of 4 reasonably peaceful years. Did you vote, and for whom? We chose Truman at the last minute, as the votes for Wallace would only have benefited Mr Dewey with the moustache.

340

Meanwhile Thomas Mann's daughter Monika[5] has asked me to give her literary advice. Coming on Saturday.

Norah found your new apartment quite delightful, a great improvement on the last. That makes us glad and grateful. I hope you feel very much at ease there, my animal.

Heartiest kisses from your old child
Teddie

Original: typewritten letter.

1 Presumably 'Freudian Theory and the Pattern of Fascist Propaganda'. The essay was published only in 1951, in *Psychoanalysis and the Social Sciences*, vol. 3, ed. G. Róheim (see *GS* 8, pp. 408–33).

2 See Charles J. Rolo, 'Mann and his Mephistopheles', *Atlantic Monthly*, vol. 182, no. 5, November 1948, pp. 92–4. Or perhaps also: Alfred Kazin, 'Doom of Dr. Faustus, demon of the absolute: Thomas Mann offers searching fictional study of deep-rooted conflict in German spirit and culture', *New York Herald Tribune Weekly Book Review*, 31 October 1948.

3 On 23 July there had been an anonymous review in *Aufbau*. Bruno Raudszus's review 'Das Gesetz der Serie. Beiträge zur Kritik der Zeit' [The Law of the Series: Contributions to a Critique of our Times] appeared on 9 October 1948 in the *Frankfurter Rundschau*.

4 The presidential election had been won by the Democrat Harry S. Truman (1884–1972); his Republican opponent was the governor of New York, Thomas Edmund Dewey (1902–71). Henry A. Wallace (1888–1965), originally a Republican, who had been vice-president during Roosevelt's third term of office, was the candidate of the newly founded Progressive Party, which had a pro-Soviet programme.

5 Monika Mann (1910–92).

229 LOS ANGELES, 2.12.1948

2 December 1948

My dear Hippo Cow,
thank you kindly for your sweet letter. Today I have good news: Teddie's lecture at the university yesterday (on Heine) was a great success. The students applauded for minutes, and the professors from the English department made very positive comments. It would be nice if something more were to come of it, but sadly that is uncertain, to say the least, even though we could certainly do with the extra money. – If you continue to make such good progress with your English, I daresay you will soon write us English letters; I am sure your eagerness would have been a tremendous source of joy to Oscar. – Next week Archie will be speaking about music sociology[1] for a seminar

341

at the other Los Angeles university. On Sunday we were at Miss Massary's place for tea, and collected our records once more. Although she is an old lady now, she still has great charm and grace; I would like to look like that myself when I am 70.

Many hugs and kisses from your lanky

Giraffe

Mumma my animal, so, tout allait bien – incidentally, I spoke entirely freely, without a script, which made the lecture much more lively. One of the students recorded it all gramophonically with the new method. The lecture is to appear in a journal.

Yesterday was generally a good day: I finally received the definitive contract from Harpers for the big Berkeley book. There is only one more little thing to sort out, then I will send the signed document to New York. According to the terms of the contract, the publisher is obliged to print the book no later than 1 July. I think it will have a considerable effect. I am listed as co-author together with the 3 Berkeley colleagues, but for alphabetical reasons my name is the first.

I received a 16-page letter from Charlotte, who is in a wretched state. She sends you her heartfelt apologies for not visiting you yet, but she is in such a bad way that she did not want you to get the wrong impression of her.

Heartiest kisses from your old child

Teddie

Original: typewritten letter.

1 Adorno seems to have spoken freely once again; no manuscript has survived among his belongings.

---

230   LOS ANGELES, 8.12.1948

8 December 1948

My dearest Hippo Cow,

a thousand thanks for your very sweet letter. Of our friends and acquaintances, Max,[1] Mendelssohn, Felix Weil and his new flame, Pollock's secretary, Frau Krenek and a friend of hers, and Lily Latté were at Archie's Heine lecture; Max was unable to come that day. Yesterday at the University of Southern California things also went very well; it was only a very intimate seminar. First one girl gave an utterly lousy presentation on an essay by Teddie, then he spoke, and there was quite an active discussion. It was initiated by Ingolf Dahl,[2] a conductor who teaches there; he was born in Sweden and grew up in Switzerland. We received a letter from Luli, saying that she plans to

arrive here around Christmas. Lisa Minghetti was ill, and will probably not be able to visit you, as she has only a few more days in New
York. I enclose a letter from Franz. If we could only see some of
our German assets at last, so that things could at least be easier for
you. Max has decided not to go to Europe for now; instead, he will
probably resume the joint work with Teddie. At the moment it is
unbelievably cold here, by Californian standards; the temperature
drops below zero at night, and there is snow up in the mountains.
Hopefully you are not having too unpleasant a winter.

Many hugs and kisses from your lanky
Giraffe

Mumma my animal, Giraffe has snatched away everything worth
reporting – yesterday my debut at USC was very pleasant – an effect
of my essays about the radio, which are starting to get some attention
now, after 8–10 years. Otherwise, the only thing worth mentioning is
a rather strong earthquake; I was just playing the piano, and the
instrument started swaying about under my hands. But nothing happened. I am in the middle of writing an essay for a psychoanalytical
yearbook; a 'technical' study. Do be very careful with the cold weather.

Heartiest kisses from your old child
Teddie

Original: typewritten letter.

1 Presumably a slip of the pen; perhaps Maidon Horkheimer is meant, as
Horkheimer was unable to attend.

2 The composer, conductor and pianist Ingolf Dahl (1912–70), whom
Adorno seems to have met for the first time at the house of Thomas Mann,
had taught at the aforementioned university since 1945.

231   LOS ANGELES, 15.12.1948

15 December 1948

My dear Hippo Cow,
a thousand thanks for your letter and the splendid Christmas
package. The handkerchiefs are exactly as I had imagined, and the
towels are so especially large that it is a true joy to dry oneself with
them. The little writing pad also arrived in good shape. Today we
enclose your Christmas present; hopefully it will help to put your
radio in working order again. Please give Jenny our warmest greetings
– we always have so much to do that we never get around to writing.
You need not worry at all about Germany;[1] I already wrote to you that

343

Max is 95% unlikely to go to Europe now, that at least means that the business will be postponed by another two years, and a great deal can still happen before then. If Ilse Mayer pays you another visit sometime, ask her to take a few pictures of you for us, they do not all look like those of Archie, and many are even quite good. Thomas Mann's little book 'The Genesis of a Novel', the story of how the Faust novel was written, is going to press now, and will be out in about two months. – William Dieterle is going to Europe within the next few days to shoot some films there, first in France, then also in other countries. He is very happy about the assignment,[2] for things are very quiet here in Hollywood, incredible numbers of people are without work, and the atmosphere is gloomy in the whole film industry. We do not notice anything ourselves, as we have nothing to do with all that.

Many hugs and kisses

from your lanky
Giraffe

Mumma my animal, a thousand thanks for the letter. As for Else's, it means nothing to me, though I do think that you can safely write to her that you do not understand her attitude, above all that, through silence, she evades addressing the matter instead of helping to clarify it. – We listened to Mahler's 2nd from the end of the 2nd movement on; it was not all that bad by Walter's standards, and above all properly rehearsed, but in the last movement *before* the choir entry I felt it quite fell apart this time, a choral finale is only possible in real polyphony – the structure is simply not sufficient. – Heartiest kisses from your old child

Teddie

Original: typewritten letter.

1 Maria Wiesengrund had written: 'Is a journey there directly imminent? I completely share Franz's grave reservations about that and am quite convinced that he is right. – The poisonous plants thrive under the manure, following the motto "The Jews will be hanged or burned".' (The letter dates from 13 December 1948.)

2 *assignment*: EO.

232   LOS ANGELES, 21.12.1948

21 December 1948

My dear Hippo Cow,
    just imagine what a special Christmas present we received: through a formal error on the part of our landlady, the eviction has become invalid, which meant that she had to send us a new one and the whole

344

business will be postponed for another two months. We were so amazed at the decision that we could not believe it at first. We made immediate use of our high spirits to go for a magnificent drive on Sunday: first to the desert, then back through a 1,300-metre pass with a great deal of snow. We have hardly ever been so happy here in California, and then in the evening we ate at a nice little Mexican restaurant in Hollywood. – The Pollocks have meanwhile returned from Argentina in a state of great satisfaction, while Ilse Mayer has just set off there for 5/6 months with several assignments, but then intends to return to New York. We are working as hard as always, Teddie is trying to finish a psychological essay before Christmas. Hopefully you will have a nice peaceful Christmas, with many hugs and kisses from
your lanky
Giraffe

Mumma my animal, I send you my heartiest Christmas wishes, and am deeply sad that we cannot celebrate together – it is on such occasions that I become most painfully aware of our spatial (*only* spatial) separation. Hopefully it will not be lonely for you this time. We are naturally in a much more festive mood than we would otherwise have been through the new delay in our housing business. Christmas Eve at the Horkheimers, Christmas Day Lang and Lily here, Boxing Day at Norah's. New Year's Eve at the Pollocks. We all plan to relax completely from the end of the week until the start of the new year, Max too – we are all very much in need of it.

If I might make a Christmas wish, then it is that you might receive Charlotte, who will soon contact you, in a friendly manner. You need not warn me of her failings, for no one knows them better than I do and they are clear enough – but, aside from that, she is still one of the most delightful people I know, and also very sweet. We have had another great reconciliation, pourvu que ça dure, and I am sure she will get in touch; she was feeling miserable.

Heartiest kisses from your old child
Teddie

Original: typewritten letter.

233   LOS ANGELES, 27.12.1948

27 December 1948

My dear Hippo Cow,

so, we had a lovely cosy Christmas up at the Horkheimers, Maidon had made a special effort with the preparations, and later in the evening there was even a Santa Claus who came and brought everyone an extra parcel. On Sunday we just had Lily and Lang over here for goose with a Christmas tree, it was very peaceful. Yesterday an idiotic party at Norah's with a lot of people we did not know, but entirely uninteresting. She is in the best of spirits, for Anina has finally managed it, and hopes to have her child in June. Apropos children: I feel sorry for Louische with his grandchildren; the only consolation we could offer is that, as Archie has taken his name,[1] he will no doubt become immortal and is no doubt in better hands than with Franz's brats. Tonight, Anita Alexander has invited her daughter to stay here for three nights, apparently she is very independent and Anita merely wants to know that we are looking after her at night.

Dear Hippo Cow, have a good start to the new year with hearty kisses from your lanky

Giraffe

Mumma my animal, the holidays were very pleasant, especially last night, après Norah, at Lang's with champagne and foie gras. We received wonderful presents, terribly luxurious ones from Luli, but also charming and especially affectionate ones from Lix, who is incidentally in New York to have a look at his grandchildren – that is how old we have become. I still managed to finish my big essay for the yearbook Psychoanalysis and Society before the holidays; now I am having a little rest. It is raining cats and dogs. Hopefully you are not having such a rough time with the New York weather, which is apparently quite indescribable this time. – Mietze is back in San Francisco, still living with Robert and Anita, but is looking for a little house of her own in the country, to everyone's relief. We are spending more time than ever with Max, who really is the closest and the only one for us – aside from the massive Hippo Cow. Make a good start to the new year, and think of us as we are thinking of you. We are celebrating at the Pollocks. Hopefully poor Julie is finally feeling better.

The very heartiest of kisses from your old child

Teddie

Original: typewritten letter.

1 A reference to Adorno's middle name, Ludwig.

1949

3 January 1949

My dear Hippo Cow,
hopefully you got the new year off to a good start. We had a very
peaceful New Year's Eve party at the Pollocks', just the four of us,
except for Lisa Minghetti, who came by around midnight, looking
more beautiful than ever. On Saturday we first dropped by to see
Norah, then up with Lang and Lily for good champagne and foie gras,
yesterday afternoon at the Maaskoffs. Luli is back again; sadly only
for a short while, six weeks, she came to us straight away with Ali
Baba, who is nice and fat, and when I took him for a walk he still knew
the area very well. He is an old gentleman now, will be 12 years old
this year. Meanwhile Anita's daughter Corinna was also here for three
nights – she spent almost all day doing things with her friends from
Berkeley. She is so conventional and well adjusted that we could
hardly believe it. Quite seriously, the way she talks about herself when
one recommends a book to her: 'o, that is not good for my education'
or – she went to a Catholic school – 'yes I am religious, but not too
much'. In cases such as this, one is glad not to have children. Lix is
back from New York, very satisfied with his trip,[1] we shall be seeing
him tomorrow.
      Many hugs and kisses from your
                        Giraffe,
                              who is equally lanky in the new year

Mumma my animal, happy New Year! Ours had a pleasant and peaceful start, as Giraffe reported, and now Max and I will still take about

another week off, which will unfortunately be disturbed only by a lousy New York research Jew. Otherwise, just that Charlotte told me of her engagement yesterday, to a doctor – after writing me the most glowing love letters only a few days earlier. But, as the German folk song goes, I don't begrudge the girl a thing, and, for all her bourgeois small-mindedness, she has every right to long for order and someone to provide for her – she got into the relationship with me entirely by chance. I congratulated her, but am putting an end to our correspondence (until the next disaster in her life). Otherwise nothing new. Now I am very curious to see Else's reaction[2] after all. Heartiest kisses from your old child

Teddie

Original: typewritten letter.

1 *trip*: EO.

2 On 19 December 1948, Maria Wiesengrund had written to Adorno: 'I shall write to Else and bring up the bone of contention once more for *your* sake. I have already mentioned it to her a few times. The only answer she gave me was "Teddie disappointed me!" How and why?' When Adorno met Else Herzberger's nephew in late October near Paris, he told him that his aunt had been disappointed by Adorno's lack of support for Walter Benjamin.

235   LOS ANGELES, 11.1.1949

L.A., 11 January 1949

Mumma my animal,

a thousand thanks for your very sweet letter. Just think, we are having a real winter here now, for the first time since we moved here – hills and gardens completely covered in snow, an extremely strange contrast to the almost tropically southern formation of the landscape. But the fresh air is most pleasant. Meanwhile, we went to Luli's highly official dinner party,[1] with all sorts of very interesting people – she looked indescribably beautiful and elegant. Her husband was not there . . . Saturday night at Norah's, also very pleasant. On Sunday I played with Lisa Minghetti, with whom I am now working regularly and very seriously on some Beethoven sonatas. But the main thing is that, yesterday, Max and I finally got back to our really important things, after being kept away from them these last years through all the anti-Semitism work. We are very happy about it. 'May from our quill / flow sweetest words',[2] i.e. precisely *not* sweet words.

I will do my best to make my letters double-spaced from now on, my animal.

348

To answer your question: Philosophie der neuen Musik will be published in German, but the big book for Harpers, and the various essays connected to it, in English. – The university has invited me to give another lecture, this time on historical-philosophical aspects of the Nibelungenlied.[3] On 9 March.

When Charlotte finally gets her husband, the problem will take care of itself. It is certainly not my duty to 'defend' her; but I did, after all, make her – as indescribably bourgeois as she is – my mistress, and draw her into a situation that she is in no way equal to, and if she wants to find shelter and security in every relationship then I cannot reproach her for it, as that is precisely what I cannot give her – as alien to me as such wishes and the sphere of the Jewish 'schittich'[4] might be. On the other hand, she clings to me to such a degree that she comes running after every unsuccessful hunt – yet without being able to stop hunting. – It is strange how distance can lend such relatively primitive matters a 'dangerous' aspect that they do not have in themselves.

Heartiest kisses from your old child
Teddie

The Horkheimers did not send any Christmas cards this year.
Many kisses Giraffe

Original: typewritten letter with additional handwritten note by Gretel Adorno.

1 *dinner party*: EO.

2 The two last lines of Goethe's poem 'Selige Sehnsucht' [Blessed Yearning], which concludes 'Das Buch des Sängers' [The Book of the Singer] from *West-Östlicher Divan*: 'Möge meinem Schreibe-Rohr / Liebliches entfließen' [May from my quill / flow sweetest words].

3 A five-page typescript, presumably made from a shorthand dictation or a tape recording, has survived among Adorno's belongings. The title is: 'The Nibelungenlied and the Problem of the Epic'.

4 The Yiddish word *schidech* means 'marriage', or a 'good catch'.

236 LOS ANGELES, 20.1.1949

20 January 1949

My dearest Hippo Cow,
yes, the Nibelungen lecture is connected to the successful one on Heine, and has been postponed until 16 March, as Mrs Roosevelt will probably be giving a lecture here on the 9th, which Teddie wants to

attend. Otherwise we have an indescribable amount of things to do, even in the evenings and on Sundays. On four afternoons every week, Teddie works with Max on the follow-up to their big text, in the mornings on the Heine, which is to be published in the Pacific Spectator, and then there are still countless technical matters that also need to be taken care of. Years ago Archie once wrote 19 articles[1] for a music dictionary, but the whole thing turned out to be a fraud, and only one article on jazz appeared. Now another dictionary[2] has contacted him and asked for a contribution, but instead of writing something new he has sent them twelve of the old articles, which will now be published. The whole thing was originally called 'The Nineteen-Teat Pig', and it is nice that at least 13 teats have now had the honour after all. Dear Hippo Cow, how was your visit to the ophthalmologist, what did she think of your eyes? – Have you heard from Dr Liefmann how he is finding it back in Germany? How is Julie? So please do not worry about us, if something is really the matter I will let you know.

Hugs and kisses

from your lanky
Giraffe

In dreadful haste! Therefore only the heartiest kisses, and I wish those dear Hippo Cow eyes a good recovery

your child   Teddie

Original: typewritten letter with additional handwritten note by Adorno.

1 See letter no. 51, note 5.

2 Unknown.

237   LOS ANGELES, 27.1.1949

27 January 1949

Mumma, my animal,

on Wednesday of last week we had a farewell dinner at Norah's, as she was flying to New York on Thursday and then on to Europe to celebrate her mother's eightieth birthday. On Saturday her housekeeper called us to say that Norah had fallen down a flight of stairs that morning and died instantly. It is unclear whether the fall was caused by a stroke or the whole thing was an accident, but either way it is terrible and gave us an awful shock. We had become very closely attached, and in a sense Norah had taken on the role in our lives that Else used to have. We shall miss her greatly, and I know that you will feel with us.

We are very glad that the business with your eyes is nothing serious, and the symptoms of fatigue can certainly be kept at bay. The Afghan is certainly very pretty, but I do not especially like the humour of singing dogs.[1] – Naturally not a word from Else. – Luli, who had put me in contact with a publisher who is quite important for me,[2] had to fly back to New York. I am not well disposed towards flying, and I think that Norah's terrible misfortune would not have happened if she had taken the old-fashioned option of the train. But she had lived an incredibly hectic life during the last few months.

I have not written any more to Charlotte. Her marriage candidate is called Dr Violin. That speaks for itself. At the moment our common friends, the Moses[3] from San Francisco, are here; it is from them that I heard about it. I went to visit Vicki Baum[4] with them and Lily last night.

Heartiest kisses

from your old child
Teddie

Kisses Gi

Original: typewritten letter with handwritten greeting from Gretel Adorno.

1 An allusion to the 'Singing Dogs', which were trained to render popular songs such as 'Jingle Bells'. There seems to have been a veritable flood of such performances on the radio.

2 This is probably Duell, Sloan and Pearce, who published Luli Kollsman's novel *Come, Take my Hand*. As an unpublished letter from Adorno to Horkheimer written on 12 April 1949 reveals, Adorno had contact with a representative of the house by the name of Kennedy. Adorno had spoken to Kennedy about the following projects: '1. A book that integrates my essays about the radio, some of which were printed by this publisher and are now out of print. 2. An English edition of "Dialektik der Aufklärung" translated by Norden, who has already heard about the plan. 3. A translation of Philosophie der neuen Musik. 4. The joint book on anti-Semitism you suggested.'

3 The doctor and psychologist Paul J. Moses (1897–1965), who published the book *The Voice of Neurosis* in 1954, specialized in vocal physiognomy. Upon Moses' death, Adorno wrote to his widow: 'Paul was a friend in the very rare sense that he was there and showed solidarity in a situation when I was at rock bottom, and that is not something one forgets.' Adorno reviewed the German translation of Moses' book, which was published in 1956, for the *Frankfurter Allgemeine Zeitung* the following year (see *GS* 20.2, pp. 510–14).

4 The writer Vicki Baum (1888–1960), author of the novel *Menschen im Hotel* [People in the Hotel/in Hotels], had lived in Hollywood since 1931.

11 February 1949

Mumma, my animal,
  a thousand thanks for your very sweet Hippo Cow letter. The last week has involved several commitments – on Monday Klaus Pringsheim (Thomas Mann's brother-in-law) conducted a somewhat improvised performance of Bruckner's 7th, on Wednesday we went to Lix's to celebrate his birthday, last night we were at the Horkheimers with Lang and Lily, tonight I am playing with Lisa Minghetti. You remembered quite correctly: I know her through Norah, and already did in Germany, but she has attached herself to us much more strongly. Her husband has been feeling astoundingly well for the last year; there is no doubt about the diagnosis, but it seems possible that the course of this particular illness could perhaps be substantially delayed. He is a truly significant artist. Lix very movingly agreed to correct the whole of 'Philosophie der neuen Musik'. Naturally you will receive the first copy I can get hold of. The book is almost as long as the Kierkegaard, and is being set in the same way. – Charlotte is already marrying on Tuesday, Anita called about it, but I am not going to react. My animal, as we are constantly sending packages to the Adornos and as all of us, as you know, are living off *very* restricted means, I would ask you *not* to send any more packages to Germany. The people in question receive enough, and it would only make the situation more complicated than it already is. I need hardly tell you that my request is not based on pettiness or ill will, only the necessity of the situation. I truly wish we had more money, so that there would not be any problem with all these things. But *we*, after all, are the exiled and dispossessed. Hopefully your eyes are still better – your writing, if anything, is clearer than it used to be. Heartiest kisses
from your old child
Teddie

Friedel[1] turned 60 on the 8th!
  Kisses Giraffe

Original: typewritten letter with handwritten postscript and handwritten greeting from Gretel Adorno.

1 Siegfried Kracauer.

2 March 1949

Mumma my animal,
   a thousand thanks for your letter. Unfortunately I have bad news[1] today: we lost our court case. It would be superfluous to mull over the details: the essence is that our main argument, namely that the landlady wants to move into our inhabited apartment and rent out the uninhabited one purely for reasons of profit, was not even disputed, but that the judge took the position that this did not legally constitute 'bad faith' – despite a contradictory decision by the court of appeal. It was clear to me at the start of the proceedings that we had lost. What makes matters particularly difficult is that we have to clear our stable as early as 15 March, i.e. in 2 weeks. We only narrowly escaped having to pay compensation. The matter is extremely unpleasant. Not only because we had grown so fond of our househalf, which had become so pretty, comfortable and a part of our life, but also because it is quite impossible, even for double the money, to find something at all comparable. At present the matter looks rather hopeless. Gretel and I are searching day and night. So forgive us if you do not hear from us until the 15th – that is the only reason, everything is fine otherwise.
   You will meanwhile have received Thomas Mann's essay,[2] which contains over 4 pages about me. On Saturday he told me mischievously that this was only the beginning – the main thing, namely that I thought up Leverkühn's compositions, only comes up in the 2nd part, though it is already hinted at. It will amuse you to find that you also appear in it.
   Yes, Lisa Minghetti is a professional concert violinist and we are working very seriously on some Beethoven sonatas.
   Keep your dear fingers crossed that we might find a bearable stable, my animal – we are in dire need of it.
   Heartiest kisses from your old child
                                        Teddie

Giraffe is apartment-hunting and sends her fond regards!

Original: typewritten letter with handwritten postscript.

1 *bad news*: EO.

2 The first eight chapters of *Genesis of a Novel* had been printed in the January 1949 issue of the *Neue Rundschau*.

803 Yale Street
Santa Monica, Calif.
18 March 1949

Mumma my animal,

so, we moved house smoothly, without incident and very comfortably, without even a gramophone record or a glass being damaged; and the packers were perfectly charming. The apartment is delightful – very close to the previous one (the other side of the street already belongs to Brentwood), so that we have a view of the same little monastery church in the mountains – directly in front of us is the golf course, which cannot be built on, everything green; the apartment is bright, as friendly as can be. It takes up the whole first storey of the house, but with a separate entrance, so that one really has the feeling of a house of one's own, at least as much for us as previously. Every one of our friends finds it prettier, especially the living room and the studies; the bedrooms are slightly smaller, just as we generally have slightly less space. First one enters a huge, beautiful sun porch – once we have a door built in, it will be a room of its own. Then our very large living room, which comfortably holds the grand piano and the large cupboard, then the dining room, slightly larger than the previous one, so that some of our books fit in there; our rooms towards the back, very quiet and more or less closed off. The plans enclosed[1] will give you an idea of the furnishings – Fritz Lang drew them up for us, so that we knew exactly where to put every piece of furniture. Everyone helped; Lily tirelessly, but also Lix and Frau Mendelssohn. Everything is finished except for storing the reference books, as the shelves for those are only being built in tomorrow. It was a terrible commotion, but all concerned got through it intact. Lily was all the more moving for being strongly handicapped by a hip injury and limping about. But the 2 weeks of searching after the unexpectedly lost court case were ghastly, especially for poor Giraffe, who was chasing apartments from morning till night the way Charlotte chases husbands.

In the middle of all that, on Wednesday (the first day after the move), I also gave my lecture at UCLA on the Nibelungenlied, which we rehearsed amid the wreckage. It went superbly and was a most excellent success, with at least 200 students present. Afterwards, the people from the English department (which had organized the event) said it is a scandal that I have not long since been given a professorship at their university. We shall have to see whether anything further occurs, and what.

Last night Lang invited us to see the Nibelungen *film*, his most famous one, which was shown – quite by chance – the day after my lecture. Full of ideas and talent. Shot in 1922!

Why did you have the main passage from Th. M.'s essay read out to you?[2] Are your dear hippo eyes *so* weak? I am worried about them. Do write.

Among our sheet music, along with some other things, we discovered the Borodin songs dedicated to you,[3] to my immense delight.

I wish I could show you everything, my animal.

Giraffe, who is rummaging about in the dirt (as zoologically unlikely as that may sound), sends her heartiest greetings.

Kisses from your faithful old child

Teddie

Provisional telephone number: Santa Monica 5-4922

The American singer is not a singer, but rather a highly talented pianist by the name of Pesha Kagan, with whom I have worked on various things.

The family connection to Benjamin is based on a confusion with Egon Wissing, whose first wife[4] was a childhood friend of the Mann children and who is indeed a cousin of Benjamin.

Original: typewritten letter.

1 Not preserved.

2 On 15 March, Maria Wiesengrund had written: 'Meanwhile I have read on in the essay (Julie already read me the 4 pages about my boy before I read any further), almost up to your bit. Magnificent!! Th. Mann is very clever and has *no* intellectual limits at all. [Paragraph] How did he come to suggest a family connection with Walter Benjamin? And who is the American singer you worked with and who said: "It is unbelievable, he knows every note in the world". I hope to finish the essay in 1–3 days. But I am proud and happy about his judgement, for Thomas Mann is after all someone special! . . .[. . .] Our WK would also have been happy and proud of Th. M.'s words about you! He loved you so very much.'

3 These are two songs by Alexander Borodin (1833–1887) which bear the maiden name of Adorno's mother on the title page, printed in Cyrillic writing. It could not be ascertained where or when Maria Wiesengrund and the Russian composer and chemist met; possibly during her time at the opera house in Riga or Borodin's stay in Germany in the early 1880s.

4 See letter no. 30, note 4.

803 Yale Street
Santa Monica, Calif.
5 April 1949

Mumma my animal,
a thousand thanks for your very sweet letter. There is quite a confusion here, as Max and Fritz may, though it has still not been decided,
be going to Frankfurt in the next few days regarding a rebuilding of
the institute and similar matters – all very sudden, and a strain on all
our nerves. I expect you know that Leo has meanwhile taken a very
good and honourable government position as director of the research
department of the Voice of America.
    Our big party was most successful, as was a little one on Saturday
with the former Hungarian foreign minister Scytowsky[1] – Liesl and
I played the Spring Sonata[2] genuinely well, I think. I am doing a
number of smaller technical articles, I simply lack the concentration
for bigger things. The apartment is delightful, albeit slightly more
difficult for Gretel to manage than the old one, but then we do not
have to climb any stairs now. It very suddenly became incredibly hot
yesterday.
    I just received a terribly sad letter from Margot Rocholl,[3] who
wants to go back to Frankfurt, as she evidently sees no prospects for
herself in Portugal. Utterly resigned, a tired old woman, grown very
fat – you would not recognize her any more in the picture. The mess
she made of her own life was brought to completion by Hitler and his
gang. How much better off we all are.
    We can read your writing superbly – I would sooner say it is clearer
than it has been for a while. And how are those dear Hippo Cow
eyes?
    Forgive my own messy writing – but my own typewriter is rather
out of order, so I am using Giraffe's one.
    Heartiest kisses
    from your old child
                                    Teddie

Kisses Giraffe

Original: typewritten letter with handwritten greeting from Gretel Adorno.

1 Tibor Scitovszky (1875–1959), who was Hungarian foreign minister in the
Bethlen government from November 1924 until March 1925, had moved to
the USA in 1947.

2 Beethoven's op. 24.

3 See letter no. 171, note 4.

25 April 1949

My dear Hippo Cow,
a thousand thanks for your letter. It is still uncertain whether Max and Fred (for that is Fritz's name now) are going to Germany. En attendant I have countless institute matters to sort out. But we are fine with it. Yesterday we went for a long drive through the blossoms. Last Friday I started a teaching course[1] for the psychoanalytical candidates to great success.

Following Else's letter I wrote to her again,[2] and enclose a copy. Perhaps, with your Corsican dignity, you consider it wrong, but I am not ashamed to admit that, even though Else's later development is as clear to me as it is to you, breaking with a person who was so close not only to me, but in particular to you and the Tigress, is very painful for me, and as I do not 'want anything' from her, I have no fear of losing anything. What really goes on in her head is still a mystery to me, incidentally, she probably has a completely fantastic notion of my life; one of the things she had imagined, for example, was that I must be able to find a job for Arnold,[3] who is really quite incapable of any serious intellectual work.

I am glad that you are still well – let us know the result of the eye examination soon. Please give the blank cheques enclosed to Julie, with my warmest regards.

Heartiest kisses
from your old child
Teddie

Kisses Giraffe. Please extend our fond greetings to your housekeeper.

Original: typewritten letter with additional handwritten note by Gretel Adorno.

1 No further information.

2 Adorno wrote the letter the same day.

3 Else Herzberger's nephew Arnold Levy-Ginsberg, who lived as an antiquarian bookseller in France and had assumed the name Arnold Levilliers.

6 May 1949

My dear Hippo Cow,
today I have a little surprise for you: the pictures enclosed were taken especially for you by Franz Roehn, so that you can at least gain some impression of our apartment. The grand piano is naturally in the living room, the bureau is in Archie's room, and the two stupid horses play their daft 66 peacefully with all those books behind them. – On Wednesday Max and Fritz finally departed on the Mauretania to Europe-Frankfurt after all, to see if one can rebuild the institute there. Come August we will know much more. Leo has naturally not left the institute entirely, but at the moment he simply has a very good government position. The course for the analytical candidates (young doctors who want to become psychoanalysts) is proceeding well. That has nothing to do with Heine and Nibelungen, those were at the university. I am frightfully happy about the oph-thalmologist's findings,[1] and especially that you do not have to change anything about your life. The new Rundschau arrived intact. – The landlords are still pleasant, we hear nothing from the neigh-bours (thank God), and we are enjoying the apartment quite espe-cially now with the lovely weather. I always do the driving, and I enjoy it a great deal as long as it is not too far or too exhausting. Last Sunday we were off again, this time in the mountains, on Mt. Wilson with the big observatory, and on the way back ate downtown in Chinatown. Lily and Lang had just gone for a few days to look for suitable places for outside shots, and we will probably spend the coming Sunday with her. – Martha Everett-Lehner, whose husband died of lung cancer in April, plans to come here with her daughter in the summer. Hugs and kisses from
     your lanky Giraffe
                              Gretel

Heartiest kisses from your
                    old child
                    Teddie

Original: typewritten letter with handwritten greeting from Adorno.

1 In her letter of 1 May, Maria Wiesengrund writes: 'My two dear, best chil-dren, a thousand thanks for your dear letter, my boy, and for your dear kisses, my Gretelein. – Yesterday I was too tired and worn out from the very stren-uous eye examination. The result: my vision has unfortunately deteriorated!

But I will not lose it. "That is quite impossible and is out of the question." The only trouble is that I cannot read very fine writing any more or do fine embroidering! [. . .] That is a great comfort. And I can go out *alone*, I simply have to be very careful. Julie is looking after me quite touchingly. The doctor is quite extraordinary in every respect. I am supposed to come back in July. – So for heaven's sake, my two dears, do *not* worry about me.'

244   LOS ANGELES, 11.5.1949

11 May 1949

Mumma, my animal,

I hear from dear Julie that you have not been feeling so well these last few days, and am writing to you very quickly to give you a sniff with my hippo snout, and wish with all my love that you might very soon be quite fresh and lively again. Probably the rapid climatic shift in New York during the change of season is giving you trouble, but once the organism has adapted I am sure that, with your nature, the complaints will quite definitely pass. I hope you have meanwhile received the pictures and Giraffe's letter, and that the pictures – some of which are rather funny, after all – are bringing you a little joy.

Otherwise I simply wanted to tell you that my friend Dr Friedgood is in New York at the moment. He is my doctor, but much more than that; there is a true intellectual and personal relationship between us, I am greatly indebted to him for my heart business and have complete faith in him. I shall therefore ask him to look you up if he can; though it is not certain that I will still reach him in the East, but you should at any rate not be amazed if he contacts you, and you should have as much faith in him as I do.

Max and Fred should be arriving in Paris today. My course is proceeding nicely and is well attended. Otherwise we have nothing new to report. Golde is coming here at the end of June and will be staying with Maidon for a few weeks.

So, make sure you get completely well soon, with heartiest kisses from your old child

Teddie

Many kisses from the lanky Giraffe   Get well very soon!

Original: typewritten letter with additional handwritten note by Gretel Adorno.

359

16 May 1949

Mumma, my animal,
   a thousand thanks for your lengthy letter.[1] We are *overjoyed* that the Wondrous Hippo Cow is feeling better. Did you actually have real pains, or simply feel wobbly? And what did the doctor order?
   The living room has light coming in from three sides, so you need not worry regarding the piano. I am working quite intensively. Next week the rector of Frankfurt University, Hallstein,[2] is coming here. I have arranged lectures for him at the university here and in Berkeley. Saturday night we went with Lily to see two university opera productions, Milhaud's pauvre matelot[3] and Mozart's Schauspieldirektor, but it was all frightfully provincial.
   It is a shame that you cannot hear my piano playing now. Practising daily for almost three months has had such an effect that it finally sounds pianistic and quite balanced again. I am enjoying it a great deal; learned eight Beethoven sonatas quite thoroughly with Lisa Minghetti, now we are taking on the remaining two, the Kreutzer and the last one, but I have already studied the Kreutzer a little. Compared to my other, completely different, work of sociological essays and lectures, it is extremely relaxing.
   Continue your recovery, my animal, and be sure to write soon!
   Heartiest kisses
                    from your old child
                    Teddie
Many hugs and kisses, and a very, very speedy recovery
                    Your lanky Giraffe

Original: typewritten letter.

1 This reads:

   My dear boy and my dear Gretel, a thousand heartiest thanks for your love, which does my old heart so much good. – Children, the pictures just came on Monday, one day before I became ill, so I was able to enjoy them to my heart's content. – And I did!! They are so delightful, and I cannot think of any better picture of my Gazelle, – they are all so lively and natural that I can almost hear you speak. The indoor pictures are also quite lovely. But is the grand piano not standing *against* the light? But I am sure you know that better, and if necessary you can turn it and perhaps gain some space? It was a great joy to see my crocheted tablecloth again – our WK always helped me measure it. – Please give Herr Röhn my warm regards. You will meanwhile also have received, *read* and forwarded my two letters. I do not know the addresses of Maidon and Carlotta and are in the picture. – My dear Julie is doing everything she can once again. I myself was not in such good shape! But now it is much better again, no pains and I am allowed to get up! Not to go out yet, of course. Your friend Dr Friedgood has not contacted me yet. My Dr Ulrich has proved most valuable, and I am extremely content with him. He is only coming back on Monday.

Yesterday I had a letter from Herbert Levi. Poor Hermann, after a complete reconciliation with Herbert, died. It is a relief, for he had long been mentally unsound. Persecution mania. – Write soon to your old Mumma, who sends you her heartiest kisses. – P.S. Have you heard from Max yet; Golde has not got in touch yet.

(14 May 1949, Maria Wiesengrund to the Adornos)

2 From 1946 to 1948, the jurist and politician Walter Hallstein (1901–82) served as the first elected rector of Frankfurt University following the war.

3 Darius Milhaud (1892–1974) set the text *Le Pauvre Matelot* by Jean Cocteau, with whom he collaborated on several occasions.

18 May 1949

My dear Hippo Cow,

a thousand thanks for your sweet letter; a shame that Harry Friedgood did not see you, then he could have reported back to us about you. Today I am sending you a few little pictures that the Pollocks took a few months ago during a walk with us in the hills around here; they are quite good, and perhaps you will have some fun with them. Otherwise we have little news. Lix's Scotch terrier Mackie has had 6 puppies, and Lix is very proud. I feel a little tired, probably the menopause gradually setting in with the semi-tropical climate here. I am rapidly nearing fifty, after all, and am well on the way to becoming a dignified old lady, completely mild and serene. But Archie says that I am still in full possession of my faculties. The weather here is completely mad at the moment, another rainy season with genuinely constant rain, something almost unheard of in California at this time of year.

You just carry on like that, dear animal, in good old hippo tradition, and you will go far in life!

Hugs and kisses

from your lanky Giraffe
Gretel

Mumma my animal, I am *overjoyed* that you are feeling better once more. Truly an admirable and heroic Hippo Cow – I am now entirely reassured. The first corrections for the big Berkeley book will be

coming within the next few days. In all haste, so that the letter can still be sent off. Heartiest kisses from your old child
Teddie

Original: typewritten letter.

247   LOS ANGELES, 24.5.1949

24 May 1949

Mumma, my animal,
a thousand thanks for your letter[1] with that most vivid description. Thank God that you are back to normal again; it must have been dreadful. Just be careful with the heat. Is your room at least somewhat cool?
Hallstein had not yet come to the university in my time, a relatively young jurist who acted as rector for a few years. Last night Maidon put on a little party for him, and today he has already left. An infinitely skilled politician.[2]
We passed on your letters to Carlota and Maidon immediately. I expect you have read that poor Klaus Mann,[3] whom I also knew quite well, has died. A poor soul! His parents are in Europe at present, in Stockholm.
We enclose a letter from Helenchen. Evidently it is a case of septicaemia, as I had suspected.
Otherwise we have absolutely nothing to report, except that poor Giraffe had a severe migraine attack, but is now crawling about again. Meanwhile midsummer has arrived here.
Heartiest kisses
from your old child
Teddie

and the lanky stupid Giraffe

Original: typewritten letter.

1 This reads:

My dear boy and my dear Gazelle, you must have received my letter of dismissal [from medical care] by now? Meanwhile I am feeling fine again, and I thank you heartily for your sweet letter. – My beloved boy, to answer your questions: I did not have *any* pains in the usual sense, nor any very thorough examinations, stomach etc.! Only, soon after breakfast, I was just about to take my digitalis, I suddenly had a shivering fit and *stomach cramp*, such that I could hardly breathe and hardly dared breathe. Julie alerted the Dr from the shop, having been called at once by my housekeeper, and he came a few minutes later. Examined me gave me an injection at once, which worked wonders – heart attack that spread to the inner vessels. I was given tablets for that awful stomach muscle cramp and they worked immediately. So a few days in bed. In the evening the Dr came again and then just once daily and was very pleased with my progress. He ordered my medicine himself. I thought I was done for! – Now you know what it was. – I hope to go out again soon. With *such* hot weather I cannot. This afternoon Golde [Löwenthal] was here. Very sweet. Her son [Daniel] is getting married in the autumn.

Gretel my child, dear, *I beg you* not to over-exert yourself with the driving. I would like to join you sometime. It is so hot here at the moment, no rain and it is so close and humid. I cannot go out with this weather, nor am I allowed to. *Everything* sticks to one.

How are the Lyx-dogs? What holiday plans do you have? – Forgive the writing. Can you still read it? Hearty hugs from your old faithful Hippo Cow Marinumba.

I never heard the name Hallstein mentioned. Was he already in Frankfurt in your time? The last time we, that is to say I, heard the Kreutzer Sonata was at our place with Kolisch and Steuermann!! I am so happy that you can practise and play more again. How is the grand piano? How are your listeners? You speak in English? How many do you have to give? Heartiest kisses from your faithful old happy Mumma P.S. did you send the little letters?'

(19 May 1949, Maria Wiesengrund to the Adornos)

2 *politician*: EO.

3 He had died on 21 May in Cannes from an overdose of sleeping pills.

248   LOS ANGELES, 14.6.1949

14 June 1949

Mumma, my animal,

thank you kindly for your letter.[1] Naturally you can keep the little picture, I am happy to hear that you like it. Gretel has meanwhile written to Julie, and I ask you to tell her once again how glad we are that she has finally found a decent home of her own. On the other hand, I get the impression that the housing problems are gradually becoming much simpler.

Else did not respond to my last letter either. How old is she now? Gretel says 73, I think 71.

I have meanwhile written a new introduction to my part of the Berkeley book (which is a book in itself). My joint course with

Max[2] at the Jewish College is finished, and all our students wrote enthusiastic letters of thanks. My course with the psychoanalytical candidates is also a great success.

On the evening of Gretel's birthday we went for a very good Chinese meal with Lang and Lily. He is in the middle of shooting a film and under terrible strain, but insisted on celebrating with us – touching. The two of us drank one of the last bottles of our Palatinate wine, Deidesheimer Rennpfad, and thought of you. The wine, from 1934, has kept superbly and was still magnificent. On Sunday we went for a long drive, and it was very good for us to get some air and take a break from our daily routine.

Do be careful with the heat – I know that June is a particularly unpleasant month in New York due to the humidity.

Heartiest kisses

from your old child
Teddie

Kisses Gretel

Original: typewritten letter with handwritten greeting from Gretel Adorno.

1 The letter of 23 May reads:

> My two dear, dear horse-children, you cannot imagine how happy you made me with the two excellent little pictures! A thousand thanks for those and for your very sweet letter! –
>
> You will meanwhile have received my doctor's report, and I am still very well. –
>
> I read today that Thomas Mann lost his son Klaus. Terrible for his old parents! I hear he was also very talented and diligent. –
>
> I wrote to Else once again, but now I will not write any more on the matter if she does not write. –
>
> Dear little Gazelle you must take things a little easy and *not* over-exert yourself and eat *properly*. You asked your doctor, after all, a good one? I cannot say anything on the matter myself, as I did not feel *anything*, I mean of the menopause. – long, long ago. –
>
> Are you receiving good news from Max and Fred?
>
> The weather here is so bad that I have still not been able to go out. Music here practically zero. – What have you heard from Lotte and Mellie?
>
> So, Gretel my child, take certain days v e r y quietly! – How are your lectures going, my boy? Is the big 'psychology essay' the big joint project with Max? –
>
> Heartiest kisses from your old Mumma!

2 The themes could not be ascertained.

30 June 1949

Mumma, my animal,
    a thousand thanks for your letter. I was very distressed to
hear that the evidently very pleasant Mrs Wood had died, and hope
with all my heart that you can nonetheless keep your lovely stable,
which had made such an impression on everyone. At the same time
as your letter I received a second, from Hermann Grab's wife,
that was extraordinarily depressing for me. He is *very* gravely ill.
After one kidney had to be removed last year and he never properly
recovered, he is now paralysed in both legs, and has therefore had an
operation on his spine. The operation seems to have gone well,
but the combination of these two operations leads me to fear the
very worst. I feel indescribably sorry for him, one of the very few
people in my life who mean something to me. I know you understand.
    Luli is back, was here for a long time yesterday, as charming as ever.
Baba, who is now twelve-and-a-half – as old as you, so to speak – got
through a bout of pneumonia in good shape. And who is Luli's doctor
in New York? Herr Dr Violin, Charlotte's husband! Luli had strongly
advised him to marry, without knowing Charlotte or anything about
the connections. The fact that the world is so small does not, by any
means, always make it more agreeable.
    We saw Golde and she passed on your greetings, to our joy.
    The proofs of the Berkeley book are now all here, and I have fin-
ished all but two chapters. Lix helped me quite touchingly. I still have
to do the revision corrections, but that is a purely technical matter,
whereas the work of the last few weeks has really been that of ensur-
ing the coherence and uniformity of the whole. This giant book,
which Gretel compares to a Hippo Cow, is extraordinarily impressive, and should get quite some attention. I am very proud that I
managed, through the greatest of insistence, to force the later addition of a very important introduction to my part (which is almost a
book in itself).
    But my 'Philosophie der neuen Musik', which I am expecting to
appear in Germany any day now, means incomparably more to me than
the whole of that huge research tome, even though it is barely 150 pages
long.
    I also wish to thank you most warmly for the pan-fried steak recipe.
Gretel has a very similar way of making veal cutlets. Despite all the work
we are getting a relative amount of fresh air, and are greatly enjoying
our light-flooded porch, which really serves as our summer living room.

Our faithful Julie will almost be back again by the time you receive this letter. Continue to be careful with the heat and look after yourself very well, my animal. Heartiest kisses

from your old child
Teddie

Kisses Giraffe

Original: typewritten letter with handwritten greeting from Gretel Adorno.

250 LOS ANGELES, 11.7.1949

11 July 1949

Dear Hippo Cow,
    your last letter made me very sad; how are your dear eyes now? What did the doctor say? It really is a poor show that cars cannot hop about, otherwise I could visit you every day and read to you. Julie is back now; I hope she had a good break, for she was urgently in need of one. Apart from still having a lot of work, we have nothing at all to report. Last night there was a chamber music evening at Lisa Minghetti's, first a Haydn quartet, then some Mozart with piano, naturally with Archie, who kept the whole thing together, and last of all some Schumann. – Teddie is still having a great deal of trouble with the corrections for the Berkeley book and the revision of the labor study; if one wants the job done properly, one has to do it oneself. – Did I already tell you that Archibald has made me an Honorary Hippo Cow called Stuta von Schnicko-Bello, how do you like the name? Lix is having a big barbecue party next Sunday afternoon, 36 people; one simply has to go along to these things once a year.
    So, my animal, write very soon, with fondest regards
your old
Giraffe

Still under terrible pressure, mostly because of the Berkeley corrections, but we shall have fun in the end. The very difficult Mozart (E flat major Piano Quartet, with a concertante piano part) went amazingly well, considering we had only played through it once. A shame you cannot hear me now – I think I have never played as decently as I am now, especially in terms of the balance between the fingers (I am systematically doing technical exercises). –

Hopefully those dear fat hippo eyes will soon be feeling better.
Heartiest kisses from your old child

Teddie

Original: typewritten letter.

251 LOS ANGELES, 18.7.1949

18 July 1949

Mumma, my animal,

a thousand thanks for your sweet letter. I am so dreadfully sorry for
your poor Hippo Cow eyes, and I only hope that soon, as has now
often been the case, they will improve once again. I am sending you
'The Genesis of a Novel' in book form, so that dear Julie can read you
the parts you find interesting. You already know everything from
p. 90 onwards from the 'Neue Rundschau'.

Today I received a sample of the jacket design for 'Philosophie der
neuen Musik', and it looks quite impressive. The book is now being
printed, and is to appear in August.

Luli has written a frightful novel[1] with the Courths-Mahleresque
title 'Come, Take my Hand'. I gave her my opinion, which cannot have
come as any surprise to her, in all frankness, and she received it very
pleasantly. Ali Baba is very old and sick. When he tried to get up and
do the honours for us he had a terrible coughing fit – he never properly recovered from his pneumonia. Hopefully the good animal will
get back to normal.

Yesterday there was a big party at Lix's, almost exclusively with rich
Jews from Frankfurt, all called Meyer, Pickard etc., the sort of people
that made me run a mile back home. But it was all pleasant enough.
Golde is going back at the end of the week via San Francisco; she is
very proud that her son is getting married on 7 August. Fred Pollock
will, if all goes well, be here in one week, Max only in mid-August.

Heartiest kisses

from your old child
Teddie

Sadly no news of Hermann yet. –
Kisses Giraffe

Original: typewritten letter with handwritten postscript and handwritten
greeting from Gretel Adorno.

1 See Luli Kollsman, *Come, Take my Hand* (New York: Duell, Sloan &
Pearce, 1949).

26 July 1949

Mumma, my animal,
    a thousand thanks for your letter. We could read it superbly, but are
naturally sad that you are still having difficulties with your eyes. I
enclose the book jacket. The print is as large as if someone had already
thought of those Hippo Cow eyes. I am to receive the first copies in
August. We also enclose a letter for you and Julie from Helenchen.
Fred came back yesterday, after leaving Frankfurt only on Saturday,
and if he had not stopped over in New York he would already have
been here on Sunday. He was also together with Franz, and will tell us
about it at length in the next few days. Max, who is coming by rail
and by boat, is to arrive here on 15 August.
    We spent a day with some nice Americans in Carpenteria, having
been invited there to the beach 75 miles north of here, and enjoyed it
very much.
    Yesterday Luli appeared unannounced for lunch with four dogs.
Baba seems to be feeling a little better; it seems the cough is nothing
serious. We have a tacit agreement not to say another word about the
novel. Lisa Minghetti is separating from her husband; I am very sorry
for both of them, not least considering his serious illness, but the relationship between the much older man and Liesl, who is still highly
neurotic despite going through analysis, is beyond repair. The one who
suffers most, as always, is the child.
    No word from Hermann or his wife – surely not a good sign. I sent
him a card together with a mutual friend so as to make it less obvious.
Hopefully your indestructible optimism will prove justified. Heartiest
kisses
                    from your old child
                    Teddie

and Giraffe Gazelle

Original: typewritten letter with handwritten greeting from Gretel Adorno.

9 August 1949

Mumma, my animal,
    a thousand thanks for your very sweet letter. Just think: Hermann
has indeed died.[1] I had already expected the worst following a letter

from Blanche stating that the doctors had given up hope, and then her silence, and last night Lily showed Gretel an issue of Aufbau with his obituary – that is how we found out. I need hardly tell you what a blow it is to me. Not only one of those people closest to me, but also a surviving part of my youth. Whenever I saw him again, even after a very long time, it seemed like yesterday, and I really cannot imagine the world without him. I feel as if I have been knocked down. And not even the news that 'Philosophie der neuen Musik' has been printed, and that the first copies are on the way to me, can bring me any joy.

It saddens me that it is still so hot that you are confined to your room. Do you not gasp for air, my animal? Always indoors – surely that is not good for you.

Max is expected here on Sunday.

Frau Frenkel's illness also looks very worrying. Hermann evidently had cancer of the kidney, but we do not know any details. Eduard is not coming here this summer, as he is teaching at Juilliard and taking a trip to Europe; we have not heard anything from Rudi, he seems to be tied to his house in Madison, if he does not turn up at Schönberg's 75th birthday after all – but it is uncertain whether we will be here then.

Your writing seems to have improved again.

Heartiest kisses from your faithful child
Teddie

and the stupid Giraffe

Original: typewritten letter with handwritten greeting from Gretel Adorno.

1 Adorno published an obituary, 'Hermann Grab', in the fourth issue of the *Neue Rundschau*; see GS 20.2, pp. 465f.

254   LOS ANGELES, 26.8.1949

26 August 1949

Mumma, my animal,

a thousand thanks for your letter, the birthday present and the most welcome waistcoats, which Julie announced to us. It has meanwhile become frightfully, quite uncommonly hot here too, but we cope quite well on our airy porch, and also go to the beach[1] as often as our work permits. What is less pleasant is the fact that once again our house threatens to be sold – yesterday a horde of prospective buyers came to look at it. Our contract extends to next spring, but what then?

If everything goes smoothly, we hope to go to Tahoe on 6 September. Address: Tahoe Cedars Lodge, Box 69, Tahoma P.O., Lake Tahoe, Calif. It depends partly on when we receive the page proofs for the Berkeley book and when Max takes his holidays.

We went to see two quite nice French films,[2] one of them with the great actress Rosay, who now, as an old woman, reminds me very strongly of Agathe – it is strange how distinctively she developed that southern French quality, despite being psychologically much more German than you. The second film was entitled 'The Puritan', with the important Barraud, who maintains a strange balance between dancing and acting, giving a veritably clinical portrayal of a paranoid moralist. Although French films have a strong air of export articles, they do give the impression of mirroring something of unregimented life compared to the polished products of the monopoly here.

The day before yesterday the psychoanalyst Hacker, with whom I have started a research project[3] dealing with the psychology of artistic production, took Max and myself to the restaurant Romanoff, the most luxurious one here. The owner achieved his incredible career by pretending for years to be a certain Prince Romanoff, even though he has probably never seen Russia, but comes from Chicago. It was only after he had found complete success that he publicly abandoned the fiction. This bizarre man, who is as famous for his brawls with troublesome guests as for his excellent fodder, sat at our table for the whole evening, spoke to us about philosophy and proved amazingly well versed. One does encounter the strangest things.

There is much to discuss with Max concerning the matters relating to Germany. Otherwise there is nothing to report.

Heartiest kisses from your faithful child
Teddie

Many kisses

from your stupid lanky
Giraffe

Original: typewritten letter.

1 *beach*: EO.

2 The film with Françoise Rosay (1891–1974) could not be traced with certainty; around that time she had featured in the film *Macadam* from 1946 and in the English production *Sarabande for Dead Lovers* from 1948. The film *Le Puritain*, with Jean-Louis Barrault (1910–1994), was made in 1938.

3 The Vienna-born psychiatrist and psychoanalyst Frederick J. Hacker (1914–89) had been director of the Hacker Clinic in Beverly Hills since 1945. The project mentioned in the letter was not realized on account of Adorno's return to Frankfurt.

Tahoe Cedars Lodge
Chambers P.O.
LAKE TAHOE, CALIFORNIA

18 September 1949

Mumma my animal,
'all too briefly' – tomorrow we are going home, with one stop in the middle (for the distance between here and L.A. is roughly equivalent to that between Frankfurt and Vienna). It was indescribably enjoyable, and we both feel more refreshed, despite the brevity of the holiday, than ever before; also made the most careful use of the time, outside all day. Lily somewhat less, unfortunately (she stayed with us until the end and is going home with us); for she is having trouble with her angiospasms. One of the highlights was a very long drive to the Sierra Buttes, a mountain range that is not especially high, yet very baroque and reminiscent of the Dolomites, situated in the most deserted of regions. It is peculiar, incidentally, how little one otherwise has the feeling of high mountains, even though we are 2100 metres (6300 feet) above sea level here, which is much higher than the Engadin or Lake Carezza – but there is no snow, and one generally has the impression of a low mountain range, albeit often in the deepest solitude. Our accommodation was very pleasant, only most of our good restaurants were already shut. A small sensation: a man from San Francisco who lives here on his property had crabs from the lake, proper ones, the first since Paris, admittedly very small, like those in Amorbach, but still a reminder of the real taste.

Otherwise there is no news. I expect you know that the daughter of the conductor Erwin Stein,[1] whom you also know (he visited us once in Frankfurt), is to marry the nephew of the king of England; the papers are full of it. – I enclose the wrap-around band and brochure[2] for Philosophie der neuen Musik; they make very shrewd use of the Thomas Mann business, and with his full consent. (Do you know, incidentally, that you are also mentioned in 'The Genesis of a Novel'? And Oscar's apricot brandy?)[3]

Did I tell you that Frankfurt University has officially invited me to return?

We have not heard from you since our arrival here; but we assume that everything is fine, as dear Julie would no doubt have informed us otherwise.

Take care my good animal and write soon.
Heartiest kisses from your old child
Teddie

Many kisses Giraffe

Original: typewritten letter with printed letterhead and handwritten greeting from Gretel Adorno.

1 Erwin Stein (1885–1958), who had studied composition with Schoenberg and musicology with Guido Adler in Vienna, published the text 'Neue Formprinzipien' [New Formal Principles], the first treatment of the twelve-tone technique, in 1925. Stein had emigrated to England in 1938. His daughter Countess Marion (Maria) Donata Stein (b. 1926) married George Lascelles, earl of Harewood.

2 Neither of these have survived among Adorno's belongings. The brochure contained the central passages from Thomas Mann's letter of 29 May 1948 to the publisher: 'I was particularly interested to hear that you intend to publish Theodor Adorno's book "Philosophie der modernen Musik" and wish to extend to you my sincere congratulations for seeking to further the reputation in Germany of this author, whose important book on Kierkegaard you already published previously, through this equally significant publication. [Paragraph] Dr Adorno is one of today's finest, sharpest and most critically profound thinkers. Himself a musician and composer, he is at once blessed with an analytical ability and capacity for verbal expression whose precision and illuminating force are beyond compare, and I can think of no one who could give the public more astute and experienced instruction as to the present state of music. I know his work very well: he provided suggestions and assistance for certain parts of my musician's novel "Doktor Faustus", and I wish most sincerely that he might be given the recognition he deserves in the country in whose language it was written' (cited from the duplicate in the Theodor W. Adorno Archiv; the complete letter is in Thomas Mann, *Tagebücher 28.5.1946–31.12.1948*, ed. Inge Jens [Frankfurt am Main: Fischer, 1989], p. 924).

3 The reference to Maria Wiesengrund is in the fifth chapter: 'His mother, herself a singer, is the daughter of a French officer [. . .] of Corsican – originally Genoese – extraction and a German singer'; the fruit liqueur mentioned in the twelfth chapter is the famous apricot brandy.

29 September 1949

Mumma, my animal,
    accept my very heartiest congratulations on your birthday – the eighty-fourth. You are now a true Wondrous Ancient Hippo Cow, and the name Marinumba is not even sufficient to describe your palaeontological quality; you have already become an Archinumba, the well-known collective term for all venerable Ancient Hippo Sows. You just carry on like that, my animal.

We have little to report. All the problems relating to Germany are still in the balance. On Monday evening Stiedry and his wife, Erika Wagner,[1] whom you also know, were here for dinner, very stimulating and interesting, as he knows both Mahler and especially Strauss very well and had many amusing things to tell about the latter. Unfortunately Rudi does not seem too happy in Madison.

I spent all day yesterday at Republic Studios for the recording of the music to Lang's new film 'The House by the River'. The music is by George Antheil,[2] a rather interesting man whom I get on with quite well. – Unfortunately not as good a composer as his overall quality would suggest. But it was informative and productive for me in many respects. The technology is so perfect that as soon as a piece of music is recorded it can immediately be synchronized with the film and the dialogue, which means that one can directly check whether the recording was successful. If only the indescribably advanced technology were matched by the quality of that which it serves.

Meanwhile we have almost finished the final revision of the Berkeley book. It will now be over 900 pages long after all, the institute's most representative publication since the authority volume, of which it is in some respects a continuation. And indeed it is called 'The Authoritarian Personality'. Lix is being a very good helper, as always. Tonight we are all having dinner at his place.

Once again all my best wishes, my animal, especially for your health and the improvement of your eyes. We are writing this on the Erika so that you can read it better.

Heartiest kisses

from your old child
Teddie

My dear Hippo Sow,

I too must send you my very best birthday wishes, and the little cheque from both of us. Buy yourself something nice and warm for the winter, my animal. We shall think of you when we celebrate on Saturday, the birthday of the Wondrous Hippo Cow. Hugs and kisses from your lanky Giraffe

Gi

Original: typewritten letter.

1 Regarding Fritz Stiedry, see letter no. 71, note 6. The actress Erika Stiedry-Wagner had taken the part of reciter in several performances of Schoenberg's *Pierrot Lunaire*, most recently for the gramophone recording conducted by Schoenberg in 1942.

2 The New Jersey-born composer George Antheil (1900–59) had worked for the film industry since 1936. He had gone to Europe in 1922, met Stravinsky

in Berlin and worked with Artur Schnabel before moving to Paris for almost three years.

28 October 1949

HOTEL LUTETIA
BOULEVARD RASPAIL
PARIS

Mumma my animal,
   this is just to tell you and Julie of my safe arrival – by hand, as the typewriter is being repaired. Despite a turbulent crossing – we arrived an entire day late – no sea-sickness, thanks to the new remedy.
   Seeing Paris again after 12 years was deeply moving for me. It is indescribably beautiful amid all the poverty.
   On Wednesday 2 November I am going to Frankfurt. My initial address there is:
   Pension Haus Zeppelin
   Zeppelinallee Ecke Bockenheimer Landstrasse.
   Frankfurt a. M., Germany,
   American Zone.
I was *so* happy with you![1]
   Hopefully you are both well!
Heartiest kisses from your old child
                              Teddie

Original: handwritten letter with printed letterhead.

1 Adorno had departed from Los Angeles on 11 October without Gretel Adorno and spent 14–20 October in New York, where he visited, among others, his mother and Julie Rautenberg.

258   FRANKFURT, 12.11.1949

Frankfurt a. M.
Address from 21 November: c/o Irmer, Liebigstrasse 19, III.
12 November 1949

Mumma my animal, a thousand thanks for your two very sweet letters. You can imagine how much it moved me to arrive here. At the first lecture I was officially received by the deacon himself, in full gown, and the whole faculty. I was a little excited after all. I have a seat and a vote in the faculty. Lecture overcrowded, more than 150 students; seminar and lessons very well attended. The students highly

374

intelligent, an incredibly high intellectual standard, but lack of education. Get on with them superbly.

Saw old Annachen, who is quite well, as her husband is retired and she herself is also receiving a pension. She has become a pleasant old woman, not stupid at all, and was touchingly pleased to see me. I asked her straight out about her relationship to the two of you, and she replied quite honestly: she would truly have loved to see you, but she was so frightfully scared. And one really cannot imagine the terror to which people here were subjected (and not only Jews). I cannot hold it against old Annachen, and you will understand me.

Spent the last weekend in Auerbach, stayed the night with Franz. Louis, at the age of 83, is extraordinarily fit in every respect, seems 10 years younger than he actually is, and apart from his extended beard he has hardly changed at all. Franz has become a devout Catholic, but very kind and warm; Helenchen unchanged and pleasant. Agathchen[1] sweet, a distinguished face, though sadly with the stature of a dwarf and rather too much like a little granny for a nineteen-year-old girl; also devout. It was a thoroughly pleasant day; we played a great deal of piano four hands, some Mahler. Poor Louis's hearing dangerously impaired; not only weak, but also so distorted that he cannot hear anything properly. He would so love to see you again. He has really become very melancholy since Helene's death.

I am extremely well in every respect, and everything is starting up nicely. A few exceptional people here, in particular my closest departmental colleague Gadamer[2] and a man by the name of Podszus,[3] reader at the Suhrkamp publishing house, who knows every line I have written. Also saw Kurt Bruck,[4] who has dried up somewhat.

At first the city, in the area around Bockenheimer Warte, did not seem in such a bad state, but the old town centre is a desolate dream where everything is in a terrible mess. The Fahrgasse, for example, no longer exists at all. Avoided seeing our houses until now; am handing over all our matters, incidentally, to a capable man.[5] In spite of it all, it is still Frankfurt, and the feeling of coming home is stronger than everything else. A miracle that this city, of which three-quarters has been destroyed, nonetheless almost conveys an impression of normality. Food excellent, room overheated, as is my large one at the university. Only the people's clothes are shabby, and there are no elegant women at all any more.

I am so terribly sorry for poor Julie.

I am writing in a mad rush, just so that you can have a few words from me and know that I am well, think of you all the time, and love you indescribably my Hippo Cow.

Heartiest kisses

from your old child

Teddie

375

Original: typewritten letter.

1 This is Agathe, the daughter of Helene and Franz Calvelli-Adorno, born in 1930.

2 The philosopher Hans-Georg Gadamer (1900–2002) taught in Frankfurt from 1947 to 1949.

3 The poet and writer Friedrich Podszus (1899–1971) worked for Suhrkamp as reader from 1950 to 1956; he co-edited the two-volume edition of the writings of Walter Benjamin, whose acquaintance he had made in Heidelberg in 1921.

4 A friend from Adorno's youth; he later became a public prosecutor.

5 This was the Frankfurt tax adviser Joseph Christ, who represented Adorno's compensation claims.

259 FRANKFURT, 24.12.1949

Frankfurt a. M.
Liebigstrasse 19 III, c/o Irmer   24 December 1949

Mumma my animal,
    the only reason for my long silence is the indescribable turbulence of the first weeks in Frankfurt – I relied on Gretel to keep you informed, and you must know that, even when I do not write, I have still not forgotten you for one second. Now we have three weeks of holidays, I have had a massive lie-in (in fact from yesterday afternoon until 10 this morning), and Christmas Eve, the first one in my life that I have spent alone, among strangers, is the best of all times to tell you how much I love you. I send you the best possible wishes for the new year, that you may remain healthy and have as much joy as is still possible in this world. And that we might see each other again. I know the letter from Ännie Rath, and if we do end up staying here for a long time, then her suggestion is not at all bad. She, and naturally also Erich,[1] received me in the most charming fashion, and I am *truly* convinced that they were – and are – absolutely decent, and that you misinterpreted that situation in the tram. If you wish to do me a favour, then write her a genuinely friendly letter. It is so easy, in one's bitterness about what was done, to attack the wrong people, while true villains (I here include, among others, the Graus,[2] who grabbed the Schöne Aussicht house) get off scot-free.
    You really cannot imagine the extent of my success at the university. It was a natural formality that the faculty immediately and unanimously accepted my appointment as senior lecturer, but beyond that they want to employ me here full-time in connection with the plans to

376

reopen the institute. Whether and under what conditions that will happen is still unclear, and also depends very much on the institute, for Max and I do not under any circumstances ever want to separate again, even temporarily. The students cling to me in a way that I would never have thought possible. Lectures and seminars full to bursting; the participants in the Kant seminar never wanted it to end, and even asked me to continue it during the holidays. They put on a charming seminar party with my colleague Gadamer and myself as guests of honour. Also very close contact with the professors, the old ones such as Reinhardt[3] and Schwietering,[4] but also new ones such as Hartner,[5] who still remembers me from Amorbach during our childhood. The radio people also want to have me for all sorts of things, and I was invited[6] to speak at the TH[7] in Darmstadt, as well as receiving invitations to Marburg, Stuttgart and God knows where. – Max will, I hope, arrive here before the end of winter.

Of the old people I saw Annachen, you know that, Franz and Helenchen several times, and also visited Alois at work, who sends you many regards. The compensation business is very drawn-out, and is not looking very good. My father made every mistake he could possibly have made – and on top of that the misfortune that the Schöne Aussicht house was destroyed completely and the one in Oberrad mostly. I visited both – your lovely old dressing table was still there in Oberrad, as well as some other things of ours (a picture by Hall and one by Agnes Meyerhof);[8] they seemed so very peculiar amid the petty bourgeois conventionality and the ruins. Was also in the garden, which has had a large piece of property added to it – very alien. The quarter around Schöne Aussicht is the most miserable of them all – not only houses, but entire stretches of road destroyed, so that I no longer know my way around at all, unless a single house, such as that of the Mannskopfs, suddenly accosts me in my childhood area. In place of number 9, absolute nothingness; no. 7 replaced by an entirely new building. I had a sharp altercation with the young Grau, a Nazi, and will not show the slightest consideration in such matters. Things are more peaceful in Oberrad, and with the Seeheim house there will be meetings first. Mali Völckers[9] asked after you in a letter, is still alive, eighty years old. Nothing from Sanna or Drescher[10] – are presumably dead. It is very pleasantly quiet where I am living, I have a Bechstein grand, and my health is better than it has been in years; feel three times as fresh and productive as in LA; only it can sometimes be very depressing to be a stranger in one's homeland. I often see Kurt Bruck, who has now settled here altogether as high district court administrator, like Franz.

Unfortunately I could hardly decipher your last two letters, my animal. Please try to space the lines as widely as you can, they often cross and render each other illegible. – I shall write to Julie in the next few days, for today just send her the heartiest of greetings.

Heartiest sniffs and kisses
from your old child

Teddie

Original: typewritten letter with handwritten greeting.

1 Erich Rath, who had been Adorno's friend since their school days, worked in Bonn as an internist. He died at the end of 1962 or the start of 1963. Nothing is known about his mother, Ännie Rath.

2 See letter no. 220.

3 The classicist Karl Reinhardt (1886–1958).

4 The Germanist Julius Schwietering (1884–1962) taught at Frankfurt University from 1932 to 1938, and held a professorship in Berlin from 1938 to 1945; he had returned to Frankfurt in 1946.

5 Willy Hartner (1905–81), who had studied chemistry and astronomy at Frankfurt University and gained his PhD there in 1928, taught science history there from 1946 onwards.

6 In connection with the 'Darmstädter Gemeindestudie' [Darmstadt Community Study], in which the Institute of Social Research was involved, Adorno gave a lecture on 'Urban Development and Social Order'.

7 Translator's note: this stands for Technische Hochschule, meaning 'technical college'.

8 Neither the picture by Hall – who could not be traced – nor that by Agnes Meyerhof – the Frankfurt painter, sculptress and illustrator, born in Hildesheim in 1858 – could be identified.

9 Presumably the wife of the Frankfurt architect and dialect poet Adolf Völckers (1859–1919).

10 Sanna (Susanna) Drescher (1867–1965) was Adorno's first piano teacher. She was a daughter of the Frankfurt poet Adolf Stoltze (1842–1933); following her studies in music and singing – she had received her first lessons in the latter from Hans Pfitzner's mother – she taught piano at the Raff Konservatorium; she also gave private tuition until 1922, when she married the privy councillor Otto Drescher. Otto Drescher had died on 4 May 1946. (See Lydia Lerner-Stoltze, *Adolf Stoltze. Ein Dichterleben für Frankfurt* [A Poet's Life for Frankfurt], revised and completed by Luise Bodensohn [Frankfurt am Main, 1983], p. 123.) The Stoltzes were friends of the Wiesengrund family.

1950

15 July 1950

Mumma my animal, today is E's 50th birthday – we are celebrating together in Heidelberg at Pfälzer's and (hopefully) with good fodder, and all three of us thinking of the Wondrous Hippo Cow Marinumba with the most faithful love. With this in mind, heartiest kisses from your faithful old child
  Teddie

Dear Maria, we are thinking of you a great deal and drinking your health with a glass of Pfälzer's fine wine. See you in New York[1] Egon

Dear Hippo Cow, I am happy because E told me what a nice place you are now living in, and hopefully I can see it for myself before too long, and then tell you all about things here.
  Hugs from your Gretel Giraffe

Original: picture postcard: Heidelberg. Manuscript.

1 *See you in New York*: EO.

Amorbach, Hotel Post   24 September 1950

Mumma my animal,
  it was not intentional, but now it does strike me as symbolic that I am spending your eighty-fifth birthday in Amorbach. It is, after all, the

379

last trace of a homeland I still have – externally quite unchanged, and possibly even quieter than it used to be –, and it is here, if anywhere, that I feel as if you were with me as in the old days, with the Tigress. I am truly spending your grand and joyous birthday entirely with you in spirit, and can hardly imagine that these most hearty congratulations I have for you first have to travel all the way across the ocean and through the air before they reach you.

I know you will now say, with quiet reproach: so, you went to the Hotel Post? But listen: it is no longer owned by Hilde and Ludwig. It was taken from them due to their fanatical Nazism. Hilde, whom I have not yet seen (I will not make the first move, and she has not showed her face yet), lives over in the house that once belonged to the Gilloths and plays the piano furiously. Ludwig, the decent one, who was not a Nazi, died in June following a prostate operation. The hotel now belongs to the former Carlchen. He looks very much like Heinrich, is pleasant, only a little inhibited and grim. Has a wife and two children. Emmy – to continue with the family – is also here, the wife of a ghastly seventy-two-year-old hairdresser named Stöcklin, whom she had to marry; a slightly feeble-minded, worn-out creature. Willy is chief post inspector in Stuttgart, but is apparently not happy there.[1]

We know all this from the three Burkharths,[2] who are still unchanged and pray and tell tales of noble ladies, and furthermore have rather simple notions of the justice of the world's ways, with the good being rewarded and the evil punished. Their beer is better than ever, and a true delight to Gretel. We also know everything else from them, for example that Berthold Bührer,[3] who used to be a musical child, is now the abbey organist; that Niedbauer's idiotic son died of septicaemia because they treated a scab of his with manure, and the various other atrocities one encounters. Gretel Spörer and Josef Fischer[4] are also dead. He, a prominent *Zentrumsmann*, was severely hounded by the Nazis, lost all his little positions, and during the last years they were very badly off. Gretel, a kind and pretty girl to whom I was very attached, died of stomach cancer. Both daughters are actresses.

We have already done a good many things in the week that we have been here. We went to Wolkmann and Schafhof, Gotthard, were in Neudorf, almost reached Boxbrunn on foot. Two big tours in a private bus. The first through the Spessart, Mespelbrunn and Rohrbrunn, to the indescribably beautiful Wertheim. Yesterday a trip through the Odenwald, Vielbrunn (do you remember?), Hainehaus (with the fehmic[5] chairs, which made a great impression upon me as a child), Michelstadt, Erbach, returning via Kailbach. The chauffeur was grim and hardly answered any questions. When I asked the owner about him upon our return, I learned that it was Loisl Rossmann, the son of Max Rossmann.[6] I told him who I was, and the poor fellow, who has made an utter mess of his life, showed a certain joy. Everyone here remembers you two and thinks of you.

Nonetheless, it is not the old Hotel Post, and that is down to Carl. They were on the point of bankruptcy at the start of the Nazi regime, and he wants to work his way out of decades of mismanagement, which is understandable – but he does so by saving money on the guests, on food and heating, us too, and that is foolish of him. His old largesse has disappeared and one does not feel half as comfortable any more. The weather here is bad, but until the pouring rain today we had not let it put us off, and plan, if possible, to go on another big bus tour to Rothenburg, where Gretel has not yet been. She will also like the food at Stang's. The owner of Engel's, Nikolaus Deufel, has a new tenant – and his name is Judas. I am not making it up: Herr Judas, from Vienna.

We are having a good and systematic rest. Something wonderful that I was not familiar with is Schloss Steinbach-Fürstenau, near Michelstadt. Laid aside all work. I only have to proof-read Minima Moralia, which will be a thick book and should still be published before Christmas by Suhrkamp. We are also trotting a great deal through the Wiesental like you and the Tigress, and we go to the Burkharths when it is time for our pre-dinner drink.

Our little present is enclosed – buy yourself something pretty with it. And celebrate your birthday as much in our spirit as we celebrate it in yours. Keep your health and your wits and keep us in your heart. My greatest wish: for us to see each other again. Who knows, maybe even in Amorbach . . .

My heartiest greetings to Julie, for whom this letter is also intended. We are happy about every line she writes us. If Gretel wrote more than I did of late, that was purely due to my truly excessive workload – as well as the university and institute also a pile of radio commitments. But now I am forgetting everything, apart from when Max and I discuss the most urgent institute matters on the telephone.

Heartiest kisses

from your old child

Teddie

Dear Hippo Cow,

85 years – a stately age! We will devote next Sunday entirely to birthday thoughts and be with you in everything you do. Here, the two of you – Agathe and you – are always with us.

Hugs and kisses

from your daughter-in-law
the lanky Giraffe

Original: typewritten letter with additional handwritten note from Gretel Adorno.

1 No details could be found regarding the Spoerer family, who manage the Hotel Post in Amorbach to this day.

2 These were the three sisters Marie (b. 1875), Magdalen (Lenchen) (b. 1877) and Anna Burkharth. As they remained unmarried, they were known as the three Burkharth maidens. They ran the Brauereigaststätte Burkharth on the marketplace in Amorbach, which was known for its excellent and affordable food, as well as its good beer. As an adult, Adorno went there almost daily for a pre-dinner drink.

3 The organist Berthold Bührer (1908–96), son of the sawmill-owner Rudolf Bührer (1872–1947), whose works was located in the Schneeberger Strasse, was a childhood friend of Adorno from Amorbach. On 31 January, Adorno wrote the following to Berthold Bührer: 'I kept hearing about you, and I can well imagine how happy you must be to have the Amorbach church organ under your command now. I wish with all my heart that you might play to me upon it – play Bach – to both our hearts' content when I am in Amorbach again. Do you think that would be possible? Please make sure to let me know. I daresay you know how strongly my own work has remained tied to music; although, in the narrow professional sense, I am defined as a philosopher and sociologist, I never stopped feeling equally like a musician. Our days together in Amorbach, even the whirring of your sawmill that I was so fond of, have remained unforgettable for me.'

4 No further information.

5 The *Feme* was the imperial court of justice in Westphalia until 1808.

6 Adorno remembered the painter and sculptor Maximilian Rossmann (1861–1926), who lived in Amorbach, as 'the true rediscoverer' of Amorbach. Rossmann fashioned the decorations for Bayreuth and 'brought the singers of the festival ensemble' to Amorbach (see Adorno, 'Amorbach', *GS* 10.2, p. 303).

1951

21 Jan. 1951

Mumma, my animal,

I think it has been an eternity since I wrote you a letter 'of my own', but the quotation marks enclosing this phrase at the same time express the state of affairs, namely that Gretel and I are so completely identified with each other that every word she writes to you is like my own, and that she simply sees to the technical side of the correspondence to take a little work off my hands. For you can really barely imagine how many things I have to do, and when I return home in the evening, like a real office worker, I am generally so utterly exhausted that I can hardly manage more than a few finger exercises (which I have been practising conscientiously since October) and a daft little game of 66. The institute has developed with such incredible speed in the last months, and because Max, as dean of the faculty, may be even more tied up than I am, the entire burden of current institute business, with countless conferences, dictations, the execution and monitoring of projects etc., is on my shoulders. Even my course on aesthetics, which I am enjoying a great deal, has to be virtually improvised for lack of time, that is to say I prepare each lecture the same day I give it. For the first time in my life, I have not managed to produce anything of my own in the last nine months; the only thing I wrote was the big commemorative essay[1] for Walter Benjamin in the Neue Rundschau.

Nonetheless, I have so far managed to stay on top of everything, and I know that this will not always be the case. I even hope to have evaded the rather rampant influenza through a vaccination and similar things.

I am most reassured that you have now found somewhere decent to live, all the more so because I was by no means charmed by Mrs Clark, as I can tell you now, and I am not even sure whether she fed you properly, whereas everything seems to have been arranged in the most pleasing fashion with your new hosts. I do not doubt that you would be incomparably more comfortable here in Germany (it by no means has to be Amorbach) and could truly live a pleasant and honourable life. I do not want to urge you to do anything against your will, but at the same time I do ask, if you feel your health is at all up to it, that you think the matter over thoroughly once more with dear Julie. The thought that we could then see each other again soon is naturally a considerable factor in my considerations, for while it is certainly possible that I could visit you anytime, I really cannot foresee when that will be the case. My teaching success at the university, incidentally, is quite unusual: even now, approaching the end of term, my lectures on aesthetics are still as overcrowded as they were at the start. I try to imagine what you might say if Giraffe smuggled you into the university and you sat there with everyone like a true Hippo Cow. Are you not at all tempted to come to your child? If I were in your position, I would make the decision exclusively dependent on whether the doctor approved a Hippo Cow air transport after he has examined you again in March. Naturally I would not come now, during the very wet winter, but only in the spring.

On Tuesday I am to give an introductory lecture[2] to Krenek's Orestes at the opera house here. I generally have so many invitations and offers of every kind that it is quite impossible for me to take up even a fraction of them – I turn down almost everything, and only took on the opera business thinking of the Ancient Hippo Cow.

I have just been elected by the faculty as one of the representatives of the non-professorial staff, an example of the faith that even my colleagues have in me. I am also on the committee that is formulating the new constitution for Frankfurt University. These are all things that I was not born for, and which feel to me like a masquerade, but those are precisely the things one cannot evade, and they constitute a further strain on my time.

Could you not dictate Julie a special letter to me sometime! I send her my very heartiest thanks in advance.

You know that I am always thinking of you, my animal, but today in particular.

Heartiest kisses

from your faithful Hippo King

Original: unsigned typewritten letter.

1 'Charakteristik Walter Benjamins'; see *GS* 10.1, pp. 238–53.

2 On 23 January, in the university auditorium, Adorno gave an introduction to the work of Ernst Krenek, whose opera *The Life of Orestes* was premiered on 28 January in Frankfurt. No notes have survived among Adorno's belongings; it seems likely that he spoke without a script.

Index

Adelaer family 237, 239
Adorno, Gretel (*née* Karplus) vii; on American clothes 4; on anti-Semitism 11; birthdays 100, 139, 187, 223, 286, 327; on California 69, 72, 74–5; health of 51, 184, 212; cold and conjunctivitis 273, 274; dramatic improvement 217–18; gall bladder attack 96–7, 98; lumbago 132; migraines 10, 31, 47, 117, 340; sciatica 160, 161–2, 163, 164, 166–7, 170, 172, 205; naturalization process 141, 160; working hard 37
Adorno, Joseph A. 7, 267, pl. 6
Adorno, Paola 23, pl. 2
Adorno, Theodor Wiesengrund: accompanies the violinist Lisa Minghetti 348, 352, 353, 356, 360, 363, 366; on advertising 93; advice on the New World 1–2; affair with Charlotte Alexander 276, 277–9, 281–3, 349; affair with Renée Nell 123–5, 131, 134–5; 'Aldous Huxley and Utopia' 338; apartment-hunting for parents 81, 82–3; on being an alien 54, 87–8, 97, 101, 104, 115, 258–9, 352; Benjamin and 348; birthdays 109, 336, 337; on California 69–71, 75, 79, 334–5; CIO meeting 148, 149; evicted 332, 336, 353; health of 23, 24; chronic cold 150; diabetes 249, 250, 251, 268, 282; headache

cure 193; heart problems 241, 242–3, 247, 249, 251; influenza 175; neuralgia 191, 215, 221; stomach ulcers 271, 273, 274, 276; tonsillectomy 239, 247; wisdom teeth pulled 223–4, 226, 228; at Lake Tahoe 294–8; Mann's *Doctor Faustus* 327; Mann's *The Genesis of a Novel* 328–9; military status in USA 134; money matters 60–1; moves house 240, 337–8; name change 161, 163; naturalization process 141, 143, 160; nicknames 3, 6; on philosophical language 174, 176; on post-war anti-Semitism 248–9; property in Frankfurt 337; on psychoanalysis 189; relationship with parents vi; return to Frankfurt 374–8; speaking against fascism 51; teaches music 289; teaches psychoanalytical candidates 357, 363–4; teaches with Horkheimer 363, 364; travel permit 136, 142; wish to return to Germany 40–2; works: address to JLC 166; 'Aldous Huxley and Utopia' 340; *Anti-Semitism: A Social Disease* 271, 272; 'Anti-Semitism and Fascist Propaganda' 186, 187–8; anti-Semitism project 10–11, 61, 128, 131, 132, 136, 142, 180, 204, 321, 348; arts dictionary project 83; *The Authoritarian Personality* (with Horkheimer) 129, 373; *Beethoven: The Philosophy of Music* 56, 165; on Benjamin 43, 98, 327, 329, 383; Columbia lecture 75, 76; *Composing for the Films* (with Eisler) 119, 121, 129, 170, 172, 224, 267, 277, 294; 'Culture Industry' 158; 'Das Schema der Massenkultur' 106, 108, 109; 'Democratic Leadership and Mass Manipulation' 339; *Dialectic of Enlightenment* (with Horkheimer) 92, 95, 118, 120, 125, 274, 293, 317, 340; dictionary of music 350; the F-scale 206, 207; on George 46; Heine lecture 341, 342; on Hofmannsthal 46; on Kierkegaard 37, 57, 61, 292, 293; 'Kulturkritik und Gesellschaft' 340; *Minima Moralia* 151, 212, 213, 235, 274; music education project 43; musical compositions 90, 91, 168, 169; 'On a Social Critique of Radio Music' 10, 17–18, 23; 'Philosophical Fragments' (with Horkheimer) 184, 219; on popular music 5, 93, 94, 101, 102; 'Private Morale in Germany' (with Marcuse) 88; psychoanalysis lectures 254, 285, 326; 'Reason and Survival' (with Horkheimer) 86, 87; 'Reflections upon the Theory of Class' 108; report for Washington 106; response to Tillich 170, 171; *In Search of Wagner* 34–5, 43; on Simmel 45; 'Spengler after the Decline' 168, 169, 171, 172, 174; study for US government 118; 'The Musical Climate for Fascism in Germany' 196; 'The Radio Symphony' 84, 86; Theory of Needs seminar 101, 102; 'Theses on Art and Religion' 232; 'Träume in Amerika' 110, 114; on Veblen 71, 72, 73; on Wagner 349, 354; 'Why Are We Still Barbarians?' (with Horkheimer) 207; 'Zur Philosophie der neuen Musik' 293, 315, 316, 317, 318, 319, 320, 321, 322, 324, 326, 327, 349, 352, 365, 367, 371

Adorno family 23–4 *see also under* Calvelli-Adorno; Wiesengrund
Alaska 10
Alcan, Felix 49
Alexander, Charlotte 212, 213, 214, 316, 327, 333–4; affair with Adorno 274, 277–83; character of 345; divorces Robert 301; keeps married name 335; letters and 300; looking for security 348, 349; and Maria 329, 339, 342; marries Dr Violin 351, 352, 365; in Nevada 286, 297; Robert's wedding and 312
Alexander, Robert 220, 226; and Anita Lothar 217, 219; car accident 310; divorces Charlotte 277, 278, 281, 283; marries Anita 312, 316; medical advice 204, 212, 213, 214, 221, 231, 237; uncertainty about remarriage 301, 304
Allmeier 43
American Jewish Committee (AJC) 128, 129, 193, 286; Adorno's role with 229, 323; childhood anti-Semitism study 220; effect of war's end 236; hires Horkheimer as consultant 197–8, 199; *Jewish Record* 234; post-war anti-Semitism 248–9
Anders (Stern), Günther 101, 102
Andor, Paul (Wolfgang Zilzer) 107
Andor-Palfi, Lotte 107
Andreae, Norah (*née* Hahn) 108, 125, 150; character of 72–3, 81, 89; Christmas with 345, 346; comforts Adornos 259; with daughter in Mexico 167, 299, 319; death of 350; Gretel's birthday 100, 223; help for ailing Gretel 162; husband 73, 236; Levi and 73, 214–15, 317; makes Adorno executor 136, 139; and Mietze Seligmann 159, 300; music and 111; New Year's day 347; news from Germany 245; parents 90, 326; separated from children 118, 128–9; visits Europe 285, 290; visits New York 338–9
Annachen (Wiesengrunds' maid) 9, 375, 377

Antheil, George 373–4
Asch, Scholem 175, 177
Attlee, Clement 227
Auber, Stefan 21
Auchinleck, General Claude 103

Bacon, Lloyd 57
Badarzewska-Baranowska, Tekla 212
Barrault, Jean-Louis 370
Bartók, Béla 236; *Contrasts* for
  Benny Goodman 94; personality of
  47, 51, 52
Bary, Helene de 293, 294, 300
Baudelaire, Charles 43, 234, 235
Baum, Vicki 351
Beck, Maximilian 7
Beethoven, Ludwig van 56; Adorno
  and Minghetti play 348, 352, 353,
  356, 360, 363
Beit, Elisabeth 128, 129
Benjamin, Dora (sister of Walter)
  245, 246
Benjamin, Dora (wife of Walter) 246
Benjamin, Walter 12, 97, 348, 376;
  Adorno's work on 383; in danger
  51, 53; essay on Baudelaire 43; in
  Lourdes 62; peculiarity 137;
  Wiesengrund family connection
  355
Bentley, Eric 285
Berg, Alban 54
Berlau, Ruth 205, 206
Berlin, Isaiah 65–6
Bernekker, Frau 265
Bernfeld, Siegfried 186, 188, 189
Beroldingen, Count Egon von 139,
  140
Beuschel (childhood friend) 325
Beutler, Ernst 222, 223
Bissing, Hans-Ulrich von 262
Bloch, Ernst 119, 121
Bloch, Trude 37, 39, 98
Bloom, Leonard 324
Bodenhausen, Christa von 318, 319
Bodenhausen, Julie von *see* Kollsman,
  Luli
Bohm, Gertrud (daughter) 244
Bohm, Gertrud (*née* Pie) 239, 243,
  244
Bohm, Hans 244
Böker, Alexander 30, 31–2
Bolongaro-Crevenna, Alfred 319

Borchardt, Rudolf 138
Borodin, Alexander 355
Boyer, Charles 186
Brecht, Bertolt 78, 80, 108, 139, 143,
  150, 187; affair with Ruth Berlau
  205, 206; ignores wife 175–6;
  poem 'Hollywood' 106; Theory of
  Needs seminar 101, 102; visited by
  FBI 97
Brecht (Weigel), Helene 135, 175–6;
  help for ailing Gretel 162
Brentano, Baroness 310, 318
Briggs, Laura 78
Britain: appeasing Hitler 58; post-
  war 226, 227, 299; wartime 17,
  48, 63, 99, 100
Bruck, Kurt 375, 376, 377
Bruckner-Karplus, Susi 115
Bruckner-Karplus, Wilhelm 115
Brunswik, Egon 201–2
Bührer, Berthold 380, 382
Burkharth maidens 380, 382
Busch, Adolf 13–14

Cahn, Rosa 107
Calvelli-Adorno, Agathe 42, 296,
  375, 376
Calvelli-Adorno, Anton 18, 19
Calvelli-Adorno, Elisabeth (*née*
  Henning) 78, 80
Calvelli-Adorno, Franz 18, 110, 274,
  276; Adorno's stay with 375;
  children of 346; German property
  and 255, 256; on property claims
  316; on Reparations Committee
  233
Calvelli-Adorno, Helene (Franz's wife,
  née Mommsen) 110, 244, 276,
  288, 362; disappoints Adorno
  316
Calvelli-Adorno, Helene (Louis's wife,
  née Katz) 225; death of 244
Calvelli-Adorno, Louis Prosper 16,
  18; criticism of vi; death of wife
  244; family of 18–19, 211, 237;
  grandchildren of 346; hell of
  Germany 252; later years 375
Calvelli-Adorno, Ludwig 109, 110
Chamberlain, Neville 27, 58, 59
Chaplin, Charlie 310; private
  showing of *Mr Verdoux* 279, 280
Chart, Frederick G. 215

Child Welfare Institute 220, 226
Christ, Joseph 376
Christians, Mady 167, 169, 170, 173
Churchill, Winston S. 63; speeches of 26, 29, 176, 177; succeeds Chamberlain 59
Colonna family 229, 231
Columbia Broadcasting System 17
Columbus, Christopher 36, 38
Committee for Industrial Organization (CIO) 148, 149
Coolidge, Elizabeth Sprague 53
Coolidge Quartet 52, 53
Copland, Aaron 94
Coryan, Irina 134
Coughlin, Father Charles 58, 60
Crevenna, Hilda (née Plieninger) 318–19
Cuba: Adorno's parents leave 26; radio 17

Dahl, Ingolf 342, 343
Damrosch, Walter J. 28, 29
Darrieux, Danielle 186
Debussy, Claude 48
Deste, Luli see Kollsman, Luli
Deufel, Nikolaus 381
Deutsch, Monroe E. 203, 204
Dewey, Thomas E. 341
Dieterle, William and Charlotte 81, 83, 93, 95, 139, 143, 299, 344; big shot gathering 141; social life 200
Drescher, Otto 377, 378
Drescher, Sanna 377, 378
Drevermann, Ria 327
Drevermann, Wolf 327
Dreyer, Carl 106
Dreyfuss, Carl 119, 120
Dreyfuss, Willi 326

Eden, Anthony 220
Eisler, Gerhart 269
Eisler, Hanns 93, 94, 100, 288; Composing for the Films (with Adorno) 119, 121, 129, 170, 172, 224, 267, 277, 294; family in the news 268, 269; housewarming party 128; as neighbour 108; social visits 111, 114, 134, 143, 144–5, 208; Theory of Needs seminar 101, 102; Virgil Thomson

reviews book 306; threat of deportation 310; at victory party 228
Eisler, Lou 125, 186–7, 306
Epstein, Alice (née Wiesengrund) 159, 232
Epstein, Fritz T. 232
Epstein, Paul 159, 232
Epstein, Peter 158, 159
Everett-Lehner, Martha 147, 150, 358

Farrow, John: The Hitler Gang 152
fascism: hope for collapse of 40–1; speaking against 50–2
Feiss, Gertrud 49, 50
Fenichel, Otto 169, 186, 189, 204
Ferrier, Kathleen 314
Feuchtwanger, Lion and Marta 175, 315
Fischer, Josef 380
Fischer, Ruth (née Eisler) 269
Flesch, Carl 120
Föh, Frau 160
France 17, 56, 58, 59
Frank, Liesel 325
Frankfurt University 360; Adorno returns to 268, 269, 371, 374–5, 376–7
Franz Joseph, Kaiser 184
Franzos, Karl Emil: Der Pojaz 125, 126
Frenkel, Frau 369
Frenkel, George: personality 40
Frenkel, Hilde 119
Frenkel, Leo 1, 3, 24, 75, 91, 159, 161, 358; and emigrating Adornos 27, 33; job with Voice of America 356; and Julie Rautenberg 37; legal adviser 200; money matters 43–4, 48; personality 40
Frenkel-Brunswik, Else 180, 200
Friedberg, Carl 329, 330
Friedgood, Harry 245, 246, 359, 361
Fritz, Hanna (née Hofer) 143, 162, 288
Froeschel, Georg 211, 212
Fromm, Erich 62–3
Fürth, Lore 102–3

Gadamer, Hans-Georg 375, 376, 377
Galsworthy, John 302

Gans, Elisabeth von (née Keller)
  89–90
Gans, Ludwig von 237, 238
Garbo, Greta 170
George, Stefan 10, 46, 257
Germany: Allied invasion 187; anti-
  Hitler groups within 165, 190;
  attack on Britain 63; bombardment
  of 99, 100; citizenship of refugees
  26; death of Hitler 216–17;
  expected fall of 40–1, 156; internal
  wartime situation 95–6, 130;
  invades the Low Countries 55;
  occupation of 222; pact with Soviet
  Union 16, 17; post-war offers to
  Jews 249; post-war partying 245;
  property of emigrants 195–6,
  199–200, 202, 255, 262; war
  damage 221; wishing revenge
  against 149 see also Hitler
Goebbels, Josef 151, 152
Goerdeler, Carl Friedrich 100
Goerz, Countess see Kollsman, Luli
Goldbeck, Céline 329, 330
Goldbeck, Fred 63, 64, 329
Goodman, Benny 94
Gould, Mr 128–9, 136
Grab, Blanche (née Smullyan) 127,
  128
Grab, Hermann 63, 64, 127, 128,
  156, 181, 182, 255, 365
Grable, Betty 157, 158
Graf, Dr Herbert 1, 3
Gräfenberg, Ernst 69, 72
Graham, Raymond 54
Granach, Alexander 125, 126, 182,
  196, 267; autobiographical novel
  265, 266; death of 213–14
Grau family 333, 376, 377
Greissle, Felix 99
Grünebaum 28, 30
Guilbert, Yvette 316
Gumperz, Julian 127
Gumperz, Lotte 125
Günther, Alois 219, 220, 377
Gurland, A. R. L. 76

Habsburg, Rudolf von 186
Hacker, Frederick J. 370
Haggin, B. H. 100, 104
Hahn, Albert 34, 35
Hahn, Anna Gertrude 89, 90

Hahn, Ludwig Arnold 89, 90, 150,
  154, 159, 181; German property
  248; longevity of 183; looks after
  Hermann Levi 214–15; music and
  111
Hahn family 237
Hallstein, Walter 269, 360, 361, 362,
  363
Hartmann, Johann Georg 223
Hartner, Willy 377, 378
Haskin, Byron 57
Hawkins, Richard Laurin 7
Hebbel, Friedrich 50, 52
Herbert, Walter 153
Herlé, Frau 160
Hermann, Eva 235, 315
Herz, Frau 236
Herzberger, Alfons 28, 29–30
Herzberger, Else 28, 29–30, 34, 37,
  206, 207, 266, 344; Adorno's
  second letter to 357;
  disappointment revealed 348;
  friendship with Maria Wiesengrund
  310, 312; and Grünebaum 74; old
  sourpuss letter to 330–1, 333;
  unresponsive 317, 320, 335, 363,
  364
Herzberger, Gretel 317, 318
Herzberger, Julius 194, 195
Herzog, Herta 6
Heymann/Heimann family 14, 15,
  245
Heyneman, Anne 173, pl. 3
Hindemith, Paul 94, 309
Hirsch, Donald von 63, 64
Hitler, Adolf: agreement with
  Chamberlain 27; assassination
  attempt 190; death of 216–17;
  facing defeat 79–80; invades
  Poland 16–17; pact with USSR 16;
  pocketing Europe 56
Hoare, Viscount Samuel 329, 330
Hobson, Wilder 7
Hofer, Johanna 205, 206
Hoffmann, Heinrich 100; Der
  Struwwelpeter 193
Hoffmann von Fallersleben, Heinrich
  227
Hofmannsthal, Hugo von 10, 46,
  138
Hölderlin, J. C. F. 261
Horenstein, Jascha 115

Horkheimer, Maidon 14, 49; admires blanket 116; attends Heine lecture 342; birthday of 172; bursitis 309, 313; farewell dinner 200; Gretel's birthday 223; help for ailing Gretel 162; holidays with 17; learning bridge 162; Lix's birthday party 315; Max misses 208; New York and California 199; social time 5, 6, 109, 134, 286; special occasions 68, 89, 100, 269, 271; visits the parents 214

Horkheimer, Max: and Adorno's parents 112, 313; burden of work 143, 210–11, 231, 236, 286, 320; in California 69–71, 188, 343, 344; comforts Adornos 259; as 'enemy alien' 88; 'exploratory tour' 60; farewell dinner 200; Granach's party 125; health of 172, 173, 219, 243; gout 178, 183, 288; improves in Europe 334–5; helps Adorno's emigration 2; learning bridge 162; military status in USA 134; misses wife 208; in New York 233; reads Hugo 139; *The Revolt of Nature* (lectures) 173, 174; social times 5, 6, 14, 17, 56, 286; special occasions 68, 89, 100, 117, 269, 271, 315; surviving the war 54; view of war 144; working with Adorno 62, 79, 136, 150; works and roles: on anti-Semitism 11, 46, 180, 186, 187–8, 204, 348; *The Authoritarian Personality* (with Adorno) 129, 373; 'Authoritarian State' 37, 38; 'Betrachtung zum curfew' 110; CIO meeting 148, 149; consultant for AJC 197–8, 199; 'Culture Industry' 158; *Dialectic of Enlightenment* (with Adorno) 92, 95, 118, 120, 125, 274, 293, 317, 340; 'Die Juden und Europa' 5, 7; *Eclipse of Reason* 167, 169; at Frankfurt University 356, 357, 358, 383; lectures in New York 193; music education project 43; 'Philosophical Fragments' (with Adorno) 184, 219; 'Reason and Survival' (with Adorno) 86, 87; report for Washington 106; in Simmel's *Anti-Semitism* 272;

speaking against fascism 51; speech on Simmel 308, 309; teaches at La Habra 289; teaches with Adorno 363, 364; 'The End of Reason' 71, 72; 'Why Are We Still Barbarians?' (with Adorno) 207; works with Adorno 49

Hugo, Victor 139
Hüpeden, Frau 218, 219
Husserl, Edmund 176
Huxley, Aldous 158, 338

Institute of Social Research: Columbia lectures 76; post-war revival 356, 357, 358, 383; 'Walter Rosenthal' figure 16, 19
Italy 144

Japan 228
Jaspers, Karl 250
Jewish College 363
Jewish Labor Committee (JLC) 129, 169; Adorno's address to 166, 168
Jewish people: Alaska as refuge 10; 'country' Germans 36, 38, 47; dangers in Nazi Germany 20; fascism and anti-Semitism 40–1; Madagascar plan 12; refuges for 11–12; territorial problem 58
Jochman, Carl Gustav 43
Johnson, Osa 170, 172
Jones, Harold E. 222, 287

Kagan, Pesha 329, 330
Kahn, Salomon 194, 195
Kainz, Josef 316
Kaltenborn, Hans von 17
Kant, Immanuel 125
Kappel, Hugh 173, pl. 3
Karplus, Albert 21
Karplus, Amalia (Melly, *née* Jacak) 20, 21, 22, 45, 328; missing 196, 221; property in Germany 195–6; silence from 200; survives 239, 243; in touch with Adornos 255
Karplus, Gretel *see* Adorno, Gretel
Karplus, Liselotte *see* Wissing, Liselotte
Karplus and Herzberger company 284, 285
Kaschnitz, Marie Luise 250

Kaus, Regina Wiener 115, 116, 125, 128
Khuner, Felix 21
Klein, Bertha 170
Klemperer, Otto 48, 52, 53
Klemperer, Victor 88
Knöll, Dr 284
Kolisch, Lorna 290, 295
Kolisch, Rudolf 6, 7, 43, 127, 128, 244, 289, 291; at Lake Tahoe 295; performs Bartók 47
Kolisch Quartet 52
Kollsman, Luli (Julie von Bodenhausen, then Deste) 143, 162; Adornos' affection for 247; character of 137–9, 140, 150, 187, 302; Come, Take my Hand 367; custody discussions 199, 203; divorce of 174, 176; and Dr Violin 365; health and emotional state of 148, 229–30, 300, 304, 313; impostor princess and 310; Mann and 321, 322; marriage to Kollsman 194, 195, 267, 282; sister of 318; social time 144, 145, 348; takes the dog 226, 228, 230, 255, 290; visits with dog 282, 283, 347
Kollsman, Paul 194, 195, 313
Kömff, Otto 323, 324
Korngold, Erich Wolfgang 314
Kortner, Fritz 143, 162, 205, 288, 303, 305, 306
Kortner, Hanna (née Hofer) 306, 309
Kracauer, Elisabeth 64
Kracauer, Siegfried 63, 64, 147; From Caligari to Hitler 284, 285
Kramer, Beate 8, 9, 19, 91
Kramer, Ferdinand 18, 19, 91
Kramer & Rosenstein 215
Kraus, Karl 18
Kreisler, Fritz 10, 12, 157, 304, 321, 322
Krenek, Ernst 301, 306, 320, 323; The Life of Orestes 384
Krenek, Frau 342
Kullman, Charles 306, 307
Kuszowski, Wera von 317

La Habra College 289, 301, 302, 303; Adorno leaves 314, 317;

money problems 308, 312; short of money 304
Laidlaw, Estella 6, 7, 8, 11, 22
Landshoff, Fritz H. 323
Lang, Frita: Secret Beyond the Doors 302
Lang, Fritz: Adorno on studio set 277; Christmases with 269, 271, 309, 310, 345–6; Fury 279; guest Fritzi Massary 325; helps Adornos move 354; The House by the River 373; relationship with Lily Latté 298; social time 228, 306, 319, 321, 327, 336; stag invades garden 300; strained at work 364; visits Pioneer Town 318
Lanskoronski 234
Lascelles, George (earl of Harewood) 371, 372
Latté, Elisabeth Lily (née Schaul): angiospasms 371; appendectomy 321; attends Heine lecture 342; birthdays with 286, 336; Christmases with 269, 271, 276, 309, 310, 345–6; close friendship of 297–8; Gretel's birthday 327; helps Adornos move 354; reports on Maria Wiesengrund 299–300; social time 228, 256, 264, 319, 364; visits Pioneer Town 318
Lazarsfeld, Paul Felix 2, 5
Lefébure, Yvonne 329
Lehmann, Jules/Julius 128–9, 136
Lehmann, Walter 316
Leibowitz, René 308, 309
Lenya, Lotte (Karoline Blamauer) 14–15, 173
Lester, Conrad Henry 115, 116
Levi, Blanche 369
Levi, Herbert 319, 320, 361
Levi, Hermann 18, 214–15, 317, 318, 319, 361; death of 368–9
Levi, Samson 18
Levy-Ginsberg (Levilliers), Arnold 357
Lewis, Leon 145
Lewis, Sinclair: It Can't Happen Here 41
Ley, Robert 237, 238
Liefmann, Dr Emil 271; background of 53; returns to Germany 337, 350; travel permit and 136, 142;

treats Gretel Adorno 51; treats
Maria Wiesengrund 174; treats
Oscar Wiesengrund 177–8, 257
Lind, Jenny 296
Lindbergh, Charles A. 58, 60, 190
Loeb, Anna 107, 112, 135, 151
London, Jack: *Iron Heel* 41
Lothar, Anita (*née* Seligmann, later
Alexander) 34, 35, 146, 153, 167,
254, 301, 346; marriage to Robert
Alexander 316; marries Alexander
217, 219, 301
Lothar, Corinna 347
Lothar, Hans 167, 169
Low, Sir David Alexander 104, 105
Löwenthal, Erman 103
Löwenthal, Golde 359, 365
Löwenthal, Leo 26, 28, 94, 100, 279;
illness 136; in *Jewish Record* 234,
235; report on Oscar Wiesengrund's
funeral 261
Löwenthal, Rosie 98, 99
Löwenthal, Victor 98, 99; death of
100, 101
Lukács, Georg 268
Lynd, Helen Merrell: *Middletown*
(with R. Lynd) 6
Lynd, Robert S.: *Middletown* (with H.
Lynd) 5, 6

Maaskoff, Anton 114, 115, 123, 125,
291; illness 312, 321, 352; musical
talent 157; separates from Lisa
368
Maaskoff, Liesel *see* Minghetti, Lisa
McCormick, Robert Rutherford 190
MacManus, George 224
Madariaga, Salvador de: *Christopher
Columbus* 36, 38
Mahler, Gustav 92; performance of
338; radio broadcasts of 97, 310,
312, 313–14; recordings of 305,
306, 307; score gone astray 99,
103, 104
Maier, Ilse *see* Mayer, Ilse
Maier, Josef 38, 39
Mallarmé, Stéphane 123
Mann, Katia 330
Mann, Klaus 362, 363
Mann, Monika 341
Mann, Thomas: broken shoulder
318; chamber music evening 337;

doesn't warm to Luli Kollsman
321, 322; forms friendship with
Adorno 153, 154; and Emil
Liefmann 178; lung operation
253–4, 260; and *Minima Moralia*
234, 313; music discussion 151,
152; Nietzsche lecture 279, 280; on
post-war Germany 299; social time
131, 144, 185, 246, 315; support
for Adorno's book 371, 372; at
victory party 228; Walter and 314;
Warner premier 150; works:
Adorno and *Doctor Faustus* 243,
257, 258, 274, 275, 323, 327; *Der
Zauberberg/The Magic Mountain*
266, 268; *Doctor Faustus* 154,
155; *Felix Krull* 334; finishes
Doctor Faustus 280; *On the
Genesis of a Novel* 328–9, 340,
344, 353, 355, 367, 371;
publication of *Doctor Faustus* 304;
reads from *Doctor Faustus* 165
Mannerheim, General C. G. E. F. 26
Mannheimer, Jakob 37, 98
Manuilski, Dimitri 220, 222
Marcuse, Herbert 75, 76, 102, 143,
144, 299; 'Private Morale in
Germany' (with Adorno) 88;
work on German chauvinism 118,
120
Marcuse, Ludwig 111, 134; Theory
of Needs seminar 101, 102
Massary, Fritzi 325
Matray, Ernst 316
Mayer, Ilse 37, 39, 98–9, 115, 116,
174, 175, 321, 334, 344
Mendelssohn, Felix Bartholdy 98
Mendelssohn, Margot von 97, 99,
160, 342, 354
Menuhin, Hephzibah 337
Meyerhof, Agnes 377
Michaelis, Karin 82, 181
Michaelis firm 215
Milhaud, Darius 94, 360, 361
Minghetti, Lisa 322, 343, 347;
Adorno accompanies 123, 167,
348, 352, 353, 356, 360, 363;
background 113, 114–15, 312;
chamber evening 366; Alexander
Granach's party 125; separates
from Maaskoff 368; social time
281, 291, 316

Mitropoulos, Dimitri 307, 310
Moissi, Alexander 316
Molotoff, Vyacheslav 220
Mommsen, Helmut 244
Morgenstern, Soma 73, 74, 115
Mosbacher, Lotte 208 see Zilzer,
    Lotte
Moses, Paul J. 351
Mozart, Wolfgang Amadeus 337, 360
Mussert, Anton A. 12
Mussolini, Benito 186–7; death of
    218, 219; dismissed from
    government 144, 145

National Broadcasting Company 17
National Centre for Jewish
    Emigration 11
Nell, Renée 117, 204; Adorno's affair
    with 124–5, 131, 135;
    reconciliation party 137–8
Neufville, Otto de 150, 157
Neufville, Robert de 26, 28–9, 30,
    225
Neumann, Franz 40, 42, 76;
    Behemoth 92
Nietzsche, Friedrich 125
Nürnberg, Ralph: Theory of Needs
    seminar 101, 102

Odets, Clifford 280
Opie, Kathrin (*née* Taussig) 284,
    285
Opie, Redvers 18, 19, 22, 284, 285
Oporto, Thora d' (Countess Boxberg)
    257, 258
Oppenheim, Paul 22, 23, 40, 120,
    136, 139
Oppenheim-Errera, Gabrielle 22, 23
Oppenheimer family 118–19, 120

Palfi, Victor 107, 143, 144, 208, 239,
    309; at victory party 228
Pallenberg, Max 184, 316, 325
Pastern, Frau 315
Patti, Adelina 296
Patzak, Julius 314
Petacci, Clara 218, 219
Pfeiffer-Belli, Erich 270
Piper's Opera House 296, pl. 8
Plaut, Clara (*née* Mayer) 334
Podszus, Friedrich 375, 376
Poland 16–17

Pollock, Andrée (Dée) 5, 6, 8, 49;
    death of 14
Pollock, Carlota (*née* Bernekker) 247,
    321, 323, 327; in Argentina 339,
    345; mother of 309, 365
Pollock, Frederick (Fritz) 5, 6, 8, 14,
    63, 188, 327; anti-Semitism project
    204; apricot brandy and 85; in
    Argentina 339, 345; Columbia
    lecture 76; government
    consultation 135; Gretel's birthday
    223; holidays 17, 89; in Los
    Angeles 290; marries Carlota 246,
    247; new house 308; new mother-
    in-law 265; in New York 320;
    rebuilding institute in Frankfurt
    356, 357, 358; social time 109,
    118, 230; special occasions 100;
    visits California 75; working
    relations 79
Portugal 63
Pringsheim, Klaus 352
Psychoanalytical Society 186, 187–8

Radbruch, Gustav 222, 223
Rainer, Luise 193–4, 195, 280
Rath, Ännie 376
Rath, Erich 376, 378
Raudszus, Bruno 340
Rauschning, Hermann 306, 307,
    308
Rautenberg, Julie 3, 33, 91, 182,
    363; Adorno inheritance 339;
    emigrates to USA 25, 35–7, 40;
    home of her own 332, 333, 339,
    363; and Horkheimers 49, 52;
    Maria Wiesengrund's 81st birthday
    264; money matters 48; social
    relationship 63; visits California
    320, 330–1
Ravel, Maurice 48
Rebner, Adolf 309
Rebner, Wolfgang Edward 308, 309,
    318
Reichenbach, Hans 97, 99
Reinhardt, Gottfried 96
Reinhardt, Karl 377, 378
Reinhardt, Max 81, 96, 316
Reinheimer, Jane Constance 148,
    149, 174, 175
Reis, Ludwig 173
Reynolds, Robert Rice 189, 190

Robinson, Edward G. 56, 57
Rocholl, Margot 270, 356
Rockefeller Foundation 21, 22, 37, 287
Roehn, Franz 256, 358
Roosevelt, Eleanor 349
Roosevelt, Franklin D. 205
Rorty, James 232, 233
Rosanska (Kolisch), Josefa 6, 7, 44, 329, 330
Rosay, Françoise 370
Rossmann, Loisl 381
Rossmann, Max 381, 382
Rottenberg, Ludwig 78, 80
Rumpf, Josefine (Juliette) 270
Runes, Dagobert David 83, 85

Sade, Marquis de 125
Sadie (maid) 15–16
Salomon, Bernhard 270
Salomon, Mé 112, 113
Salomon-Delatour, Gottfried 28, 30
Sanford, R. Nevitt 133
Schildkraut, Joseph 303, 304, 306
Schildkraut, Rudolf 303
Schneider, Mischa 125
Schoenberg, Arnold 73, 79, 100, 108, 151, 171, 309
Schoenberg, Gertrud (Mitzi, née Kolisch) 289, 290
Schröder, Alexander 138
Schröder Hanfstängel, Marie 170, 172
Schubert, Franz 261
Schwietering, Julius 377, 378
Scitovszky, Tibor 356
Seele, Frau 14, 15, 244, 269, 278
Seligmann, Maria (née Kolisch) 146
Seligmann, Marie (Mietze, née Gans) 146, 187, 300–1, 346
Seligmann, Milton 35, 146, 154, 268, 271; death of 326; golden anniversary 277; in Switzerland 295
Seligmann, Walter Herbert 146
Serkin, Rudolf 13–14
Sevilla, Emeranja 36
Siebeck (publisher) 292, 324
Simmel, Ernst 180, 187–8, 204; *Anti-Semitism: A Social Disease* 272
Simmel, Georg 45
Simmel, Joseph 308, 309

Simpson, George 21, 34
Simpson, Wallis W. 59
Sinn, Carrie (née Frenkel) 1, 3, 26
Slawson, John 263
Smith, Gerald L. K. 190
Smith, 'Whispering' Jack 8, 9
Social Science Research Council 287
Sohn-Rethel, Alfred 63, 64
Solveg, Maria 316
Soviet Union: Hitler's campaign in 80; pact with Hitler 16, 17, 26–7, 58
Spain 63
Speyer, Willi 318, 319
Spier, Julius 204
Spoerer family 380, 382
Stalin, Josef 26
Stein, Countess Marion Donata 371, 372
Stein, Erwin 371, 372
Steinberg, William 171, 172
Stern (Anders), Günther: Theory of Needs seminar 101, 102
Sternberger, Dolf 250
Steuermann, Augusta 78, 80, 86, 111, 125; election party 205; at the piano 115; social visits 134
Steuermann, Eduard 38, 39, 51–2, 108, 135, 300, 317, 336; comforts Adornos 259; daughter's mental health 315–16, 335; family of 78, 96; performs Bartók 47; teaching at Juilliard 369; Theory of Needs seminar 101, 102
Steuermann, Mausi 316, 317, 335
Steuermann, Salka *see* Viertel, Salomea
Stiedry, Fritz 115, 116, 373
Stiedry-Wagner, Erika 373
Stokowski, Leopold 173
Stoltze, Adolf 378
Stravinsky, Igor 320
'Swabian Railway' 152–3, 154
Szell, George 115, 116

Taft, Robert A. 58, 60
Taubler, Frau 14
Taylor, Davidson 141, 143, 147
Theory of Needs seminar 101, 102
Thomas, Martin Luther 156, 158, 162, 165

Thomson, Virgil 84, 85, 86, 143, 155, 306, 307, 320; letter of advice 104
Tillich, Paul 170, 171
Torberg, Friedrich 284, 285
Toscanini, Arturo 48
Tracy, Spencer 279
Truman, Harry S. 341
Tucholsky, Kurt 3

Umberto II of Italy 226, 227
United States: Adorno on southern places 30–1; 'enemy aliens' 87–8; enters the war 54, 79–80; Japanese attack 84, 85; neutrality of 17; wartime immigrants and 97; wartime scarcities 130–1
University of California, Los Angeles 354
University of Southern California 343

Vandenberg, Arthur 58, 60
Vercors (Jean Bruller) 155
Verlaine, Paul 257
Vetsera, Baroness Maria 186
Victor Emmanuel III, king of Italy 145
Viertel, Berthold 78, 80, 125, 126, 134
Viertel, Salomea (Salka, née Steuermann) 78, 79, 80, 96, 167, 208; election party 205; Garbo for tea 170
Villinger, Arnold 14, 15, 19, 218, 219
Villinger, Franz 18, 165, 218, 219, 231
Villinger, Jenny (née Wiesengrund) 14, 15, 19, 191, 192, 218, 219, 231
Villinger, Leonore A. 168, 169
Violin, Dr 351, 352, 365
Vittorio Emanuele of Italy 227
Vlissi, Jascha 21
Völckers, Mali 377, 378

Wagner, Richard 43, 349; Nibelungen 354–5; Tristan und Isolde 281
Wallace, Henry A. 341
Walter, Bruno 97, 173, 306, 312; Adorno's view of 313–14, 315
Wamba, king of the Visigoths 94
Warburg, Anita 10, 11

Warburg, Max 10, 11
Watt, Ian 286
Weber, Alfred 250
Weber, Carl Maria von 337
Webern, Anton 54, 236
Weigel, Helene see Brecht, Helene
Weil, Felix 112, 269; Adorno 'looks after' 233, 321; in Argentina 37; birthdays of 315, 352; character of 40, 109, 230, 275; divorces fourth wife 288, 336, 339; emigrates to USA 34; entertains rich Frankfurters 367; first wife, Katharina 64; fourth wife, Helen 90, 275, 276; has puppies 361; helps Adornos move 354; helps with The Authoritarian Personality 365, 373; more zeal than understanding 232; as neighbour 104; new girlfriend 342; in New York 108; re-establishing institute 52; social time 306, 346
Weil, Helen (née Knopping) 90, 91, 275, 276
Weil, Katharina (née Bachert) 64
Weil, Lucille (née Jakobowitz) 90, 91
Weil, Margot (Motte) 34; death of 125–6
Weill, Kurt 48–9, 173
Weinberg, Arthur 112, 113
Weinberg, May (née Forbes) 118
Wertheimber, Maus 234
Wertheimber family 215
Weygand, General Maxime 53, 55
Wheeler, Burton Kendall 189, 190
Wiesengrund, Bernhard (Bernard Wingfield) 220, 243
Wiesengrund, Maria Calvelli-Adorno: Adorno inheritance 339; Adorno visits en route to Paris 374; birthdays 21, 110, 112–13, 197–8, 233–4, 262, 381; Borodin and 355; emigrates to Cuba vi, 1–2, 24; emigrates to USA 33; health of 130; eye problems 276, 281, 284, 301–2, 351, 358–9, 366; gastric troubles 206, 208; stomach cramp 362–3; housing problem 332; Lily's report on 299–300, 301; makes blanket 116; and Mann 355, 372; responds to photos 360–1; singing career 80, 86, 87, 296; US

citizenship 216; worries about post-war anti-Semitism 344

Wiesengrund, Oscar: birthdays 64–5, 67, 105–6, 144–5, 190, 225–7; death of 258–61, 288; emigrates to Cuba vi, 1–2, 24; emigrates to USA 33; father's firm 220; health of 109; eye troubles 235; final illness 250–3, 256, 257; heart attack and recovery 177–86, 195, 202–3; nose 159–60; thrombosis 192; money matters 43–4, 48; nicknames 9; on post-war anti-Semitism 248–9

Wilkie, Wendell 58, 60

Windsor, Duke of 58

Wingfield, Alexander Louis 18, 19

Wingfield, Bernard Theodore 18, 19

Wingfield, Lina 152

Wissing, Dr Egon 167, 169, 379; in Chicago 67; first wife 49; marries Lotte 45, 46, 55; related to Benjamin 355; travelling home 244; wartime travels 148, 149, 239

Wissing, Liselotte (Lotte, née Karplus) 45, 46, 49, 55; in Chicago 67; visits Adornos in Los Angeles 289, 291, 292

Wittfogel, Karl August 51, 53

Wohlauer, Eric J. 84, 85, 90

Wolf, Max 11

Zickel, Lenore 138, 140

Zickel, Reinhold 140

Zilzer, Lotte (née Mosbacher) 107, 112, 134, 141, 143, 151

Zilzer, Wolfgang (Paul Andor) 107